Fodor's

SAN DIEGO

T0048994

Welcome to San Diego

San Diego is a vacationer's paradise, with year-round temperatures in the 70s and near-constant sunshine. One of America's most family-friendly cities, it's home to LEGOLAND, the New Children's Museum, and the San Diego Zoo. Sunbathers and surfers are guaranteed to find their perfect beach, and foodies find delights in craft breweries, local bistros, and gourmet restaurants. From the European feel of Little Italy to the nouveau-chic of the Gaslamp Quarter, San Diego has something for everyone. As you plan your upcoming travels, please confirm that places are still open and let us know when we need to make updates by writing to us at editors@fodors.com.

TOP REASONS TO GO

★ **Sun and Surf:** Legendary beaches and surfing in La Jolla, Coronado, and Point Loma.

★ **Golf:** A concentration of beautiful courses with sweeping ocean views and light breezes.

★ **Outdoor Sports:** A perfect climate for biking, hiking, sailing—anything—outdoors.

★ **Family Time:** Fun for all ages at LEGOLAND, Balboa Park, the San Diego Zoo, and more.

★ **Great Eats:** Brewpubs, a wide mix of ethnic cuisines, and modern cafés delight diners.

★ **Shopping:** From hip boutiques to fine Mexican crafts.

Contents

Fodor's Features

Lions and Tigers and Bears:
The World-Famous San Diego Zoo....101

MAPS

Chapter 1

EXPERIENCE
SAN DIEGO

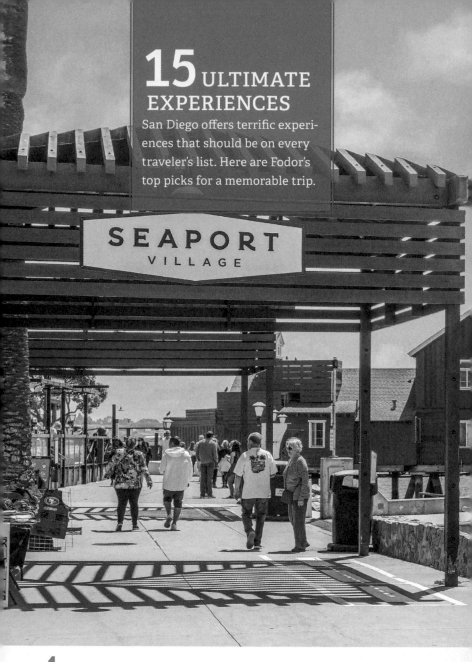

15 ULTIMATE EXPERIENCES

San Diego offers terrific experiences that should be on every traveler's list. Here are Fodor's top picks for a memorable trip.

SEAPORT
VILLAGE

1 Shop and Dine in Seaport Village

Situated along the water, the recently revitalized Seaport Village is a 14-acre, open-air shopping and dining complex that's home to shops and eateries, special events, and winding walking paths. *(Ch. 3)*

2 Bet on a Horse

The Del Mar Racetrack sees about 12 races a day, July through early September. Be prepared for loud cheering, boozy cocktails, and dapper attire. *(Ch. 10)*

3 Explore Old Town

The city's oldest and most storied neighborhood is home to Mexican restaurants, souvenir shops, and cultural and historical attractions and celebrations. *(Ch. 5)*

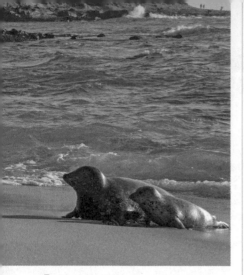

4 Seals in La Jolla Cove

Seals and sea lions love the Children's Pool Beach, but keep your distance. For good views from Coast Boulevard, walk along the sea cliffs toward the seawall. *(Ch. 7)*

5 Shop at a Farmers' Market

Thanks to California's bounty of fresh produce, San Diego's farmers' markets boast a cornucopia of foodstuff. Visit Little Italy on Saturday and Wednesday, and Hillcrest on Sunday. *(Ch. 3, 5)*

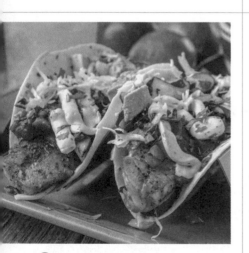

6 Eat Baja-style Fish Tacos

Featured on countless menus across town, fish tacos—battered and fried whitefish fillets, cabbage, pico de gallo, crema, fresh lime, corn tortillas—are San Diego's unofficial, must-try meal. *(Ch. 6, 8)*

7 Hike Mount Woodson

Mount Woodson is best known for a picturesque 6.4-mile loop that goes past well-known Potato Chip Rock. It's not an easy hike, taking most people about three hours to complete. *(Ch. 10)*

8 Book a Kayak Tour or Surf Lesson in La Jolla

One of the best local beaches for water sports, La Jolla Shores has rental and tour companies located just steps from the sand. There's surf or SUP lessons, as well as snorkel and kayak tours. *(Ch. 7)*

9 Take the Ferry to Coronado

The 15-minute ferry ride between Downtown San Diego and Coronado provides great views of Downtown and Naval Air Station North Island. *(Ch. 9)*

10 The Beauty of Untouched Nature

You'll find the rare Torrey pine at Torrey Pines State Natural Reserve; there's also hiking trails, spectacular bluffs, sweeping ocean views, and access to Torrey Pines State Beach. *(Ch. 7)*

11 Visit a Local Craft Brewery

With more than 150 craft breweries spread throughout San Diego County, it's safe to say you'll have an easy time finding quality beer. *(Ch. 3, 5, 8, 10)*

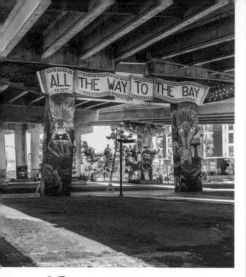

12 Colorful Mexican-American History

Designated a National Historic Landmark in 2017, Barrio Logan's Chicano Park features large murals that depict Mexican-American history and Chicano activism. *(Ch. 3)*

13 Panoramic Views and Whale Sightings

The 144-acre Cabrillo National Monument contains rugged cliffs, beautiful overlooks, the Old Point Loma Lighthouse, and great tide pools. *(Ch. 8)*

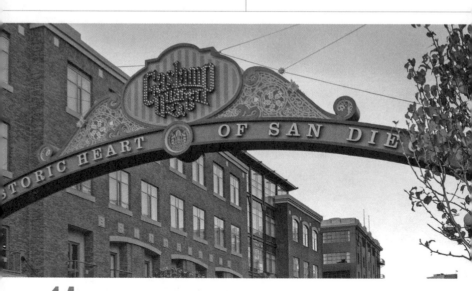

14 Explore the Gaslamp Quarter

Covering more than 16 city blocks, this bustling neighborhood is great for shopping, dining, and nightlife. Guided walking tours of the historic district are available. *(Ch. 3)*

15 Spend a Day Exploring Balboa Park

This 1,200-acre urban park houses 18 museums, performing arts venues, gardens, sculptures, and other attractions like the San Diego Zoo. *(Ch. 4)*

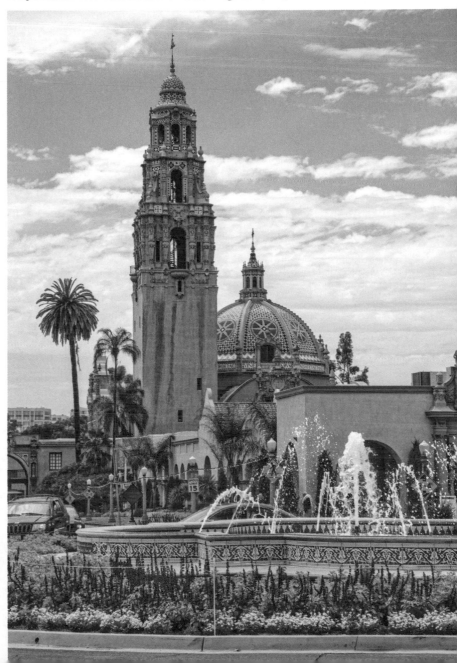

WHAT'S WHERE

1 Downtown. Streets are lined with night-clubs, boutiques, and restaurants, from the glam Gaslamp Quarter to the edgier East Village (home to Petco Park). Seaport Village, the Embarcadero, and Little Italy are nearby.

2 Balboa Park, Bankers Hill, and San Diego Zoo. This park has museums, performing arts venues, stunning Spanish revival architecture, and the San Diego Zoo. Bankers Hill, on the park's west side, is an affluent neighborhood home to numerous eateries.

3 Old Town and Uptown. Old Town's state park has historic buildings, galleries, and Mexican eateries. Uptown's a cluster of trendy neighborhoods north of Balboa Park. Hillcrest is the heart of the city's LGBTQ community, while hip North Park has boutiques, eateries, and bars. South Park has charming shops and cafés. Historic Mission Hills is between Old Town and Hillcrest; northeast lie the Mission Valley and Fashion Valley shopping hubs.

4 Mission Bay and the Beaches. Home to SeaWorld and a 4,600-acre aquatic park perfect for water activities. Mission Beach and Pacific Beach—full of surf shops, casual cafés, and beach bars—are nearby.

5 La Jolla. Picturesque cliffs and beaches, the famous seals, and a bevy of hotels, restaurants, galleries, and shops. Kearney Mesa's home to San Diego's Asian food mecca, Convoy District; nearby Clairemont also has good Asian food.

6 Point Loma Peninsula. The peninsula has grand houses, seafood eateries, Liberty Station, and Cabrillo National Monument. Harbor Island and Shelter Island are between the peninsula and Coronado, and farther north is Ocean Beach's Sunset Cliffs.

7 Coronado. An island-like peninsula across from the San Diego waterfront, the upscale area has the fabled Hotel del Coronado, two naval bases, and lots of shopping, dining, and sand.

8 North County and Around. Beach towns like Del Mar, Encinitas, Carlsbad; family attractions like LEGOLAND and the San Diego Zoo Safari Park; wineries in Temecula; and the Anza-Borrego Desert.

10 Best Beaches in San Diego

CORONADO
Often praised for its sparkling sand, the island is home to the Hotel del Coronado, a 135-year-old luxury hotel perfect for postbeach snacks; Del Beach, which is open to the public; and Dog Beach where pooches can run free sans leash.

MISSION BEACH
Located near SeaWorld San Diego, Mission Beach is home to a bustling board-walk that's frequented by walkers, cyclists, and people-watchers. The bay is popular for water sports such as stand-up paddle-boarding and Jet Skiing, but the beach is best known for Belmont Park, its ocean-front amusement park.

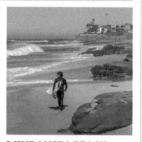

WINDANSEA BEACH
Seasoned surfers should head to La Jolla's Windan-sea Beach for powerful waves. Tucked away in a residential area, Windan-sea's entrance is marked by large rocks that make for a great place to watch or dry out, but recreational swimming is not advised here due to the strong surf.

TORREY PINES STATE BEACH
Situated at the base of a 1,500-acre natural reserve, La Jolla's Torrey Pines State Beach offers a long, narrow stretch of pristine beach framed by picturesque sea cliffs. Beachgoers can add a hike to their itinerary that starts or finishes on the sand, with plenty of lookout areas for great photo ops. Beyond the bluffs, a salt marsh provides seclusion from businesses and their associated street noise.

LA JOLLA SHORES
Pack up the whole family for a beach day in La Jolla Shores, which is known for its calm waves, two parks, and playground. Sea caves and underwater canyons that are part of La Jolla Underwater Park and Ecological Reserve—a marine protected area— attract kayakers and scuba divers.

DEL MAR CITY BEACH
In the upscale coastal neighborhood of Del Mar lie two beach parks that are popular for special events because of their stunning views of the Pacific. Seagrove Park is perched on the hill at the end of 15th Street, with benches for ocean gazing and winding paths along the bluffs. Farther north across the railroad tracks, Powerhouse Park offers easy beach access, a playground area, and a volleyball court.

SWAMI'S STATE BEACH
West of the magnificent Self-Realization Fellowship Temple and Meditation Gardens in Encinitas, this

La Jolla Shores is the best beach in San Diego for water sports.

beach draws surfers and yogis in with its Zen vibes, while others treat the steep staircase leading down to the beach as a workout, with a rewarding view of sea cliffs waiting at the bottom. At low tide, shells and other sea creatures are left behind for beachcombers to easily discover.

FLETCHER COVE BEACH PARK

Nestled in the heart of Solana Beach, Fletcher Cove Beach Park doubles as a recreational park and beach access area. Here you'll find a basketball court, playground, lawn area, and picnic tables. A paved ramp leads down to the crescent-shape beach that's flanked by cliffs on both sides.

MOONLIGHT STATE BEACH

Fans of active beach days should head to this Encinitas beach. Volleyball courts, picnic tables, and playgrounds line the beach, with a concession stand, equipment rentals, and free Sunday concerts in high season.

For sweeping views of the ocean, position yourself at one of the lookouts outfitted with seating and/or binoculars—yup, binoculars are waiting for you.

BEACON'S BEACH

Follow the windy dirt path laden with switchbacks down to find Beacon's Beach in Encinitas, a well-known beach spot and favorite locals' hangout; on maps it may be labeled Leucadia State Beach. Since its entrance is hidden below sea cliffs on a one-way residential street, Beacon's Beach has an air of exclusivity. With plenty of space to spread out here, you won't have to infringe on sun-worshipping neighbors.

What to Eat and Drink

CRAFT BEER

Dubbed the "Capital of Craft," San Diego has more than 150 craft breweries, a movement that began with Karl Strauss Brewing Company in 1989. Since then, the San Diego Brewers Guild established an annual San Diego Beer Week every November, and a few neighborhoods have become craft brewery destinations in their own right including "Beeramar" (Miramar) and North Park's "Beer Boulevard" (30th Street).

MEXICAN FOOD

California burritos, carne asada fries, and fish tacos are common staples at the city's Mexican restaurants. If you can't make the trip to Tijuana, the most authentic San Diego alternative is Las Cuatro Milpas, a no-frills eatery that typically draws a line of people around the corner at lunchtime. For exceptional tacos of many varieties, head to Puesto, Galaxy Taco, or Lola 55.

ASIAN FOOD

The Convoy District in Kearny Mesa is San Diego's Asian food mecca. Here you'll find Chinese, Vietnamese, Thai, Japanese, Korean, and Filipino restaurants—all within a stone's throw of one another.

SEAFOOD FRESH FROM THE OCEAN

You don't have to go far to find a bounty of fresh seafood in San Diego, most likely sourced from the waters off Southern California and Baja California. Always check out the day's catch—usually served as a sandwich, salad, or plate—and what's been shucked on ice.

SUSHI

Sushi should be a no-brainer when visiting San Diego, especially for tourists from landlocked states who don't often get fresh fish.

FISH TACOS

There's a great debate about who makes the best fish tacos in town. There are numerous options, but Rubio's Coastal Grill is credited with popularizing fish tacos in the United States; the original location is still in Pacific Beach. The original tacos have fried pollock, white sauce, salsa, cabbage, and a corn tortilla.

DISTILLERIES

This is a craft beer town, but that hasn't stopped distilleries from popping up. Cutwater Spirits has nine types of spirits and 26 ready-to-drink canned cocktails; Malahat Spirits specializes in small-batch, handcrafted rum, whiskey, bourbon, and vodka; and You & Yours Distilling offers gin and vodka.

A trip to San Diego isn't complete without fish tacos.

VEGETARIAN FOOD

Californians are generally known to be health conscious, eating lots of fresh local produce (including adding avocado to everything) and exercising outdoors year-round. There are plentiful vegetarian and vegan options throughout the city.

SWEETS

Calories don't count on vacation, right? There are plenty of options to indulge in here including exquisite layered cakes, cookies, and classic French pastries. And we'd be remiss if we didn't mention the local chocolatiers. Artisanal chocolate, bonbons and truffles, and flavored chocolate bars are yours for the tasting.

COFFEE

You'll be hard-pressed to find a San Diego neighborhood that lacks a proper coffee shop these days, as many of the local roasters have recently expanded their operations and added new locations. Dark Horse Coffee Roasters, a handcrafted, small-batch roaster, has six San Diego locations. James Coffee Co. brews single-origin beans and custom blends at its four coffee shops. Bird Rock Coffee Roasters brews ethically sourced java at its three San Diego spots.

TIKI COCKTAILS

Tiki culture has obvious parallels to San Diego's tropical, laid-back vacation vibe, so it's no surprise that the concept took root here with rum as the star spirit. Sure bets include The Grass Skirt, False Idol, and Fairweather Bar.

MARGARITAS

San Diego's mixologists have elevated the burgeoning cocktail scene, and margaritas can come skinny, spicy, or standard, with house-made sours and fresh-squeezed juices.

San Diego on Tap

CUTWATER SPIRITS

Created as an offshoot of Ballast Point, Cutwater is best known for its 26 flavors of canned cocktails, including a tequila margarita and a vodka mule. Their Tasting Room & Kitchen in Miramar is a full-service restaurant and bar with mixed drinks, neat pours, and tasting flights. ⊕ *cutwaterspirits.com*

BALLAST POINT BREWING COMPANY

The popularity of its gold medal–winning Sculpin IPA helped launch Ballast Point to its position as a nationwide favorite. With tasting rooms and restaurants in Little Italy and Miramar—plus a home brew mart and tasting room in Morena—Ballast Point is a must-visit stop on any San Diego brewery tour. ⊕ *ballastpoint.com*

BORDER X BREWING

San Diego's first Mexican-owned brewery delivers creative pours like the Blood Saison, a spinoff of the traditional Mexican *agua fresca* drink. Located in the predominantly Mexican-American neighborhood of Barrio Logan, there's a spacious back patio and it's close to great taco shops. ⊕ *borderxbrewing.com*

STONE BREWING

Best known for its Arrogant Bastard Ale, Stone is viewed as a pioneer of West Coast IPA and Double IPA styles. Stone Brewing World Bistro & Gardens locations in Point Loma and Escondido serve up eclectic worldly cuisine alongside hoppy pints, wine, and brewery merch. ⊕ *stonebrewing.com*

EPPIG BREWING

With arguably the most scenic brewery location in town, Waterfront Biergarten in Point Loma overlooks the San Diego Bay and a nearby marina. There's a diverse spread of lagers, pilsners, ales, sours, and stouts. Better yet, try a taster flight and watch the sunset over the water. ⊕ *eppigbrewing.com*

YOU & YOURS DISTILLING CO.

Specializing in gin and grape-based vodka, You & Yours also sells their spirits as canned cocktails such as flavored gin and tonics and vodka sodas. Head to their East Village tasting room for cocktails, flights, and a limited food menu. ⊕ *youandyours.com*

KARL STRAUSS BREWING COMPANY

Touted as San Diego's first craft brewery in 1989, Karl Strauss continues to produce innovative new beers like their 31st-anniversary whiskey barrel–aged scotch ale, aged for 12 months. The Red Trolley Ale is a trusted old favorite, as are the beer pretzels and beer sausages served in their restaurants; there's a location in Little Italy. ⊕ *karlstrauss.com*

MODERN TIMES BEER

California's first employee-owned brewery, Modern Times is easily recognized by its consistently cool retro decor: think VHS and cassette tapes, lampshades, and cross-stitched tennis rackets. Modern Times also roasts its own coffee—get a taste of both specialties in their Black House coffee stout. There are locations in Point Loma and North Park. ⊕ *moderntimesbeer. com*

SOCIETE BREWING COMPANY

Societe's tasting room in Kearny Mesa offers a prime view of their adjacent barrel room and brewing facility. While you can't go wrong with The Pupil IPA, wine lovers shouldn't miss The Thief feral ale, made with grenache blanc grapes. The Harlot Belgian blonde ale is used to marinate the juicy carnitas served at their on-site food truck, Chacho's Tacos. ⊕ *societe-brewing.com*

San Diego Today

Although most visitors know little about San Diego beyond its fun-in-the-sun reputation, locals are talking about much more than the surf forecast and their tan lines. Concerns about the city's public infrastructure, budget woes, and homeless population are all topics of local debate. After a tumble during the last recession, housing prices have once again skyrocketed and affordability has become a renewed issue. However, San Diegans have managed to keep the city's overall forecast sunny. Several large companies, including Qualcomm, Petco, and Sony Electronics continue to call San Diego home base. The buzz around San Diego's science and biotech industry continues to grow, along with the flourishing craft beer trade. San Diego has been busy shedding its image as L.A.'s less sophisticated neighbor, and coming into an urban identity of its own. Across the region, residents are embracing new trends in the local art, shopping, dining, and cultural scenes.

TODAY'S SAN DIEGO

Eating well. All over town, new and exciting restaurants are popping up, celebrating both the local bounty and the region's diversity. Healthy and fresh California Modern cuisine remains a feature on many menus, while neighboring Baja Mexico has given rise to BajaMed, a fusion of Mexican and Mediterranean styles. San Diego's sizable Asian population has introduced everything from dim sum carts to Mongolian hot pot, while local sushi chefs take advantage of San Diego's reputation for some of the finest sea urchin in the world. The locavore trend has become somewhat of an obsession for San Diegans, and many restaurants are happy to highlight how and where they source their ingredients.

Toast of the town. San Diego continues to gain recognition as one of the most exciting beer towns in the nation. Craft brewers creating a buzz include Ballast Point, Societe, and Modern Times, just to name a few, and Stone Brewing Company, creator of the notorious Arrogant Bastard Ale, has several locations. All this enthusiasm for San Diego's suds has given rise to a beer tourism industry, from bus tours of local brewers to large beer-theme events such as the popular San Diego Beer Week. There's even an app to help you find the perfect pint: inspired by the local brewing scene, a San Diego couple created the TapHunter website and mobile application, which helps beer lovers find what's on tap and where.

Building for the future, and conserving its past. A drive around San Diego reveals a huge range of architecture, from hip to historic to downright hideous. Urban planning from half a century ago, such as the decision to run Interstate 5 right through Little Italy and Downtown, is hard to undo, but other efforts to conserve the city's architectural integrity have been more successful. Downtown's Gaslamp Quarter is the most famous conservation area, but the residential neighborhoods of Uptown, Kensington, and South Park delight early-20th-century architecture buffs with streets full of historically designated homes. Projects making waves in San Diego today include the revitalization of the Embarcadero and the opening of The Rady Shell outdoor music venue.

Get outside. San Diego's near-perfect climate and gorgeous natural landscape make it hard to find an excuse not to get outside and exercise. In fact, San Diego is home to one of the most active populations in the country. Year-round opportunities to surf, sail, bike, or hike offer something for everyone. On weekends and throughout the summer, beaches and parks teem with locals enjoying the great weather and fresh air. Gas barbecues, bouncy houses, and huge shade tents take the concept of the picnic to a whole new level. So when visitors hailing from harsher climates wonder if San Diegans appreciate how good they have it, the answer is a resounding yes.

WHAT WE'RE TALKING ABOUT

After years of back and forth over funding and new stadium proposals, Chargers fans learned in early 2017 that their NFL team would be leaving San Diego and heading north to Los Angeles. The new Snapdragon Stadium site is now home to San Diego State University's football team as well as soccer and rugby leagues.

The buzz surrounding San Diego's craft beer community is growing louder. The sales of local breweries Ballast Point to Constellation Brands—for a whopping $1 billion—Saint Archer to MillerCoors, and Stone Brewing to Sapporo USA made international headlines, and solidified San Diego's reputation as one of the nation's best beer cities. The sales ignited the aspirations of nearly 160 other local brewers, demonstrating the ability to turn their passion into profit.

San Diego loves its markets, and the Liberty Public Market and Little Italy Food Hall are no exceptions. Housed within Liberty Station, the mixed-use redevelopment of the old San Diego Naval Training Center, Liberty Public Market buzzes with residents and tourists alike. Vendors sell fresh meat, seafood, pasta, and other ingredients alongside a variety of prepared foods such as empanadas,

lobster rolls, tostadas, and baked goods. Situated within a 10,000-square-foot piazza, Little Italy Food Hall has eight rotating food stations including pizza, tacos, and gelato, plus a full bar. Indoor and outdoor seating areas throughout both markets make these popular lunch spots.

WHAT WE'RE LOOKING FORWARD TO

■ The opening of SeaWorld San Diego's highly anticipated straddle coaster, Arctic Rescue.

■ The newest addition to LEGOLAND California Resort, a LEGO version of San Diego called Miniland U.S.A.: San Diego.

■ The reopening of Lafayette Hotel and Swim Club and its three new restaurants, two bars, a vintage bowling alley, game room, and new pool bar.

■ The transformation of Horton Campus downtown, an innovation hub with office and lab space, plus parks and retail shops.

San Diego with Kids

BEACH FUN

A pail and shovel can keep kids entertained for hours at the beach—**Coronado Beach** is especially family-friendly. Be liberal with the sunscreen, even if it's cloudy.

If you're visiting in summer, check out Imperial Beach's **Sun and Sea Festival.** This sand castle competition in July even has a kids' contest.

Drop off the tweens and teens for a morning **surf lesson** and enjoy some guilt-free grown-up time. Or rent bikes for a casual family ride along the **Mission Bay boardwalk.** If that's not enough of an adventure, take your daring offspring on the **Giant Dipper,** an old wooden roller coaster at Mission Bay's **Belmont Park,** also home to a huge arcade and the Beach House.

TOP ATTRACTIONS

LEGOLAND California is a full day of thrills for kids 12 and under, while the **San Diego Zoo** and **San Diego Zoo Safari Park** satisfy all age groups and every kind of kid, from the curious (plenty of educational angles) to the boisterous (room to run around and lots of animals to imitate). They even have family sleepover nights in summer.

WINTER SIGHTINGS

If you're visiting in winter, try a **whale-watching** tour. Even if you don't see any migrating gray whales, the boat ride is fun. La Jolla's **Birch Aquarium** has enough glowing and tentacled creatures to send imaginations plummeting leagues under the sea.

MUSEUMS GEARED TO KIDS

An afternoon at the museum might elicit yawns until they spy all the neat stuff at Balboa Park's **San Diego Air & Space Museum,** which celebrates aviation and flight history with exhibitions that include actual planes. The **Fleet Science Center** inspires budding scientists with interactive exhibits and its IMAX dome theater. The **San Diego Model Railroad Museum** features miles and miles of model trains and track, including an incredibly detailed reproduction of the Tehachapi railroad circa 1952.

Downtown's **New Children's Museum** appeals to all age groups. With installations geared just for them and dry and wet art-making areas (less mess for you), kids can channel all that excess vacation energy into something productive. While they color and craft, you can admire the museum's ultracontemporary, sustainable architecture.

TAKE ME OUT TO THE BALL GAME

Baseball buffs will have a blast at **Petco Park,** where the San Diego Padres play all spring and summer. Petco's Gallagher Square, a grassy elevated area outside the stadium, offers stellar center-field views—plus all the action on a big screen—with a sandy play space if your kids get bored after a few innings.

TREATING YOUR TOTS

With locations in Pacific Beach and Encinitas, **The Baked Bear** (⊕ *www.thebakedbear.com*) offers customized ice cream sandwiches that are sure to please. If toys trump sweet treats, check out the classics at **Geppetto's** (⊕ *www.geppettostoys.com*), a family-run business with nine locations throughout San Diego, including Old Town, La Jolla, and the Fashion Valley Mall.

Free Things to Do in San Diego

San Diego may levy an unofficial "sunshine tax," but it makes up for it with plenty of free stuff. Aside from the beaches, backcountry trails, and verdant city parks—all as free as the steadfast sun and endless blue skies—a little careful planning can land you cost-free (or very cheap) fun for the whole family.

FREE IN BALBOA PARK

Balboa Park hosts its one-hour **Twilight in the Park** concert series from June through August, Tuesday through Thursday at 7 pm. Sit under the stars and take in everything from Dixieland jazz to Latin salsa. Also at the park, check out the **San Diego International Organ Festival** concerts Monday at 7:30 pm, from June to September, as well as 2 pm Sunday matinee concerts throughout the year. Balboa Park's **Screen on the Green,** an outdoor movie screening, runs on Thursday throughout August. The **Timken Museum of Art** in Balboa Park is free but a donation is suggested.

FREE CONCERTS

The **Del Mar Racetrack Summer Concert Series** features big-name local and national bands; it's technically free, though you still have to pay a few bucks for racetrack admission.

Also worth catching: Carlsbad's **TGIF Concerts in the Parks,** Friday at 6 pm; **Coronado Summer Concerts in the Park,** Sunday at 6 pm, May through September; the **Del Mar Summer Twilight Concert Series,** Tuesday at 7 pm, June through August; and Encinitas's **Sunday Summer Concerts by the Sea,** 3 pm, July and August.

The annual **Adams Avenue Unplugged** festival in April and **Adams Avenue Street Fair** in September both hit pay dirt: blues, folk, country, jazz, indie, world, and more—all for free.

FREE (OR INEXPENSIVE) TASTINGS

Beer aficionados can take a $15, 60-minute tour of the 55,000-square-foot **Stone Brewing Company**—groups fill up fast, maybe because of the free tastings at the end. At **Alpine Beer Company,** it's not free, but it's cheap: up to four tasters are just $2 each. Wine lovers might grab lunch from the on-site food truck at **Orfila Vineyards & Winery**, where picnic tables dot the pastoral landscape—the wine's not free, but the views are. Or spend an entire afternoon in **Temecula Wine Country**. Tastings typically aren't free, but you can find twofer coupons and other discounts online (⊕ *www.temeculawines.org*).

OCTOBER FREEBIES

October is Kids Free month for tots at the **San Diego Zoo, SeaWorld, Balboa Park Museums, San Diego Zoo Safari Park**, and more than 50 museums. Little ones can also snag meals on the house and more than 100 other perks throughout San Diego.

FREE MUSEUMS

The **MCASD** is always free for military families and all patrons under 25, and for everyone else the third Thursday of the month.

In February, you can pick up a free **Museum Month Pass** at San Diego libraries that offers half-off admission to 60 museums for the entire month.

Many of San Diego's museums offer a once-a-month free Tuesday, on a rotating schedule (see ⊕ *www.balboapark.org* for the schedule) to San Diego city and county residents and active military, and their families; special exhibitions often require separate admission.

What to Read and Watch

THE HOUSE OF BROKEN ANGELS
Centered on three generations of a Mexican-American family, with a history in the California Territories since World War I, this novel written by Luis Alberto Urrea is about family love and heartbreak, teeming with big personalities and vivid characters.

THE GANGSTER WE ARE LOOKING FOR
The characters of Le Thi Diem Thuy's novel are Vietnamese refugees in the late '70s, adjusting to life in crowded bungalows and apartments of Normal Heights, Linda Vista, and East San Diego. The protagonist, a young girl, flees Vietnam with her father and is sponsored by a churchgoing family in San Diego after their long journey. The novel is based on the author's own childhood.

TIJUANA STRAIGHTS
Set in San Diego, San Ysidro, and the area around the Mexican border, the cast of characters is made up of washed-up surfers, gangsters, down-and-outs, and others in dire straits. Kem Nunn's novel has a suspenseful and entertaining storyline, full of chases, crimes, and mysterious circumstances across borders; it's also a glimpse at the gritty violence and adventures in the land between California and Mexico.

TOP GUN (1986, 2022)
This famous late '80s flick, starring a cocky Tom Cruise in pilot school, filmed most of its base scenes at the elite pilot school that it fictionalizes, the Naval Air Station Miramar in San Diego (it's since moved to Nevada). Other key scenes were filmed throughout San Diego County, in Oceanside, and at Kansas City Barbeque, a divey sports bar in San Diego's Embarcadero (the bar proudly displays memorabilia from the movie). The movie's 2022 sequel, *Top Gun:*

Maverick was also filmed in Coronado and Point Loma.

ANCHORMAN (2004)
In this raunchy comedy, Will Ferrell plays Ron Burgundy, a beloved San Diego news anchor who faces challenges to his job and sexist way of thinking when a female news anchor (Christina Applegate) comes on the scene. While the loud comedy boasts San Diego as its setting, much was filmed in L.A., with great pains taken to make everything look like San Diego.

TRAFFIC (2000)
This complex and moving film tackles the war on drugs through several different points of view and experiences of the people within it. San Diego scenes include the ritzy Ranch Bernardo Inn, La Jolla coast, the Hall of Justice courthouse in Downtown San Diego, Balboa Park and the botanical gardens, and the San Ysidro/Tijuana border crossing just south of San Diego.

FAST TIMES AT RIDGEMONT HIGH (1982)
This humorous coming-of-age film has become something of a cult classic, but many people don't know it's based on the book and journalistic efforts of Cameron Crowe (the young *Rolling Stone* prodigy reporter). Cameron spent a year undercover in Clairemont High School in San Diego, and the book and movie tell the account of this wild, adolescent year and the characters he meets.

VERONICA MARS
A drama series starring Kristen Bell as a young crime-solver wrapped up in the (many) mysteries of her wealthy beachside town, seasons of *Veronica Mars* were filmed almost entirely in and around San Diego.

Chapter 2

TRAVEL SMART

Updated by
Claire Deeks van der Lee

POPULATION
1,390,000

LANGUAGE
English

$ CURRENCY
U.S. dollar

AREA CODES
619 and 858

⚠ EMERGENCIES
911

🚗 DRIVING
On the right

⚡ ELECTRICITY
120–240 v/60 cycles;
plugs have two or three
rectangular prongs

🕐 TIME
Pacific Daylight Time (three
hours behind New York)

🌐 WEB RESOURCES
www.sandiego.org

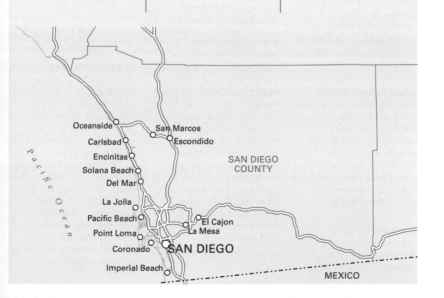

Know Before You Go

A desirable destination for beachgoers, outdoor enthusiasts, and culture seekers, San Diego attracts more than 35 million visitors annually. Take the guesswork out of packing and planning for your trip with these insider tips on what to expect, what to bring, and what to avoid.

BRING LAYERS

Known for having one of the most temperate climates in the country, San Diego's typical weather forecast is 70s and sunny. But tourists who have never visited the Southern California paradisical city are often surprised to find out how cool it gets at night. Many businesses and residences—particularly older buildings—do not have central heating or air-conditioning, so it's advised to bring a light jacket or sweater for summer evenings, and heavier knits during winter. Coastal neighborhoods can turn particularly chilly from ocean breezes.

WEAR COMFY SHOES

San Diego's a walkable town, and based on the traffic and lack of parking, you should walk as much as possible. Balboa Park and the Zoo are walkers' paradises, and all of Downtown is pedestrian-friendly.

SUNRISE, SUNSET

The beaches can't be beat, but battling the crazy summer crowds for a spot on the sand is far from relaxing. Take a stroll just after dawn, or find a secluded spot on the cliffs, for a more serene sunset.

IF YOU DECIDE TO GO TO MEXICO, BRING YOUR PASSPORT

San Diego's an international border city, located only 17 miles from Tijuana, making it easy to plan a trip to both cities in a single visit. But gone are the days when Americans could cross the border into Mexico and return by simply showing their driver's license. For the last decade, U.S. Customs and Border Protection has required Americans to show a valid passport to return home after a day of tacos and margaritas in Mexico. From San Diego, the easiest way to travel to the border is by taking the trolley ($5 round-trip) to San Ysidro on the blue line, and then walk across—retracing your steps on the way back. Check the CBP Border Wait Times mobile app for estimated wait times around the clock.

SAN DIEGO IS A NAVY TOWN

With more than 143,000 active-duty service members and another 241,000 veterans, San Diego has the largest military concentration in the world. While in town (especially Coronado), you will likely see service members walking in uniform, or catch them driving special military vehicles. The best opportunity to interact with them or visit an active military base is during Fleet Week San Diego, held each fall. Visitors can also take self-guided tours of decommissioned aircraft carrier USS *Midway* Museum, open to the public year-round. Naval Air Station North Island is the birthplace of naval aviation. Naval Base San Diego is home to the largest contingency of ships in the U.S. Pacific Fleet, and Naval Amphibious Base Coronado is headquarters to elite special forces commands including the U.S. Navy SEALs.

GOOD LUCK FINDING A HOTEL IF YOU'RE VISITING DURING COMIC-CON INTERNATIONAL

More than 130,000 people, including big-name celebrities, flock to San Diego Convention Center each July for Comic-Con International. You can expect area lodging prices to be at an all-time high during the convention (which lasts for about five days), with hotel rooms and Airbnb rentals booked several months in advance. People in cosplay take over the streets of Downtown, with additional spectators there to people-watch—inevitably causing heavy traffic into and out of the Downtown area. Check the Comic-Con website for event dates to plan accordingly.

AVOID RUSH HOUR

San Diego does not have a good public transit system to effectively help the thousands of people who commute across the city every day, causing bad weekday traffic from about 7 to 10 am and 3 to 7 pm. The I–5 and I–805 that run north and south are arguably the worst, and the I–15 and I–8 can also get bad during peak drive times. But as the locals say, it's still never as bad as driving in Los Angeles.

IT'S THE CRAFT BEER CAPITAL FOR A REASON

Sure, you could drink mainstream beer like Budweiser in San Diego, but you'll be hard-pressed to find it on tap at local bars or restaurants. San Diego is proud of its booming craft beer industry, evidenced by the more than 150 craft breweries throughout the county that are loyally supported by locals. India Pale Ales are the most common brews, but you'll find other varieties being poured to please your palate, in addition to ciders, hard kombucha, and mead.

SAN DIEGO IS HOME TO MAJOR THEME PARKS

If you're bringing kids to San Diego, there won't be a shortage of places to entertain them. Take a day off from the beach to visit local amusement parks, including San Diego Zoo and Safari Park, SeaWorld, and LEGOLAND. Adjacent to San Diego Zoo, Balboa Park houses 17 museums, as well as restaurants, gardens, and other attractions. Expect larger crowds during the summer months, and shop for multipark passes if you plan to park hop.

■ TIP→ **Adult beverages are available for purchase at all area theme parks.**

"MAY GRAY, JUNE GLOOM"

This common phrase in San Diego essentially means don't expect to see the sun during those months. An offshore marine layer that forms overnight is typically burned off by midmorning sun, but until then, it leaves a blanket of thick fog over much of the coastal area. During May and June, the marine layer often doesn't burn off, leaving the city with fall-like temps and cloud-covered beaches. For the warmest weather, visit during high season, between July and September.

PARKING CAN BE TRICKY

The electric scooter trend continues to be a divisive topic in San Diego, with some communities like Coronado banning them, while other areas encourage their use to get cars off the road and free up parking spots. There's an abundance of scooters sprinkled throughout Downtown, Balboa Park, and the beach communities, which are all accessed through a mobile app (depending on the brand) and cost $1 to activate. In San Diego, adults 18 years and older are no longer required to wear a helmet while riding, but it's still illegal to ride electric scooters on sidewalks.

TACO TUESDAYS ARE A WEEKLY TRADITION

If you like happy hour, then you'll love Taco Tuesdays in San Diego. Many local restaurants offer discounts on Tuesday that may also include drink specials. And it's not just Mexican restaurants that join in the tradition—eateries of all types and every price point have tempting deals. Browse Instagram for drool-worthy #TacoTuesday posts to begin plotting out your next tortilla-filled meal.

STAY AWAY FROM THE SEALS

They might look cute and cuddly, but keep away from the seals and sea lions that congregate at La Jolla's Children's Pool Beach. Do not feed them, and go with the knowledge that these playful creatures often leave a strong odor of feces in their wake.

FLIP-FLOPS AND SHORTS ARE THE NORM

You won't find a more casual big city. Flip-flops are the favored footwear, shorts and beachy skirts comprise the summer uniform, and designer jeans qualify as dressing up. Dining out warrants a little research; some eateries barely toe the "no shirt, no shoes" rule, while others require more elegant attire.

Getting Here and Around

When traveling in the San Diego area, consider the big picture to avoid getting lost. Water lies to the west of the city. To the east and north, mountains separate the urban areas from the desert. If you keep going south, you'll end up in Mexico.

Walking (or riding the bus or trolley) is the way to go once you've reached a destination area. Balboa Park and the Zoo are walkers' paradises, and all of Downtown, including the Gaslamp Quarter, Little Italy, Seaport Village, and Embarcadero, is pedestrian-friendly. In the heart of the city, numbered streets run west to east and lettered streets run north to south. The business district around the Civic Center, at 1st Avenue and C Street, is dedicated to local government and commerce.

 Air

Flying time to San Diego is 5 hours from New York, 4 hours from Chicago, 3 hours from Dallas, and 45 minutes from Los Angeles.

AIRPORT

The major airport is San Diego International Airport (SAN), formerly called Lindbergh Field. Most airlines depart and arrive at Terminal 2. Southwest, Frontier, JetBlue, and a handful of smaller carriers are reserved for Terminal 1. Free, color-coded shuttles loop the airport and match the parking lot they serve. The long-term parking lot on Harbor Drive and Liberator Way is a shuttle ride to the terminals. The Terminal 2 Parking Plaza services both terminals 1 and 2, charges $38 per day and has covered parking as well as charging stations. There is no longer a Terminal 1 parking lot due to a multiyear new Terminal 1 construction project. With limited parking, advanced reservations for the Terminal 2 Parking Plaza are recommended. The Cell Phone Lot for attended vehicles is convenient when picking up passengers. With only one runway serving two main terminals, San Diego's airport is too small to accommodate the heavy traffic of busy travel periods. Small problems including fog and rain can cause congested terminals and flight delays. Delays of 20–30 minutes in baggage claim aren't unusual.

If you have a flight delay, consider catching a 10-minute cab ride to the Gaslamp Quarter for last-minute shopping or a stroll around Downtown.

If you need travel assistance at the airport, Airport Ambassadors are stationed at the information centers in both terminals.

GROUND TRANSPORTATION

San Diego International Airport is 3 miles from Downtown. Shuttle vans, buses, and taxis run from the Transportation Plaza, reached via the skybridges from Terminals 1 and 2. The cheapest and sometimes most convenient shuttle is the Metropolitan Transit System's Flyer Route 992, red-and-white-stripe buses that serve the terminals at 10- to 15-minute intervals between 5 am and midnight. These buses have luggage racks and make a loop from the airport to Downtown along Broadway to 9th Avenue and back, stopping frequently within walking distance of many hotels; they also connect with the San Diego Trolley and Amtrak. The $2.50 fare includes transfer to local transit buses and the trolley, and ticket vending machines are located in both terminals. Information about the Metropolitan Transit System's shuttles and buses, the San Diego Trolley, and Coaster commuter train can all be found on the joint transit website, San Diego 511 (⊕ *www.511sd.com*).

If you're heading to North County, the MTS route 992 can drop you off across from the Santa Fe Depot, where you can take the Coaster commuter train as far north as Oceanside for $6.50.

Ground shuttle service is available between LAX and San Diego, but can be prohibitively expensive, with rates for the two-hour trip starting at $365, so a car rental may be a more economical option.

Taxis departing from the airport are subject to regulated fares—($4 initial fee, $4.10 per mile, $3 airport surcharge). Taxi fare is about $23 plus tip to most Downtown hotels. The fare to Coronado runs about $38 plus tip. Limousine rates vary and are charged per hour, per mile, or both, with some minimums established.

Rideshare services such as Uber and Lyft operate from designated pickup points at each terminal.

Boat

Many hotels, marinas, and yacht clubs rent slips short-term. Call ahead, because available space is limited. The San Diego and Southwestern yacht clubs have reciprocal arrangements with other yacht clubs.

Flagship Cruises takes you between Downtown and Coronado in a nostalgic, old-school ferry every hour from 9 am to 9 pm. The ride lasts about 15 minutes and costs $7 each way; bicycles and Segways are free.

Car

To fully explore sprawling San Diego— especially with kids in tow—consider renting a car. Nearly everything of interest can be found off I–5 or I–163, and the county's freeways are wide and easy to use. Traffic isn't a major issue if you avoid rush hour. Parking in urban areas is typically metered, Monday through Saturday, 10 to 8, unless otherwise marked. You may park for free outside those hours, and on Sunday and holidays.

■ TIP→ **Yellow commercial loading zones are fair game for parking after 6 pm.**

During special Downtown events, such as Padres games, you'll likely have to settle for one of the many paid parking structures—they cost around $30 close to the action. Parking at beaches is free for the most part, though tough to come by on sunny days unless you stake out a spot early.

A car is necessary for getting around greater San Diego on the sprawling freeway system and for visiting the North County beaches, mountains, and desert. Driving around San Diego County is pretty simple: most major attractions are within a few miles of the Pacific Ocean. Interstate 5, which stretches north–south from Oregon to the Mexican border, bisects San Diego. Interstate 8 provides access from Yuma, Arizona, and points east. Drivers coming from the Los Angeles area, Nevada, and the mountain regions beyond can reach San Diego on I–15. During rush hours there are jams on I–5 and on I–15 between I–805 and Escondido.

There are a few border inspection stations along major highways in San Diego County, the largest just north of

Getting Here and Around

Oceanside on I–5 near San Clemente. Travel with your driver's license, and bring your passport if you're an international traveler.

Gas is widely available in San Diego County, except in rural areas. Outlets are generally open 24 hours and accept major credit cards that can be processed at the pump. Full service is not available, but you will usually find window-washing tools next to a pump. with water and air available somewhere on the property. All fuel in California is unleaded and sold at three price levels. Pricing is per gallon pumped and varies widely by season, location, and oil company provider. In San Diego gas tends to cost about 15% more than it does in many other California cities.

There are nearly 60 charging stations for electric vehicles in San Diego, located at Balboa Park, recreation centers, libraries, upscale hotels, and entertainment districts. A map of EV charging stations is available at ⊕ www.sandiego.gov.

PARKING

Meters in Downtown usually cost $1.25 to $2.50 an hour; enforcement is generally 10–8 every day but Sunday. Be extra careful around rush hour, when certain on-street parking areas become tow-away zones. Violations in congested areas can cost $45 or more. In the evening and during events in Downtown, parking spaces are hard to find. Most Downtown hotels offer valet parking service. The Convention Center has nearly 2,000 spaces that go for $15 to $35 for event parking. On game day at Petco Park, expect to pay $15 to $35 for a parking space a short walk from the stadium. Other Downtown lots cost $10–$45 per day.

Balboa Park and Mission Bay have huge free parking lots, and it's rare not to find a space, though it may seem as if you've parked miles from your destination. Old Town has large lots surrounding the transit center, but parking spaces are still hard to find. Parking is more of a problem in La Jolla and Coronado, where you generally need to rely on hard-to-find metered street spots or expensive by-the-hour parking lots.

RENTAL CARS

In California you must be 21 to rent a car, and rates may be higher if you're under 25. Some agencies will not rent to those under 25; check when you book. Children up to age eight or under 4 feet, 9 inches in height must be placed in safety or booster seats. For non–U.S. residents an international license is recommended but not required.

Rates fluctuate with seasons and demand, but generally begin at $39 a day and $250 a week for an economy car with air-conditioning, automatic transmission, and unlimited mileage. This doesn't include an 8.75% tax.

ROAD CONDITIONS

Highways are in good condition in the San Diego area. From 6 to 8:30 am and 3:30 to 6 pm, traffic is particularly heavy on I–5, I–8, I–805, and I–15. Before venturing into the mountains, check on road conditions; mountain driving can be dangerous. Check Caltrans or listen to radio traffic reports for information on the length of border waits from Mexico. For roadside assistance, dial 511 from a mobile phone.

Ⓜ Public Transport

Visit ⊕ www.511sd.com, which lists routes and timetables for the Metropolitan Transit System and North County Transit District. Local/urban bus fare is $2.50 one way, or $6 for an unlimited day pass (exact change only; pay when you board). A one-way ride on the city's iconic red trolleys is $2.50; get your ticket at any trolley vending machine.

Under the umbrella of the Metropolitan Transit System, there are two major transit agencies in the area: San Diego Transit and North County Transit District (NCTD). You will need to download the PRONTO app or buy a $2 PRONTO card, available when you board for the first time, on which are loaded your destinations to use MTS. Day passes, available for 1 to 30 days and starting at $6, give unlimited rides on nonpremium regional buses and the San Diego Trolley. You can buy them from most trolley vending machines, at the Downtown Transit Store, and at Albertsons markets. A $12 Regional Plus Day Pass adds Coaster service and premium bus routes.

The bright-red trolleys of the San Diego Trolley light-rail system operate on three lines that serve Downtown San Diego, Mission Valley, Old Town, South Bay, the U.S. border, UCSD, and East County. The trolleys operate seven days a week from about 5 am to midnight, depending on the station, at intervals of about 15 minutes. The trolley system connects with San Diego Transit bus routes—connections are posted at each trolley station. Bicycle lockers are available at most stations and bikes are allowed on buses and trolleys though space is limited. Trolleys can get crowded during morning and evening rush hours. Schedules are posted at each stop; on-time performance is excellent.

NCTD bus routes connect with Coaster commuter train routes between Oceanside and the Santa Fe Depot in San Diego. They serve points from Del Mar north to San Clemente, inland to Fallbrook, Pauma Valley, Valley Center, Ramona, and Escondido, with transfer points within the city of San Diego. The Sprinter light rail provides service between Oceanside and Escondido, with buses connecting to popular North County attractions.

San Diego Transit bus fares range from $2.50 to $5; North County Transit District bus fares are $2.50. You must have exact change in coins and/or bills. Pay upon boarding. Transfers are not included; the $6 day pass is the best option for most bus travel and can be purchased onboard.

San Diego Trolley tickets cost $2.50 and are good for two hours, but for one way travel only. Round-trip tickets are double the one-way fare.

Tickets are dispensed from self-service machines at each stop; exact fare in coins is recommended, although some machines accept bills in $1, $5, $10, and $20 denominations and credit cards. Ticket vending machines will return up to $5 in change. For trips on multiple buses and trolleys, buy a day pass good for unlimited use all day.

FRED (FREE RIDE EVERYWHERE DOWNTOWN)

These open-air electric vehicles offer free rides throughout the Downtown area 7 days a week. Riders can make a pickup request through the Ride Circuit app (⊕ www.ridecircuit.com/fred), or simply flag one down.

Getting Here and Around

Ride-Sharing

App-driven ride-sharing services such as Uber and Lyft are popular in San Diego. Drivers are readily available from most in-town destinations and also service the airport.

Taxi

Cabs are a fine choice for trips to and from the airport and short jaunts around town. The approximate rates are: $2.80 for the first 1/10 mile, $3 each additional mile, and $24 per hour of waiting time. You can find taxi stands at the airport, hotels, major attractions, and shopping centers. Downtown, your best bet is to flag one down.

If you are heading to the airport from a hotel, ask about the flat rate, which varies according to destination; otherwise you'll be charged by the mile (which works out to $20 or so from any Downtown location). Taxi stands are at shopping centers and hotels; otherwise you must call and reserve a cab.

PEDICABS

These pedal-powered tricycles with a rear passenger area are a great way to get around Downtown. Just be sure to agree on a price before you start moving, or you could get taken for the wrong kind of ride.

Train

Amtrak serves Downtown San Diego's Santa Fe Depot with daily trains to and from Los Angeles, Santa Barbara, and San Luis Obispo. The scenic "Pacific Surfliner" route delights with coastal views for much of the journey. Connecting service to Oakland, Seattle, Chicago, Texas, Florida, and points beyond is available in Los Angeles. Amtrak trains stop in San Diego North County at Solana Beach and Oceanside. You can obtain Amtrak timetables at any Amtrak station, or by visiting the Amtrak website. Recent track stabilization work has resulted in service modifications, so be sure to check the website for the most current schedules.

Coaster commuter trains, which run daily between Oceanside and San Diego, stop at the same stations as Amtrak as well as others. The frequency is about every half hour during the weekday rush hour, with four trains on Saturday (with additional Friday and Saturday night service in spring and summer). One-way fares are $5 to $6.50, depending on the distance traveled. The Oceanside, Carlsbad, and Solana Beach stations have beach access. The Sprinter runs between Oceanside and Escondido, with many stops along the way.

Train vending machines accept all major credit cards. Reservations, which you can make online, are suggested for trains running on weekends between San Diego and Santa Barbara. Make your reservations early to get the best fares. For security reasons, Amtrak requires ticket holders to provide photo ID.

Essentials

🏃 Activities

With average daily temperatures of 70.5°F, San Diego is built for outdoor activities year-round. As you'd expect, the ocean is one of San Diego's most popular natural attractions. Surfers, swimmers, kayakers, divers, snorkelers, and paddleboarders have 70 miles of shorefront to explore. What might surprise you is there is also great hiking, horseback riding, rock climbing, biking, and more.

The possibilities for outdoor activity really are endless and evidence of San Diego's outdoorsy spirit is apparent everywhere; you'll likely see runners swarming the waterfront and Balboa Park, groups of surfers bobbing in the water at dawn, hang gliders swooping off sandstone cliffs, and white sails gliding gracefully along the shore. Outdoor enthusiasts are as much a part of San Diego's landscape as the sea, sand, and hills, and if you want to get in on the action, it's easy. Companies offering kayak and snorkeling tours and rentals are prevalent, especially in the beach communities of La Jolla, Mission Beach, and on Coronado. If you want to learn to surf, sign up for a lesson at one of the many surf schools in La Jolla or rent a board in Mission Beach and go out on your own. If sightseeing is more your style you can head out on a fishing or whale-watching excursion aboard a charter boat or take a sunset stroll on a wide, sandy beach. At the end of the day at any beach in the county, you'll surely see a local ritual: everyone stops what they're doing to watch the sun's orange orb slip silently into the blue-gray Pacific.

🍴 Dining

San Diego is a notable culinary destination, thanks to its stunning Pacific Ocean setting, proximity to Mexico, diverse population, and the area's extraordinary farming community. Increasingly the city's veteran top chefs are being joined by a new generation of talented chefs and restaurateurs who are adding stylish restaurants with innovative food and drink programs to the dining scene at a record pace. Yes, visitors still are drawn to the San Diego Zoo and miles of beaches, but now they come for memorable dining experiences as well.

The city's culinary scene got a significant boost when San Diego emerged as one of the world's top craft beer destinations, with artisan breweries and gastropubs now in almost every neighborhood. San Diego also was on the cutting edge of the farm-to-table, Slow Food movement. Local sourcing is possible for everything from seafood to just-picked produce from a host of nationally recognized producers like Chino Farms and Carlsbad Aquafarm. The city's ethnically diverse neighborhoods with their modest eateries offering affordable authentic international cuisines add spice to the dining mix.

San Diego's distinct neighborhoods have their own dining personalities with friendly restaurants and bistros catering to every craving in this sun-blessed city. The trendy Gaslamp Quarter delights visitors looking for a broad range of innovative and international dining and nightlife, while bustling Little Italy offers a mix of affordable Italian fare and posh new eateries. Modern restaurants and cafés thrive in East Village, amid the luxury condos near Petco Park.

Essentials

The Uptown neighborhoods centered on Hillcrest—an urbane district with San Francisco flavor—are a mix of bars and independent restaurants, many of which specialize in ethnic cuisine. North Park, in particular, has a happening restaurant and craft beer scene, with just about every kind of cuisine you can think of, and laid-back prices to boot. And scenic La Jolla offers some of the best fine dining in the city with dramatic water views as an added bonus.

DINING HOURS
Unless otherwise noted, the restaurants listed in this guide are open daily for lunch and dinner. Lunch is typically served 11:30 am to 2:30 pm, and dinner service in most restaurants begins at 5:30 pm and ends at 10 pm, though a number of establishments serve until 11 pm or later on Friday and Saturday nights.

WHAT TO WEAR
In San Diego restaurants, generally a "come-as-you-are" attitude prevails. It's a casual city for men and women alike, but going-out dress is generally fashionable and fun, especially for celebratory or upscale dining. Very few dress-up places remain.

CHILDREN
Most San Diego restaurants welcome children and many have special kids' menus with food offerings targeted to younger palates and parents' pocketbooks. Some high-end and bar-oriented establishments may not be appropriate for children—if unsure, call the establishment for confirmation.

PARKING
With the boom of new apartments and condominiums Downtown and in Little Italy, street parking near many restaurants can be frustrating, especially in the evenings and on weekends. Valet ($10–$15) parking in front of many major restaurants is easy and convenient. Some valet parking is subsidized by restaurants; call ahead for parking offers and suggestions. There are several parking garages and lots throughout Downtown with prices that fluctuate depending on events. For major Downtown events where parking is impossible, consider parking for free at the Old Town transit center and get a quick San Diego Trolley ride to stops in Little Italy, East Village, and the Gaslamp Quarter.

SMOKING
Smoking is banned in restaurants in California. It is also forbidden on outdoor patios in the cities of San Diego, Chula Vista, Del Mar, El Cajon, Encinitas, National City, and Solana Beach.

PRICES
Meals in San Diego popular dining spots can be pricey, especially in areas like La Jolla and the Gaslamp Quarter. Many other restaurants are very affordable or offer extra value with fixed-price menus, early-dining specials and early and late happy hours.

⇨ *Prices in the reviews are the average cost of a main course at dinner or, if dinner is not served, at lunch. Restaurant reviews have been shortened. For full information, visit Fodors.com.*

What It Costs in U.S. Dollars			
$	$$	$$$	$$$$
RESTAURANTS			
under $20	$20–$30	$31–$40	over $40

➕ Health and Safety

San Diego is generally a safe place for travelers who observe all normal precautions. Downtown can get a little rowdy at night, especially toward 2 am, when bars boot drunken patrons out on the sidewalks. The city also has a large homeless population, who often camp out on side streets not far from East Village. Most are harmless, aside from the occasional panhandling, but it's safest to stick to well-lighted, busy areas. Certain pockets of Balboa Park are frequented by drug dealers and prostitutes after hours; if you're attending a nighttime theater performance or art event, park nearby or use the valet.

At the beach, check with lifeguards about any unsafe conditions such as dangerous riptides or water pollution. The San Diego Tourism Authority offers a print and Web version of visitor safety tips, providing sensible precautions for many situations.

For police, fire, or ambulance, dial ☎ 911 (0 in rural areas).

🛏 Lodging

In San Diego, you could plan a luxurious vacation at the beach, staying at a resort with panoramic ocean views, private balconies, and a full-service spa. Or you could stay Downtown, steps from the bustling Gaslamp Quarter, in a modern hotel featuring lively rooftop pools, complimentary wine receptions, and high-tech entertainment systems. But with some flexibility—maybe opting for a partial-view room a quick drive from the action—it's possible to experience San Diego at half the price. And, even in the most expensive areas, you can find affordable rooms. High season is summer, and rates are lowest in fall. If an ocean view is important, request it when booking, but it will cost you.

Sharing the city's postcard-perfect sunny skies are neighborhoods and coastal communities that offer great diversity; San Diego is no longer the sleepy beach town it once was. In action-packed Downtown, luxury hotels cater to solo business travelers and young couples with trendy restaurants and cabana-encircled pools. Budget-friendly options can be found in smaller neighborhoods just outside the Gaslamp Quarter such as Little Italy and Uptown (Hillcrest, Mission Hills, and North Park).

You'll need a car if you stay outside Downtown, but the beach communities are rich with lodging options. Across the bridge, Coronado's hotels and resorts offer access to a stretch of glistening white sand that's often recognized as one of the best beaches in the country. La Jolla offers many romantic, upscale ocean-view hotels and some of the area's best restaurants and specialty shopping. But it's easy to find a water view in any price range: surfers make themselves at home at the casual inns and budget stays of Pacific Beach and Mission Bay. If you're planning to fish, check out hotels located near the marinas in Shelter Island, Point Loma, or Coronado.

For families, Uptown, Mission Valley, and Old Town are close to SeaWorld and the San Diego Zoo, offering good-value accommodations with extras like sleeper sofas and video games. Mission Valley is ideal for business travelers; there are plenty of well-known chain hotels with conference space, modern business centers, and kitchenettes for extended stays.

When your work (or sightseeing) is done, join the trendsetters flocking to Downtown's Gaslamp Quarter for its eateries, lounges, and multilevel clubs that rival L.A.'s stylish scenes.

Where Should I Stay?

	NEIGHBORHOOD VIBE	PROS	CONS
Downtown	Downtown's hub is the Gaslamp Quarter, an action-packed area with many hotels, boutiques, restaurants, and clubs. Little Italy and Embarcadero areas are quieter, but trendier and home to some of the city's hottest restaurants.	Close to food and nightlife options for every age and taste. Quick walk or trolley ride to convention center. Won't need a car to get to many attractions.	Streets can be congested and noisy at night, particularly in the Gaslamp Quarter and East Village. Overnight parking is expensive.
Uptown and Old Town	Quieter area north of Downtown with more budget-friendly hotels. Old Town has a busy stretch of Mexican restaurants and historic sites.	Central location that's close to Balboa Park and major freeways. Good for business travelers. More inexpensive dining options.	Feels more removed from San Diego's beachy vibe. Mission Valley area lacks character; it's filled with malls and car lots.
Mission Bay, Beaches, and SeaWorld	Relaxed and casual beachside area with many resorts, golf courses, and parks. Largest man-made aquatic park in the country.	Right on the water. Can splurge on Jet Skis and other water sports or stick to barbecues and public playgrounds. Close to SeaWorld.	Resorts are spaced far apart, and area is somewhat removed from central San Diego. Watch for high resort fees and other not-so-obvious charges.
La Jolla	The "jewel" of San Diego, an affluent coastal area with a small-town atmosphere. Has a range of luxury hotels and a few value choices.	Gorgeous views. Close to or right on the beach. Some of the best seafood restaurants and high-end shopping in the state. Safe area for walking.	Often congested, and parking can be nearly impossible in summer. Very expensive area. Has few hotels that cater to children.
Point Loma and Shelter Island	Areas by the bay have historic and resort hotels, beaches, and tourist-oriented restaurants. Point Loma is residential and home to many military families.	Great views of the city, bay, and beaches. Near the airport. Convenient for boaters. Hotels tend to be family-friendly, with large rooms and pools.	Isolated from the rest of the city; you'll spend significant time commuting to other parts of San Diego, such as La Jolla and Balboa Park.
Coronado	Coronado, home to the iconic Hotel del Coronado, is residential, home to many military families. It's the perfect place to bike, or relax on the beach.	Quiet, lovely neighborhood feel on an island with easy access to Downtown San Diego. Great beaches, restaurants, shopping, and nightlife.	This is an island, so you'll spend significant time commuting to other parts of San Diego, and parking can be tough.

Essentials

PARKING

Given the distances between attractions and limited public transportation routes, a car is almost a necessity for visitors to San Diego. That being said, a vehicle can significantly add to your expenses if you stay in the ritzier areas. Overnight parking in Coronado, La Jolla, and Downtown's Gaslamp Quarter can be as high as $50 per night; in Uptown and Mission Bay it usually runs $10 to $20.

PRICES

⇨ *Prices in the reviews are the lowest cost of a standard double room in high season. Hotel reviews have been shortened. For full information, visit Fodors. com.*

What It Costs in U.S. Dollars			
$	$$	$$$	$$$$
HOTELS			
under $200	$200– $350	$351– $500	over $500

RESERVATIONS

Book well in advance, especially if you plan to visit in summer, which is the busy season for most hotels. In spring and fall, conventions and sports events can fill every Downtown hotel room. When you make reservations, ask about specials. Several properties in the Hotel Circle area of Mission Valley offer reduced rates and even free tickets to the San Diego Zoo and other attractions. You can save on hotels and attractions by visiting the San Diego Tourism Authority website (⊕ *www. sandiego.org*) for special seasonal offers.

STAYING WITH KIDS

The area is full of hotels suited to a family's budget and/or recreational needs, and many allow kids under 18 to stay free with their parents. You'll find the most choices and diversity in and around Carlsbad near LEGOLAND, and Mission Bay, which is close to SeaWorld, beaches, parks, and Old Town.

SERVICES

Downtown hotels once catered primarily to business travelers, though the new boutique hotels are attracting hip leisure travelers to the area, while those at Mission Bay, in coastal locations such as Carlsbad and Encinitas, and at inland resort areas offer golf and other sports facilities, spa services, children's activities, and more. If you're traveling with pets, note that pet policies do change and some hotels require substantial cleaning fees of $50 to $100. At many San Diego hotels, even smoking outdoors is frowned on or prohibited.

Ⓢ Money

With the mild climate and proximity to the ocean and mountains, San Diego is popular with tourists and conventioneers and, accordingly, is a relatively expensive place to visit. Three-star rooms average between $200 and $280 per night in high season, but there is also a good variety of modest accommodations available. Meal prices compare to those in other large cities, and you can usually find excellent values by dining in smaller, family-run establishments. Admission to local attractions can cost anywhere from $10 to $90. Thankfully, relaxing on one of the public beaches or meandering through the parks and neighborhoods is free—and fun.

Prices here are given for adults. Substantially reduced fees are almost always available for children, students, and senior citizens. Most museums in Balboa Park offer free admission to residents on Tuesday.

Essentials

☯ Nightlife

The San Diego nightlife scene is much more diverse and innovative than it was just a decade ago. Back then, options were limited to the pricey singles-heavy dance clubs Downtown, the party-hearty atmosphere of Pacific Beach, and a handful of charmingly musty neighborhood dive bars popular with locals. Today, options in San Diego have expanded dramatically, boasting more than 150 craft breweries throughout the county, not to mention several stylish cocktail lounges.

The Gaslamp Quarter is still one of the most popular areas to go for a night on the town. Named for actual gaslights that once provided illumination along its once-seedy streets (it housed a number of gambling halls and brothels), the neighborhood bears only a trace of its debauched roots. Between the Gaslamp and nearby East Village, Downtown San Diego mostly comprises chic nightclubs, tourist-heavy pubs, and a handful of live music venues. Even most of the hotels Downtown have a street-level or rooftop bar—so plan on making it a late night if that's where you intend to bunk. Nearby, Little Italy offers a more subtly chic bar scene. On weekends, parking can be tricky; most lots run about $20, and though there is metered parking (free after 6 pm and all day Sunday), motorists don't give up those coveted spots so easily. Some restaurants and clubs offer valet, though that can get pricey.

Hillcrest is a popular area for LGBTQ nightlife and culture, whereas just a little bit east of Hillcrest, ever-expanding North Park features a diverse range of bars and lounges that cater to a twenty- and thirtysomething crowd, bolstering its reputation as the city's hipster capital. Nearby Normal Heights is a slightly less pretentious alternative, though whichever of these neighborhoods strikes your fancy, a cab from Downtown will run about the same price: $15.

Nightlife along the beaches is more of a mixed bag. Where the scene in Pacific Beach might feel like every week is spring break, La Jolla veers toward being more cost-prohibitive. And although Point Loma is often seen as a sleepier neighborhood in terms of nightlife, it's coming into its own with some select destinations.

If your drink involves caffeine and not alcohol, there's no shortage of coffeehouses in San Diego, and some of the better ones in Hillcrest and North Park stay open past midnight. Many of them also serve beer and wine, if the caffeine buzz isn't enough.

THE LOWDOWN

Step outside to smoke. Smoking is strictly outlawed indoors in public places in San Diego, and since 2014 that includes e-cigarettes or vaporizer pens.

What to wear. In the Gaslamp, East Village, and some of North Park's more upscale spots, dress code is strictly enforced: no flip-flops, ball caps, jerseys, or shorts at any of the city's swankier bars.

Last call for alcohol. The last chance for nightcaps is theoretically 2 am, but most bars stop serving around 1:30. Listen for the bartender's announcement.

WHAT'S GOING ON?

The city's daily paper, *The San Diego Union-Tribune* (⊕ *www.sandiegouniontribune.com*), has up-to-date entertainment listings, as well as the paper's more nightlife-heavy sister site *Pacific San Diego* (⊕ *www.pacificsandiego. com*), which provides event listings and editorial suggestions. San Diego's alt-weekly *The Reader* (⊕ *www.sandie-goreader.com*) boasts extensive online listings.

San Diego Magazine (⊕ *www.sandiego-magazine.com*) is a mainstream read for all walks of life; *Modern Luxury* (⊕ *www.modernluxury.com/san-diego*) is younger, more upscale, and au courant.

📷 Packing

Plan on warm weather at any time of the year. Cottons, walking shorts, jeans, and T-shirts are the norm. Pack bathing suits and shorts regardless of the season. Few restaurants require a jacket and tie for men. Women may want to also bring something a little dressier than their sightseeing garb.

Evenings are cool, even in summer, so be sure to bring a sweater or a light jacket. Rainfall in San Diego isn't usually heavy; you won't need a raincoat except in winter, and even then, an umbrella may suffice.

Be sure you have comfortable walking shoes. Even if you don't walk much at home, you will probably find yourself covering miles while sightseeing on your vacation. Also bring a pair of sandals or water shoes for the beach.

Sunglasses and sunscreen are a must in San Diego. Binoculars can also come in handy, especially if you're in town during whale-watching season, from December through mid-April, or planning to stargaze in the desert in the summer. If you plan on surfing, consider packing or renting a wet suit or rash guard depending on the season. In winter, water temperatures drop into the 50s and average around 72°F in the summer.

🎭 Performing Arts

A diverse and sophisticated arts scene probably isn't the first thing that visitors—or even locals—associate with San Diego. It's a destination for those who seek out its perennial sunshine, gorgeous beaches, and beautiful scenery. Even those within the arts scene readily admit their fiercest competition is the beach! But just a little to the right of the Pacific Ocean, there are some amazing and diverse artistic offerings to prove that San Diego can hold its own.

The theater scene in San Diego may not have the commercial appeal that Broadway does, but it more than makes up for it with talent. In fact, a long list of Broadway-bound productions started right here, including *Jersey Boys,* The Who's *Tommy, Dirty Rotten Scoundrels,* and *Memphis.*

Balboa Park's Old Globe Theatre is modeled after the Shakespearian Globe Theatre in England, and hosts both an annual Shakespeare Festival as well as contemporary plays. A little bit north is La Jolla Playhouse, which was founded by Gregory Peck in 1947, and has hosted dozens of world-premiere productions, in addition to star actors like Laura Linney and Neil Patrick Harris. The playhouse has also launched the Without Walls initiative, which places theater in a new context by removing the theater entirely.

Music also has a major presence in San Diego, courtesy of the world-class San Diego Opera, which performs major works by Puccini and Mozart, and the San Diego Symphony, which caters to a diverse audience thanks to both its classical concerts and its more accessible Summer Pops series.

Essentials

Whether you fancy *rond de jambes* or something a bit more modern, San Diego's scene is *en pointe* for dance fans.

There's always something new and exciting happening with visual arts in San Diego. No longer limited to a collector's market, younger urban artists are making inroads with warehouse gallery spaces in Barrio Logan, while galleries in La Jolla and Little Italy showcase bold works of contemporary art on their walls. The annual San Diego Art Prize highlights rising figures in the visual arts realm, and in the field of architecture, Orchids and Onions honors the best and worst in structural design—and with a sense of humor at that.

GALLERY AND MUSEUM NIGHTS

The art gallery and museum experience in San Diego isn't limited to the daytime—at night, a number of different museums and venues host after-business-hours events that attract a younger, cosmopolitan crowd.

TICKETS

Plan ahead and buy tickets early—ideally around the same time that you book your hotel. Not that you can't find an outlet that sells day-of-show tickets, but you'll run the risk of paying a grossly inflated price, and might not end up with good seats.

🛍 Shopping

San Diego's retail landscape has changed radically in recent years with the opening of several new shopping centers—some in historic buildings—that are focused more on locally owned boutiques than national retailers. Where once the Gaslamp was the place to go for urban apparel and unique home decor, many independently owned boutiques have decided to set up shop in Little Italy and the charming neighborhoods east of Balboa Park known as North Park and South Park. Although Downtown is still thriving, any shopping trip to San Diego should include venturing out to the city's diverse and vibrant neighborhoods.

Old Town is a must for pottery, ceramics, jewelry, and handcrafted baskets. Uptown is known for its mélange of funky bookstores, offbeat gift shops, and nostalgic collectibles and vintage stores. The beach towns offer the best swimwear and sandals. La Jolla's chic boutiques offer a more intimate shopping experience, along with some of the classiest clothes, jewelry, and shoes in the county. Point Loma's Liberty Station shopping area in the former Naval Training Center has art galleries, restaurants, and home stores. Trendsetters will have no trouble finding must-have handbags and designer apparel at the world-class Fashion Valley mall in Mission Valley, a haven for luxury brands such as Hermès, Gucci, and Jimmy Choo. The Carlsbad Outlets near LEGOLAND have nearly 100 designer outlet stores including Barneys New York, Coach, Kate Spade, Michael Kors, and Nike.

Enjoy near-perfect weather year-round as you explore shops along the scenic waterfront. The Headquarters at Seaport is an open-air shopping and dining center in the city's former Police Headquarters building. Here there are some big names, but mostly locally owned boutiques selling everything from gourmet cheese to coastal-inspired home accessories. Just next door, Seaport Village is still the place to go for trinkets and souvenirs.

Most malls have free parking in a lot or garage, and parking is not usually a problem.

OPENING HOURS

Shops near tourist attractions and the major shopping malls tend to open early and close late. Standard hours are typically 10 to 9 on weekdays and 10 to 10 on weekends. Smaller shops may close as early as 5 on weekdays and Sunday. It's best to call ahead to confirm hours if you have your heart set on visiting a particular shop.

OUTLET MALLS

Some hotels offer free shuttles to shopping centers, outlet malls, and nearby casinos. Check with the concierge for schedules.

Visitor Information

For general information and brochures before you go, contact the San Diego Tourism Authority, which publishes the helpful *San Diego Visitors Planning Guide*. When you arrive, stop by one of the local visitor centers for general information.

For a dining and entertainment guide to San Diego's most popular nightlife district, the Gaslamp Quarter, check out ⊕ *www.gaslamp.org*. For information on the birthplace of California, search the Old Town San Diego organization's site (⊕ *www.oldtownsandiego.org*).

ONLINE RESOURCES

Browse the website of San Diego's premier upscale lifestyle magazine, *Ranch and Coast*. *San Diego Magazine* also has a useful site. Search the site of ArtsTix for half-price show tickets. For a comprehensive listing of concerts, performances, and art exhibits, check out the local alternative paper *San Diego Reader*.

When to Go

San Diego's weather is so ideal that most locals shrug off the high cost of living and relatively low wages as a "sunshine tax." Along the coast, average temperatures range from the mid-60s to the high 70s, with clear skies and low humidity. Annual rainfall is minimal, less than 10 inches per year.

The peak season for sunseekers is July through October, but the best months for surfing are August through November. In July and August, the mercury spikes and everyone spills outside. Beaches are a popular daytime destination, as is Balboa Park, thanks to its shady groves and air-conditioned museums. Summer's nightlife scene thrives with the usual bars and clubs, plus outdoor concerts, theater, and movie screenings. Early fall is a pleasant time to visit, as many tourists have already left town and the temperature is nearly perfect. If you're into sportfishing, June through October is tuna season. From mid-December to mid-March, whale-watchers can glimpse migrating gray whales frolicking in the Pacific.

San Diego has miles of beaches and bays, numerous lakes, mountains, and deserts to explore. With balmy average temperatures and less than a foot of rain per year, the lure to go play outside is hard to resist. That said, Southern California isn't as seasonless as some claim. Although the weather is generally mild and sunny year-round, the seasons do bring different outdoor activities.

Check WaveCast (⊕ *www.wavecast.com/tides*) for tide schedules, wave reports, and water temperatures.

Essentials

Hotels. If you're planning to book a hotel, the best months (for low cost and occupancy) are January, September, November, and December. Avoid July when Comic-Con takes over the city and August when visitors from warmer states escape their summer swelter.

Summer. This is the best time to plan your trip from an outdoor activities point of view (this is peak tourist season for a reason). San Diego's proximity to the ocean offers an almost endless selection of water activities. Rent kayaks at La Jolla Cove, take a charter boat off Point Loma for deep-sea tuna fishing, or simply hit the beach and go for a swim. Action Sport Rentals, operating out of the Catamaran Resort at Mission Bay, offers paddleboards and sailboat rentals to help you enjoy the shimmering bay. This is also when the Del Mar Races kick into full swing, running mid-July through Labor Day.

Visitors planning a trip in early summer should be aware of the phenomenon known as "May Gray and June Gloom," when fog often blankets the coast in the morning. Things usually clear up by the afternoon, but occasionally the fog lasts all day, making a trip to the beach a damp and chilly affair.

Fall. The temperature begins to cool down for winter, but before it does, Santa Ana winds usher in a warm dry spell throughout Southern California through the fall. Santa Ana winds generally bring in offshore winds, a favorite for surfers. Fall is the perfect time to shoot 18 holes at the Park Hyatt Aviara in Carlsbad, or take a hike at the Bayside Trail at Cabrillo National Monument—fall's cloudless skies allow for a crisp, clear vision of the Pacific. And although the foliage in San Diego doesn't turn into burnished reds and golds, you can appreciate the rare species of evergreen at Torrey Pines State Reserve.

Winter. This time of year in California is hardly bitter or harsh, but the weather certainly gets too cold for water sports. Serious surfers love the breaks best in winter, when the swells are high. Thick wet suits are a must, because water temperatures can drop into the high 50s. Black's Beach continues to be one of the most challenging surfing beaches in San Diego. Winter is also when gray whales migrate to warmer waters. Charter boats offer whale-watching trips between December and April. View the whales with San Diego Harbor Excursion or with one of the more intimate sailboat charters offered around town. Sunsets can be particularly spectacular during the winter months.

Spring. Southern California's best wildflower display begins to appear in the Anza-Borrego Desert. At the Carlsbad Ranch, Southern California's largest bulb farm, 60 acres of Tecolote Giant Ranunculus bloom mid-March through early May. At its peak, there are more than 70 million blooms.

Contacts

Air

AIRPORT SHUTTLES
SuperShuttle. ✉ *San Diego* ☎ *800/258–3826* ⊕ *www. supershuttle.com.*

AIRPORTS San Diego International Airport. ✉ *3225 N. Harbor Dr., off I–5, San Diego* ☎ *619/400–2400* ⊕ *www.san.org.*

Public Transport

North County Transit District. ☎ *760/966–6500* ⊕ *www. gonctd.com.* **San Diego 511.** ✉ *San Diego* ☎ *855/467– 3511* ⊕ *www.511sd. com.* **San Diego Metropolitan Transit System.** ✉ *102 Broadway, San Diego* ☎ *619/234–1060* ⊕ *www. sdmts.com.*

🚕 Taxi

Silver Cabs. ✉ *San Diego* ☎ *619/280–5555.* **Yellow Cab.** ✉ *San Diego* ☎ *619/444–4444* ⊕ *driveu. com.*

🚆 Train

Amtrak. ☎ *800/872–7245* ⊕ *www.amtrak.com.* **Coaster.** ☎ *760/966–6500* ⊕ *www.gonctd.com/ coaster.* **Metrolink.** ☎ *800/371–5465* ⊕ *www. metrolinktrains.com.* **Pacific Surfliner.** ✉ *San Diego* ⊕ *www.pacificsurfliner.com.*

🔵 General Interest

ArtsTix. ⊕ *www.sdartstix.com.* **Ranch & Coast.** ⊕ *www.ranchandcoast. com.* **San Diego Magazine.** ⊕ *www.sandiegomagazine.com.* **San Diego Reader.** ⊕ *www.sandiegoreader.com.* **San Diego Union-Tribune.** ⊕ *www. sandiegouniontribune. com.*

📍 Visitor Information

Borrego Springs Chamber of Commerce. ✉ *Borreo Springs* ☎ *760/767–5555* ⊕ *www.borregospringschamber.com.* **California Welcome Center Oceanside.** ✉ *Oceanside* ☎ *760/721– 1101, 800/350–7873* ⊕ *www.visitoceanside. org.* **Coronado Visitor Center.** ✉ *1100 Orange Ave., Coronado* ⊕ *www. coronadovisitorcenter. com.* **Encinitas Chamber of Commerce.** ✉ *535 Encinitas Blvd., Suite 116, Encinitas* ☎ *760/753–6041* ⊕ *www. encinitaschamber.com.* **The Gaslamp Quarter Association.** ⊕ *www.gaslamp.org.* **Julian Chamber of Commerce.** ☎ *760/765– 1857* ⊕ *www.visitjulian. com.* **Old Town San Diego.** ⊕ *www.oldtownsandiego. org.* **San Diego Tourism Authority.** ✉ *750 B St., Suite 1500, San Diego* ☎ *619/232–3101* ⊕ *www. sandiego.org.* **Visit Carlsbad.** ✉ *Carlsbad* ⊕ *visitcarlsbad.com.*

Tours

Bike Tours

The Bike Revolution

BICYCLE TOURS | Biking is very popular in San Diego. You can find trails along the beach, in Mission Bay, and throughout the mountains. Pedal your way around San Diego with The Bike Revolution, which delivers and rents bikes. ☒ *San Diego* ☏ *352/817–8564* ⊕ *www.thebik-erevolution.com.*

⏻ Boat Tours

City Cruises By Hornblower

BOAT TOURS | Sixty- and 90-minute tours around San Diego Harbor depart from the Embarcadero several times a day and alternate between the northern and southern portion of the bay. If you're hoping to spot some sea lions, take the North Bay route. Dinner and brunch cruises are also offered, as well as whale-watching tours in winter. ☒ *970 N. Harbor Dr., San Diego* ☏ *619/686–8700, 855/552–9059* ⊕ *www.cityexperiences. com* ☒ *From $35.*

Everyday California

SPECIAL-INTEREST TOURS | On these hour-long, eco-friendly kayak tours of the La Jolla Ecological Reserve, guests get to explore one of the world's top-ten kayaking destinations as well as get up close and personal with leopard sharks, dolphins, turtles, and more. ☒ *San Diego* ⊕ *www.everydaycalifornia.com* ☒ *From $64.*

Flagship Cruises and Events

BOAT TOURS | One- and two-hour tours of the San Diego Harbor loop north or south from the Broadway Pier through-out the day. Other offerings include dinner and dance cruises, brunch cruises, and winter whale-watching tours December–mid-April. ☒ *990 N. Harbor Dr., Embarcadero* ☏ *619/234–4111* ⊕ *www.flagshipsd.com* ☒ *From $32.*

H&M Landing

BOAT TOURS | From mid-December to mid-March, this outfitter offers three-hour tours to spot migrating gray whales just off the San Diego coast. ☒ *2803 Emerson St., San Diego* ☏ *619/222–1144* ⊕ *www.hmlanding.com* ☒ *From $55.*

San Diego SEAL Tours

BOAT TOURS | This amphibious tour drives along the Embarcadero before splashing into the San Diego Harbor for a cruise. The 100-minute tours depart daily from 10 am to 5 pm from Seaport Village and the Embarcadero. Call for daily departure times and locations. ☒ *500 Kettner Blvd., Embarcadero* ☏ *619/298–8687* ⊕ *www. sealtours.com* ☒ *$49.*

Seaforth Boat Rentals

BOAT TOURS | For those seeking a private tour on the water, this company can provide a skipper along with your boat rental. Options include harbor cruis-es, whale-watching, and sunset sails. Seaforth has four locations and a diverse fleet of sail and motorboats to choose from. ☒ *1641 Quivira Rd., Mission Bay* ☏ *888/834–2628* ⊕ *www.seaforthboat-rental.com* ☒ *From $200.*

🚌 Bus and Trolley Tours

DayTripper Tours

BUS TOURS | **FAMILY** | Single- and multiday trips throughout Southern California, the Southwest, and Baja depart from San Diego year-round. Popular day trips include the Getty Museum, and theater performances in Los Angeles. Call or check the website for pickup locations. ☏ *619/334–3394* ⊕ *www.daytripper.com* ☒ *From $99.*

Five Star Tours

BUS TOURS | Private and group sightseeing bus tour options around San Diego and beyond include everything from the San Diego Zoo and brewery tours to city tours and trips to Baja, Mexico. ⊠ *1050 Kettner Blvd., San Diego* ☎ *619/232–5040* ⊕ *www.fivestartours.com* ✉ *From $50.*

Old Town Trolley Tours

GUIDED TOURS | **FAMILY** | Combining points of interest with local history, trivia, and fun anecdotes, this hop-on, hop-off trolley tour provides an entertaining overview of the city and offers easy access to all the highlights. The tour is narrated, and you can get on and off as you please. Stops include Old Town, Seaport Village, the Gaslamp Quarter, Coronado, Little Italy, and Balboa Park. The trolley leaves every 30 minutes, operates daily, and takes two hours to make a full loop. ⊠ *San Diego* ☎ *866/754–0966* ⊕ *www. trolleytours.com/san-diego* ✉ *From $49.*

General Interest Tours

Go Car Tours

DRIVING TOURS | Tour the city in a bright yellow three-seater, equipped with GPS navigation and accompanying narration. Go Car Tours offers multiple routes: choose from Downtown, Balboa Park, Uptown, and Old Town; Point Loma, Cabrillo National Monument, and Ocean Beach; or Coronado. The tours can be driven straight through, or visitors can park and explore any of the sights en route. In addition to their classic GoCars, newer electric vehicles and sporty Blackjacks offer increased speed and style. ⊠ *3918 Mason St., Old Town* ☎ *800/914–6227* ⊕ *www.gocartours.com* ✉ *From $85.*

Walking Tours

Balboa Park Walking Tours

GUIDED TOURS | On Tuesday and select Fridays at 11 am, free, hour-long walks start from the Balboa Park Visitor Center. Tours explore the history of Balboa Park, its gardens and architecture. Reservations are not required, but no tours are scheduled between Thanksgiving and the New Year. Private, custom tours are also available for a fee, with proceeds going to the Balboa Park Conservancy. Contact the visitor center for details and to schedule. ⊠ *Balboa Park Visitor Center, 1549 El Prado, Balboa Park* ☎ *619/239–0512* ⊕ *www.balboapark.org* ✉ *Free; custom private tours from $60.*

Gaslamp Quarter Historical Foundation

WALKING TOURS | Ninety-minute walking tours of the Downtown historic district depart from the William Heath Davis House at 1 pm on Thursday and 11 am on Saturday. ⊠ *410 Island Ave., San Diego* ☎ *619/233–4692* ⊕ *gaslampfoundation. org* ✉ *$25.*

Great Itineraries

One Day in San Diego

If you've only got 24 hours to spare, start at **Balboa Park,** the cultural heart of San Diego. Stick to El Prado, the main promenade, where you'll pass by peaceful gardens and soaring Spanish colonial revival architecture. Unless you're a serious museum junkie, pick whichever piques your interest—choices range from photography to folk art.

If you're with the family, don't even think of skipping the **San Diego Zoo.** You'll want to spend the better part of your day there, but make an early start of it so you can head for one of San Diego's **beaches** afterward while there's still daylight. Kick back under the late afternoon sun and linger for sunset. Or wander around **Seaport Village** and the **Embarcadero** before grabbing a bite to eat in the **Gaslamp Quarter.**

Alternate plan: Start at **SeaWorld** and end with an ocean-view dinner in **La Jolla.**

Four Days in San Diego

DAY 1

The one-day itinerary also works for the first day of an extended visit. If you're staying in North County, though, you may want to bypass the zoo and head for the **San Diego Zoo Safari Park.**

Here, you'll see herds of African and Asian animals acting as they would in the wild. Not included in the general admission, but worth it, are the park's "special experiences"—guided photo caravans, behind-the-scenes tours, and the Flightline, a zipline soaring above the animal enclosures.

Another North County option for families with little ones: **LEGOLAND** in Carlsbad. **Note:** the San Diego Zoo, the San Diego Safari Park, and LEGOLAND are all-day, wipe-the-kids-out adventures.)

DAY 2

You might want to ease into your second day with a leisurely breakfast, followed by a 100-minute tour aboard the **San Diego SEAL Tours,** which departs from Seaport Village and Embarcadero daily. The bus-boat hybrid explores picturesque San Diego neighborhoods before rolling right into the water for a cruise around the bay, all with fun-facts narration.

Back on land, you can devote an hour or so to **Seaport Village,** a 14-acre waterfront shopping and dining complex. Meant to look like a 19th-century harbor, Seaport features 4 miles of cobblestone pathways bordered by lush landscaping and water features.

From there, stroll north to the **Embarcadero,** where you'll marvel at the **Maritime Museum's** historic vessels, including the *Star of India* (the world's oldest active sailing ship).

Explore San Diego's military might at the **USS *Midway* Museum;** the permanently docked aircraft carrier has more than 60 exhibits and 29 restored aircraft.

Spend the rest of your afternoon and evening in **Coronado,** a quick jaunt by ferry or bridge, or walk a few blocks north to the **Gaslamp Quarter,** where the shopping and dining will keep you busy for hours.

DAY 3

Set out early enough, and you might snag a parking spot near **La Jolla Cove,** where you can watch sea lions lounging on the beach at the **Children's Pool.** Then head up one block to Prospect Street, where you'll find the vaunted **La Valencia** hotel (called the "Pink Lady" for its blush-hue exterior) and dozens of posh boutiques and galleries.

If you're with kids, head for **La Jolla Shores,** a good beach for swimming and making sand castles, followed by a visit to the **Birch Aquarium** and a bite to eat at the popular **El Pescador Fish Market.**

Once you've refueled, head for **Torrey Pines State Natural Reserve,** where you can hike down the cliffs to the state beach with breathtaking views in every direction. (If you're with small children, the trek might prove too challenging.)

For dinner, swing north to **Del Mar**; during racing season, the evening scene is happening.

DAY 4

Start the day with a morning visit to **Cabrillo National Monument,** a national park with a number of activities. Learn about 16th-century explorer Juan Rodríguez Cabrillo, take a gentle 2-mile hike on the beautiful Bayside Trail, look around the Old Point Loma Lighthouse, and peer at tide pools.

■TIP→ Find out when low tide is before planning your itinerary.

After Cabrillo, head to **Old Town,** where San Diego's early history comes to carefully reconstructed life. Old Town's Mexican restaurants aren't the city's best, but they're definitely bustling and kid-friendly, and frosty margaritas make an added incentive for grown-ups.

After that, spend a few hours exploring whatever cluster of neighborhoods appeals to you most. If you like casual coastal neighborhoods with a youthful vibe, head to **Pacific, Mission,** or **Ocean Beach,** or venture up to **North County** for an afternoon in **Encinitas,** which epitomizes the old California surf town.

If edgy and artsy are more your thing, check out the hip and ever-changing neighborhoods in **Uptown,** where you'll find supercool shops, bars, and eateries.

Tips

■ It's easy to add a theater performance or a concert to any of these days. Some of the city's top venues are in Balboa Park, Downtown, and La Jolla.

■ If you plan to tour many of Balboa Park's museums, buy the **Balboa Park Explorer Pass,** which gets you into 16 attractions for $67. Passes are valid for seven consecutive days. Buy them online or at the **Balboa Park Visitor Center** (☎ 619/239–0512).

■ The **Trolley** and the **Coaster** are great ways to access foot-friendly neighborhoods up and down the coast. You can head almost anywhere from the **Santa Fe Depot** in Downtown.

Alternatives

You can easily fill four days or more with every imaginable outdoor activity, from swimming and surfing to hiking and stand-up paddleboarding. San Diego is an athletics-enthusiast's heaven—unless you're a skier.

In **winter,** include more indoor activities—the museums are fantastic—as well as a whale-watching trip.

In **summer,** check local listings for outdoor concerts, theater, and movie screenings.

A Walk Through San Diego's Past

Downtown San Diego is a living tribute to history and revitalization. The Gaslamp Quarter followed up a long stint of seediness, emerging as a glamorous place to live and play. Little Italy, once a bustling fishing village, also got a face-lift.

WHERE IT ALL STARTED

Begin at the corner of 4th and Island. This is the location of the 150-year-old **Davis-Horton House,** a saltbox structure shipped around Cape Horn and assembled in the Gaslamp Quarter. Among its famous former residents: Alonzo Horton, the city's founder. Take a tour, keeping a lookout for the house's current resident: a lady ghost.

From there walk a block east to 5th Avenue and head north. Along the way, you'll see some of the 16½-block historic district's best-known Victorian-era commercial beauties, including the Italianate **Marston Building** (at F Street), the **Keating Building,** the **Spencer-Ogden Building,** and the **Old City Hall.** Architecture buffs should pick up a copy of *San Diego's Gaslamp Quarter,* a self-guided tour published by the Historical Society.

At E Street, head back over to 4th Avenue and you'll behold the **Balboa Theatre,** a striking Spanish Renaissance–style building that was constructed in 1923 and restored in 2007. Pop across Broadway to check out the stately **U.S. Grant Hotel,** built in 1910 by the son of President Ulysses S. Grant.

Follow Broadway west to Kettner Boulevard and the **Santa Fe Depot**, San Diego's main train station built for the influx of passengers to the 1915 Panama-California Exposition and stunning visitors with its domed towers and tiled arches.

A Walk Through San Diego's Past

HIGHLIGHTS:
Restored gas lamps that give the Gaslamp its name; the contrast of old and new architecture; Little Italy's sidewalk cafés.

WHERE TO START:
The Davis-Horton House, at the corner of 4th and Island Avenues, is a short walk from most Downtown hotels.

LENGTH:
About 3 miles and three to four hours roundtrip with stops. Take the Orange Line trolley from Santa Fe Depot back if you're tired.

WHERE TO STOP:
From Little Italy head down Laurel Street to Harbor Drive and wander along the Embarcadero until you hit Broadway.

BEST TIME TO GO:
Morning or early afternoon.

WORST TIME TO GO:
During rush hour.

WHERE TO REFUEL:
If your stomach is growling, head to Little Italy: mangia, mangia! Try Little Italy Food Hall (550 W. Date Street), or Ironside Fish and Oyster (1654 India Street).

FROM FISHERMEN TO FASHIONISTAS

From there, head north on Kettner to A Street, make a quick right, and then take a left on India Street. This is the heart of **Little Italy,** which, at the turn of the 20th century, was a bustling Italian fishing village. The area fell into disarray in the early 1970s due to a decline in the tuna industry and the construction of I–5, which destroyed 35% of the area. In 1996, a group of forward-thinking architects—commissioned by the city—developed new residential, retail, and public areas that coexist beautifully with the neighborhood's historic charms. Now, it's a vibrant urban center with hip eateries, bars, and shops. There are remnants of retro Little Italy, from authentic cafés (check out **Pappalecco,** a popular gelateria) to bocce ball matches played by old-timers at **Amici Park.**

On the Calendar

January

Farmers Insurance Open. This is the Holy Grail for golf fans; the celeb-heavy tourney has been held at the scenic Torrey Pines Golf Course for decades. ⊕ *www.farmersinsuranceopen.com*

San Diego Brew Festival. More than 70 breweries are joined with a bevy of food trucks for a day of fun in the sun. ⊕ *www.sandiegobeerfest.com*

February

Gaslamp Quarter Mardi Gras. This block party invites revelers to let the good times roll. ⊕ *www.gaslamp.org*

Museum Month. Half-price admission (with free pass) to more than 40 museums throughout the city. ⊕ *www.sandiego.org*

March

Carlsbad Flower Fields. More than 60 acres of giant ranunculus flowers bloom mid-March through early May. ⊕ *www.theflowerfields.com*

Cherry Blossom Festival. The Japanese Friendship Garden at Balboa Park celebrates spring in bloom with cherry trees, cultural performances, Japanese street food, and beer and tea tastings. ⊕ *www.niwa.org*

April

Adams Avenue Unplugged. The free event features 50-plus live musical performances staged inside 20 restaurants, bars, coffeehouses, and galleries on Adams Avenue. ⊕ *www.adamsavenuebusiness.com*

Humphreys Concerts by the Bay. Outdoor concerts—from rock and jazz to comedy and folk and everything in between—run through October on Shelter Island. ⊕ *www.humphreysconcerts.com*

Mission Federal ArtWalk. Little Italy's annual event showcases local art talent on tent-lined streets. ⊕ *artwalksandiego.org*

May

Cinco de Mayo. Old Town is home to one of the country's biggest Cinco de Mayo celebrations with live music, *lucha libre* matches, lots of food, and much more. ⊕ *www.cincodemayooldtown.com*

Gator By The Bay. New Orleans comes to San Diego with blues, jazz, Louisiana food, and crawfish. ⊕ *www.gatorbythebay.com*

Temecula Valley Balloon and Wine Festival. Usually the last weekend of the month, the annual event has concerts with headliner entertainment, wine tasting and food pairings, and an evening Balloon Glow. ⊕ *www.tvbwf.com*

June

San Diego County Fair. Over 1 million visitors come for a month of fun attractions including rides, concerts, and greasy fair favorites. ⊕ *sdfair.com*

San Diego Festival of the Arts. More than 190 award-winning artists display watercolors, sculpture, fine jewelry, photography, and more. ⊕ *www.sdfestivalofthearts.org*

July

Del Mar Races. Place your bets on your favorite horse at the Del Mar Racetrack from mid-July to Labor Day. ⊕ *www.dmtc.com*

Comic-Con International. At this four-day comic book convention, thousands of fans unite for all things comics, sci-fi, fantasy, and anime. ⊕ *www.comic-con.org*

San Diego Pride. The city's vibrant LGBTQ Pride Festival celebrates diversity with four stages of live entertainment, cultural presentations, and vendor booths. ⊕ *sd-pride.org*

Summer Shakespeare Festival. The Old Globe's summer theater festival is the best way to enjoy Shakespeare under the stars. ⊕ *www.theoldglobe.org*

September

MCAS Miramar Air Show. The annual marine air show often features the Blue Angels. ⊕ *www.miramarairshow.com*

October

Día de los Muertas Old Town. Ofrendas and decorations adorn the plaza and buildings throughout Old Town in late October. A two-day festival with face painting, crafts, food, and entertainment takes place the last weekend of the month. ⊕ *www.dayofthedeadsd.com*

Fleet Week San Diego. Military men and women are honored and celebrated with parades, entertainment, and daily events. ⊕ *fleetweeksandiego.org*

HalGLOWeen. Halloween-theme music and dance parties, glowing "Boolahoops," special treats, and more entertain zoo visitors on weekend evenings throughout October. ⊕ *zoo.sandiegozoo.org*

Kids Free San Diego. Discounts, free meals, and free admission to attractions for kids throughout October. ⊕ *www.sandiego.org/promotions/kids-free*

November

San Diego Bay Wine & Food Festival. The West Coast's largest wine and culinary classic features wine-tasting seminars, cooking classes, and celebrity chef dinners. ⊕ *www.sandiegowineclassic.com*

San Diego Beer Week and Guild Fest. Hosted by the San Diego Brewers Guild, this 10-day event celebrates craft breweries throughout the county and kicks off with more than 60 independent breweries descending upon the Embarcadero for the Guild Fest celebration. ⊕ *www.sdbeer.com*

Wonderfront. A 3-day music, food, and arts festival along the Embarcadero waterfront. ⊕ *wonderfrontfestival.com*

December

Balboa Park December Nights. Drawing 350,000 visitors the first Friday and Saturday of December, this event offers festive carolers, food, music, and dance. ⊕ *www.sandiego.gov/december-nights*

San Diego Bay Parade of Lights. Boats decked out for the holidays light up the harbor. ⊕ *www.sdparadeoflights.org*

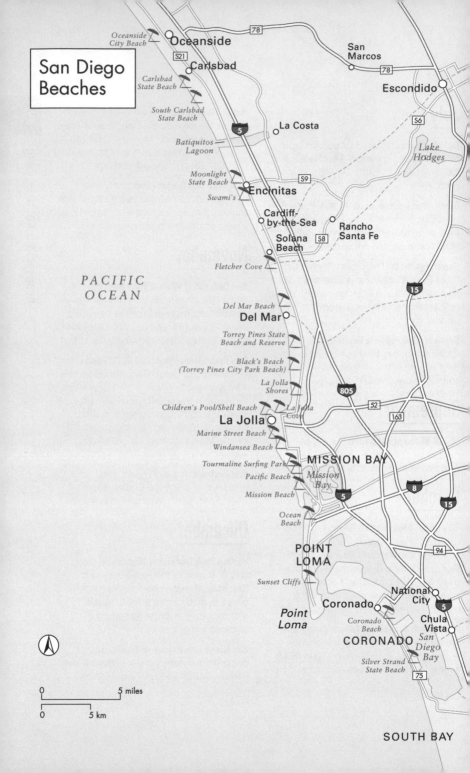

San Diego Beaches

Oceanside City Beach — Oceanside

[78]

[S21]

Carlsbad

San Marcos

Carlsbad State Beach

Escondido

[78]

South Carlsbad State Beach

[5]

La Costa

[S6]

Batiquitos Lagoon

Lake Hodges

Moonlight State Beach

[S9]

Encinitas

Swami's

Cardiff-by-the-Sea

Solana Beach

Rancho Santa Fe

[S8]

Fletcher Cove

PACIFIC OCEAN

[15]

Del Mar Beach

Del Mar

Torrey Pines State Beach and Reserve

Black's Beach (Torrey Pines City Park Beach)

La Jolla Shores

[805]

[52]

Children's Pool/Shell Beach

La Jolla Cove

[163]

La Jolla

Marine Street Beach

Windansea Beach

Tourmaline Surfing Park

MISSION BAY

Pacific Beach

Mission Bay

[8]

Mission Beach

[5]

[15]

Ocean Beach

POINT LOMA

[94]

Sunset Cliffs

National City

[5]

Coronado

Point Loma

Coronado Beach

Chula Vista

CORONADO

San Diego Bay

Silver Strand State Beach

[75]

0   5 miles

0   5 km

SOUTH BAY

Chapter 3

DOWNTOWN

WITH THE EAST VILLAGE, EMBARCADERO, THE GASLAMP QUARTER, LITTLE ITALY, AND BARRIO LOGAN

3

Updated by
Jeff Terich

 Sights
★★★★★

 Restaurants
★★★★★

 Hotels
★★★★★

 Shopping
★★★★☆

 Nightlife
★★★★☆

NEIGHBORHOOD SNAPSHOT

TOP EXPERIENCES

■ **Waterfront delights:** Stroll along the Embarcadero, explore Seaport Village, or enjoy a harbor cruise.

■ **Contemporary art for all ages:** From the stunning galleries of the Museum of Contemporary Art to the clever incorporation of art and play at the New Children's Museum, Downtown is the place for art.

■ **Maritime history:** Climb aboard and explore a wide array of vessels from sailing ships to submarines.

■ **Delicious dining:** The hip and high-style restaurants of Little Italy, the Gaslamp Quarter, and the East Village make Downtown San Diego a diner's delight.

■ **Happening Gaslamp:** It's hard to believe this hip neighborhood filled with street art, galleries, restaurants, and buzzing nightlife was once slated for the wrecking ball.

GETTING HERE

It's an easy drive into Downtown, especially from the nearby airport. There are reasonably priced parking lots (about $10 per day) along Harbor Drive, Pacific Highway, and lower Broadway and Market Street. Most restaurants offer valet parking at night, but beware of fees of $15 and up.

If you tire of exploring Downtown on foot, hop aboard a pedicab, hail the Free Ride Everywhere Downtown (FRED) shuttle, or rent a GoCar (three-wheel cars equipped with a GPS-guided audio tour).

PLANNING YOUR TIME

Most Downtown attractions are open daily, but the New Children's Museum is closed on Tuesday during the school year. For guided tours of the Gaslamp Quarter Historic District, visit on Saturday. A boat trip on the harbor, or at least a hop over to Coronado on the ferry, is a must at any time of year. From December through March, when gray whales migrate between the Pacific Northwest and southern Baja, consider booking a whale-watching excursion from the Broadway Pier.

PAUSE HERE

Adjacent to the Little Italy Food Hall, **Piazza della Famiglia** is a 10,000-square-foot European-style piazza at the center of Little Italy. A perfect gathering place, visitors can gather around the marble fountain or at one of the piazza's tables with coffee, lunch or a snack, or simply enjoy being serenaded by a nearby busker.

GONE TO THE DOGS

In 2007 two life-size dog statues took center stage in San Diego's Downtown park next to the William Heath Davis House on the corner of 4th and Island Avenues. Dedicated to San Diego's official town dog, "Bum," the bronze statue shares a prominent place alongside "Greyfriars Bobby," the official dog of Edinburgh, Scotland. When the citizens of Edinburgh discovered that, like them, San Diego had an official town dog, they presented a Greyfriars Bobby replica. In 2008, a replica of Bum was installed in Edinburgh, symbolizing the friendship between the sister cities.

Nearly written off in the 1970s, today Downtown San Diego is a testament to conservation and urban renewal. Once derelict Victorian storefronts now house the hottest restaurants, and the *Star of India*, the world's oldest active sailing ship, almost lost to scrap, floats regally along the Embarcadero. Like many modern U.S. cities, Downtown San Diego's story is as much about its rebirth as its history. Although many consider Downtown to be the 16½-block Gaslamp Quarter, it actually comprises eight neighborhoods, including East Village, Little Italy, and Embarcadero.

Gaslamp Quarter

Considered the liveliest of the Downtown neighborhoods, the Gaslamp Quarter's 4th and 5th Avenues are peppered with trendy nightclubs, swanky lounge bars, chic restaurants, and boisterous sports pubs. The Gaslamp has the largest collection of commercial Victorian-style buildings in the country. Despite this, when the move for Downtown redevelopment gained momentum in the 1970s, there was talk of bulldozing them and starting from scratch. In response, concerned history buffs, developers, architects, and artists formed the Gaslamp Quarter Council to clean up and preserve the quarter.

The majority of the quarter's landmark buildings are on 4th and 5th Avenues, between Island Avenue and Broadway. If you don't have much time, stroll down 5th Avenue, where highlights include **Louis Bank of Commerce** (No. 835), **Old City Hall** (No. 664), **Nesmith-Greeley** (No. 825), and **Yuma** (No. 631) buildings. The Romanesque revival **Keating Hotel** at 432 F Street was designed by the same firm that created the famous Hotel del Coronado, the Victorian grande dame that presides over Coronado's beach. At the corner of 4th Avenue and F Street, peer into the **Hard Rock Cafe,** which occupies a restored turn-of-the-20th-century tavern with a 12-foot mahogany bar and a spectacular stained-glass domed ceiling.

Sights ▼

1 Coronado Ferry **B5**
2 Gaslamp Museum at the Davis-Horton House..... **F6**
3 Museum of Contemporary Art San Diego (MCASD)..... **C4**
4 The New Children's Museum (NCM)........ **E6**
5 Petco Park............... **G7**
6 Santa Fe Depot........... **C4**
7 Seaport Village........... **C7**
8 USS *Midway* Museum **B5**
9 You & Yours............... **I6**

Restaurants ▼

1 Animae.................... **C5**
2 The Blind Burro **G7**
3 Breakfast Republic **G6**
4 Cowboy Star............. **G6**
5 Eddie V's Prime Seafood **C6**
6 Havana 1920.............. **F6**
7 Lionfish Modern Coastal Cuisine **F6**
8 The Mission **H6**
9 Puesto.................... **C6**
10 Tajima East Village...... **G5**
11 Taka **F6**
12 Top of the Market........ **A6**
13 The Westgate Room..... **E4**

Quick Bites ▼

1 Carnitas' Snack Shack **B4**
2 The Invigatorium........ **G6**
3 Lola 55.................... **H5**
4 Parfait Paris **F6**

Hotels ▼

1 The Bristol................ **E4**
2 Courtyard San Diego Downtown................ **F4**
3 Gaslamp Plaza Suites ... **F5**
4 Hard Rock Hotel San Diego................. **F7**
5 Hilton San Diego Bayfront................. **G9**
6 Hilton San Diego Gaslamp Quarter......... **F7**
7 InterContinental San Diego................. **C4**
8 Kimpton Alma San Diego................. **F4**
9 Manchester Grand Hyatt San Diego............... **D6**
10 Omni San Diego Hotel..................... **G7**
11 Pendry San Diego **F6**
12 San Diego Marriott Gaslamp Quarter........ **G7**
13 The Sofia Hotel........... **E4**
14 The U.S. Grant, a Luxury Collection Hotel...................... **F4**
15 The Westgate Hotel **E4**

The Gaslamp is a lively place—during baseball season, the streets flood with Padres fans, and festivals, such as Mardi Gras in February, ShamROCK on St. Patrick's Day, and Monster Bash in October, keep the party atmosphere going throughout the year.

◉ Sights

Gaslamp Museum at the Davis-Horton House

HISTORIC HOME | The oldest wooden house in San Diego houses the Gaslamp Quarter Historical Foundation, the district's curator. Before developer Alonzo Horton came to town, Davis, a prominent San Franciscan, had made an unsuccessful attempt to develop the waterfront area. In 1850 he had this prefab saltbox-style house, built in Maine, shipped around Cape Horn and assembled in San Diego (it originally stood at State and Market Streets). Ninety-minute walking tours ($25) of the historic district leave from the house on Thursday at 1 pm (summer only) and Saturday at 11 am (year-round). If you can't time your visit with the tour, a self-guided tour map ($2) is available. ✉ 410 Island Ave., at 4th Ave., Gaslamp Quarter ☎ 619/233–4692 ⊕ www. gaslampfoundation.org ⊠ $5 self-guided, $10 with audio tour ☉ Closed Mon.

🍴 Restaurants

The historic heart of Downtown spread across 4th, 5th, and 6th Avenues, the Gaslamp Quarter satisfies foodies, conventioneers, and night-clubbers with a wide choice of eateries and nightlife. Many are pricey, upscale chains and tourist-driven concepts, while others are stylish restaurants or casual gastropubs with local roots, featuring everything from sushi to authentic Mexican and aged steaks.

Trolley Dances

During the fall in San Diego, the commuter experience comes alive with dance performances at select trolley stops. A partnership between the Jean Isaacs Dance Theater and the city's Metropolitan Transit System, these dancers (⊕ www.sandiegodancetheater.org/trolley-dances) give site-specific performances inspired by their environments, from historic Barrio Logan to the modern Downtown library. Get on the trolley for a tour ($40) to see the performances at each site.

Breakfast Republic

$ | **AMERICAN** | Just because it's the most important meal of the day doesn't mean it can't also be flashy or innovative. Breakfast Republic adds some hipster flair to typical brunch fare with a menu that combines hearty Southern staples (grits, jambalaya), Mexican food (chilaquiles, breakfast burritos), and over-the-top treats such as Oreo pancakes and s'mores French toast. **Known for:** rich, gooey pancakes and French toast; kombucha flights; kitschy decor. $ Average main: $12 ✉ 707 G St., Gaslamp Quarter ☎ 619/501–8280 ⊕ www.breakfastrepublic.com ☉ No dinner.

Havana 1920

$$ | **CUBAN** | A short walk up a flight of stairs transports diners into old Havana as Hemingway once knew it. True to its name, this still-young restaurant specializes in classic Cuban fare, such as empanadas, croquettes, and, of course, the Cubano sandwich. **Known for:** Cubano sandwich with fresh Cuban bread; strong yet refreshing daiquiris and mojitos; Latin jazz performers and salsa dancing. $ Average main: $20 ✉ 548 5th Ave., Gaslamp Quarter ☎ 619/369–1920 ⊕ www.havana1920.com.

Lionfish Modern Coastal Cuisine

$$$$ | SEAFOOD | One of several options inside the Pendry Hotel, Lionfish is a showcase for chef Jojo Ruiz's seafood-centric cuisine inside of a spacious, two-story room. The atmosphere is hip, yet aesthetically pleasing, though the menu itself is what's worth returning for, from the butter-poached king-crab leg to the wild mushroom and potato gnocchi. **Known for:** fresh seafood, including oysters and crab; nigiri (special sushi rice treated with vinegar) flights; elegant yet unconventional craft cocktails. $ *Average main: $42 ☒ 435 5th Ave., Gaslamp Quarter ☎ 619/738–7200 Pendry Hotel ⊕ www.lionfishsd.com.*

Taka

$$ | JAPANESE | Pristine fish imported from around the world and presented creatively attracts crowds nightly to this intimate Gaslamp restaurant. Table service is available inside and outside where an *omakase* (tasting menu) or eight-piece rolls can be shared and savored; take a seat at the bar to watch one of the sushi chefs preparing appetizers. **Known for:** uni sushi topped with wasabi; omakase tasting menu; upscale sake offerings. $ *Average main: $21 ☒ 555 5th Ave., Gaslamp Quarter ☎ 619/338–0555 ⊕ www.takasushi.com ☺ No lunch.*

The Westgate Room

$$ | FRENCH | Normandy-born chef Fabrice Hardel oversees the preparation of three meals a day at the Westgate Hotel, writing seasonal menus that mix French and Asian flavors. At dinner you're likely to find specials like grilled salmon with spring onions and shiitake mushrooms, as well as classics like Dover sole meunière and steak frites. **Known for:** opulent Sunday brunch buffet is one of the best in town; regal, formal setting; French-inspired cuisine with California flavors. $ *Average main: $29 ☒ Westgate Hotel, 1055 2nd Ave., Gaslamp Quarter ☎ 619/238–1818 ⊕ www.westgatehotel. com.*

☕ Coffee and Quick Bites

Parfait Paris

$ | BAKERY | Two French transplants have brought sleek Parisian style to Downtown San Diego and rows of eclairs, tarts, croissants, colorful macarons, and the aroma of espresso greet patrons as they enter a minimalist space. For something more substantial, look to their menu of crepes, panini, salads, and quiches; caffeinated drinks range from teas and coffee to a sweet lavender honey latte. **Known for:** open until midnight on Friday and Saturday, offering a more low-key postdinner alternative in the neighborhood; extensive macaron selection; pillow-soft pastries and chocolate-filled breads. $ *Average main: $10 ☒ 555 G St., Gaslamp Quarter ☎ 619/245–4457 ⊕ parfaitparis.com.*

🛏 Hotels

Smack in the middle of Downtown is the Gaslamp Quarter where you'll find nightlife options for every night of the week, ranging from gastropubs to clubs with celebrity DJs. For years, lodging options in this neighborhood were lacking in character, but the hotels themselves are becoming destinations in their own right, from the luxurious accommodations of the historic U.S. Grant to the EDM party scene at the Hard Rock or the stylish and trendy appeal of the Pendry, which opened in 2017. And though there are still a handful of budget hotels in the area, the Gaslamp is quickly becoming a go-to spot for glamorous accommodations.

The Bristol

$$$ | HOTEL | Mod pop art inspired by artists such as Andy Warhol and Ed Ruscha sets the tone at this casual boutique hotel. **Pros:** modern rooms; centrally located; good value. **Cons:** no restaurant; somewhat seedy area; street noise. $ *Rooms from: $234 ☒ 1055 1st Ave., Gaslamp Quarter ☎ 619/232–6141*

⊕ *www.thebristolsandiego.com* 🛏 *114 rooms* ⊙ *No Meals.*

Courtyard San Diego Downtown

$$ | **HOTEL** | **FAMILY** | This is not your typical Courtyard by Marriott as the building has a historic past—it was the home of San Diego Trust and Savings Bank in 1928. **Pros:** historic charm; rooms have been recently renovated; 24-hour market. **Cons:** a little far from convention center and Petco Park; expensive valet parking; rooms are a bit small. ⑤ *Rooms from: $229* ✉ *530 Broadway, Gaslamp Quarter* ☎ *619/446–3000* ⊕ *www.sandiegocy. com* 🛏 *245 rooms* ⊙ *No Meals.*

Gaslamp Plaza Suites

$ | **HOTEL** | One of San Diego's first "skyscrapers," this 11-story structure has a central location and a vintage feel. **Pros:** historic building; good location a block from Horton Plaza; well priced. **Cons:** books up early; small, dated rooms; no room service. ⑤ *Rooms from: $200* ✉ *520 E St., Gaslamp Quarter* ☎ *619/232–9500* ⊕ *www.gaslampplaza. com* 🛏 *64 rooms* ⊙ *Free Breakfast.*

★ Hard Rock Hotel San Diego

$$ | **HOTEL** | Self-billed as a hip playground for rock stars and people who want to party like them, the Hard Rock near Petco Park overlooks glimmering San Diego Bay with an interior that oozes laid-back sophistication and guest rooms that include branded Sleep Like a Rock beds and the option of renting a guitar. **Pros:** central location; energetic scene; luxurious rooms. **Cons:** pricey drinks; some attitude; party scene tends to be loud. ⑤ *Rooms from: $249* ✉ *207 5th Ave., Gaslamp Quarter* ☎ *619/702–3000, 866/751–7625* ⊕ *www.hardrockhotelsd. com* 🛏 *420 rooms* ⊙ *No Meals.*

Hilton San Diego Bayfront

$$ | **HOTEL** | **FAMILY** | This contemporary 30-story hotel overlooking San Diego Bay strives for a boutique feel. **Pros:** close to the convention center and Petco Park; allergy-friendly rooms available; excellent

views. **Cons:** expensive valet parking; not as family-friendly as other area hotels; no fridge or minibar in the rooms. ⑤ *Rooms from: $220* ✉ *1 Park Blvd., Gaslamp Quarter* ☎ *619/564–3333* ⊕ *hilton-bay-front.thehotelsinsandiego.com* 🛏 *1190 rooms* ⊙ *No Meals.*

Hilton San Diego Gaslamp Quarter

$$ | **HOTEL** | The moment you experience the cozy lounge spaces and wood accents of the Hilton's modern and sophisticated lobby, you realize this isn't your run-of-the-mill chain hotel—room perks include pillow-top mattresses, down comforters, and spacious work desks. **Pros:** nice decor; upscale lofts; near restaurants and shops. **Cons:** noisy area; pricey parking; Wi-Fi is free for Hilton's Honors loyalty program members. ⑤ *Rooms from: $289* ✉ *401 K St., Gaslamp Quarter* ☎ *619/231–4040, 800/445–8667* ⊕ *www3.hilton.com* 🛏 *283 rooms* ⊙ *No Meals.*

Kimpton Alma San Diego

$$ | **HOTEL** | A few blocks from the heart of the Gaslamp Quarter, this swanky Kimpton hotel features luxurious guest rooms and a popular rooftop lounge. **Pros:** modern rooms; centrally located; complimentary evening wine hour. **Cons:** expensive parking; noisy part of town; most rooms' views leave something to be desired. ⑤ *Rooms from: $294* ✉ *1047 5th Ave., Gaslamp Quarter* ☎ *619/515– 3000* ⊕ *www.stayalma.com* 🛏 *211 rooms* ⊙ *No Meals.*

Omni San Diego Hotel

$$ | **HOTEL** | Business travelers who also want to catch a baseball game flock to this modern masterpiece that occupies the first 21 floors of a 32-story high-rise overlooking Petco Park. **Pros:** great views; good location; modern setting. **Cons:** busy; crowded during baseball season; pricey valet parking. ⑤ *Rooms from: $235* ✉ *675 L St., Gaslamp Quarter* ☎ *619/231–6664, 800/843–6664* ⊕ *www. omnihotels.com* 🛏 *511 rooms* ⊙ *No Meals.*

★ Pendry San Diego

$$$$ | **HOTEL** | Opened in early 2017, the Pendry San Diego is the Gaslamp's newest stunner. **Pros:** well situated in Gaslamp Quarter; excellent dining options; complimentary coffee in the mornings. **Cons:** pricey room rates; meals are expensive; not very family-friendly. ⑤ *Rooms from: $510* ✉ *550 J St., Gaslamp Quarter* ☎ *619/738–7000* ⊕ *www.pendry.com* ⇥ *317 rooms* ⦿ *No Meals.*

San Diego Marriott Gaslamp Quarter

$$$ | **HOTEL** | The 22-story Marriott sits amid the Gaslamp's restaurants and boutiques, near a trolley station, the convention center, and Petco Park. **Pros:** good views; modern decor; central location. **Cons:** rooftop bar can get rowdy; no pool; small rooms. ⑤ *Rooms from: $356* ✉ *660 K St., Gaslamp Quarter* ☎ *619/696–0234* ⊕ *www.sandiegogaslamphotel.com* ⇥ *306 rooms* ⦿ *No Meals.*

★ The Sofia Hotel

$$ | **HOTEL** | This stylish and centrally located boutique hotel may have small rooms, but it more than compensates with pampering extras like motion-sensor temperature controls, a Zen-like 24-hour yoga studio, an updated lobby, and a brand-new spa suite. **Pros:** upscale amenities; historic building; near shops and restaurants. **Cons:** busy area; small rooms; spotty Wi-Fi. ⑤ *Rooms from: $257* ✉ *150 W. Broadway, Gaslamp Quarter* ☎ *619/234–9200, 800/826–0009* ⊕ *www.thesofiahotel.com* ⇥ *211 rooms* ⦿ *No Meals.*

★ The U.S. Grant, a Luxury Collection Hotel

$$ | **HOTEL** | The U.S. Grant may be more than 100 years old (it first opened in 1910) but thanks to a top-to-bottom renovation in 2017, this grand old dame is now one of the most glamorous hotels in Southern California. **Pros:** sophisticated rooms; great location; near shopping and restaurants. **Cons:** street noise can be heard from the guest rooms; no in-room minibars or coffeemakers; surrounded by many major construction projects Downtown. ⑤ *Rooms from: $334* ✉ *326 Broadway, Gaslamp Quarter* ☎ *619/232–3121, 800/325–3589* ⊕ *www.marriott.com* ⇥ *270 rooms* ⦿ *No Meals.*

The Westgate Hotel

$$ | **HOTEL** | A modern high-rise near Horton Plaza hides San Diego's most opulent old-world-style hotel—the lobby is outfitted with bronze sculptures and Baccarat chandeliers—where staff greet guests with old-fashioned charm and politeness; other Downtown hotels have flashier amenities but you won't find one with greater class. **Pros:** affordable luxury; serene rooftop pool deck; San Diego Trolley stops right outside the door. **Cons:** dated guest rooms; mandatory facility fee; next to courthouse. ⑤ *Rooms from: $289* ✉ *1055 2nd Ave., Gaslamp Quarter* ☎ *619/238–1818, 800/522–1564* ⊕ *www.westgatehotel.com* ⇥ *223 rooms* ⦿ *No Meals.*

Nightlife

The Gaslamp Quarter is still one of the most popular areas to go for a night on the town. Named for actual gaslights that once provided illumination along its once-seedy streets (it housed a number of gambling halls and brothels), the neighborhood bears only a trace of its debauched roots. Partygoers line up behind velvet ropes to dance inside Downtown's most exclusive clubs.

BARS

Altitude Sky Lounge

PIANO BARS | Location is everything at this sophisticated lounge on the roof of the 22-floor San Diego Marriott Gaslamp Quarter. The views of the Downtown skyline and Petco Park will give you a natural high. ✉ *San Diego Marriott Gaslamp Quarter, 660 K St., Gaslamp Quarter* ☎ *619/696–0234* ⊕ *altitudeskylounge.com.*

barleymash

BARS | This gigantic space can resemble either a raucous club or a sports bar, depending on what night you're there. But the drinks are strong and reasonably priced, and the reclaimed wood decor makes for an intimate atmosphere, even when the DJs are spinning mostly Top 40. ⊠ *600 5th Ave., Gaslamp Quarter* ☎ *619/255–7373* ⊕ *www.barleymash. com.*

Coin Op

THEMED ENTERTAINMENT | Step back into the '80s with this kitschy yet vibrant hybrid of bar and video arcade. The room is stocked with vintage arcade cabinet games like Galaga and Pac-Man, as well as Skee-Ball and other childhood favorites. Yet unlike those trips to the arcade, Coin Op features a rotating menu of craft cocktail creations, including punch bowls, to make those pinball tournaments even more spirited.

■TIP➔ **Come on the first Sunday of the month for free games all day long.** ⊠ *789 6th Ave., Gaslamp Quarter* ☎ *619/546– 6441* ⊕ *www.coinopgaslamp.com.*

★ The Grant Grill

COCKTAIL LOUNGES | Though the Grant Grill—located on the ground floor of the historic U.S. Grant Hotel—is a full-service restaurant, it's built up a reputation in recent years for stepping up San Diego's craft cocktail game. The cocktail menu is updated seasonally with fresh ingredients and themes (one recently featured a mini "Voodoo" doll frozen inside of a large ice cube), all of which are both innovative and palate pleasant. The atmosphere is comfortable and elegant, even on its busiest nights. ⊠ *U.S. Grant Hotel, 326 Broadway, Gaslamp Quarter* ☎ *619/744–2077* ⊕ *www.grantgrill.com* ☾ *No dinner on Sun. and Mon.*

Hard Rock Hotel

DANCE CLUBS | A-list wannabes (and a few real celebs) gather in two bars, the loungey 207 off the lobby and the rooftop Float. The latter's Intervention and Wintervention daytime parties feature some of the world's biggest DJ names, or if you prefer a rock show, head to Maryjane's Underground at 207. Maybe you can't be a rock star, but you might as well party like one. Just be prepared to spend like one, too. ⊠ *207 5th Ave., Gaslamp Quarter* ☎ *619/702–3000* ⊕ *hardrockhotelsd. com.*

The Nolen

BARS | Panoramic views, warm and welcoming firepits, and beer-forward "hop-tails" (cocktails that have beer in them) are the attraction at this rooftop destination, situated atop the Courtyard by Marriott San Diego Gaslamp/Convention Center. ⊠ *453 6th Ave., Gaslamp Quarter* ☎ *619/796–6536* ⊕ *www.thenolenrooftop.com.*

Prohibition

PIANO BARS | This underground jazz lounge lives up to its name with a slinky speakeasy style. Red lighting, dark wood, and leather-tufted couches provide a cozy 1920s–'30s-inspired backdrop to the live jazz on weekends. There's a "cocktail attire" dress code and cell phones are not allowed at the bar. ⊠ *548 5th Ave., Gaslamp Quarter* ☎ *619/501–1919* ⊕ *prohibitionsd.com.*

DANCE CLUBS

Oxford Social Club

DANCE CLUBS | A luxurious Downtown nightclub beneath the Pendry Hotel, Oxford Social Club has become one of San Diego's trendiest new clubs, with a predictably ample-size line outside on weekends. But once inside, the place is spacious and comfortable, with plush bench seating and strong cocktails, plus table reservations and bottle service for the high rollers. ⊠ *Pendry Hotel, 435 5th Ave., Gaslamp Quarter* ☎ *619/738–7040* ⊕ *www.theoxfordsd.com.*

MUSIC CLUBS
House of Blues

LIVE MUSIC | The local branch of the renowned music chain is decorated floor to ceiling with colorful folk art and features three different areas to hear music. There's something going on here just about every night of the week, and the gospel brunch on select Sundays is one of the most praiseworthy events in town. Can we get a hallelujah? ⊠ *1055 5th Ave., Gaslamp Quarter* ☎ *619/299–2583* ⊕ *www.houseofblues.com.*

★Westgate Hotel Plaza Bar

PIANO BARS | The old-money surroundings, including leather-upholstered seats, marble tabletops, and a grand piano, supply one of the most elegant and romantic settings for a drink in San Diego. ⊠ *1055 2nd Ave., Gaslamp Quarter* ☎ *619/238–1818* ⊕ *www.westgatehotel.com.*

WINE BARS
★Vin de Syrah

WINE BARS | This "spirit and wine cellar" sends you down a rabbit hole (or at least down some stairs) to a whimsical spot straight out of Alice in Wonderland. Behind a hidden door (look for a handle in the grass wall), you'll find visual delights (grapevines suspended from the ceiling, vintage jars with flittering "fireflies," cozy chairs nestled around a faux fireplace and pastoral vista) that rival the culinary ones—the wine list is approachable and the charcuterie boards are exquisitely curated.

■TIP→ **More than just a wine bar, the cocktails are also worth a try.** ⊠ *901 5th Ave., Gaslamp Quarter* ☎ *619/234–4166* ⊕ *www.syrahwineparlor.com* ⊗ *Closed Mon.*

🎭 Performing Arts

DANCE

Whether you fancy *rond de jambes* or something a bit more modern, San Diego's scene is *en pointe* for dance fans.

City Ballet

BALLET | The ballet holds performances at the Spreckels Theatre and a few other area venues from November through May. At Christmastime, they dance a mean *Nutcracker.* ⊠ *Spreckels Theatre, 121 Broadway #600, Gaslamp Quarter* ☎ *858/272–8663* ⊕ *www.cityballet.org.*

MUSIC
Balboa Theatre

MUSIC | This renovated theater offers a variety of performances including ballet, music, plays, and even stand-up comedy. In addition to architectural splendor, the space offers unsurpassed acoustics. ⊠ *868 4th Ave., Gaslamp Quarter* ☎ *619/615–4000* ⊕ *www.sandiegotheatres.org.*

★Copley Symphony Hall

MUSIC | The great acoustics here are surpassed only by the incredible Spanish baroque interior. Not just the home of the San Diego Symphony Orchestra, the renovated 2,200-seat 1920s-era theater has also hosted major stars like Elvis Costello, Leonard Cohen, and Sting. ⊠ *750 B St., Gaslamp Quarter* ☎ *619/235–0804* ⊕ *www.sandiegosymphony.org.*

★San Diego Opera

MUSIC | Drawing international performers, the opera's season runs January–April. Past performances have included *Die Fledermaus, Faust, Idomeneo,* and *La Bohème,* plus solo concerts by such talents as Renée Fleming. ⊠ *Civic Theatre, 1100 3rd Ave., Gaslamp Quarter* ☎ *619/533–7000* ⊕ *www.sdopera.com.*

San Diego Symphony Orchestra

MUSIC | The orchestra's events include classical concerts and summer and winter pops, nearly all of them at Copley Symphony Hall. Their outdoor summer concerts are held at the newly opened **Rady Shell at Jacobs Park** at the Embarcadero (⊠ *222 Marina Park Way*), on North Harbor Drive beyond the convention center. ⊠ *Box office, 750 B St., Gaslamp*

Quarter ☎ *619/235–0804* ⊕ *www.sand-iegosymphony.org.*

Spreckels Theatre

THEATER | A landmark theater erected in 1912, the Spreckels hosts comedy, dance, theater, and concerts. Good acoustics and old-time elegance make this a favorite local venue. ✉ *121 Broadway, Suite 600, Gaslamp Quarter* ☎ *619/235–9500* ⊕ *www.spreckels.net.*

THEATER

Horton Grand Theatre

THEATER | After being home to the long-running *Triple Espresso*, the Horton Grand Theatre hosts productions from the likes of San Diego Musical Theatre as well as Intrepid Theatre Company, whose shows include *Who's Afraid of Virginia Woolf?* and *Woody Guthrie's American Song.* ✉ *Hahn Cosmopolitan Theatre, 444 4th Ave., Gaslamp Quarter* ☎ *858/560–5740.*

San Diego Civic Theatre

THEATER | The home of the San Diego Opera, the Civic Theatre is the city's largest performing arts venue, with musicals, theatrical productions, and concerts held throughout the year. ✉ *1100 3rd Ave., Gaslamp Quarter* ☎ *619/615–4000* ⊕ *www.sandiegotheatres.org.*

🛍 Shopping

The mix of retailers in the historic heart of San Diego changes frequently, but there are always boutiques in the Victorian buildings and renovated warehouses along 4th and 5th Avenues. Also in the quarter are the usual mall stores and gift shops. Some stores close early, starting as early as 5 pm, and many are closed Sunday or Monday.

CLOTHING AND ACCESSORIES

Blends

SHOES | Minimalist decor provides a perfect backdrop for the wild colors and patterns featured on original sneakers from Adidas, Nike, Vans, and other in-demand brands. Prices are steep, but many of the urban styles are unique. ✉ *919 6th Ave., Gaslamp Quarter* ☎ *619/233–6126* ⊕ *blendsus.com.*

Goorin Bros. Hats

HATS & GLOVES | Established in Pittsburgh in 1895, this company has helped make hats hip again with its stylish takes on fedoras, bowlers, and Panama hats. The San Diego location occupies the first floor of the historic Yuma building, a former brothel in the red light district. ✉ *631 5th Ave., Gaslamp Quarter* ☎ *619/450–6303* ⊕ *www.goorin.com.*

FOOD AND WINE

Wine Bank

WINE/SPIRITS | This overwhelmingly stocked emporium with a large selection of wines also features a long list of other beverages, from rums and tequilas to mezcals and local craft beers. ✉ *363 5th Ave., #100, Gaslamp Quarter* ☎ *619/234–7487* ⊕ *www.sdwinebank.com.*

MUSIC STORES

FeeLit Records

MUSIC | This all-vinyl record shop features a wide selection, from curated new releases to budget used records, that crosses a wide spectrum of genres: rock, pop, dance, punk, metal, R&B, and hip-hop. ✉ *909 E St., Gaslamp Quarter* ☎ *707/733–3548* ⊕ *www.feelitrecords.com.*

Embarcadero

The Embarcadero cuts a scenic swath along the harborfront and connects today's Downtown San Diego to its maritime routes. The bustle of Embarcadero comes less these days from the activities of fishing folk than from the throngs of tourists, but this waterfront walkway, stretching from the Convention Center to the Maritime Museum, remains the nautical soul of the city. There are several seafood restaurants here, as well as sea vessels of every variety—cruise ships, ferries, tour boats, and Navy destroyers.

On the north end of the Embarcadero at Ash Street you'll find the **Maritime Museum.** South of it, the **B Street Pier** is used by ships from major cruise lines while tickets for harbor tours and whale-watching trips are sold at the foot of **Broadway Pier.** The terminal for the Coronado Ferry lies in between. Docked at the Navy Pier is the decommissioned **USS** *Midway*. At the foot of G Street, **Tuna Harbor** was once the hub of one of San Diego's earliest and most successful industries, commercial tuna fishing. The pleasant Tuna Harbor Park offers a great view of boating on the bay and across to any aircraft carriers docked at the North Island naval base. A few blocks south, **Embarcadero Marina Park North** is an 8-acre extension into the harbor from the center of **Seaport Village.** It's usually full of kite fliers, in-line skaters, and picnickers. Seasonal celebrations, including San Diego's Parade of Lights, the Port of San Diego Big Balloon Parade, and the Big Bay July 4 Celebration, are held here and at the similar **Embarcadero Marina Park South.** The **San Diego Convention Center,** on Harbor Drive between 1st and 6th Avenues, is a waterfront landmark designed by Canadian architect Arthur Erickson. The backdrop of blue sky and sea complements the building's nautical lines. The center often holds trade shows that are open to the public, and tours of the building are available.

A recent revitalization project along the northern Embarcadero transformed the area with inviting parks, walkways, and public art installations. The redevelopment plan is now focused south along the waterfront, with plans underway for a major overhaul of the entire Central Embarcadero and Seaport Village, with a target date of completion set in 2028.

Sights

Coronado Ferry

TRANSPORTATION | Fifteen-minute ferries connect two locations along the Downtown San Diego waterfront with the Coronado Ferry Landing. Boats depart on the hour from the Broadway Pier on the Embarcadero and on the half hour from Coronado Ferry Landing to the Embarcadero during operating hours. Between the San Diego Convention Center and the Coronado Ferry Landing, service departs every 30 minutes during operating hours. Buy tickets at the Broadway Pier, 5th Avenue Landing, or Coronado Ferry Landing. To reach the heart of downtown Coronado from the Ferry Landing, you can rent a bike at the landing (or bring one with you), or catch the 904 shuttle bus that runs along Orange Avenue. Ferry service is operated by Flagship Cruises. ⊠ *Broadway Pier on the Embarcadero, 990 N. Harbor Dr., Embarcadero* ☎ *619/234–4111, 800/442–7847* ⊕ *www.flagshipsd.com* ⊠ *Ferry $5 one-way.*

★ Museum of Contemporary Art San Diego (MCASD)

ART MUSEUM | At the Downtown branch of the city's contemporary art museum (the space is under renovation so best to call ahead for hours), explore the works of international and regional artists in a modern, urban space. The Jacobs Building—formerly the baggage building at the historic Santa Fe Depot—features large gallery spaces, high ceilings, and natural lighting, giving artists the flexibility to create large-scale installations. MCASD's collection includes many pop art, minimalist, and conceptual works from the 1950s to the present. The museum showcases both established and emerging artists in temporary exhibitions, and has permanent, site-specific commissions by Jenny Holzer and Richard Serra. ⊠ *1100 and 1001 Kettner Blvd., Embarcadero* ☎ *858/454–3541* ⊕ *www.mcasd.org* ⊠ *$10; free 3rd Thurs. of month 5–7* ☉ *Closed Wed.*

★ The New Children's Museum (NCM)

CHILDREN'S MUSEUM | FAMILY | The NCM blends contemporary art with unstructured play to create an environment that appeals to children as well as adults. The 50,000-square-foot structure was constructed from recycled building materials, operates on solar energy, and is convection-cooled by an elevator shaft. It also features a nutritious and eco-conscious café. Interactive exhibits include designated areas for toddlers and teens, as well as plenty of activities for the entire family. Several art workshops are offered each day, as well as hands-on studios where visitors are encouraged to create their own art. The studio projects change frequently and the entire museum changes exhibits every 18 to 24 months, so there is always something new to explore. The adjoining 1-acre park and playground is across from the convention center trolley stop. ⊠ 200 W. Island Ave., Embarcadero ☎ 619/233–8792 ⊕ www.thinkplaycreate.org ⊴ $20 ⊙ Closed Tues.

Santa Fe Depot

TRANSPORTATION | The Mission-style Santa Fe Depot, which replaced the original 1887 station on this site when it opened in 1915 for the Panama–California International Exposition, serves Amtrak and Coaster passengers. A booth here has bus schedules, maps, and tourist brochures. Formerly an easily spotted area landmark, the graceful, tile-dome depot is now overshadowed by **1 America Plaza,** the 34-story office tower across the street. At the base of this skyscraper, designed by architect Helmut Jahn, is a center linking the city's train and bus systems, as well as MTS's red trolleys, which run from the station all the way to the Mexico border. The building's signature crescent-shape, glass-and-steel canopy arches out over the trolley tracks. ⊠ Broadway and Kettner Blvd., Embarcadero.

Seaport Village

PEDESTRIAN MALL | FAMILY | You'll find some of the best views of the harbor at Seaport Village, three bustling shopping plazas designed to reflect the New England clapboard and Spanish Mission architectural styles of early California. On a prime stretch of waterfront the dining, shopping, and entertainment complex connects the harbor with hotel towers and the convention center. Specialty shops offer everything from a kite store and swing emporium to a shop devoted to hot sauces. You can dine at snack bars and restaurants, many with harbor views.

Live music can be heard daily from noon to 4 at the main food court. Additional free concerts take place every Sunday from 1 to 4 at the East Plaza Gazebo. The Seaport Village Carousel (⊴ rides $3) has 54 animals, hand-carved and hand-painted by Charles Looff in 1895. Across the street, the Headquarters at Seaport Village converted the historic police headquarters into several trendsetting shops and restaurants. ⊠ 849 W. Harbor Dr., Embarcadero ☎ 619/530–0704 office and events hotline ⊕ www.seaportvillage.com.

★ USS *Midway* Museum

MILITARY SIGHT | FAMILY | After 47 years of worldwide service, the retired USS *Midway* began a new tour of duty on the south side of the Navy pier in 2004. Launched in 1945, the 1,001-foot-long ship was the largest in the world for the first 10 years of its existence. The most visible landmark on the north Embarcadero, it now serves as a floating interactive museum—an appropriate addition to the town that is home to one-third of the Pacific fleet and the birthplace of naval aviation. A free audio tour guides you through the massive ship while offering insight from former sailors. As you clamber through passageways and up and down ladder wells, you'll get a feel for how the *Midway*'s 4,500 crew members lived and worked on this "city at sea."

Though the entire tour is impressive, you'll really be wowed when you step out onto the 4-acre flight deck—not only the best place to get an idea of the ship's scale, but also one of the most interesting vantage points for bay and city skyline views. An F-14 Tomcat jet fighter is just one of many vintage aircraft on display. Free guided tours of the bridge and primary flight control, known as "the Island," depart every 10 minutes from the flight deck. Many of the docents stationed throughout the ship served in the Navy, some even on the *Midway*, and they are eager to answer questions or share stories. The museum also offers multiple flight simulators for an additional fee, climb-aboard cockpits, and interactive exhibits focusing on naval aviation. There is a gift shop and a café with pleasant outdoor seating. This is a wildly popular stop, with most visits lasting several hours.

⚠ **Despite efforts to provide accessibility throughout the ship, some areas can only be reached via fairly steep steps; a video tour of these areas is available on the hangar deck.** ⊠ *910 N. Harbor Dr., Embarcadero* ☎ *619/544–9600* ⊕ *www.midway.org* ⊠ *$31.*

🍴 Restaurants

This walkable Downtown bay-front strip between the iconic County Administration building and the convention center offers visitors access to historic maritime destinations and dining options served up with spectacular views.

★ Animae

$$$$ | **ASIAN FUSION** | The large, plush booths and elegant decor at Animae suggest an air of sophistication, while the soundtrack of '90s-era hip-hop adds a flash of casual cool to keep it from ever being too stuffy. Not that such a thing is at risk at this dazzling Embarcadero bistro, which pairs indulgent, tender Wagyu beef steak cuts with a variety of dishes inspired by Japan and Southeast Asia. **Known for:** wide variety of Japanese whiskeys; whole branzino; aged Wagyu beef filet. ⑤ *Average main: $41* ⊠ *969 Pacific Hwy., Embarcadero* ☎ *619/432–1225* ⊕ *www.animaesd.com* ⊗ *Closed Sun. and Mon. No lunch.*

★ Eddie V's Prime Seafood

$$$ | **SEAFOOD** | Don't be put off by the name, or that it is part of a small chain. This fine-dining restaurant at the Headquarters at Seaport in Downtown has won a devoted following for classic seafood, casual but sophisticated settings, and nightly live jazz. **Known for:** the shellfish tower, featuring oysters, crab, shrimp and Maine lobster; wallet-friendly happy hour deals; indulgent truffled mac and cheese. ⑤ *Average main: $40* ⊠ *789 W. Harbor Dr., Embarcadero* ☎ *619/615–0281* ⊕ *www.eddiev.com* ⊗ *No lunch.*

★ Puesto

$ | **MEXICAN** | Bold graffiti graphics, chandeliers with tangled telephone wires, and beat-heavy music energize this Downtown eatery that celebrates Mexican street food with a modern twist. Settle into one of the interior rooms or the sunny patio under orange umbrellas to sip margaritas and other specialty cocktails, Baja wines, or fruity aguas frescas made daily. **Known for:** taco trio plates; unique Parmesan guacamole; fruit-infused margaritas made in-house. ⑤ *Average main: $16* ⊠ *789 W. Harbor Dr., Embarcadero* ☎ *619/233–8880* ⊕ *www.eatpuesto.com.*

Top of the Market

$$$ | **SEAFOOD** | With its bay views from Point Loma to the Coronado Bridge, this upscale seafood house is just right for a memorable evening. The romantic teak-paneled dining room and a deck that sits over the water are popular spots for visitor splurges and locals celebrating special occasions. **Known for:** romantic atmosphere; smoked fish appetizers. ⑤ *Average main: $35* ⊠ *750 N. Harbor Dr., Embarcadero* ☎ *619/234–4687* ⊕ *www.topofthemarketsd.com.*

Coffee and Quick Bites

Carnitas' Snack Shack

$ | **AMERICAN** | Carnitas Snack Shack got a start further inland in North Park, but eventually brought their signature pork tacos westward to provide a side of bayfront views with their modern Mexican cuisine. Indulge in some carnitas tacos, a BLT, or the "Triple Threat" pork sandwich at the Embarcadero outpost of this popular swine-heavy dining spot. **Known for:** the "Triple Threat" pork sandwich; amazing tacos; crispy golden French fries. ⑤ *Average main: $12* ✉ *1004 N. Harbor Dr., Embarcadero* ☎ *619/696–7675* ⊕ *www.carnitassnackshack.com.*

🛏 Hotels

★ InterContinental San Diego

$$ | **HOTEL** | A new addition to the waterfront skyline, InterContinental San Diego provides a more luxurious and stylish option for travelers in what's generally an area populated by more family-friendly lodging. **Pros:** stunning waterfront views; excellent dining options at Vistal and Garibaldi; close to both airport and attractions. **Cons:** a bit on the pricier side; pedestrian traffic can be hectic because of nearby shopping/boating areas; entrances and elevators are a bit confusing. ⑤ *Rooms from: $278* ✉ *901 Bayfront Ct., Embarcadero* ☎ *619/501–9400* ⊕ *www.intercontinentalsandiego.com/* ⊷ *400 rooms* ⦿ *No Meals.*

Manchester Grand Hyatt San Diego

$$ | **HOTEL** | **FAMILY** | Primarily a draw for business travelers, this hotel between Seaport Village and the convention center also works well for leisure and family travelers. **Pros:** great views; spacious rooms; good location. **Cons:** lots of convention goers; some trolley noise; not as stylish as many other Downtown hotels. ⑤ *Rooms from: $259* ✉ *1 Market Pl., Embarcadero* ☎ *619/232–1234* ⊕ *www.hyatt.com* ⊷ *1628 rooms* ⦿ *No Meals.*

Nightlife

Scenic drinking spots and higher bar tabs overlook tall ships and naval history.

The Lion's Share

PIANO BARS | Hemingway would have loved this exquisitely designed brick-and-wood bar that serves up equally exquisite craft cocktails that, while pricey, are definitely made for sipping. The place attracts a sophisticated crowd and is highly recommended for those looking to impress a special someone. ✉ *629 Kettner Blvd., Embarcadero* ☎ *619/564–6924* ⊕ *lionssharesd.com.*

Top of the Hyatt

COCKTAIL LOUNGES | This lounge at the Manchester Grand Hyatt crowns the tallest waterfront building in California, affording great views of San Diego Bay, including Coronado to the west, Mexico to the south, and Point Loma and La Jolla to the north. It's pricey and pretentious (don't you dare wear flip-flops), but this champagne-centric bar is great for catching a sunset or celebrating an anniversary. ✉ *1 Market Pl., Embarcadero* ☎ *619/232–1234* ⊕ *topofthehyatt.com.*

🎭 Performing Arts

Rady Shell at Jacobs Park

MUSIC | The glamorous new home for outdoor summer and spring concerts presented by the San Diego Symphony sits on the same spot where its former outdoor concert space sat, but with a dazzling new upgrade. An $85 million, two-year project, the Rady Shell is a large and stunning space to catch a concert or symphony performance during the warm summer months—or any time of year, really—with space for up to 10,000 attendees, with typical seated performances accommodating around 3,500. In addition to the sounds and bayside sights, the Shell also has top-notch dining options, including a prix-fixe menu from Blais by the Bay, tacos from Lola 55, and sandwiches from Biga. ⊠ *222 Marina Park Way, Embarcadero* ☎ *619/235–0804* ⊕ *www.theshell.org.*

Shopping

The new Headquarters at Seaport shopping district is breathing new life into the somewhat touristy San Diego waterfront. Spanning 14 acres and offering more than 50 shops and 17 restaurants, Seaport Village remains popular for souvenirs and entertainment.

★ The Headquarters at Seaport

MARKET | This new upscale shopping and dining center is in the city's former police headquarters, a beautiful and historic Mission-style building featuring an open courtyard with fountains. Restaurants and shops, many locally owned, occupy former jail facilities and offices. Pop into **Urban Beach House** for coastal-inspired fashion from popular surf brands for men and women, including accessories and home decor. **Perfume Gallery** offers more than 1,000 different scents in its extensive collection. **Madison San Diego** offers a great selection of leather goods and accessories, from apparel and handbags to belts and travel accessories. ⊠ *789 W. Harbor Dr., Embarcadero* ☎ *619/235–4013* ⊕ *theheadquarters.com.*

Seaport Village

SHOPPING CENTER | FAMILY | If you're looking for trinkets and souvenirs, this is the place. This complex of kitschy shops and waterfront restaurants has upped its hip factor with boutiques like **San Pasqual** wine bar and bamboo clothing–maker **Cariloha**. While there, keep an eye out for **Urban Girl Accessories** to find an eclectic mix of clothing and gifts from name brands and local artisans, and stop by **Village Hat Shop** to browse their collection of 50,000 fedoras, bowlers, cowboy, and custom-embroidered hats. In addition to shopping, the village has views of the bay, fresh breezes, and great strolling paths. A hand-carved historic carousel

and frequent public entertainment are among the attractions. Seaport Village is within walking distance of hotels, the San Diego Convention Center, and the San Diego Trolley. ⊠ *849 W. Harbor Dr., at Pacific Hwy., Embarcadero* ☎ *619/530–0704* ⊕ *www.seaportvillage. com/shopping.*

Activities

BIKING

Wheel Fun Rentals

BIKING | Surreys, cruisers, mountain bikes, and tandems, among other two-, three-, and four-wheeled contraptions, are available at the Wyndham San Diego Bayside and a number of other locations around San Diego; call or visit the website for details. ⊠ *1355 N. Harbor Dr., Embarcadero* ☎ *619/342–7244* ⊕ *www. wheelfunrentals.com* 🖭 *From $20 per hr.*

TOURS AND CRUISES

Whale-watching season peaks in January and February, when thousands of gray whales migrate south to the warm weather, where they give birth to their calves. If you want a closer look, charter boats and cruises like City Cruises and Flagship host whale-watching excursions.

City Cruises

BOATING | FAMILY | This outfit operates harbor cruises, sunset cocktail and dining cruises, and yacht charters, as well as whale-watching excursions with live narration provided by experts from the San Diego Natural History Museum. ⊠ *970 N. Harbor Dr., Embarcadero* ☎ *619/686–8700, 800/459–8105 toll-free* ⊕ *www. cityexperiences.com* 🖭 *From $35.*

Flagship Cruises & Events

BOATING | FAMILY | Get on board here for harbor tours, two-hour dinner and brunch cruises, and a ferry to Coronado. Twice-daily whale-watching tours run from December through April, with narration provided by experts from Birch Aquarium at Scripps. ⊠ *990 N. Harbor Dr., Embarcadero* ☎ *619/234–4111,*

800/442–7847 reservations ⊕ *www.
flagshipsd.com* ⊡ *From $24.*

East Village

The most ambitious of the Downtown
projects is **East Village,** not far from the
Gaslamp Quarter, and encompassing 130
blocks between the railroad tracks up to
J Street, and from 6th Avenue east to
around 10th Street. Sparking the rebirth
of this former warehouse district was
the 2004 construction of the San Diego
Padres' stunning 42,000-seat baseball
stadium, **Petco Park,** where games are
rarely rained out.

The **Urban Art Trail** has added pizzazz to
drab city thoroughfares by transforming
such things as trash cans and traffic
controller boxes into works of art. As the
city's largest Downtown neighborhood,
East Village is continually broadening
its boundaries with its urban design of
redbrick cafés, spacious galleries, rooftop
bars, sleek hotels, and warehouse
restaurants.

Sights

Petco Park
SPORTS VENUE | FAMILY | Petco Park is
home to the city's major league baseball
team, the San Diego Padres. The ballpark
is strategically designed to give fans
a view of San Diego Bay, the skyline,
and Balboa Park. Reflecting San Diego's
beauty, the stadium is clad in sandstone
from India to evoke the area's cliffs and
beaches; the 42,000 seats are dark
blue, reminiscent of the ocean, and the
exposed steel is painted white to reflect
the sails of harbor boats on the bay. The
family-friendly lawnlike berm, "Park at
the Park," is a popular and affordable
place for fans to view the game. The ballpark underwent a huge effort to improve
dining in the park, and local food vendors
and craft breweries now dominate the

Western Metal Supply

Initially scheduled for demolition
to make room for Petco Park, the
historic Western Metal Supply Co.
was instead incorporated into the
ballpark and supports the left-field
foul pole. Great care was taken to
retain the historic nature of the
building's exterior despite extensive
interior renovations. Built in 1909,
the four-story structure originally
manufactured wagon wheels and
war supplies, and today holds the
Padres' Team Store, food and bever-
age outlets, and rooftop seating.

dining options. Behind-the-scenes guided
tours of Petco, including the press box
and the dugout, are offered throughout
the year. ⊠ *100 Park Blvd., East Village*
☎ *619/795–5011 tour hotline* ⊕ *sandiego.
padres.mlb.com* ⊡ *$30 tour.*

You & Yours
DISTILLERY | A refreshing alternative to
the sensory overload in some of the bars
Downtown, You & Yours is a local gin
and vodka distillery that also serves up a
number of excellent cocktails inside its
tasting room. The atmosphere is modern,
relaxed, and airy; the clientele low-key;
and the gin itself is outstanding. ⊠ *1495
G St., East Village* ☎ *619/955–8755*
⊕ *www.youandyours.com.*

🍴 Restaurants

Revived with the opening of the San
Diego Padres stadium, Petco Park, this
trendy high-rise residential area is an
eclectic mix of hip gastropubs, wine bars,
and cafés serving everything from French
bistro fare to Baja-Mexican, burgers, and
artisan-baked bread.

Home of the San Diego Padres, Petco Park offers behind-the-scenes tours.

The Blind Burro

$$ | **MODERN MEXICAN** | **FAMILY** | East Village families, baseball fans heading to or from Petco Park, and happy-hour-bound singles flock to this airy restaurant with Baja-inspired food and drink. Traditional margaritas get a fresh kick from fruit juices or jalapeño peppers; other libations include sangria and Mexican beers, all perfect pairings for house-made guacamole, ceviche, or salsas with chips. **Known for:** house margarita with fruit infusions; surf-and-turf Baja-style tacos; gluten-free menu. ⑤ *Average main: $21 ⌧ 639 J St., East Village* ☎ *619/795–7880* ⊕ *www. theblindburro.com.*

Cowboy Star

$$$$ | **STEAKHOUSE** | Special-occasion diners, conventioneers on expense accounts, and meat-loving locals haunt this surprisingly intimate dining room for great beef expertly prepared. The wood-and-brick interior has leather accents, Western landscapes, and vintage Old West photos, and servers wear white shirts and stylish denim aprons, all creating a relaxed urban-cowboy ambience. **Known for:** on-site butcher shop selling premium steaks, sausages, and charcuterie; Western decor, with leather booths and steer skulls; 35-day dry-aged beef. ⑤ *Average main: $53 ⌧ 640 10th Ave., East Village* ☎ *619/450–5880* ⊕ *www.cowboystarsd.com* ⊗ *No lunch.*

The Mission

$ | **AMERICAN** | Healthy, creative dishes and a friendly staff make this art-filled East Village café a local favorite for breakfast and lunch. Hungry San Diegans wait 30 minutes or more to enjoy fluffy scrambled eggs with chicken apple sausage or strawberry banana pancakes with a side of eggs and bacon. **Known for:** Mexican-influenced breakfast dishes like chilaquiles; French toast made with house-baked cinnamon bread; busy breakfast scene especially on weekends. ⑤ *Average main: $12 ⌧ 1250 J St., East Village* ☎ *619/232–7662* ⊕ *www.themissionsd.com* ⊗ *No dinner.*

Tajima East Village

$ | **JAPANESE** | With four other locations in the city—Hillcrest, North Park, and two outposts in Kearny Mesa—Tajima has become a favorite source for ramen-hungry San Diegans. Climb into a cozy booth and order a Japanese craft beer or sake before diving into one of the five types of ramen—all of which come in hefty portions with affordable price tags—including an excellent vegan version with spinach noodles. **Known for:** spicy sesame ramen with spicy ground pork and fried garlic; affordable and hefty portions; karaage fried chicken. $ *Average main: $14* ⊠ *901 E St., East Village* ☎ *619/431–5820* ⊕ *www.tajimaramen.com.*

Coffee and Quick Bites

The Invigatorium

$ | **CAFÉ** | Decked out in dinosaurs and featuring a mosaic dragon on the wall, The Invigatorium is as much a showcase for tasteful whimsy as it is for tasty treats. A partnership between brewery/coffee roaster Modern Times and local restaurateurs Consortium Holdings, the East Village spot is essentially two small eateries in one: the eponymous coffee and breakfast bite purveyors as well as its sibling bar, J & Tony's, which serves up Italian cold-cut sandwiches and classic cocktails while vintage vinyl spins on the hi-fi. **Known for:** breakfast tacos; Lavender London fog latte; Tony's Negroni. $ *Average main: $10* ⊠ *631 9th Ave., East Village* ☎ *855/634–7664* ⊕ *www.theinvigatorium.com* ⊘ *No dinner.*

Lola 55

$ | **MEXICAN** | This is the place for exceptional, elevated tacos that won't break the bank. Don't miss happy hour, Sunday–Friday from 2 to 6 pm, where margaritas and Modelos are $4. **Known for:** great cocktails; great tacos; gluten-free and vegan options. $ *Average main: $5* ⊠ *1290 F St., East Village* ☎ *619/542–9155* ⊕ *lola55.com* ⊘ *Closed Mon.*

▼ Nightlife

East Village, just outside of the Gaslamp, is a little more cutting edge. This up-and-coming urban hood has upscale style mashed with hip, underground dives. Most of its destinations are within close quarters to Petco Park, so on game night, the neighborhood is particularly lively. Not that it's quiet any other night; popular hangouts like East Village Tavern & Bowl, and Bar Basic are reliably crowded haunts, so show up early.

BARS

Bar Basic

BARS | This spot is always bustling, in part because it's *the* place to be seen for Padres fans or anyone else attending events at Petco Park. True to its name, Basic reliably dishes up simple pleasures: strong drinks and hot, coal-fired pizza. The garage-style doors roll up and keep the industrial-chic former warehouse ventilated during the balmy summer. ⊠ *410 10th Ave., East Village* ☎ *619/531–8869* ⊕ *www.barbasic.com.*

East Village Tavern & Bowl

THEMED ENTERTAINMENT | Twelve bowling lanes means no more hauls to the suburbs to channel one's inner Lebowski. Lane rental is pricey during prime times, but reasonable if you consider that some nearby clubs charge a Jackson just for admission, though reservations are definitely recommended. From the expansive bar area you can watch sports on 33 flat screens, and the satellite radio plays an assortment of alt- and classic rock. ⊠ *930 Market St., East Village* ☎ *619/677–2695* ⊕ *www.tavernbowl.com.*

Fairweather Rooftop Bar

BARS | The star of the show here is the rooftop bar; it's a great place to meet for a drink, specializing in tropical treats like Singapore slings and piña coladas, but its location right next to the ballpark makes it such a sweet spot during baseball season. On the main floor, Rare

Form is another bar and dining area that serves great tacos and local beers on tap. ✉ *793 J St., East Village* ☎ *619/578–2392* ⊕ *www.fairweatherbar.com.*

★ Noble Experiment

PIANO BARS | There are a handful of speakeasy-style bars in San Diego, though none deliver so far above and beyond the novelty quite like this cozy-yet-swank cocktail lounge hidden in the back of a burger restaurant. Seek out the hidden door (hint: look for the stack of kegs), tuck into a plush leather booth next to the wall of golden skulls, and sip on the best craft cocktails in the city. For even more exclusivity, check out the speakeasy-within-a-speakeasy Young Blood, which is an all-inclusive cocktail experience in an adjacent space for the up-front fee of $67. ■**TIP➔ Reservations are almost always a must, so be sure to call ahead.** ✉ *777 G St., East Village* ☎ *619/888–4713* ⊕ *nobleexperimentsd.com.*

Punch Bowl Social

GATHERING PLACES | Punch Bowl Social—which also has locations in Atlanta, Austin, and Denver—is essentially three different concepts all wrapped up in one wildly entertaining time. It's a cocktail bar, boasting favorites including mules and daiquiris, along with modern twists and even spiked milkshakes. It's also a diner, with fare that ranges from breakfast nachos to fried-chicken sandwiches. And most importantly, it's a game room, complete with darts, pinball, and even a bowling alley. No matter what, though, get one of those milkshakes—they're dangerously good. ✉ *1485 E St., East Village* ☎ *619/452–3352* ⊕ *www.punchbowlsocial.com.*

Little Italy

Home to many in San Diego's design community, Little Italy exudes a sense of urban cool. The main thoroughfare, India Street, is filled with lively cafés, chic shops, and many of the city's trendiest restaurants. Little Italy is one of San Diego's most walkable neighborhoods, and a great spot to wander. Art lovers can browse gallery showrooms, while shoppers adore the Fir Street cottages. The neighborhood bustles each Saturday during the wildly popular Mercato farmers' market, and at special events throughout the year such as Artwalk in spring and FESTA! each fall. The website Little Italy San Diego (⊕ *littleitalysd.com*) has detailed info about neighborhood shops and events.

The neighborhood is also authentic to its roots and marked by old-country charms: church bells ring on the half-hour, and Italians gather daily to play bocce in Amici Park. After an afternoon of gelati and espresso, you may just forget that you're in Southern California.

Sights

Little Italy Mercato

MARKET | Each Saturday tourists and residents alike flock to the Little Italy Mercato, one of the most popular farmers' markets in San Diego. More than 150 vendors line Date Street selling everything from paintings and pottery to flowers and farm-fresh eggs. Come hungry, as several booths and food trucks serve prepared foods. Alternatively, the neighborhood's many cafés and restaurants are just steps away. The Mercato is a great opportunity to experience one of San Diego's most exciting urban neighborhoods. ✉ *Date and India Sts., Little Italy* ⊕ *www.littleitalysd.com/events/mercato.*

Built in 1863, the Maritime Museum's *Star of India* is often considered to be a symbol of San Diego.

★ Maritime Museum

MARINA/PIER | FAMILY | From sailing ships to submarines, the Maritime Museum is a must for anyone with an interest in nautical history. This collection of restored and replica ships affords a fascinating glimpse of San Diego during its heyday as a commercial seaport. The jewel of the collection, the *Star of India*, was built in 1863 and made 21 trips around the world in the late 1800s. Saved from the scrap yard and painstakingly restored, the windjammer is the oldest active iron sailing ship in the world. The newly constructed *San Salvador* is a detailed historic replica of the original ship first sailed into San Diego Bay by explorer Juan Rodriguez Cabrillo back in 1542, and the popular HMS *Surprise* is a replica of an 18th-century British Royal Navy frigate. The museum's headquarters are on the *Berkeley*, an 1898 steam-driven ferryboat, which served the Southern Pacific Railroad in San Francisco until 1958.

Numerous cruises of San Diego Bay are offered, including a daily 45-minute narrated tour aboard a 1914 pilot boat and three-hour weekend sails aboard the topsail schooner the *Californian*, the state's official tall ship, and 75-minute tours aboard a historic swift boat, which highlights the city's military connection. Partnering with the museum, the renowned yacht *America* also offers sails on the bay, and whale-watching excursions are available in winter. ✉ *1492 N. Harbor Dr., Little Italy* ☎ *619/234–9153* ⊕ *www.sdmaritime.org* 🖃 *$20.*

★ Waterfront Park

CITY PARK | FAMILY | Adjacent to San Diego's County Administration Center is one of the city's most playful destinations—this 12-acre, family-friendly space is a great place to stretch out and cool off with fountain jets that are operational during the warmer months and a playground where children can climb, swing, and slide to their hearts' content. Even if you're just taking a moment to rest, the seaside view is worth the stop. ✉ *1600 Pacific Hwy., Little Italy* ☎ *619/232–7275* ⊕ *sdparks.org* 🖃 *Free.*

🍴 Restaurants

One of San Diego's oldest and liveliest neighborhoods, steeped in the city's Italian and Portuguese fishing culture, Little Italy is known for its bustling nightlife and Italian fine and casual dining mixed with trendy new eateries, dessert destinations, sidewalk cafés, and a few late-night bars.

Ballast Point Brewing Co.

$ | **AMERICAN** | **FAMILY** | Until recently, you had to head to the Miramar/Scripps Ranch area for a tasting at Ballast Point, but now there's a spacious (and popular) local taproom in Little Italy. The Sculpin IPA is outstanding, as are the blue cheese duck nachos. **Known for:** duck nachos; truffalo wings; more than three-dozen beers on tap. Ⓢ *Average main: $18* ⊠ *2215 India St., Little Italy* ☎ *619/255–7213* ⊕ *www.ballastpoint. com.*

Bencotto

$$ | **ITALIAN** | The ultramodern Italian eatery with young Milanese owners gets cheers for its design and cuisine from hip Little Italy residents and visitors alike. Diners linger over drinks and house-made pasta at the friendly long bar and more intimate upstairs dining room. **Known for:** mix-and-match pasta entrées; gluten-free pasta options; traditional Italian tiramisu. Ⓢ *Average main: $24* ⊠ *750 W. Fir St., Little Italy* ☎ *619/450–4786* ⊕ *www. lovebencotto.com* ⊗ *No lunch Mon.*

★ Born and Raised

$$$$ | **STEAKHOUSE** | The name is cheeky if a little morbid; the title refers to the restaurant's speciality—steak. It's a twist on a classic steak house, with a menu full of aged, prime cuts of beef served with a number of sauces, or perhaps try the table-side-prepared steak Diane with flambéed jus. **Known for:** table-side Caesar salad; aged New York steak; cheeky, glamorous decor. Ⓢ *Average main: $45* ⊠ *1909 India St., Little Italy* ☎ *619/202–4577* ⊕ *www.bornandraisedsteak.com.*

Cloak and Petal

$$ | **JAPANESE FUSION** | More than simply a sushi restaurant, Cloak and Petal offers up "Japanese tapas," with a menu of small bites that range from fresh sashimi to Wagyu beef lettuce cups. Even more stunning is the visual appeal, including a giant cherry blossom tree behind the bar. **Known for:** tiki drinks with Far East ingredients; unconventional sushi rolls; decor that's a feast for the eyes. Ⓢ *Average main: $21* ⊠ *1953 India St., Little Italy* ☎ *619/501–5505,* ⊕ *www.cloakandpetal. com* ⊗ *No lunch weekdays.*

★ The Crack Shack

$ | **AMERICAN** | **FAMILY** | Next to his successful fine-dining restaurant, Juniper and Ivy, celebrity chef Richard Blais has opened this more casual eatery complete with a walk-up counter, picnic-style tables, a bocce court, and a giant rooster—a nod to the egg- and chicken-theme menu. Ingredients are sourced from high-quality vendors and used for sandwiches, of which the fried chicken varieties shine, as well as salads and sides like fluffy minibiscuits with a miso-maple butter and a Mexican spin on poutine. **Known for:** Señor Croque fried chicken sandwich with smoked pork belly; biscuits with miso-maple butter; all-outdoor seating with bocce court. Ⓢ *Average main: $13* ⊠ *2266 Kettner Blvd., Little Italy* ☎ *619/795–3299* ⊕ *www.crackshack.com.*

Craft & Commerce

$$ | **AMERICAN** | The redesigned Little Italy restaurant-bar oozes slightly surreal cool. Crammed bookshelves line the walls, banquettes and mirrors are scrawled with sayings, and taxidermy appears in odd settings like a lion preying on a hog above the bar. **Known for:** wood-fired cuisine including grilled oysters and fire-roasted eggplant dip; refreshing craft cocktails infused with cucumber, grapefruit, or apple. Ⓢ *Average main: $22* ⊠ *675 W. Beech St., Little Italy* ☎ *619/269–2202* ⊕ *www.craft-commerce.com.*

Sights ▼

1 Little Italy Mercato **E5**
2 Maritime Museum...... **B6**
3 Waterfront Park..........**C6**

Restaurants ▼

1 Ballast Point
  Brewing Co. **D3**
2 Bencotto................. **D5**
3 Born and Raised **E4**
4 Cloak and Petal **E4**
5 The Crack Shack.........**C3**
6 Craft & Commerce...... **D6**
7 Herb & Wood............ **D3**
8 Ironside
  Fish & Oyster............. **E5**
9 Juniper and Ivy **C3**
10 Karl Strauss' Brewing
  Company................. **E8**
11 Morning Glory............ **E5**

Quick Bites ▼

1 Extraordinary
  Desserts **F7**
2 James Coffee Co........ **D2**
3 Little Italy Food Hall...... **E5**
4 Pappalecco............... **E6**

Hotels ▼

1 Found Hotel............... **E4**
2 Hilton Garden Inn/
  Homewood Suites **C4**
3 La Pensione Hotel **E5**
4 Porto Vista Hotel......... **E5**

★ Herb & Wood

$$ | **AMERICAN** | Design lovers will fall for celebrity chef Brian Malarkey's sprawling restaurant, a former art store that has been refashioned into four luxe spaces in one—an entryway lounge, outdoor lounge, fireplace-dotted patio, and the main dining room, which is flanked by beaded chandeliers, lush banquettes, and paintings in rich jewel tones. The menu is heavy on wood-roasted dishes, many of which are apt for sharing, like the roasted baby carrots or hiramasa with crispy quinoa. **Known for:** roasted baby carrots with cashew sesame dukkah; pillow-soft oxtail gnocchi; the secret menu Parker House rolls topped with Maldon sea salt. ⑤ *Average main: $22* ✉ *2210 Kettner Blvd., Little Italy* ☎ *619/955–8495* ⊕ *www.herbandwood.com* ☽ *No lunch Mon.–Sat.*

Ironside Fish & Oyster

$$ | **SEAFOOD** | Hundreds of piranhas cover one wall of this soaring, nautically themed dining room dedicated to fresh seafood in all its guises. At the raw bar with its refrigerated metal top, a half dozen or more varieties of oysters are available for slurping, along with drinks from the booklet-size cocktail menu. **Known for:** $1 oysters during weekday happy hour; extensive cocktail menu; fresh whole fish with simple sides is a bargain at less than $25. ⑤ *Average main: $30* ✉ *1654 India St., Little Italy* ☎ *619/269–3033* ⊕ *www.ironsidefishandoyster.com.*

Juniper and Ivy

$$$$ | **MODERN AMERICAN** | Celebrity chef Richard Blais's addition to San Diego's restaurant scene fills an open-beamed space with seating for 250 and an open stainless-steel dream kitchen where diners can watch the chef and team in action. Blais sources local farm-fresh ingredients for his "left coast cookery" with a molecular gastronomy twist. **Known for:** California-Baja-inspired carne crudo asada topped with quail eggs; off-menu "In & Haute" burger; very

shareable Yodel chocolate dessert. ⑤ *Average main: $42* ✉ *2228 Kettner Blvd., Little Italy* ☎ *619/269–9036* ⊕ *www.juniperandivy.com* ☽ *No lunch.*

Karl Strauss' Brewing Company

$ | **AMERICAN** | **FAMILY** | San Diego's first microbrewery now has multiple locations, but the original one remains a staple. This locale draws an after-work crowd for German-inspired pub food and pints of Red Trolley Ale and later fills with beer connoisseurs from all walks of life to try Karl's latest concoctions. **Known for:** beer pretzels with ale cheese dip; beeramisu dessert, made with Imperial Stout; more than a dozen rotating and seasonal beers on tap. ⑤ *Average main: $17* ✉ *1157 Columbia St., Little Italy* ☎ *619/234–2739* ⊕ *www.karlstrauss. com.*

★ Morning Glory

$ | **AMERICAN** | Among the plentiful and popular brunch options in Little Italy, Morning Glory stands out for not just elevating its breakfast options but making breakfast and brunch its only concern. The dazzling, pink-hue brunch palace is a luxurious sight to behold, with plush seating, a vending machine full of champagne, and a giant metal flower-shape lamp at the center of its outdoor dining area. **Known for:** fluffy and light soufflé pancakes; fried chicken and waffle; hot chocolate flights. ⑤ *Average main: $13* ✉ *550 W. Date St., Little Italy* ☎ *619/629–0302* ⊕ *www.morningglorybreakfast.com* ☽ *No lunch or dinner.*

☕ Coffee and Quick Bites

★ Extraordinary Desserts

$ | **CAFÉ** | For Paris-perfect cakes and tarts embellished California-style with fresh flowers, head to this sleek, serene branch of Karen Krasne's pastry shop and café. The space with soaring ceilings hosts breakfasts, lunches, and light dinners, accompanied by a wide selection of teas, coffee, organic wines, and craft beers. **Known for:** blueberry coffee cake for breakfast; chocolate dulce de leche cake; house-made dips including onion dip and Parmesan pesto. $ *Average main: $17* ⊠ *1430 Union St., Little Italy* ☎ *619/294–7001* ⊕ *www.extraordinarydesserts.com.*

James Coffee Co.

$ | **CAFÉ** | Housed alongside boutique retailers in The Space, a warehouse-like shopping center, James Coffee Co. and its aromas of fresh-brewed house roasts might very well prove too enticing for nearby shoppers to pass up. Take a seat while waiting for a cup of flavorful pour-over coffee, frothy espresso, or a variety of teas, and savor a morning bun or a flaky, buttery croissant. **Known for:** a wide variety of seasonal bean roasts; rich, flaky croissants; bold-flavored pour-over coffee. $ *Average main: $4* ⊠ *The Space, 2355 India St., Little Italy* ☎ *619/756–7770* ⊕ *jamescoffeeco.com* ☾ *No dinner.*

Little Italy Food Hall

$ | **FUSION** | **FAMILY** | A recently opened, chic update on the food court, Food Hall brings together a half dozen different innovative food counters to offer quick bites vastly more interesting than mall fare. Among its offerings are the fried chicken sandwiches at Coo-Coos Nest and pizza at Ambrogio15, and an update on a local delicacy, Not Not Tacos. **Known for:** fusion tacos; bustling crowds of Mercato shoppers; beer/wine cart dispensing refreshments in the outdoor seating area. $ *Average main: $10* ⊠ *550 W. Date St., Suite B, Little Italy* ☎ *619/269–7187* ⊕ *www.littleitalyfoodhall.com.*

Pappalecco

$ | **ITALIAN** | **FAMILY** | Situated in the heart of Little Italy, it's a convenient spot to drop in for coffee between boutique shopping or to tuck in for an indulgent affogato (gelato with espresso) afterward. Kids and adults alike will swoon over the addictive gelato, while those seeking something savory can choose from a selection of panini and other snacks. **Known for:** handcrafted gelato; rich, foamy cappuccinos; croissant gelato. $ *Average main: $5* ⊠ *1602 State St., Little Italy* ☎ *619/238–4590* ⊕ *www.pappalecco.com* ▭ *No credit cards.*

Hotels

Found Hotel

$ | **B&B/INN** | You'll find more amenities at other Downtown hotels but it's hard to beat this property's value and charm. **Pros:** good location; historic property; welcoming staff. **Cons:** some shared baths; no parking; not great for couples or families. $ *Rooms from: $161* ⊠ *505 W. Grape St., Little Italy* ☎ *619/230–1600* ⊕ *www.foundhotels.com* ⇌ *23 rooms* ⦿ *Free Breakfast.*

Hilton Garden Inn/Homewood Suites

$$$ | **HOTEL** | **FAMILY** | Two brands from Hilton Hotels now share a building in Little Italy two blocks from the bay, giving guests more space to spread out and be relatively within budget. **Pros:** modern guest rooms; plenty of tech conveniences; quiet neighborhood at night. **Cons:** on a busy block; valet parking only; limited amenities. $ *Rooms from: $273* ⊠ *2137 Pacific Hwy., Little Italy* ☎ *619/696–7000 Homewood Suites, 619/696–6300 Hilton Garden Inn* ⊕ *www.sandiegohiltonhotels.com* ⇌ *364 rooms* ⦿ *Free Breakfast.*

La Pensione Hotel

$ | **HOTEL** | Centrally located in the heart of Little Italy, the 67-room hotel offers boutique lodging on a budget by forgoing the extravagance of some of the larger, nearby luxury brands; thankfully, it doesn't do so at the expense of aesthetics. **Pros:** within walking distance to many restaurants and shops; comfortable, stylish rooms; great views. **Cons:** no in-hotel dining; limited space in paid garage; rooms are on the small side. $ *Rooms from: $189* ⊠ *606 W. Date St., Little Italy* ☎ *619/236–8000* ⊕ *www.lapensionehotel.com* ⇌ *67 rooms* ⦿ *No Meals.*

Porto Vista Hotel

$ | **HOTEL** | This former budget motel has transformed into a contemporary hotel-motel with modern furnishings, a stylish restaurant and lounge, a fitness center, and even a hair salon. **Pros:** great location in Little Italy; complimentary airport shuttle; scenic views from restaurant. **Cons:** can be noisy; rooms need updating; limited amenities. ⑤ *Rooms from: $149* ✉ *1835 Columbia St., Little Italy* ☎ *619/544–0164* ⊕ *www. portovistasd.com* ➥ *190 rooms* ⏏ *No Meals.*

Nightlife

Amid its art galleries and boutiques, Little Italy houses several popular open-air beer bars.

BARS
★ False Idol

COCKTAIL LOUNGES | A walk-in refrigerator harbors the secret entrance to this tiki-theme speakeasy, which is attached to the full-service restaurant Craft & Commerce. Beneath fishing nets full of puffer-fish lights and elaborate tiki-head wall carvings, the knowledgeable staff serves up creative takes on tropical classics with the best selection of rums in town. ■**TIP➔ The bar fills up quickly, especially on weekends. Make a reservation online a week or more in advance.** ✉ *675 W. Beech St., Little Italy* ⊕ *falseidoltiki.com.*

The Waterfront Bar & Grill

BARS | It isn't really *on* the waterfront, but San Diego's oldest bar was once the hangout of Italian fishermen. Most of the collars are now white, and patrons enjoy an excellent selection of beers, along with chili, burgers, fish-and-chips, and other great-tasting grub, including fish tacos. Get here early, as there's almost always a crowd. ✉ *2044 Kettner Blvd., Little Italy* ☎ *619/232–9656* ⊕ *www. waterfrontbarandgrill.com.*

San Diego's Bounty

Sunny San Diego is one of the country's premier agricultural areas. Spring is the season for cherimoyas and strawberries, summer brings peaches and boysenberries, autumn is the time for apples and pears, and winter is abundant with tangerines and grapefruit. There's a different farmers' market every day of the week, including the popular Little Italy market; a list can be found at the San Diego County Farm Bureau's website (⊕ *www.facebook.com/ SanDiegoCountyFarmBureau/*).

Wolfie's Carousel Bar

BARS | Inspired by 18th-century carousel design and with a nod to New Orleans' famed Carousel Bar, Wolfie's is an actual, operational rotating bar that makes a full 360-degree turn every 10 minutes or so, which along with its vibrant decorative motif, gives it the feel of an adult indoor amusement park. The spectacle itself is the major attraction, but the menu is no slouch either, offering new interpretations of classic cocktails as well as French bistro fare and Sunday brunch. Order a glass of bubbly or a Madame Curie cocktail (featuring bourbon and burnt sugar) and hop on for a few spins. ✉ *2401 Kettner Blvd., Little Italy* ☎ *619/255–7533* ⊕ *wolfiescarousel.com* ⊘ *Closed Mon.*

MUSIC CLUB
★ The Casbah

LIVE MUSIC | This small club near the airport, the unofficial headquarters of the city's indie music scene, has a national reputation for showcasing up-and-coming acts of all genres. Nirvana, Smashing Pumpkins, and the White Stripes all played here on the way to stardom. ✉ *2501 Kettner Blvd., Little Italy* ☎ *619/232–4355* ⊕ *www.casbahmusic. com.*

Shopping

With more than 33,500 square feet of retail, Little Italy is the place to find contemporary art, modern furniture, and home accessories. It's also an especially fun place to visit during holiday celebrations and special events like ArtWalk in April and Taste of Little Italy in June. The weekly Saturday farmers' market is one of the city's best, and brings people from all over the county to the neighborhood (⊕ *littleitalysd.com/events/mercato*). Many shops have a strong European ambience, and shoppers will find enticing wares that include colorful ceramics, hand-blown glassware, modern home accents, and designer shoes. Kettner Boulevard and India Street north of Grape Street are considered the North Little Italy Art and Design District.

FOOD AND WINE
Bottlecraft Beer Shop
OTHER SPECIALTY STORE | This boutique beer shop and tasting room stocks the best craft beer from San Diego and around the world, from double IPAs and pale ales to saisons and wheat beers. Owner Brian Jensen offers a wealth of knowledge on the local craft beer scene. Bottlecraft now has additional locations in North Park and Liberty Station. ✉ *2252 India St., Little Italy* ☎ *619/487–9493* ⊕ *bottlecraft.com.*

HOME ACCESSORIES AND GIFTS
Architectural Salvage of San Diego
ANTIQUES & COLLECTIBLES | If you have any interest in home design and renovation, this shop that specializes in reusing old materials should be top of your list. The warehouse space is filled with unusual building and decorative materials, as well as items that come from various time periods throughout the 1900s. Products range from stained-glass windows and

light fixtures to cabinets and doors in styles ranging from Victorian to Craftsman. ✉ *2401 Kettner Blvd., Little Italy* ☎ *619/696–1313* ⊕ *www.architecturalsalvagesd.com.*

Blick Art Materials
STATIONERY | Besides supplying local artists with their tools, Blick also carries art books, fine stationery and pens, ornate gift wrap, and beautiful leather-bound journals. ✉ *1844 India St., Little Italy* ☎ *619/687–0050* ⊕ *www.dickblick.com.*

Love & Aesthetics
HOUSEWARES | Located inside one of the cozy yet stylish Fir Street Cottages, this boutique offers a variety of home goods that defy conservative decor aesthetics. From trendy Jonathan Adler furnishings to psychedelic pillows, plates, lamps, and even bespoke cannabis accessories (it's legal in California), this is not your run-of-the-mill housewares emporium. ✉ *621 W. Fir St., Little Italy* ☎ *619/546–6143* ⊕ *www.loveandaesthetics.com.*

Vitreum
SOUVENIRS | The Japanese artist Takao owns this gallery-like shop that sells beautifully handcrafted home-decor items—tableware, glass vases, tea sets, and decorative gifts. ✉ *619 W. Fir St., Little Italy* ☎ *619/237–9810* ⊕ *www. vitreum-us.com.*

SHOPPING CENTERS
The Space
SHOPPING CENTER | This spacious warehouse bears the James Coffee logo on the front and the intoxicating scent of its pour-over brews inside, but the building houses considerably more than just the local coffee roaster. Its tenants include Home Ec, which sells kitchen goods and cookbooks; Specs Optometry; games-and-puzzles boutique Art of Play; and jewelry and housewares at Often Wander. ✉ *2355 India St., Little Italy* ☎ *619/756–7770* ⊕ *www.jamescoffeeco. com.*

Activities

Flagship Cruises welcomes guests aboard with a glass of champagne as a prelude to nightly dinner-dance and holiday cruises. Or take a dinner-dance cruise aboard the *Admiral Hornblower*—the trip comes with fabulous views of the San Diego skyline.

City Cruises

ENTERTAINMENT CRUISE | Take a dinner-dance cruise aboard the *Admiral Hornblower*—the trip comes with fabulous views of the San Diego skyline. ✉ *970 N. Harbor Dr., Little Italy* ⊕ *cityexperiences.com.*

Flagship Cruises and Events

ENTERTAINMENT CRUISE | Flagship Cruises welcomes guests aboard with a glass of champagne as a prelude to nightly dinner-dance and holiday cruises. ✉ *990 N. Harbor Dr., Little Italy* ☏ *619/234–4111* ⊕ *www.flagshipsd.com.*

Barrio Logan

San Diego's Mexican-American community is centered on Barrio Logan, under the San Diego–Coronado Bay Bridge on the Downtown side. Chicano Park, spread along National Avenue from Dewey to Crosby streets, is the barrio's recreational hub. It's worth taking a short detour to see the huge murals of Mexican history painted on the bridge supports at National Avenue and Dewey Street; they're among the best examples of folk art in the city. Art enthusiasts will also enjoy the burgeoning gallery scene in the Barrio Logan neighborhood, rapidly becoming a hub for artists in San Diego.

GETTING HERE AND AROUND

Barrio Logan is located right off Interstate 5, at the Cesar E. Chavez Parkway exit. Driving is the easiest way to get here, especially coming from Downtown—in fact, it's only a mile from Petco Park, and easily accessible via Imperial and Logan Avenues. However, the Blue Line trolley also stops in Barrio Logan, and several bus lines also cross through the neighborhood, including the 9, 6, 20, 705, and 923.

When staying Downtown, Barrio Logan is also just a 15-minute walk, but with its somewhat isolated location under a bridge, visitors should exercise caution visiting the Chicano Park murals after dark.

 ## Sights

Border X Brewing

BREWERY | Barrio Logan's first local craft brewery, Border X has a tap list full of brews inspired by Mexican recipes such as the Jamaica-like Blood Saison (with hibiscus) and Abuelita's Chocolate Stout, featuring cocoa and cinnamon flavors. The taproom is lively most weekends, with sounds of cumbia music soundtracking the revelry. Border X also serves tacos, which always pair well with a refreshing lager. ⊠ *2181 Logan Ave., Barrio Logan* ☎ *619/501–0503* ⊕ *www. borderxbrewing.com.*

★ Chicano Park

PUBLIC ART | **FAMILY** | The cultural center of the Barrio Logan neighborhood, Chicano Park—designated a National Historic Landmark in 2017—was born in 1970 from the activism of local residents who occupied the space after the state rescinded its promise to designate the land a park. Signed into law a year later, the park is now a protected area that brings together families and locals for both public and private events, a welcoming gathering space as well as an outdoor gallery featuring large murals

documenting Mexican-American history and Chicano activism. Every year Chicano Park Day is held on April 21, filling the park with the sights and sounds of music, dancers, vintage cars, and food and clothing vendors. ⊠ *Logan Ave. and Cesar Chavez Pkwy., Barrio Logan* ⊕ *chicano-park.com; www.chicanopark-sandiego.com.*

The Chicano Park Museum and Cultural Center

ART MUSEUM | The newly opened Chicano Park Museum and Cultural Center, adjacent to Chicano Park itself, gives the history and context behind the landmark and the political activism that inspired it. The museum also hosts galleries of rotating pieces by local Chicanx artists. The museum is free to visit but donations are accepted, and make sure to peruse the gift shop, which features items from local artists. Tours must be prearranged. ⊠ *1960 National Ave., Barrio Logan* ✉ *cpmcc.receptionist@gmail.com (to request tours)* ⊕ *chicanoparkmuseum.org* ⊗ *Closed Mon.–Thurs.*

 ## Restaurants

Las Cuatros Milpas

$ | **MEXICAN** | One of the oldest restaurants in San Diego, having opened in 1933, Las Cuatros Milpas feels like a closely held secret in Barrio Logan. Open daily until 3 pm, it almost inevitably attracts a big lunchtime rush, though the wait is worth it for the homemade tortillas, beans with chorizo, and rolled tacos. **Known for:** homemade tortillas; checkered picnic tables; chorizo con huevos. ⑤ *Average main: $5* ⊠ *1857 Logan Ave., Barrio Logan* ☎ *619/234–4460* ⊕ *www. las-cuatro-milpas.com* ⊟ *No credit cards* ⊗ *Closed Sun.*

★ ¡Salud!

$ | **MEXICAN** | The line that inevitably wraps around the building is indicative of the quality of the tacos and the large selection of local craft beers on tap.

Indeed, these are some of the best tacos in all of San Diego, ranging from the classic carne asada and Baja fish tacos to fried-shell beef tacos and Califas, which features French fries inside the tortilla. **Known for:** Baja-style street tacos; Pruno de Piña (beer and fermented pineapple); churros and ice cream. ⑤ *Average main: $4* ⊠ *2196 Logan Ave., Barrio Logan* ☎ *619/255–3856* ⊕ *saludtacos.com* ⊗ *Closed Mon.*

☕ Coffee and Quick Bites

Por Vida
$ | **MEXICAN** | **FAMILY** | A necessary stop for a pick-me-up between boutique shopping, visits to nearby art galleries, and a walk through Chicano Park, Por Vida adds some uniquely Mexican flavor to traditional coffeehouse offerings. Sweeter staples like the horchata latte and dulce de leche latte perk up the taste buds, while in warmer months, a spicy lemonade hits the spot. **Known for:** horchata latte; spicy mango lemonade with tajín rim; pan dulces. ⑤ *Average main: $4* ⊠ *2146 Logan Ave., Barrio Logan* ☎ *619/564–8568.*

🎭 Performing Arts

Bread & Salt
ARTS CENTERS | The spacious factory setting that houses Bread & Salt feels like a modern art warehouse, though its name nods to its long history as a former Wonder Bread factory. Still adorned with much of the industrial machinery and exposed brick, Bread & Salt now houses rotating exhibits from local and national artists, as well as group events such as motorcycle shows and live music showcases. It's also a partner with La Jolla Athenaeum, and puts on experimental and avant-garde concerts throughout the year. ⊠ *1955 Julian Ave., Barrio Logan* ☎ *619/851–4083* ⊕ *www. breadandsaltsandiego.com* ⊗ *Closed Mon. and Sun.*

🛍 Shopping

Hola Swim
SWIMWEAR | Before taking a brisk dip into the Pacific Ocean, swing by this local swimwear boutique where all the suits are designed in-house. A wide variety of styles are available from one-piece wonders to string bikinis for every body type. And in case of occasional clouds, peruse their selection of sweatshirts and shorts as well. The shop is open every weekend, but they also do shopping by appointment throughout the week as well. ⊠ *2159 Logan Ave., Barrio Logan* ☎ *619/997–8682* ⊕ *holaswim.com* ⊗ *Closed weekdays.*

Simón Limón
JEWELRY & WATCHES | Simón Limón doesn't have a large footprint, but what it lacks in square footage it more than makes up for with unique, colorful wares, showcasing independent, local Latinx artists from both San Diego and Tijuana. Humorous cards, stylish jewelry and t-shirts, skincare products and scented candles featuring printed affirmations are just some of the items on its shelves. ⊠ *2185 Logan Ave., #11, Barrio Logan* ☎ *619/519–0765* ⊕ *www.shopsimonlimon.com* ⊗ *Closed Mon.*

Chapter 4

BALBOA PARK, BANKERS HILL, AND SAN DIEGO ZOO

4

Updated by
Claire Deeks van der Lee

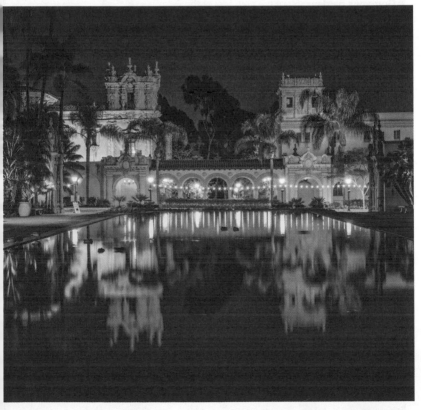

◉ Sights	🍴 Restaurants	🛏 Hotels	🛍 Shopping	🍸 Nightlife
★★★★★	★★★☆☆	★☆☆☆☆	★★★☆☆	★☆☆☆☆

NEIGHBORHOOD SNAPSHOT

TOP EXPERIENCES

■ **San Diego Zoo:** San Diego's best-loved attraction, the world-renowned zoo, is set amid spectacular scenery in the heart of Balboa Park.

■ **Museums galore:** Automobiles and spacecraft, international folk art and baroque masters, dinosaur fossils and mummified humans—there is something for everyone at Balboa Park's many museums.

■ **The great outdoors:** Escape down a hiking trail, try your hand at a new sport, or just soak in the sunshine from your own stretch of grass. You may even forget you are in the middle of the city.

■ **Gorgeous gardens:** From the lush feel of the Palm Canyon to the refined design of the Rose Garden, Balboa Park's intricate gardens and landscaping are sure to delight.

■ **Free cultural events:** The park is full of freebies, from weekly concerts at the organ pavilion to annual events like Earth Day and December Nights.

GETTING HERE

Located just north of Downtown, Balboa Park is easily reached from both Interstate 5 and Highway 163. The most spectacular approach is from 6th Avenue over the Cabrillo Bridge. There are also several entrances off Park Boulevard.

Balboa Park is served by public buses, particularly the No. 3, 7, and 120 lines. Taxis can often be found inside the park near the visitor center and lined up outside the zoo.

PLANNING YOUR TIME

Although Balboa Park is massive, many of its star attractions are located quite close to each other. That said, exploring the park can lead to a lot of walking, particularly if you throw in a trip to the zoo or take on one of the many hiking trails. The park's free tram service stops at several spots around the park, and can give tired feet a welcome rest at the end of a long day.

VISITOR INFORMATION

The House of Hospitality is an excellent resource for planning your visit to Balboa Park. Check the website (⊕ *www. balboapark.org*) before you go or spend a few minutes at the center when you arrive. They also offer a free mobile app with information on sites, special events, and useful tips to help maximize your time.

PARKING

Parking within Balboa Park, including at the zoo, is free. From the Cabrillo Bridge, the first parking area you come to is off El Prado to the right. Don't despair if there are no spaces here; you'll see more lots as you continue along toward Pan American Plaza. Alternatively, you can park at Inspiration Point on the east side of the park, off Presidents Way. Free trams run from Inspiration Point to the visitor center and museums. Valet parking is available outside the House of Hospitality on weekends.

SNACKS

Quick snacking opportunities abound throughout the park, from cafés tucked in among the museums and grounds, to hot dog, tamale, or ice-cream carts along the walkways and plazas.

Overlooking Downtown and the Pacific Ocean, 1,200-acre Balboa Park is the cultural heart of San Diego. This is where you'll find most of the city's museums, art galleries, the Tony Award–winning Old Globe Theatre, and the world-famous San Diego Zoo. Often referred to as the "Smithsonian of the West" for its concentration of museums, Balboa Park is also a series of botanical gardens, performance spaces, and outdoor playrooms dear to the hearts of residents and visitors alike.

Thanks to the "Mother of Balboa Park," Kate Sessions, who suggested hiring a landscape architect in 1889, wild and cultivated gardens are an integral part of the park, featuring 350 species of trees. What Balboa Park would have looked like had she left it alone can be seen at Florida Canyon (between the main park and Morley Field, along Park Boulevard)—an arid landscape of sagebrush, cactus, and a few small trees.

In addition, the captivating architecture of Balboa's buildings, fountains, and courtyards gives the park an enchanted feel. Historic buildings dating from San Diego's 1915 Panama–California International Exposition are strung along the park's main east–west thoroughfare, El Prado, which leads from 6th Avenue eastward over the Cabrillo Bridge (formerly the Laurel Street Bridge), the park's official gateway. If you're a cinema fan, many of the buildings may be familiar—Orson Welles used exteriors of several Balboa Park buildings to represent the Xanadu estate of Charles Foster Kane in his 1941 classic, Citizen Kane. Prominent among them was the California Building, whose 200-foot tower, housing a 100-bell carillon that tolls the hour, is El Prado's tallest structure. Missing from the black-and-white film, however, was the magnificent blue of its tiled dome shining in the sun.

The parkland across the Cabrillo Bridge, at the west end of El Prado, is set aside for picnics and athletics. Cyclists and skaters zip along Balboa Drive, which leads to the highest spot in the park, Marston Point, overlooking Downtown. At the green beside the bridge, ladies and gents in all-white outfits meet on summer afternoons for lawn-bowling tournaments.

East of Plaza de Panama, El Prado becomes a pedestrian mall and ends at a footbridge that crosses over Park Boulevard, the park's main north–south thoroughfare, to the perfectly tended Rose Garden, which has more than 1,600 rosebushes. In the adjacent Desert Garden, trails wind around cacti and succulents from around the world. Palm Canyon, north of the Spreckels Organ Pavilion, has more than 50 varieties of palms along a shady bridge. Pepper Grove, along Park Boulevard south of the museums, has lots of picnic tables as well as play equipment.

Bankers Hill is a small neighborhood west of Balboa Park, with gorgeous views ranging from Balboa Park's greenery in the east to the San Diego Bay in the west. It's home to some of San Diego's long-standing restaurant destinations.

Planning

Best Times to Visit

San Diego's ideal climate and sophisticated horticultural planning make visiting Balboa Park a year-round delight. However, summer brings longer opening hours, additional concerts at the Spreckels Organ Pavilion, and the beloved Shakespeare Festival at the Old Globe's outdoor stage.

Open Hours

Most of the park's museums and attractions are open from 10 or 11 am until 4 or 5 pm, with the zoo opening earlier. Some offer extended hours during the summer. Many of the park's museums are closed on Monday. Balboa Park is beautiful by night, with the buildings along El Prado gorgeously illuminated. The Prado restaurant and the Old Globe Theatre keep this portion of the park from feeling deserted after dark.

Planning Your Time

It's impossible to cover all of Balboa Park's museums and attractions in one day, so choose your focus before you head out. If you plan on visiting the San Diego Zoo, expect to spend at least half the day there, leaving no more than a couple of hours to explore Balboa's other attractions afterward.

⇨ See the highlighted listing for more information about the San Diego Zoo.

Otherwise, check out these itineraries.

Two Hours: To help maximize your time, rent one of the audio headsets that guide you on a 60-minute tour of the park's history, architecture, and horticulture. Pick a garden of interest to explore or drop down into Palm Canyon. Spend the remainder of your time relaxing in front of the Botanical Building or around the Bea Evenson Fountain.

Half Day: Spend a little more time at the sights above, then select a museum to explore. Alternatively, take a stroll through the Japanese Friendship Garden. Afterward, you might have time for a quick ride on the carousel or a browse around the studios of the Spanish Village Art Center. Cap things off with lunch at Panama 66 in the Sculpture Garden.

Full Day: Consider purchasing a one-day discount pass from the visitor center if you want to tackle several museums. Depending on when you visit, enjoy a free concert at the Spreckels Organ Pavilion, a cultural dance at the House of Pacific Relations International Cottages, or join a guided walking tour. Active types can hit one of the more intensive hiking trails, while others can rest their feet at an IMAX or 3-D movie in the Fleet Center. In the evening, dine at the beautiful Prado restaurant or catch a show at the Old Globe Theatre.

What's Free When

Many freebies can be found in Balboa Park, both on a weekly basis and at special times of the year. Free **volunteer-led tours** depart from the visitor center Tuesday and Friday at 11 am providing an overview of the history, architecture, and horticulture of the park. Tours on the 1st and 3rd Friday of each month focus specifically on the park's architecture. If you prefer to explore on your own, head to the visitor center to pick up a free garden tour map.

The free concerts at the **Spreckels Organ Pavilion** take place Sunday afternoon at 2 pm year-round and on Monday evening in summer. Also at the Spreckels Organ Pavilion, the **Twilight in the Park Summer Concert Series** offers various performances Tuesday, Wednesday, and Thursday from 6:30 to 7:30.

The **Timken Museum of Art, Museum of Photographic Arts,** and **San Diego History Center** offer free admission (a donation is suggested), or pay-what-you-wish admission pricing. Admission to the **House of Pacific Relations International Cottages** is also free, although they are only open on Sunday. You can explore the studios at the **Spanish Village Art Center** at no charge, although you just might be tempted to purchase a unique souvenir.

A fantastic deal for residents of San Diego County and active-duty military and their families is **Free Tuesdays in the Park,** a rotating schedule of free admission to most of Balboa Park's museums.

The **San Diego Zoo** is free for kids under 12 the whole month of October.

The **December Nights** festival on the first Friday and Saturday of that month includes free admission (and later hours) to most of the Balboa Park museums. The outdoor events during the festival make it something not to miss.

Discount: Explorer Pass

The visitor center offers a selection of Balboa Park Explorer passes that are worth considering if you plan on visiting several museums. The Explorer ($67) offers one-time admission to 16 museums and attractions over the course of seven days. The Limited Pass ($56) is good for one day for entry to 4 out of the 16 options.

Tips

Hop aboard the free trams that run every 10 to 20 minutes, 9 am to 6 pm daily, with extended summer hours.

Wear comfortable shoes—you'll end up walking more than you might expect. Bring a sweater or light jacket for the evening drop in temperature.

Don't be afraid to wander off the main drag. Discovering a hidden space of your own is one of the highlights of a trip to Balboa.

Balboa Park is a good bet for the odd rainy day—the museums are nice and dry, and many of the park's buildings are connected by covered walkways.

Make reservations for the Prado restaurant; it's popular with both visitors and locals alike.

If you aren't receiving a discount at one of the museums where San Diego residents get in for free on Tuesday, consider avoiding them on Tuesday, as they can become overcrowded.

Don't overlook the 6th Avenue side of the park, between the Marston House and the Cabrillo Bridge. There are several pathways and open fields that make for a quiet escape.

Balboa Park, the San Diego Zoo, and Bankers Hill

Sights ▼

1 Alcazar Garden **F5**
2 Balboa Park Carousel **I3**
3 Balboa Park
Miniature Railroad................ **H3**
4 Bea Evenson Fountain **I5**
5 Cabrillo Bridge **E5**
6 Comic-Con Museum **F7**
7 Fleet Science Center.............. **I5**
8 House of Hospitality.............. **H5**
9 House of Pacific Relations **F6**
10 Inez Grant Parker
Memorial Rose Garden and
Desert Garden **J5**
11 Japanese Friendship Garden **G5**
12 Marston House
Museum & Gardens.............. **B1**
13 Mingei International Museum ... **G5**
14 Museum of Photographic Arts... **H5**
15 Museum of Us..................... **F5**
16 Palm Canyon **G6**
17 San Diego
Air & Space Museum **E8**
18 San Diego
Automotive Museum.............. **E7**
19 San Diego History Center......... **H5**
20 San Diego
Model Railroad Museum **H5**
21 San Diego Museum of Art........ **G4**
22 San Diego
Natural History Museum.......... **I4**
23 San Diego Zoo **H2**
24 Spanish Village Art Center........ **I3**
25 Spreckels Organ Pavilion......... **G6**
26 Timken Museum of Art........... **H4**
27 The Zoro Garden.................. **I5**

Restaurants ▼

1 Artifact at Mingei................. **G5**
2 Azuki Sushi **B6**
3 Cucina Urbana **B5**
4 Hane Sushi **B3**
5 Mister A's **B4**
6 Panama 66......................... **G4**
7 The Prado at Balboa Park **H5**

Quick Bites ▼

1 Cafe in the Park................... **H5**
2 Craveology **I5**
3 Extraordinary Desserts **B3**
4 The Market Place................. **B4**
5 Tea Pavilion....................... **G5**

KEY

1 Sights
1 Restaurants
1 Quick Bites
P Parking
i Visitor Information

Balboa Park and the San Diego Zoo

Although Balboa Park as a whole is huge, many of its top attractions are located within reasonable walking distance. A straight shot across the **Cabrillo Bridge,** through the **Plaza de Panama,** and on to the **Bea Evenson Fountain** will take you past several of the park's architectural gems, including the **House of Hospitality.** Many of the park's museums are housed in the buildings lining the way. This route also encompasses the **Alcazar Garden** and **Lily Pond.** From the fountain, a quick jaunt across the pedestrian footbridge leads you into the **Desert Garden** and the **Inez Grant Parker Memorial Rose Garden.** Back at the fountain, your walking tour can continue by heading north toward the **San Diego Zoo.** This will take you past the **Spanish Village Art Center, Carousel,** and **Miniature Railroad.** Alternatively, double back to the Plaza de Panama and head south toward the **Spreckels Organ Pavilion.** Continuing on from here, a loop will take you past **Palm Canyon,** the **International Cottages,** the **San Diego Air and Space Museum,** several more museums, and the **Japanese Friendship Garden.**

While the aforementioned routes provide a broad overview, there are several walking opportunities for those seeking more focused explorations of the park. Those wishing to experience the numerous gardens in depth will appreciate the excellent "Gardens of Balboa Park Self-Guided Walk," available free of charge at the visitor center. History and architecture buffs might consider buying a self-guided walking tour pamphlet from the visitor center, or taking the briefer audio tour. Opportunities for hiking abound, from a brief journey through **Palm Canyon** to more strenuous hikes through **Florida Canyon** or on the **Old Bridle Trail.** Stop in the visitor center for maps and guidance before setting out.

◉ Sights

Alcazar Garden

GARDEN | FAMILY | You may feel like royalty here as you rest on the benches by the exquisitely tiled fountains—the garden's highlight—and it's no wonder: the garden's landscaping was inspired by the gardens surrounding the Alcazar Castle in Seville, Spain. The garden is open year-round, allowing for a seasonally shifting color palette. The flower beds, for example, are ever-changing horticultural exhibits featuring more than 7,000 annuals for a nearly perpetual bloom. ⊠ *1439 El Prado, Balboa Park* ⊕ *www. balboapark.org.*

★ Balboa Park Carousel

AMUSEMENT RIDE | FAMILY | Suspended an arm's length away on this antique merry-go-round is the brass ring that could earn you an extra free ride (it's one of the few carousels in the world that continue this bonus tradition). Hand-carved in 1910, the carousel features colorful murals, big-band music, and bobbing animals including zebras, giraffes, and dragons; real horsehair was used for the tails. ⊠ *1889 Zoo Pl., behind zoo parking lot, Balboa Park* ☎ *619/239–0512* ⊕ *www. balboapark.org* ⊠ *$3* ⊗ *Closed weekdays Labor Day–mid-June.*

Balboa Park Miniature Railroad

AMUSEMENT RIDE | FAMILY | Adjacent to the zoo parking lot and across from the carousel, a pint-size 48-passenger train runs a ½-mile loop through four tree-filled acres of the park. The engine of this rare 1948 model train is one of only 50 left in the world. ⊠ *2885 Zoo Pl., Balboa Park* ☎ *619/239–0512* ⊠ *$3* ⊗ *Closed weekdays Sept.–May, except during school holidays.*

Bea Evenson Fountain

FOUNTAIN | A favorite of barefoot children, this fountain shoots cool jets of water upward of 50 feet. Built in 1972 between the Fleet Center and Natural History Museum, the fountain offers plenty of room to sit and watch the crowds go by. ⊠ *Balboa Park* ✛ *East end of El Prado* ⊕ *www.balboapark.org.*

Cabrillo Bridge

BRIDGE | The official gateway into Balboa Park soars 120 feet above a canyon floor. Pedestrian-friendly, the 1,500-foot bridge provides inspiring views of the California Tower and El Prado beyond.

■ TIP→ **This is a great spot for photo-capturing a classic image of the park.** ⊠ *Balboa Park* ✛ *On El Prado, at 6th Ave. park entrance* ⊕ *www.balboapark.org.*

Comic-Con Museum

OTHER MUSEUM | FAMILY | The newest museum addition to Balboa Park celebrates San Diego's popular Comic-Con convention and all things related. Rotating exhibits explore topics such as the history of animation, Cosplay design and the evolution of Pac Man, as well as tracing the growth of Comic-Con itself from a small gathering of enthusiasts 50 years ago to the international showcase it is today. Interactive exhibits offer visitors chances to tinker, animate and game, while daily scavenger hunts offer prizes. The gift shop is worth a browse with its interesting selection of collectibles and books. ⊠ *2131 Pan American Plaza, Balboa Park* ⊕ *www.comic-con. org* ⊟ *$25; not included in Explorer Pass* ⊙ *Closed Mon.*

Fleet Science Center

SCIENCE MUSEUM | FAMILY | Interactive exhibits here are artfully educational and for all ages: older kids can get hands-on with inventive projects in Studio X, while the five-and-under set can be easily entertained with interactive play stations like the Ball Wall and Fire Truck in the center's Kid City. The IMAX Dome Theater, which screens exhilarating nature and science films, was the world's first, as was the Fleet's "NanoSeam" (seamless) dome ceiling that doubles as a planetarium. ⊠ *1875 El Prado, Balboa Park* ☎ *619/238–1233* ⊕ *www.fleetscience.org*

⊟ *The Fleet experience includes gallery exhibits and 1 IMAX film $25; additional cost for special exhibits or add-on 2nd IMAX film or planetarium show; virtual reality simulation rides $10 add-on.*

House of Hospitality

VISITOR CENTER | Originally built as the Foreign Arts Building for the Panama-California Exposition in 1915, the building was later torn down and then rebuilt using the original building as a model. Now the House of Hospitality, it's an excellent resource for planning your visit to Balboa Park. Check the website before you go or spend a few minutes at the center when you arrive. They also offer a free mobile app with information on sites, special events, and useful tips to help maximize your time. ⊠ *1549 El Prado, Balboa Park* ☎ *619/239–0512* ⊕ *www.balboapark.org.*

House of Pacific Relations

OTHER MUSEUM | FAMILY | This is not really a house but a cluster of red tile–roof stucco cottages representing three foreign countries. The word "pacific" refers to the goal of maintaining peace. The cottages, decorated with crafts and pictures, are open weekend afternoons between 11 am and 5 pm, when you can chat with transplanted people and try out different ethnic foods. Folk-song and dance performances are presented on the outdoor stage around 2 pm most Sundays—check the schedule at the park visitor center. Across the road from the cottages, but not affiliated with them, is the Spanish colonial–style United Nations Building. Inside, the United Nations Association's International Gift Shop, closed Monday, has reasonably priced crafts, cards, and books. ⊠ *2191 Pan American Plaza, Balboa Park* ☎ *619/234–0739* ⊕ *www.sdhpr.org* ⊟ *Free, donations accepted* ⊙ *Closed weekdays.*

★ Inez Grant Parker Memorial Rose Garden and Desert Garden

GARDEN | These neighboring gardens sit just across the Park Boulevard pedestrian bridge and offer gorgeous views

Balboa's Best Bets

With so much on offer, Balboa Park truly has something for everyone. Here are some best bets based on area of interest.

Architecture Buffs
Bea Evenson Fountain
Cabrillo Bridge
House of Hospitality

Arts Aficionados
Museum of Photographic Arts
San Diego Museum of Art
Spanish Village Art Center
Spreckels Organ Pavilion
Timken Museum of Art

Cultural Explorers
House of Pacific Relations
Mingei Museum

History Junkies
Museum of Us
San Diego History Center

Kids of All Ages
Balboa Park Carousel
Balboa Park Miniature Railroad
San Diego Model Railroad Museum
San Diego Zoo

Nature Lovers
Alcazar Garden
Inez Grant Parker Memorial
Rose Garden
Japanese Friendship Garden
Palm Canyon

Science and Technology Geeks
Fleet Science Center
San Diego Air & Space Museum
San Diego Automotive Museum

over Florida Canyon. The award-winning formal rose garden contains 1,600 roses representing nearly 130 varieties; peak bloom is usually in April and May but the garden remains beautiful and worthy of a visit year-round. The adjacent Desert Garden provides a striking contrast, with 2½ acres of succulents and desert plants seeming to blend into the landscape of the canyon below. ⊠ *2525 Park Blvd., Balboa Park* ⊕ *www.balboapark.org.*

★ Japanese Friendship Garden
GARDEN | A koi pond with a cascading waterfall, a cherry tree grove, and the serene Inamori tea pavilion are highlights of the park's authentic Japanese garden, designed to inspire contemplation and evoke tranquillity. You can wander the various peaceful paths spread over 12 acres, and meditate in the traditional stone and Zen garden. The garden is generally open daily from 10 am to 7 pm but check for early closures and note the final admission ends at 6 pm. ⊠ *2215 Pan American Rd., Balboa Park* ☎ *619/232–2721* ⊕ *www.niwa.org* ⊴ *$14; special exhibits are an additional $4–$5.*

Marston House Museum & Gardens
HISTORIC HOME | George W. Marston (1850–1946), a San Diego pioneer and philanthropist who financed the architectural landscaping of Balboa Park—among his myriad other San Diego civic projects—lived in this 16-room home at the northwest edge of the park. Designed in 1905 by San Diego architects Irving Gill and William Hebbard, it's a classic example of the American Arts and Crafts style, which emphasizes simplicity and functionality of form. On the 5-acre grounds is a lovely English Romantic garden, as

interpreted in California. The house may only be visited by guided tour.

■ TIP➜ Call for information about specialty tours of the gardens, historic 7th Avenue, and the Bankers Hill neighborhood. ⊠ 3525 7th Ave., Balboa Park ☎ 619/297–9327 ⊕ www.marstonhouse.org ⌨ $20 ⊗ Closed weekdays ☞ Tours offered every ½ hr and last 40–45 mins; last tour is 4 pm.

★ Mingei International Museum

ART MUSEUM | The name "Mingei" comes from the Japanese words *min,* meaning "all people," and *gei,* meaning "art." Thus the museum's name describes what's found under its roof: "art of all people." The Mingei's colorful and creative exhibits of folk art feature toys, pottery, textiles, costumes, jewelry, and curios from around the globe. Traveling and permanent exhibits in the sleek, high-ceilinged museum include everything from a history of surfboard design and craft to the latest in Japanese ceramics. The gift shop carries items related to major exhibitions as well as artwork from various cultures worldwide, such as Zulu baskets, Turkish ceramics, and Mexican objects. A major renovation unveiled in late 2021 includes a large public commons space and courtyard featuring one of the park's most exciting dining options, Artifact at Mingei. ⊠ House of Charm, 1439 El Prado, Balboa Park ☎ 619/239–0003 ⊕ www.mingei.org ⌨ $15 ⊗ Closed Mon.

Museum of Photographic Arts

ART MUSEUM | World-renowned photographers such as Ansel Adams, Imogen Cunningham, Henri Cartier-Bresson, and Edward Weston are represented in this museum's permanent collection, which includes everything from 19th-century daguerreotypes to contemporary photojournalism prints. In addition to selections from its own collection, the museum hosts excellent traveling exhibits. Photos rotate frequently, so call ahead if you're interested in something specific to find out if it is currently on display. ■ TIP➜ MOPA is also known for its film screenings. Check the website for upcoming showings. ⊠ Casa de Balboa, 1649 El Prado, Balboa Park ☎ 619/238–7559 ⊕ www.mopa.org ⌨ Pay what you wish pricing; $10 suggested donation ⊗ Closed Mon.–Wed.

★ Museum of Us

VIEWPOINT | FAMILY | Originally known as San Diego Museum of Man, the name was changed in efforts to reflect values of equity, inclusion, and decolonization. If the facade of this building—the landmark California Building—looks familiar, it's because filmmaker Orson Welles used it and its dramatic tower as the principal features of the Xanadu estate in his 1941 classic, *Citizen Kane.* Closed for 80 years, the tower was recently reopened for public tours. An additional timed ticket and a climb up 125 steps is required, but the effort will be rewarded with spectacular 360-degree views of the coast, Downtown, and the inland mountains. Back inside, exhibits at this highly respected anthropological museum focus on Southwestern, Mexican, and South American cultures. Carved monuments from the Mayan city of Quirigua in Guatemala, cast from the originals in 1914, are particularly impressive. Exhibits might include examples of intricate beadwork from across the Americas, the history of Egyptian mummies, or the lifestyles of the Kumeyaay, indigenous peoples of the present-day San Diego area. ⊠ California Bldg., 1350 El Prado, Balboa Park ☎ 619/239–2001 ⊕ www.museumofus. org ⌨ $20; tower tour $10 extra plus admission ⊗ Closed Mon. and Tues. ☞ Tower tours are timed-entry and can be booked in advance through website or on arrival at museum.

Palm Canyon

GARDEN | Enjoy an instant escape from the buildings and concrete of urban life in this Balboa Park oasis. Lush and tropical, with hundreds of palm trees representing more than 50 species, the 2-acre canyon has a shaded path perfect for those who love walking through nature. ⊠ *1549 El Prado, south of House of Charm, Balboa Park.*

★ San Diego Air & Space Museum

SCIENCE MUSEUM | FAMILY | By day, the streamlined edifice looks like any other structure in the park; at night, outlined in blue neon, the round building appears—appropriately enough—to be a landed UFO. Every available inch of space in the rotunda is filled with exhibits about aviation and aerospace pioneers, including examples of enemy planes from the World Wars. In all, there are more than 60 full-size aircraft on the floor and hanging from the rafters. In addition to exhibits from the dawn of flight to the jet age, the museum displays a growing number of space-age exhibits, including the actual *Apollo 9* command module. To test your own skills, you can ride in a two-seat Max Flight simulator or try out the Talon Racing simulator. Movies in the 3-D/4-D theater are included with admission. ⊠ *2001 Pan American Plaza, Balboa Park* ☎ *619/234–8291* ⊕ *www.sandiegoairandspace.org* ⌦ *$25; flight simulators $8–$10.*

San Diego Automotive Museum

OTHER MUSEUM | Even if you don't know a choke from a chassis, you're bound to admire the sleek designs of the autos in this impressive museum. On rotating display are gems from the museum's core collection of vintage motorcycles and cars—ranging from a pair of Steve McQueen's dirt bikes and an extremely rare Bizzarrini (only three were ever made), to a 1981 silver Delorean (remember the time machine in *Back to the Future*?)—as well as a series of visiting special exhibits. Be sure to see the *Fabulous Car of Louis Mattar,* which was ingeniously kitted out to set the cross-country endurance record in 1952 (6,320 miles nonstop from San Diego to New York City and back, refueling from

a moving gas truck); a video display shows highlights such as Mattar and his codrivers changing the tire while in motion and pouring a glass of water from the onboard tap. There's also an ongoing automobile restoration program and an extensive automotive research library.

■TIP→ **Check the calendar if visiting in December as the museum has varying early closing hours during the holiday season.** ⊠ *2080 Pan American Plaza, Balboa Park* ☎ *619/231–2886* ⊕ *www.sdautomuseum.org* ⌦ *$15* ⊘ *Closed most Mon.*

San Diego History Center

HISTORY MUSEUM | The San Diego Historical Society maintains its research library in the basement of the Casa de Balboa and organizes shows on the first floor. Permanent and rotating exhibits, which are often more lively than you might expect, survey local urban history after 1850, when California entered the Union. A 30-minute, Emmy Award-winning film, "Balboa Park- The Jewel of San Diego" plays hourly in the museum's theater. Discover the history of San Diego's craft beer scene with an interactive exhibit and tasting, offered Friday through Sunday for an additional $10. ⊠ *Casa de Balboa, 1649 El Prado, Balboa Park* ☎ *619/232–6203* ⊕ *www.sandiegohistory.org* ⌦ *Free ($10 suggested donation); beer tasting $10* ⊘ *Closed Mon. and Tues.*

San Diego Model Railroad Museum

OTHER MUSEUM | FAMILY | When the exhibits at this 27,000-square-foot museum are in operation, you can hear the sounds of chugging engines, screeching brakes, and shrill whistles. Local model railroad clubs built and maintain the four main displays, which represent California railroads in "miniature," with the track laid on scale models of San Diego County terrain. Out back, the Centennial Railway Garden features replicas of the streetcars and scenes of Balboa Park during the 1915 Exposition. The Toy Train Gallery has an interactive Lionel exhibit and whimsical vignettes. ⊠ *Casa de Balboa, 1649*

Balboa Park is home to gardens and the Spreckels Organ Pavilion, which hosts free concerts every Sunday at 2 pm.

El Prado, Balboa Park ☎ *619/696–0199* ⊕ *www.sdmrm.org* 🎟 *$20* ⊙ *Closed Mon.*

★ San Diego Museum of Art

ART MUSEUM | Known for its Spanish baroque and Renaissance paintings, including works by El Greco, Goya, Rubens, and van Ruisdael, San Diego's most comprehensive art museum also has strong holdings of South Asian art, Indian miniatures, and contemporary California paintings. The museum's exhibits tend to have broad appeal, and if traveling shows from other cities come to town, you can expect to see them here. Free docent tours are offered throughout the day. An outdoor Sculpture Court and Garden exhibits both traditional and modern pieces. Enjoy the view over a craft beer and some locally sourced food in the adjacent Panama 66 courtyard restaurant. ⊠ *1450 El Prado, Balboa Park* ☎ *619/232–7931* ⊕ *www.sdmart.org* 🎟 *$20; sculpture garden is free* ⊙ *Closed Wed.*

San Diego Natural History Museum

OTHER MUSEUM | **FAMILY** | There are 8 million fossils, dinosaur models, and even live reptiles and other specimens under this roof. Favorite exhibits include the Foucault Pendulum, suspended on a 43-foot cable and designed to demonstrate the Earth's rotation, and *Ocean Oasis,* the world's first large-format film about Baja California and the Sea of Cortés. Permanent exhibits highlight citizen scientists and the regional environment, and traveling exhibits also make a stop here. Films shown at the museum's giant-screen theater are included with admission. ■ **TIP→ Check the website for information about films, lectures, and free guided nature walks.** ⊠ *1788 El Prado, Balboa Park* ☎ *619/232–3821* ⊕ *www. sdnhm.org* 🎟 *$22* ⊙ *Closed Wed.*

★ San Diego Zoo

ZOO | **FAMILY** | Balboa Park's—and perhaps the city's—most famous attraction is its 100-acre zoo. Nearly 12,000 animals of some 650 diverse species roam in hospitable, expertly crafted habitats that replicate natural environments as closely as possible. The flora in the zoo, including many rare species, is even more dear than the fauna. Walkways wind over bridges and past waterfalls ringed with tropical ferns; elephants in a sandy plateau roam so close you're tempted to pet them.

Exploring the zoo fully requires the stamina of a healthy hiker, but open-air double-decker buses that run throughout the day let you zip through three-quarters of the exhibits on a guided 35- to 40-minute, 3-mile tour. There are also express buses, used for quick transportation, that make five stops around the grounds and include some narration. The Skyfari Aerial Tram, which soars 170 feet above the ground, gives a good overview of the zoo's layout and, on clear days, a panorama of the park, Downtown San Diego, the bay, and the ocean, far beyond the San Diego–Coronado Bridge.

■TIP→ **Unless you come early, expect to wait for the regular bus, and especially for the top tier—the line can take more than 45 minutes; if you come at midday on a weekend or school holiday, you'll be doing the in-line shuffle for a while. Don't forget the San Diego Safari Park, the zoo's 1,800-acre extension to the north at Escondido.**

⊠ *2920 Zoo Dr., Balboa Park* ☎ *619/234–3153* ⊕ *www.sandiegozoowildlifealliance. org* 🖾 *$71* ☞ *Multiday and combination tickets available.*

★ **Spanish Village Art Center**
ART GALLERY | More than 200 local artists, including glassblowers, enamel workers, wood-carvers, sculptors, painters, jewelers, and photographers work and give demonstrations of their craft on a rotating basis within and outside of these red tile–roof studio-galleries that were set up for the 1935–36 exposition in the style of an old Spanish village. The center is a

great source for memorable gifts. ⊠ *1770 Village Pl., Balboa Park* ☎ *619/233–9050* ⊕ *spanishvillageartcenter.com* 🖾 *Free.*

★ **Spreckels Organ Pavilion**
PLAZA/SQUARE | The 2,400-bench-seat pavilion, dedicated in 1915 by sugar magnates John D. and Adolph B. Spreckels, holds the 4,518-pipe Spreckels Organ, the largest outdoor pipe organ in the world. You can hear this impressive instrument at one of the year-round, free, 2 pm Sunday concerts, regularly performed by the city's civic organist Raúl Prieto Ramírez and guest artists—a highlight of a visit to Balboa Park. On Monday evening from late June to mid-August, internationally renowned organists play evening concerts. At Christmastime the park's Christmas tree and life-size Nativity display turn the pavilion into a seasonal wonderland. ⊠ *2211 Pan American Rd., Balboa Park* ☎ *619/702–8138* ⊕ *spreckelsorgan.org.*

Timken Museum of Art
ART MUSEUM | Though somewhat out of place architecturally, this small and modern structure, made of travertine imported from Italy, is a jewel box. The museum houses works by major European and American artists as well as a superb collection of Russian icons. ⊠ *1500 El Prado, Balboa Park* ☎ *619/239–5548* ⊕ *www.timkenmuseum.org* 🖾 *Museum and tours free, donations encouraged* ⊙ *Closed Mon. and Tues.*

The Zoro Garden
GARDEN | While demurely posing as a butterfly garden today, this sunken stone grotto has a racy history—tucked between the Casa de Balboa and the Fleet Center, this area showcased a nudist colony during the 1935–36 Exposition. ⊠ *El Prado, Balboa Park* ☎ *619/525–8213* ⊕ *www.balboapark.org.*

Continued on page 108

Polar bear, San Diego Zoo

LIONS AND TIGERS AND BEARS:
The World-Famous San Diego Zoo

From diving polar bears and 6-ton elephants to swinging great apes, San Diego's most famous attraction has it all. Nearly 12,000 animals representing 650 species roam the 100-acre zoo in expertly crafted habitats that replicate the animals' natural environments. Once world-famous for its Giant Panda program (they have since returned home to China), the zoo has many other celebrity residents to see, from beloved baby hippos and giraffes to its very own axolotl. But it's not all just fun and games. Known for its exemplary conservation programs, the zoo educates visitors on how to go green and explains its efforts to protect endangered species.

SAN DIEGO ZOO TOP ATTRACTIONS

Underwater viewing area at the Hippo Trail

**❶ Wildlife Explorers
Basecamp.** The newest section of the zoo delights visitors of all ages with its rope bridges and exciting play spaces set alongside its 4 distinct habitat zones: desert, marsh, woods and rainforest. Here you can observe a colony of leaf cutter ants, meet a sloth, or spot the rare resident axoltl.

**❷ Komodo Kingdom and
Hummingbird Habitat.** Get an up-close look at a pair of modern day dragons in the dry, rocky landscape of Komodo Island. Next door, observe several species of hummingbirds as you wind your way through the orchids, palms and water features of this lush habitat.

**❸ Monkey Trails and
Forest Tales (Lost Forest).**
Follow anelevated trail at treetop leveland trek through the forestfloor observing African mandrill monkeys, Asia's cloudedleopard, the rare pygmy hippopotamus, and Visayan warty pigs.

Lories at Owen's Aviary

4 Orangutan and Siamang Exhibit (Lost Forest). Orangutans and siamangs climb and swing in this lush, tropical environment lined with 110-foot-long and 12-foot-high viewing windows.

5 Scripps, Parker, and Owens Aviaries (Lost Forest). Wandering paths climb through the enclosed aviaries where brightly colored tropical birds swoop between branches inches from your face.

6 Tiger Trail (Lost Forest). The mist-shrouded trails of this simulated rainforest wind down a canyon. Tigers, Malayan tapirs, and Argus pheasants wander among the exotic trees and plants.

7 Hippo Trail (Lost Forest). Glimpse huge but surprisingly graceful hippos frolicking in the water through an underwater viewing window and buffalo cavorting with monkeys on dry land.

8 Gorilla Exhibit (Lost Forest). The gorillas live in one of the zoo's bioclimatic zone exhibits modeled on their native habitat with waterfalls, climbing areas, and an open meadow. The sounds of the tropical rain forest emerge from a 144-speaker sound system that plays CDs recorded in Africa.

9 Africa Rocks. This massive exhibit consists of six different rocky habitats designed to showcase the diversity of topography and species on the African continent. Penguins, meerkats, and a band of baboons are just a few of the animals that call this ambitious exhibit home.

10 Polar Bear Plunge (Polar Rim). Watch polar bears take a chilly dive from the underwater viewing room. There are also Siberian reindeer, white foxes, and other Arctic creatures here. Kids can learn about the Arctic and climate change through interactive exhibits.

11 Elephant Odyssey. Get a glimpse of the animals that roamed Southern California 12,000 years ago and meet their living counterparts. The 7.5-acre, multispecies habitat features elephants, California condors, jaguars, and more.

12 Koala Exhibit (Outback). The San Diego Zoo houses the largest number of koalas outside Australia. Walk through the exhibit for photo ops of these marsupials from Down-Under curled up on their perches or dining on eucalyptus branches.

MUST-SEE ANIMALS

❶ GORILLA

This troop of primates engages visitors with their human-like expressions and behavior. The youngsters are sure to delight, especially when hitching a ride on mom's back. Up-close encounters might involve the gorillas using the glass partition as a backrest while peeling cabbage. By dusk the gorillas head inside to their sleeping quarters, so don't save this for your last stop.

❷ ELEPHANT

Asian and African elephants coexist at the San Diego Zoo. The larger African elephant is distinguished by its big flapping ears—shaped like the continent of Africa—which it uses to keep cool. An elephant's trunk has over 40,000 muscles in it—that's more than humans have in their whole body.

❸ ORANGUTAN

Bornean and Sumatran orangutans have been entertaining San Diego visitors since 1928. The exhibit has rope climbing structures, a man-made "termite mound" that's often filled with treats, rocky caves, and tall "sway poles" that allow the orangutans to swing like they would in trees. Don't be surprised if the orangutans come right up to the glass to observe the humans observing them!

❹ KOALA

While this collection of critters is one of the cutest in the zoo, don't expect a lot of activity from the koala habitat. These guys spend most of their day curled up asleep in the branches of the eucalyptus tree—they can sleep up to 20 hours a day. Although eucalyptus leaves are poisonous to most animals, bacteria in koalas' stomachs allow them to break down the toxins.

❺ POLAR BEAR

The trio of polar bears is one of the San Diego Zoo's star attractions, and their brand-new exhibit gets you up close and personal. Visitors sometimes worry about polar bears living in the warm San Diego climate, but there is no cause for concern. The San Diego-based bears eat a lean diet, thus reducing their layer of blubber and helping them keep cool.

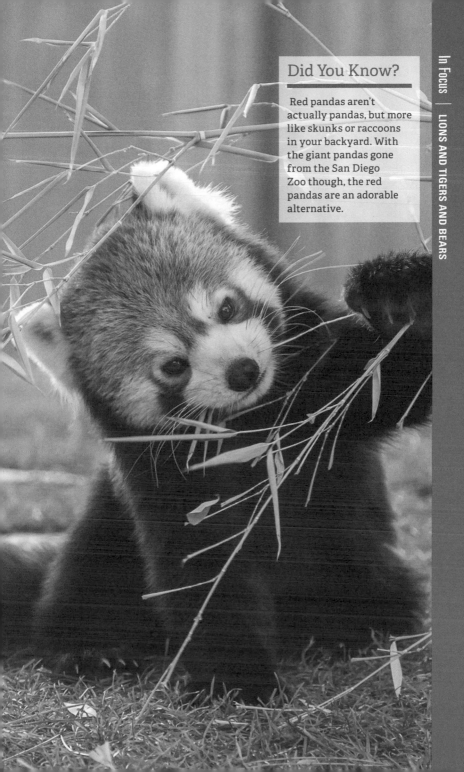

Did You Know?

Red pandas aren't actually pandas, but more like skunks or raccoons in your backyard. With the giant pandas gone from the San Diego Zoo though, the red pandas are an adorable alternative.

PLANNING YOUR DAY AT THE ZOO

Left: Main entrance of the San Diego Zoo. Right: Sunbear

PLANNING YOUR TIME

Plan to devote at least a half-day to exploring the zoo, but with so much to see it is easy to stay a full day or more.

If you're on a tight schedule, opt for the guided **35 minute bus tour** that lets you zip through three-quarters of the exhibits. However, lines to board the busses can be long, and you won't get as close to the animals.

Another option is to take the **Skyfari Aerial Tram** to the far end of the park, choose a route, and meander back to the entrance. The Skyfari trip gives a good overview of the zoo's layout and a spectacular view.

The **Elephant Odyssey,** while accessible from two sides of the park, is best entered from just below the Polar Rim.

The zoo offers several entertaining **live shows** daily. Check the website or the back of the map handed out at the zoo entrance for the day's offerings and showtimes. If traveling with children, budget some extra time to explore and play in the Wildlife Explorers Basecamp.

BEFORE YOU GO

■ To avoid ticket lines, purchase and print tickets online using the zoo's Web site.

■ To avoid excessive backtracking or a potential meltdown, plan your route along the zoo map before setting out. Try not to get too frustrated if you lose your way, as there are exciting exhibits around every turn and many paths intersect at several points.

■ The zoo offers a variety of program extras, including behind-the-scenes tours, backstage pass animal encounters, and sleepover events. The early morning cheetah experience is a favorite. Call in advance for pricing and reservations.

AT THE ZOO

Don't forget to explore at least some of the exhibits on foot—a favorite is the lush Tiger Trail.

■ If you visit on the weekend, find out when the Giraffe Experience is taking place. You can purchase leaf–eater biscuits to hand feed the giraffes!

■ Splurge a little at the gift shop: your purchases help support zoo programs.

■ The zoo rents strollers, wheelchairs, and lockers; it also has a first-aid office, a lost and found, and an ATM.

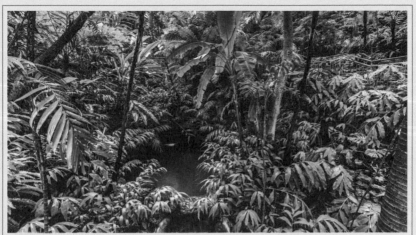

Fern Canyon, San Diego Zoo

GETTING HERE AND AROUND

The zoo is easy to get to, whether by bus or car.

Bus Travel: Take Bus No. 7 and exit at Park Boulevard and Zoo Place.

Car Travel: From Downtown, take Route 163 north through Balboa Park. Exit at Zoo/Museums (Richmond Street) and follow signs.

Several options help you get around the massive park: express buses loop through the zoo and the Skyfari Aerial Tram will take you from one end to the other. The zoo's topography is fairly hilly, but moving sidewalks lead up the slopes between some exhibits.

QUICK BITES

There is a wide variety of food available for purchase at the zoo from food carts to ethnic restaurants such as the Pan-Asian **Hua Mei Cafe**.

One of the best restaurants is **Albert's**, near the Gorilla exhibit, which features grilled fish, homemade pizza, and fresh pasta along with a full ba

SERVICE INFORMATION

✉ 2920 Zoo Dr., Balboa Park
☎ 619/234–3153
⊕ www.sandiegozoo.org

SAN DIEGO ZOO SAFARI PARK

About 45 minutes north of the zoo in Escondido, the 1,800-acre San Diego Zoo Safari Park is an extensive wildlife sanctuary where animals roam free—and guests can get close in escorted caravans and on backcountry trails. This park and the zoo operate under the auspices of the San Diego Zoo's nonprofit organization; joint tickets are available.

🍴 Restaurants

The culinary heart of this museum-filled urban park is the Prado, a stylish restaurant with a sunny patio adjacent to the Visitor Center. Panama 66 next to the Sculpture Garden and Artifact in the Mingei Commons round out the park's sit-down restaurant options. Other dining is limited to museum and zoo food stands, counter-service cafés, and food carts.

★ Artifact at Mingei

$$ | ECLECTIC | Innovative restauranteur Tracy Borkum raised the bar of in-park dining with the unveiling of Artifact, located in the Mingei commons and courtyard. Taking culinary inspirations from around the globe, flavors and spices from Morocco to Peru are on display in lunch and dinner menus billed as "craft cooking inspired by ancient methods, spices and botanicals." **Known for:** gluten-free and vegan offerings; weekend happy hour; sophisticated menu. ⑤ *Average main: $29* ✉ *1439 El Prado, Balboa Park* ⊕ *www.urbankitchengroup.com* ◷ *Closed Mon. No dinner Tues. and Wed.*

Panama 66

$ | AMERICAN | FAMILY | Adding a dose of hip to Balboa Park, this gastropub, located adjacent to the San Diego Museum of Art's sculpture garden, offers a stylish pit stop pretheater or between museum-hopping. The menu features grab-and-go options as well as dine-in upscale pub fare with several vegan options and a weekend brunch. **Known for:** varied menu including selection of shareable boards and plates; live music most nights; local San Diego brews. ⑤ *Average main: $16* ✉ *1450 El Prado, Balboa Park* ☎ *619/696–1966* ⊕ *www.panama66.com* ◷ *No dinner Mon. and Tues. Labor Day–Memorial Day.*

The Prado at Balboa Park

$$$ | ECLECTIC | This lovely restaurant in the historic House of Hospitality makes contemporary fare, friendly service, and patio dining available to legions of museum- and theatergoers who come to Balboa Park. The bar is a fashionable destination for creative drinks and light nibbles, while the dining room's specialties range from fish tacos and paella to unusual surf-and-turf combos. **Known for:** long-established park favorite; Latin-inspired cocktails heavy on rum and citrus juices; striking Spanish-Moorish architectural details. ⑤ *Average main: $33* ✉ *1549 El Prado, Balboa Park* ☎ *619/557–9441* ⊕ *www.pradobalboa.com* ◷ *Closed Mon.*

☕ Coffee and Quick Bites

Cafe in the Park

$ | SANDWICHES | Located in the Casa del Balboa building near the San Diego History Center, this café is a convenient stop for a quick breakfast or lunch, or a midday coffee break. The café offers a good selection of pastries, panini, soups, and salads, and a few indoor tables in case you find yourself there on the odd rainy day. **Known for:** convenient location along the park's main drag; all-day menu; specialty coffees. ⑤ *Average main: $11* ✉ *Casa del Balboa, 1549 El Prado, Balboa Park* ⊹ *Near San Diego History Center* ☎ *619/331–1992* ⊕ *www.balboapark.org* ◷ *No dinner.*

Craveology

$ | AMERICAN | FAMILY | Enjoy views of the Bea Evenson Fountain from the patio of this quick lunch option outside the Fleet Science Center. The menu offers everything from flatbreads, sandwiches, and soups to smoothies, specialty coffees, and soft-serve ice cream. **Known for:** fountain views; smoothies and specialty coffees; color-changing ice-cream spoons. ⑤ *Average main: $9* ✉ *1875 El Prado, Balboa Park* ⊹ *Outside Fleet Science Center* ☎ *619/238–1233* ⊕ *www.fleetscience.org.*

Tea Pavilion

$ | JAPANESE | Grab some noodles, sushi, or Japanese tea and treats at this pavilion located in the center of the park. The large outdoor patio is a great place to rest and recharge before seeking tranquility in the adjacent Japanese Friendship Garden. **Known for:** spacious patio; extensive tea selection; Japanese snacks and sweets. ⑤ *Average main: $9* ✉ *2215 Pan American Way, Balboa Park* ☎ *619/231–0048* ⊕ *www.cohnrestaurants.com* ⊘ *Closed Mon. and Tues. No dinner.*

Performing Arts

★ Globe Theatres

THEATER | This complex, comprised of the Sheryl and Harvey White Theatre, the Lowell Davies Festival Theatre, and the Old Globe Theatre, offers some of the finest theatrical productions in Southern California. Theater classics such as *Into the Woods* and *Dirty Rotten Scoundrels,* and more recent hits like *Bright Star* and *Meteor Shower*, premiered on these famed stages and went on to perform on Broadway. The Old Globe presents a renowned summer Shakespeare Festival with three to four plays in repertory. The theaters, done in a California version of Tudor style, sit between the sculpture garden of the San Diego Museum of Art and the California Tower. If you can't catch a show, daytime one-hour behind-the-scenes tours offer a close up look at the theaters as well as the intricacies of set and costume design. ✉ *1363 Old Globe Way, Balboa Park* ☎ *619/234–5623* ⊕ *www.theoldglobe.org* ☜ *Tours $7* ⊘ *Box office closed Mon.*

🛍 Shopping

Balboa Park is an excellent place to shop for unique souvenirs and gifts. In addition to the wonderful artwork for sale in the Spanish Village Art Center, several museums and the visitor center have excellent stores. Of particular note are the shops at the Reuben Fleet Science Center, Museum of Art, United Nations Association and, of course, the zoo. The Zoo Store and Ituri Forest Outpost at the San Diego Zoo carries international crafts, world music, and hats.

🏃 Activities

GOLF
Balboa Park Golf Course

GOLF | San Diego's oldest public course is five minutes from Downtown in the heart of Balboa Park and offers impressive views of the city and the bay. The course includes a 9-hole executive course and a challenging 18-hole course that weaves among the park's canyons with some tricky drop-offs. Finish off your round with biscuits and gravy and a mimosa at Tobey's 19th Hole Cafe, a greasy spoon that's also Balboa Park's best-kept secret. ✉ *2600 Golf Course Dr., Balboa Park* ☎ *619/235–1184* ⊕ *www.sandiego.gov* ☜ *18-hole from $49; 9-hole from $22* ⚐ *27 holes, 6339 yards, par 72.*

Bankers Hill

The serene neighborhood west of Balboa Park is lined with upscale condos and stately historic homes, many offering stunning vistas of the park and Downtown. This area is defined by the world-famous park, but increasingly it is known for an exceptional contemporary dining scene.

Restaurants

Bankers Hill is home to some of the city's most enduring restaurants, like the legendary Mister A's. But the eclectic area is also home to several fashionable eateries alongside divey bars and sandwich shops.

★ Azuki Sushi

$$ | **SUSHI** | Sushi should be a no-brainer when visiting San Diego, especially for tourists from landlocked states who don't often get fresh fish. This menu is based on the seasons, and you'll find innovative sushi, sashimi, and a raw bar, all utilizing the freshest local fish (some is flown in daily from Japan) and produce; there are options for nonsushi fans. **Known for:** reservations recommended; specialty rolls like the R U Kidding Me? (snow crab, diver scallops, tempura asparagus, seared tuna, white truffle oil, and mixed greens, topped with garlic ponzu and flash-fried leeks); surprising pairings with wine and sake. ⑤ *Average main: $28 ✉ 2321 5th Ave., Bankers Hill ☎ 619/238–4760 ⊕ azukisushi.com ⊗ No lunch.*

★ Cucina Urbana

$$ | **ITALIAN** | Twentysomethings mingle with boomers in this convivial Bankers Hill dining room and bar, one of the most popular restaurants in town. The open kitchen turns out innovative Italian food with a California sensibility including a selection of small plates and family-style pasta dishes alongside traditional entrées. **Known for:** in-house wine shop with reasonably priced bottles and $9 corkage fee; seasonal polenta with ragu; ricotta-stuffed zucchini blossoms. ⑤ *Average main: $27 ✉ 505 Laurel St., Bankers Hill ☎ 619/239–2222 ⊕ www.cucinaurbana.com ⊗ Closed Mon. No lunch.*

Hane Sushi

$$ | **JAPANESE** | An airy room with a sleek red-and-black Japanese aesthetic is the setting for pristine, contemporary sushi by Roger Nakamura, who spent years learning his craft from Yukito Ota of San Diego's beloved Sushi Ota restaurant. Though Hane (pronounced "hah-nay") is trendier than Ota, sushi purists will be happy with special delicacies imported from Japan. **Known for:** Japan-sourced ingredients like Kobe beef sashimi; lunch specials; innovative dishes like the crispy eggplant and spicy tuna appetizer or the Diego roll with serrano peppers. ⑤ *Average main: $27 ✉ 2760 5th Ave., Bankers Hill ☎ 619/260–1411 ⊗ Closed Mon. No lunch weekends.*

★ Mister A's

$$$$ | **CONTEMPORARY** | For decades, this venerable 12th-floor dining room with panoramic views and polished service has reigned as a celebratory fine-dining destination. A recent renovation following the passing of the torch from former owner Betrand Hug to his longtime employee Ryan Thorsen has resulted in an exciting refresh of this enduring landmark. **Known for:** iconic "special occasion" destination; popular bar and lounge space; stunning panoramic bay and city views. ⑤ *Average main: $45 ✉ 2550 5th Ave., 12th fl., Bankers Hill ☎ 619/239–1377 ⊕ www.asrestaurant.com ⊗ No lunch Mon. and Tues. ⛨ Business Casual dress code strictly enforced.*

☕ Coffee and Quick Bites

★ Extraordinary Desserts

$ | **CAFÉ** | Don't let the name fool you, there is more on offer than dessert at this popular Bankers Hill all-day dining gem. Delicious soups, salads and panini are accompanied by a variety of shareable boards and dips. **Known for:** notable hot beverage selection; deliciously light pavlova; cakes (almost) too pretty to eat. ⑤ *Average main: $16 ✉ 2870 4th Ave., Bankers Hill ☎ 619/294–2132 ⊕ www.extraordinarydesserts.com.*

The Market Place

$ | **AMERICAN** | San Diego is perfect for picnics and this popular deli just a block from Balboa Park helps turn these outdoor affairs into memorable feasts. Fans, including workers from nearby offices, rave about the ample and affordable hot and cold sandwiches, homemade soups, chili, and pizza by the slice or pie. **Known for:** deli sandwiches and salads; grocery items; wine shop. ⑤ *Average main: $11 ✉ 2601 5th Ave., Bankers Hill ☎ 619/239–8361 ⊕ themarketplacesd.com.*

Chapter 5

OLD TOWN AND UPTOWN

Updated by
Jeff Terich

● Sights	🍴 Restaurants	🛏 Hotels	⬤ Shopping	🍸 Nightlife
★★★★☆	★★★★★	★★☆☆☆	★★★★☆	★★★★☆

NEIGHBORHOOD SNAPSHOT

TOP EXPERIENCES

■ **Go back in time:** Experience the city's early days, from its beginnings as a remote military outpost and mission to the development of the first town plaza.

■ **Architectural delights:** Discover the pueblo- and clapboard-style structures of Old Town and the ornate Victorian gems in Heritage Park. Then head up the hill to view wonderfully preserved early-20th-century homes in Uptown.

■ **Scare yourself silly:** Visit the Thomas Whaley House Museum, "the most haunted house in America," at night.

■ **Tortillas and margaritas:** Enjoy one of Old Town's many Mexican eateries.

■ **Like a local:** Explore the vibrant shopping, dining, and nightlife of Uptown's unique neighborhoods.

GETTING HERE

Old Town and Uptown are northwest and north of Balboa Park, respectively. Ten bus lines stop at the Old Town Transit Center, as do the San Diego Trolley and the Coaster commuter rail line. Two large parking lots are linked to the Old Town Historic Park by an underground pedestrian walkway.

Uptown is best explored by car, although several bus routes serve the area. Both metered street parking and pay-and-display lots are available.

PLANNING YOUR TIME

It takes about two hours to walk through Old Town. Try to time your visit to coincide with one of the daily tours given by costumed park staff. Tours are free and depart at 11:30 and 2 from the Robinson-Rose House Visitor Center. If you go to Presidio Park, definitely consider driving.

The highlight of an Uptown tour is exploring the hearts of Hillcrest and North Park located at the intersections of University and 5th Avenues, and University and 30th Street, respectively. Plan to drive or catch a bus between neighborhoods, then walk.

PAUSE HERE

The 7.8-acre Heritage Park is a quiet spot with benches or grass where you can sprawl out. The park's cottages—moved here, and restored, by the Save Our Heritage Organization—are also worth exploring.

QUICK BITES

Old Town's **Fiesta de Reyes** (⊕ www.fiestadereyes.com) has several options for a quick recharge. Casa de Reyes has a mariachi band and folklorico dancers every weekend, and great margaritas and fresh guac. Old Town Jerky and Root Beer offers a good selection of snacks and mini-sandwiches, fresh lemonade, and, of course, jerky and root beer. If you're visiting between Friday and Sunday, look for the booth marked Street Tacos for a quick meal.

FESTIVALS

The Uptown neighborhoods host a variety of events throughout the year. Hillcrest hosts the annual LGBTQ Pride event every July. In late summer, Cityfest rocks the neighborhood with live music, food stalls, and beer gardens. Old Town celebrates Cinco de Mayo and the Old Town Art and Craft Show is held in early fall.

San Diego's Spanish and Mexican roots are most evident in Old Town and the surrounding hillside of Presidio Park. Visitors can experience settlement life in San Diego from Spanish and Mexican rule to the early days of U.S. statehood. Nearby Uptown is composed of several smaller neighborhoods near Downtown and around Balboa Park: the vibrant neighborhoods of Hillcrest, Mission Hills, North Park, and South Park showcase their unique blend of historical charm and modern urban community.

Dense with Mexican eateries, Old Town is the place to be for quick and easy access to house-made tortillas. The neighborhood is also home to historic adobe shops and museums. East of Old Town is Mission Valley, a suburban maze of freeways, shopping centers, and Hotel Circle, where many spacious and inexpensive lodging options are located.

San Diego's Uptown area—Hillcrest, Mission Hills, North Park, South Park, and University Heights—is close to the San Diego Zoo and Balboa Park. There are few hotels, but the area offers pedestrian-friendly shopping—it's known for its mélange of funky bookstores, offbeat gift shops, and nostalgic collectibles and vintage stores—and many of San Diego's venerable craft beer bars and breweries. The diverse communities boast bistros, gastropubs, and ethnic restaurants that range from Afghan and Indian to Russian and Vietnamese.

Hillcrest is a popular area for LGBTQ nightlife and culture, whereas just a little bit east of Hillcrest, ever-expanding North Park features a diverse range of bars and lounges that cater to a twenty- and thirtysomething crowd, bolstering its reputation as the city's hipster capital. Tucked between Hillcrest and North Park, the charming neighborhood of University Heights is home to several notable bars and restaurants. The thriving nightlife and dining scene continues down Adams Avenue and into neighboring Normal Heights, which is a more laid-back alternative. Whichever of these neighborhoods strikes your fancy, a cab from Downtown will run about the same price: $15.

Sights ▼

1 El Campo Santo
  Cemetery **B2**
2 Fiesta de Reyes **A2**
3 Heritage Park **B2**
4 Mission Basilica
  San Diego
  de Alcalá **F1**
5 Old Town San Diego.
  State Historic Park **A2**
6 Presidio Park **B1**
7 The Whaley House
  Museum **B2**

Restaurants ▼

1 Blue Water Seafood
  Market & Grill **C3**
2 El Agave **B2**
3 Fort Oak **D2**
4 Harney Sushi **B2**
5 Hash House
  A Go Go **E3**
6 Lucha Libre Gourmet
  Taco Shop **C3**
7 Ortega's Bistro **E2**
8 Saffron **C3**
9 Snooze **E2**
10 Starlite **D4**
11 Tahona **B2**

Old Town, Hillcrest, Mission Hills, and Mission Valley

Old Town

As the first European settlement in Southern California, **Old Town** began to develop in the 1820s. However, its true beginnings took place on a nearby hillside in 1769 with the establishment of a Spanish military outpost and the first of California's missions, San Diego de Alcalá. In 1774 the hilltop was declared a *presidio reál,* a fortress built by the Spanish empire, and the mission was relocated along the San Diego River. Over time, settlers moved down from the presidio to establish Old Town. A central plaza was laid out, surrounded by adobe and, later, wooden structures. San Diego became an incorporated U.S. city in 1850, with Old Town as its center. In the 1860s, however, the advent of Alonzo Horton's New Town to the southeast caused Old Town to wither. Efforts to preserve the area began early in the 20th century, and Old Town became a state historic park in 1968.

Today Old Town is a lively celebration of history and culture. The **Old Town San Diego State Historic Park** re-creates life during the early settlement, while San Diego Avenue buzzes with art galleries, gift shops, festive restaurants, and open-air stands selling inexpensive Mexican handicrafts.

 Sights

El Campo Santo Cemetery

CEMETERY | Now a peaceful stop for visitors to Old Town, the old adobe-wall cemetery established in 1849 was, until 1880, the burial place for many members of Old Town's founding families—as well as for some gamblers and bandits who passed through town. Antonio Garra, a chief who led an uprising of the San Luis Rey Indians, was executed at El Campo Santo in front of the open grave he had been forced to dig for himself. Most of the markers give only approximations of

where the people named on them are buried; some of the early settlers laid to rest at El Campo Santo actually reside under San Diego Avenue. ⊠ *2410 San Diego Ave., between Arista and Ampudia Sts., Old Town.*

★ Fiesta de Reyes

PLAZA/SQUARE | FAMILY | North of San Diego's Old Town Plaza lies the area's unofficial center, built to represent a colonial Mexican plaza. The collection of more than a dozen shops and restaurants around a central courtyard in blossom with magenta bougainvillea, scarlet hibiscus, and other flowers in season reflects what early California might have looked like from 1821 to 1872. Mariachi bands and folklorico dance groups frequently perform on the plaza stage—check the website for times and upcoming special events.

■TIP→ **Casa de Reyes is a great stop for a margarita and some chips and guacamole.** ⊠ *4016 Wallace St., Old Town* ☎ *619/297-3100* ⊕ *www.fiestadereyes.com.*

Heritage Park

NOTABLE BUILDING | A number of San Diego's important Victorian buildings are the focus of this 7.8-acre park on the Juan Street hill near Harney Street. Among the buildings is Southern California's first synagogue, a one-room classical-revival structure built in 1889 for Congregation Beth Israel. The most interesting of the park's six former residences might be the Sherman-Gilbert House, which has a widow's walk and intricate carving on its decorative trim. It was built for real estate dealer John Sherman in 1887 at the then-exorbitant cost of $20,000—indicating just how profitable the booming housing market could be. All the houses, some of which may seem surprisingly colorful, accurately represent the bright hues of the era. The synagogue and the Senlis Cottage are open to visitors daily from 9 to 5; the latter contains a small exhibit with information on the history and original locations of the houses. The

Dancers perform during the annual Dia de los Muertos celebration at the Fiesta de Reyes plaza in Old Town.

McConaughy House hosts the Coral Tree Tea House, offering traditional tea service Thursday through Sunday from 11 to 5. Save Our Heritage Organization moved the buildings to this park from their original locations and also restored them. ⊠ *2454 Heritage Park Row, Old Town* ☎ *858/565–3600* ⊕ *www.sdparks. org* ⊠ *Free.*

★ **Old Town San Diego State Historic Park**
MUSEUM VILLAGE | FAMILY | The six square blocks on the site of San Diego's original pueblo are the heart of Old Town. Most of the 20 historic buildings preserved or re-created by the park cluster are around Old Town Plaza, bounded by Wallace Street on the west, Calhoun Street on the north, Mason Street on the east, and San Diego Avenue on the south. The plaza is a pleasant place to rest, plan your tour of the park, and watch passersby. San Diego Avenue is closed to vehicle traffic here.

Some of Old Town's buildings were destroyed in a fire in 1872, but after the site became a state historic park in

1968, reconstruction and restoration of the remaining structures began. Five of the original adobes are still intact: La Casa de Estudillo, La Casa de Machado y Stewart, La Casa de Machado y Silvas, the Pedrorena-Altamirano House, and La Casa de Bandini (now the Cosmopolitan Hotel).

Facing Old Town Plaza, the **Robinson-Rose House** was the original commercial center of Old San Diego, housing railroad offices, law offices, and the first newspaper press. The largest and most elaborate of the original adobe homes, the **Casa de Estudillo** was occupied by members of the Estudillo family until 1887 and later gained popularity for its billing as "Ramona's Marriage Place" based on a popular novel of the time. Albert Seeley, a stagecoach entrepreneur, opened the Cosmopolitan Hotel in 1869 as a way station for travelers on the daylong trip south from Los Angeles. Next door to the Cosmopolitan Hotel, the **Seeley Stable** served as San Diego's stagecoach stop in 1867 and was the transportation hub of

Old Town until 1887, when trains became the favored mode of travel.

Several reconstructed buildings serve as restaurants or as shops purveying wares reminiscent of those that might have been available in the original Old Town. Racine & Laramie, a painstakingly reproduced version of San Diego's first cigar store in 1868, is especially interesting.

Pamphlets available at the Robinson-Rose House give details about all the historic houses on the plaza and in its vicinity. Free tours of the historic park are offered daily at 11:30 and 2; they depart from the Robinson-Rose House.

■ TIP → The covered wagon located near the intersection of Mason and Calhoun Streets provides a great photo op. ☒ *Visitor center (Robinson-Rose House), 4002 Wallace St., Old Town* ☎ *619/220–5422* ⊕ *www.parks.ca.gov* ☒ *Free.*

Presidio Park

CITY PARK | The hillsides of the 50-acre green space overlooking Old Town from the north end of Taylor Street are popular with picnickers, and many couples have taken their wedding vows on the park's long stretches of lawn, some of the greenest in San Diego. The park offers a great ocean view from the top, and more than 2 miles of hiking trails below. It's a nice walk from Old Town to the summit if you're in good shape and wearing the right shoes—it should take about half an hour. You can also drive to the top of the park via Presidio Drive, off Taylor Street.

If you walk, look in at the **Presidio Hills Golf Course** on Mason Street. It has an unusual clubhouse that incorporates the ruins of Casa de Carrillo, the town's oldest adobe, constructed in 1820. At the end of Mason Street, veer left on Jackson Street to reach the **presidio ruins,** where adobe walls and a bastion have been built above the foundations of the original fortress and chapel. Also on-site is the 28-foot-high **Serra Cross,** built in 1913 out of brick tiles found in the ruins.

America's Most Haunted ⊙

Built on a former gallows site in 1856, the Whaley House is one of 30 houses designated by the Department of Commerce to be haunted. Legend has it that the house is inhabited by seven spirits, making it the "most haunted house in America." Listen for the sound of heavy footsteps, said to belong to the ghost of Yankee Jim Robinson, a convict hanged on the site in 1852. Less ominous are sightings of the Whaley family's fox terrier scampering about the house.

Continue up the hill to find the **Junípero Serra Museum,** built at the sight of the original Mission San Diego de Alcalá and often mistaken for the mission. Open weekends, the Serra Museum commemorates the history of the site from the time it was occupied by the Kumeyaay Indians through its Spanish, Mexican, and American periods. Then take Presidio Drive southeast to reach the site of **Fort Stockton,** built to protect Old Town and abandoned by the United States in 1848. Plaques and statues also commemorate the Mormon Battalion, which enlisted here to fight in the battle against Mexico. ☒ *Taylor and Jackson Sts., Old Town* ⊕ *www.sdparks.org.*

★ The Whaley House Museum

HISTORIC HOME | A New York entrepreneur, Thomas Whaley came to California during the gold rush. He wanted to provide his East Coast wife with all the comforts of home, so in 1857 he had Southern California's first two-story brick structure built, making it the oldest double-story brick building on the West Coast. The house, which served as the county courthouse and government seat during the 1870s, stands in strong contrast to the

Spanish-style adobe residences that surround the nearby historic plaza and marks an early stage of San Diego's "Americanization." A garden out back includes many varieties of prehybrid roses from before 1867. The place is perhaps most famed, however, for the ghosts that are said to inhabit it. You can tour on your own during the day, but must visit by guided tour after 4:30 pm. The evening tours are geared toward the supernatural aspects of the house. Tours start at 5 pm and are offered every half hour, with the last tour departing at 9:30 pm. ⊠ *2476 San Diego Ave., Old Town* ☎ *619/273–5824* ⊕ *www.whaleyhousesandiego.com* ⊠ *From $13.*

Restaurants

Touristy but fun Mexican food reigns here with giant margaritas and heaping dishes of enchiladas, tacos, and carnitas (slow-cooked pork). You'll also find a few gourmet gems celebrating other cuisines mixed in.

El Agave
$$$ | MEXICAN | Not a typical San Diego taco shop, this Mexican eatery is upstairs in a shopping complex in the middle of a tequila museum with some 2,000 bottles dating from the 1930s. The owners are equally serious about food, calling their cuisine Hispanic-Mexican Gastronomy, which means meat and fish dishes with lots of unusual spicy chilies, herbs, spices, and moles. **Known for:** impressive tequila selection and tequila flights; variety of mole dishes; upscale option in generally casual Old Town. ⑤ *Average main: $32* ⊠ *2304 San Diego Ave., Old Town* ☎ *619/220–0692* ⊕ *www.elagave.com.*

Harney Sushi
$ | JAPANESE | One of San Diego's most popular sushi restaurants is set in a sea of touristy Mexican dining spots in the heart of Old Town. Fans young and old flock to the lively space for refreshing cocktails, sustainable California-style

sushi, and modern Asian cuisine. **Known for:** creative sushi rolls like the O'sider #55 with New York strip; specialty edamame in flavors like soy truffle and sesame bacon bonito; colorfully garnished and delicious cocktails. ⑤ *Average main: $18* ⊠ *3964 Harney St., Old Town* ☎ *619/295–3272* ⊕ *www.harneysushi.com* ☉ *No lunch.*

Tahona
$ | MEXICAN | Located next to Campo Santo Cemetery, Tahona—in its architecture and design—might suggest the illusion of a snapshot of historical San Diego, but culinarily it's anything but. Offering a dining experience that centers on mezcal, Oaxacan cuisine, and locally sourced produce and ingredients, Tahona puts a new spin on Southern California Mexican cuisine. **Known for:** mezcal flights; slow-braised beef barbacoa; gooey and rich churro s'mores. ⑤ *Average main: $18* ⊠ *2414 San Diego Ave., Old Town* ☎ *619/255–2090* ⊕ *www.tahonabar.com* ☉ *Closed Mon.*

Tuetano Taqueria
$ | MEXICAN | Located in the open-air Old Town Urban Market, the Michelin-recognized Tuetano Taqueria serves up its savory specialty: *birria* (meat stew). Grab as many napkins as you need, because these deliciously dripping birria tacos *will* make a mess. **Known for:** spicy and refreshing micheladas rojos (a Bloody Mary-type drink made with beer); bone marrow birria; birria tacos. ⑤ *Average main: $6* ⊠ *Old Town Urban Market, 2548 Congress St., Old Town* ☎ *619/856–7013.*

Hotels

Staying in Old Town makes it easy to explore the area on foot, as nearly everything is within walking distance. Old Town is also centrally located between Uptown, Downtown, and the beaches.

Best Western Plus Hacienda Hotel Old Town
$ | HOTEL | FAMILY | Perched on a hill in the heart of Old Town, this hotel is known for

Old Town is the place to go for colorful Mexican wares.

its expansive courtyards, outdoor fountains, and maze of stairs that connects eight buildings of guest rooms. **Pros:** airport shuttle; well-maintained outdoor areas; excellent location for exploring Old Town. **Cons:** some rooms need renovating; complicated layout; can be noisy in some areas. ⑤ *Rooms from: $179* ✉ *4041 Harney St., Old Town* ☎ *619/298–4707* ⊕ *www.haciendahotel-oldtown. com* ⇌ *200 rooms* ⏺ *No Meals.*

The Cosmopolitan Hotel
$ | **B&B/INN** | With antique furniture, pull-chain toilets, and a veranda overlooking Old Town State Historic Park, the Cosmo offers guests a taste of Victorian-era living. **Pros:** historic charm; huge suites; central location in Old Town State Historic Park. **Cons:** no TVs; limited on-site parking; street noise. ⑤ *Rooms from: $169* ✉ *2660 Calhoun St., Old Town* ☎ *619/297–1874* ⊕ *www.oldtowncosmopolitan.com* ⇌ *10 rooms* ⏺ *No Meals.*

Nightlife

Old-timey saloons lure tourists with margaritas, mezcal, and mariachis.

El Agave Tequileria
COCKTAIL LOUNGES | The bar of this restaurant named for the cactus whose sap is distilled into tequila stocks hundreds of top-shelf brands that are as sip-worthy as the finest cognac. ✉ *2304 San Diego Ave., Old Town* ☎ *619/220–0692* ⊕ *www. elagave.com.*

Performing Arts

Cygnet's Old Town Theatre
THEATER | A 246-seat theater operated by Cygnet Theatre Company, this is one of the more interesting small San Diego theater groups. Catch local takes on edgy classics like *Sweeney Todd* and *Little Shop of Horrors.* ✉ *4040 Twiggs St., Old Town* ☎ *619/337–1525* ⊕ *www.cygnet-theatre.com.*

🛍 Shopping

Tourist-focused Old Town has a festival-like ambience that also makes it a popular destination for locals. It's a must for pottery, ceramics, jewelry, and handcrafted baskets. At Old Town San Diego State Historic Park, you may feel like a time traveler as you visit shops housed in restored adobe buildings. Farther down the street are stores selling Mexican blankets, piñatas, and glassware. Old Town Market offers live entertainment, local artists selling their wares from carts, and a market crammed with unique apparel, home-decor items, toys, jewelry, and food. Dozens of stores sell San Diego logo merchandise and T-shirts at discounted prices, and there are great deals on handcrafted jewelry, art, and leather accessories.

HOME ACCESSORIES AND GIFTS
Cousin's Candy Shop

SOUVENIRS | Sample homemade fudge and taffy that's been cooked, stretched, and wrapped on-site at this old-fashioned confectionery shop. The old-time candies in nostalgic tins make thoughtful gifts. ✉ *2711 San Diego Ave., Old Town* ☎ *619/297–2000* ⊕ *cousinscandyshop. com.*

Tienda de Reyes

CRAFTS | This festive "store of the kings" stocks Old Town's largest selection of Day of the Dead art, and carries sculpture, handbags, and glassware from Mexico and Peru. ✉ *2754 Calhoun St., Old Town* ☎ *619/491–0611* ⊕ *www. facebook.com/tiendadereyes.*

Ye Olde Soap Shoppe

SKINCARE | The mere scent of Ye Olde's hand-fashioned soaps conjures up a relaxing bath. If you want to craft your own soaps, you'll find a full line of supplies, as well as soaps and lotions from around the world. ✉ *2497 San Diego Ave., Old Town* ☎ *619/543–1300* ⊕ *www. soapmaking.com.*

MARKETS
Old Town Harney Street Market

MARKET | San Diego's largest weekend artisan market presents live music and local artists selling jewelry, paintings, photography, handblown glass, apparel, pottery, and decorative items. The San Diego Trolley's Old Town stop is two blocks north of the market. ✉ *Harney St. and San Diego Ave., Old Town* ⊕ *www.oldtownsandiego.org/ harneystreetmarket.*

Old Town Market

MARKET | The atmosphere is colorful, upbeat, and Mexico-centric at this eclectic market. Local artisans create some of the wares for sale, including everything from dolls and silver jewelry to gourmet foods, home-decor items, and apparel. ✉ *4010 Twiggs St., Old Town* ☎ *619/278– 0955* ⊕ *www.oldtownmarketsandiego. com.*

SHOPPING CENTERS
Bazaar del Mundo Shops

SHOPPING CENTER | With a Mexican villa theme, the Bazaar hosts riotously colorful gift shops such as **Ariana,** for ethnic and artsy women's fashions; **Artes de Mexico,** which sells handmade Latin American crafts and Guatemalan weavings; and **The Gallery,** which carries handmade jewelry, American Indian crafts, collectible glass, and original silk-screen prints. The **Laurel Burch Gallerita** carries the complete collection of its namesake artist's signature jewelry, accessories, and totes. ✉ *4133 Taylor St., at Juan St., Old Town* ☎ *619/296–3161* ⊕ *www.bazaardelmundo.com.*

Hillcrest

The large, retro Hillcrest sign over the intersection of University and 5th Avenues makes an excellent landmark at the epicenter of this vibrant section of Uptown. Strolling along University Avenue between 4th and 6th Avenues and from Washington Street to Robinson Avenue will reveal a mixture of retail shops and restaurants. National chains such as Starbucks and Freshii coexist with local boutiques, bookstores, bars, and coffee shops. A few blocks east, another interesting stretch of stores and restaurants runs along University Avenue to Normal Street. Long established as the center of San Diego's gay community, the neighborhood bustles both day and night with a mixed crowd of shoppers, diners, and partygoers. If you are visiting Hillcrest on Sunday between 9 and 2, be sure to explore the exceptional Hillcrest Farmers Market.

Restaurants

From brunch to late-night snacks, Hillcrest's lively dining scene has you covered. This is a popular dining neighborhood so reservations are recommended if you don't want to wait during peak times.

Hash House A Go Go

$$ | AMERICAN | FAMILY | Big caloric portions and long lines are hallmarks of this Southern-accented comfort food destination where hungry regulars from near and far line up for an indulgent meal in the crowded (and sometimes noisy) dining room. Bring an appetite and a friend; sharing plates is a necessity here. **Known for:** decadent sage-fried-chicken eggs Benedict; huge portions perfect for sharing; inventive and generously garnished cocktails. $ *Average main: $20* ✉ *3628 5th Ave., Hillcrest* ☎ *619/298–4646* ⊕ *www.hashhouseago-go.com* ☾ *No dinner.*

Ortega's Bistro

$ | MEXICAN | FAMILY | Seafood lovers have long flocked to Puerto Nuevo, the "lobster village" just south of San Diego in Baja California, Mexico. When a family that operates several Puerto Nuevo restaurants opened Ortega's in Hillcrest, it quickly became a top draw for authentic Baja coastal cuisine, minus the long lines to cross the border. **Known for:** Puerto Nuevo–style lobster; tableside guacamole; daily happy hour including the delicious pomegranate margarita. $ *Average main: $19* ✉ *141 University Ave., Hillcrest* ☎ *619/692–4200* ⊕ *www.ortegas.com.*

Snooze

$ | AMERICAN | Bright "Brady Bunch" decor, plus plenty of sunshine and fresh air pouring through windows and skylights, are cheery wake-ups for diners at this hip neighborhood haunt for pancakes and lattes. Expect long waits for a table, especially on weekends; free coffee helps the time pass while you wait to indulge in made-from-scratch breakfast bliss. **Known for:** pineapple upside-down pancakes; half-order Benedicts; boozy brunch drinks. $ *Average main: $13* ✉ *3940 5th Ave., Hillcrest* ☎ *619/500–3344* ⊕ *www.snoozeeatery.com* ☾ *No dinner.*

★ Trust

$$ | MODERN AMERICAN | Old-school wood-fire techniques meet modern architecture in this busy bistro where comic book–style art covers the concrete walls and the bottle-lined bar beckons locals and visitors alike. Locally sourced ingredients and smoky, savory flavors feature in the well-balanced menu; be sure to save room for one of the inspired desserts. **Known for:** five-hour braised oxtail raviolini; wood-grilled cauliflower with curry vinaigrette; roomy outdoor patio. $ *Average main: $22* ✉ *3752 Park Blvd., Hillcrest* ☎ *619/795–6901* ⊕ *www.trustrestaurantsd.com* ☾ *Closed Mon. and Tues. No lunch weekdays.*

☕ Coffee and Quick Bites

Bread & Cie

$ | CAFÉ | San Diego's love affair with artisanal bread began when Charles Kaufman, a former New Yorker and a filmmaker, opened this artsy urban bakery and café two decades ago. Ovens imported from France produce irresistible aromas as you choose among classic baguettes and focaccia, delicious assorted pastries and Vienoisserie, and a wide selection of breakfast and lunch specialties. **Known for:** crusty black olive bread; traditional afternoon tea; creamy tomato soup. ⑤ *Average main: $9* ⊠ *350 University Ave., Hillcrest* ☎ *619/683–9322* ⊕ *www. breadandcie.com* ⊘ *No dinner.*

 ## Nightlife

This is San Diego's most active area for LGBTQ nightlife.

BARS
Baja Betty's

BARS | Although it draws plenty of gay customers, the festive and friendly atmosphere is popular with just about everyone in the Hillcrest area (and their pets are welcome, too). The bar staff stocks more than 100 brands of tequila and mixes plenty of fancy cocktails. ⊠ *1421 University Ave., Hillcrest* ☎ *619/269–8510* ⊕ *www.bajabettyssd. com.*

Nunu's

COCKTAIL LOUNGES | This retro-cool hangout with stiff cocktails might be one of the most popular bars in Hillcrest, but don't expect a glitzy facade. The intentionally dated decor sits within the tatty walls of a white-brick box that probably hasn't had a face-lift since the LBJ administration. ⊠ *3537 5th Ave., Hillcrest* ☎ *619/295– 2878* ⊕ *www.nunustavern.com.*

Rich's

DANCE CLUBS | The dancing and music here are some of the best in the city, making Rich's popular not only with gay men but also plenty of lesbians and straight revelers. ⊠ *1051 University Ave., Hillcrest* ☎ *619/578–9349* ⊕ *www.richs-sandiego.com.*

Urban Mo's Bar and Grill

DANCE CLUBS | Cowboys gather for line dancing and two-stepping on the wooden dance floor—but be forewarned, yee-hawers, it can get pretty wild on Western nights. There are also Latin, hip-hop, and drag revues but the real allure is in the creative drinks ("Gone Fishing"—served in a fishbowl, for example) and the breezy patio where love (or something like it) is usually in the air. ⊠ *308 University Ave., Hillcrest* ☎ *619/491–0400* ⊕ *www.urbanmos.com.*

Shopping

The Uptown neighborhood of Hill-crest hosts avant-garde apparel shops alongside gift, thrift, and music stores clustered along University Avenue at 4th and 5th Avenues, and again farther down University near 10th Avenue. Hillcrest is also well-known as home to one the city's best weekly farmers' markets.

★ Hillcrest Farmers Market

MARKET | One of the city's best farmers' markets, Hillcrest features 175 vendors that sell farm-fresh produce, handmade clothing, jewelry, and other types of handicrafts every Sunday from 9 am to 2 pm. Browse the market and plan to stay for lunch: there are several vendors selling top-notch ready-to-eat food, from fresh-made crepes and tamales to African and Indian cuisine. ⊠ *3960 Normal St., between Lincoln St. and Normal Ave., Hillcrest* ⊕ *www.hillcrestfarmers-market.com.*

Mission Hills

The route from Old Town to Hillcrest passes through the historic neighborhood of Mission Hills, with its delightful examples of early-20th-century architecture. From the top of Presidio Park, take Presidio Drive into the heart of this residential area. A left on Arista Street and a right on Fort Stockton Drive takes you past wonderfully preserved Spanish revival, Craftsman, and Prairie-style homes, to name a few. Many local residents fine-tune their green thumbs at the Mission Hills Nursery (⊠ *1525 Ft. Stockton Dr.*), founded in 1910 by Kate Sessions, the "Mother of Balboa Park." Continuing on Fort Stockton Drive, a right on Goldfinch Street leads you to several popular eateries along the neighborhood's burgeoning restaurant row. From there, a left on University Avenue will take you into the Hillcrest section of Uptown.

🍴 Restaurants

The affluent enclave of Mission Hills offers surprisingly affordable and diverse dining experiences clustered at the bottom of the hill along Washington and India Streets, and again near Washington and Goldfinch Streets at the top.

Blue Water Seafood Market & Grill

$ | SEAFOOD | FAMILY | Blame a television segment by Guy Fieri on "Diners, Drive-ins and Dives" for the long lines of fans from around the globe. But it's the fresh seafood cooked to order that keeps them coming back to this no-frills fish market and restaurant. **Known for:** beer-battered cod tacos; classic cioppino plate with mussels and clams, scallops, shrimp, and red snapper; fresh catch cooked to order. ⑤ *Average main: $17* ⊠ *3667 India St., Mission Hills* ☎ *619/497–0914* ⊕ *www. bluewaterseafoodsandiego.com.*

Fort Oak

$$$ | AMERICAN | Housed inside a converted Ford dealership that dates back to the '40s, Fort Oak is a haven for sophisticated carnivores and pescatarians alike. Chef Brad Wise's menu leans heavily on wood-fired fish, like the whole branzino, as well as aged steaks, Duroc pork, and fried chicken. **Known for:** 40-day aged rib-eye steak; hearth grilled branzino; elegant yet kitschy classic automotive design elements. ⑤ *Average main: $39* ⊠ *1011 Ft. Stockton Dr., Mission*

Hills ☎ *619/722–3398* ⊕ *fortoaksd.com* ⊙ *Closed Tues.*

Lucha Libre Gourmet Taco Shop

$ | MEXICAN | Named for a form of Mexican wrestling, this taco shop with its hot-pink walls and shiny booths was famous mostly for its lack of parking until it appeared on the Travel Channel's "Man v. Food." Then long lines of burrito-crazed fans began forming outside the walk-up window for lunch; their North Park outpost is more spacious. **Known for:** Tap Me Out taco with fried cheese; California burritos with French fries inside; lively and festive interior seating. ⑤ *Average main: $9* ⊠ *1810 W. Washington St., Mission Hills* ☎ *619/296–8226* ⊕ *www. luchalibretacoshop.com.*

Saffron

$ | THAI | Outdoor tables on a narrow sidewalk and inexpensive prices make this a standout. The simple menu by Bangkok-born chef-owner Su-Mei Yu has noodle soups; stir-fried noodles with chicken, beef, pork, or shrimp; and a couple of uncommon Vietnamese and Thai-Indian noodle dishes bathed with aromatic sauces. **Known for:** Thai grilled chicken; health-focused dishes like the Brain-Booster Stir-Fry; fresh noodle dishes. ⑤ *Average main: $10* ⊠ *3731 India St., Mission Hills* ☎ *619/574–7737* ⊕ *www.saffronthai.com.*

Starlite

$ | AMERICAN | This trendy 21-and-over establishment attracts a diverse and discerning crowd to a somewhat quiet stretch of India Street with its solid seasonal fare and understated mid-century vibe. The menu covers the gamut of comfort food from mozzarella and squash fritters to macaroni and cheese, juicy roasted chicken, and a fish of the day paired with a Thai noodle salad. **Known for:** creamy and carb-filled mac and cheese; signature Moscow Mules in copper mugs; late-night dining. ⑤ *Average main: $18* ⊠ *3175 India St., Mission*

Hills ☎ 619/618–2830 ⊕ www.starlite-sandiego.com.

 ## Coffee and Quick Bites

Gelato Vero Caffe
$ | CAFÉ | A youthful crowd gathers here for authentic Italian ice cream, espresso, and a second-floor view of the Downtown skyline. The place is usually occupied by regulars who stay for hours at a time. **Known for:** smooth and creamy gelato made with natural flavors; affogato (espresso and gelato); house-made chai. ⑤ Average main: $5 ⊠ 3753 India St., Mission Hills ☎ 619/295–9269 ⊕ www.gelatoverocaffe.com.

Karina's Ceviche and More
$ | MEXICAN | Don't miss the small walk-up window along India Street serving up delicious ceviches, seafood cocktails, and tacos. Outdoor seating is available along the adjacent terrace. **Known for:** Karina's signature spicy ceviche; choice between full-size plates or smaller tostadas; spicy marinades—ask for guidance if you want to order something mild. ⑤ Average main: $10 ⊠ 3731 India St., Suite B, Mission Hills ☎ 619/255–5900 ⊕ karinasseafood.com.

 ## Nightlife

Take your pick between unpretentious pubs or ultrastylish cocktail grottoes.

Aero Club
COCKTAIL LOUNGES | Named for its proximity to the airport, this watering hole draws in whiskey lovers for its unbeatable selection. ⊠ 3365 India St., Mission Hills ☎ 619/297–7211 ⊕ www.aeroclubbar.com.

Shakespeare Pub & Grille
PUBS | This Mission Hills hangout captures all the warmth and camaraderie of a traditional British pub—except here you can enjoy consistently sunny weather on the sprawling patio. The bar hands pour from a long list of imported ales and stouts, and the early hours for big matches make this the place to watch soccer. ⊠ 3701 India St., Mission Hills ☎ 619/299–0230 ⊕ www.shakespeare-pub.com.

 ## Shopping

The shops and art galleries in Mission Hills have a modern and sophisticated ambience that suits the trendy residents.

M-Theory Music
MUSIC | This locally owned record store in Mission Hills carries new and used vinyl and CDs. They regularly host in-store performances. ⊠ 827 W. Washington St., Mission Hills ☎ 619/220–0485 ⊕ www.mtheorymusic.com.

Mission Valley

Although Mission Valley's charms may not be immediately apparent, it offers many conveniences to visitors and residents alike. One of the area's main attractions is the Fashion Valley Mall, with its mix of high-end and midrange retail stores and dining options, and a movie theater. The Mission Basilica San Diego de Alcalá provides a tranquil refuge from the surrounding suburban sprawl.

 ## Sights

★ Mission Basilica San Diego de Alcalá
CHURCH | It's hard to imagine how remote California's earliest mission must have once been; these days, however, it's accessible by major freeways (I–15 and I–8) and via the San Diego Trolley. The first of a chain of 21 missions stretching northward along the coast, Mission San Diego de Alcalá was established by Father Junípero Serra on Presidio Hill in 1769 and moved to this location in 1774. In 1775, it proved vulnerable to enemy attack, and Padre Luís Jayme, a young friar from Spain, was clubbed to death by the Kumeyaay Indians he had been trying

Founded in 1769, Mission Basilica San Diego de Alcalá was the first of California's 21 Catholic missions.

to convert. He was the first of more than a dozen Christians martyred in California. The present church, reconstructed in 1931 following the outline of the 1813 church, is the fifth built on the site. It measures 150 feet long but only 35 feet wide because, without easy means of joining beams, the mission buildings were only as wide as the trees that served as their ceiling supports were tall. Father Jayme is buried in the sanctuary; a small museum named for him documents mission history and exhibits tools and artifacts from the early days; there is also a gift shop. From the peaceful, palm-bedecked gardens out back you can gaze at the 46-foot-high *campanario* (bell tower), the mission's most distinctive feature, with five bells. Mass is celebrated on the weekends. ✉ *10818 San Diego Mission Rd., Mission Valley* ✛ *From I–8 east, exit and turn left on Mission Gorge Rd., then left on Twain Rd.; mission is on right* ☎ *619/283–7319* ⊕ *www.mission-sandiego.org* ✍ *$8.*

🍴 Restaurants

Mission Valley, home to Hotel Circle and the area's massive malls, isn't known for groundbreaking cuisine, but it has lots of satisfying chain and casual eateries.

🛏 Hotels

Town and Country Resort

$ | **HOTEL** | **FAMILY** | Newly updated after a multimillion-dollar renovation, the Town and Country Resort—a staple of Hotel Circle for more than 60 years—has been given a second life while returning to its stylish roots. **Pros:** on-site restaurant Arlo; recently renovated with updated furnishings; lots of activities for families. **Cons:** freeway noise; not in a walkable neighborhood; snacks at the in-hotel market are still pricey but without the convenience of a minibar. $ *Rooms from: $198* ✉ *500 Hotel Circle N, Mission Valley* ☎ *619/291–7131* ⊕ *www.towncountry. com* ⇄ *671 rooms.*

▼ Nightlife

Blanco Tacos + Tequila

COCKTAIL LOUNGES | Get your margarita skinny, spicy, or standard, with house-made sours and fresh-squeezed juices, at this prime new spot within Fashion Valley Mall. Don't miss Margarita Monday ($5 classic margaritas until 6 pm) or Taco Tuesday ($4 happy hour tacos until 6 pm). ⊠ *Fashion Valley Mall, 7007 Friars Rd., Mission Valley* ☎ *619/810–2931* ⊕ *www. blancococinacantina.com/.*

⬛ Shopping

Northeast of Downtown near I–8 and Route 163, Mission Valley holds two major shopping centers and a few smaller strip malls. Fashion Valley hosts an impressive roster of high-end department stores—among them Neiman Marcus, Nordstrom, and Bloomingdale's—and a passel of luxury boutiques like Hermès, Gucci, and Fendi. Westfield Mission Valley is home to mainstays like Old Navy, plus bargain-hunter favorites like Marshalls and Nordstrom Rack. The San Diego Trolley and city buses stop at both centers.

★ Fashion Valley

MALL | San Diego's most upscale mall has a contemporary Mission theme, lush landscaping, and nearly 200 shops and restaurants. Acclaimed retailers like Nordstrom, Neiman Marcus, Bloomingdale's, and Tiffany & Co. are here, along with boutiques from fashion darlings like Michael Kors, Tory Burch, and Ted Baker. H&M is a favorite of fashionistas in search of edgy and affordable styles. Free wireless Internet service is available throughout the mall. Select "Simon WiFi" from any Wi-Fi–enabled device to log onto the network.

■ TIP→ If you're visiting from out of state, are a member of the military, or have a AAA membership, you can pick up a complimentary Style Pass at Simon Guest Services (located on the lower level beneath AMC Theaters near Banana Republic), which can get you savings at more than 70 of Fashion Valley's stores and restaurants. ⊠ *7007 Friars Rd., Mission Valley* ☎ *619/688–9113* ⊕ *www.simon.com/mall/fashion-valley.*

🏃 Activities

HIKING

A day hike through the canyons and hills of Mission Trails Park is a great way to escape to nature without leaving the city.

★ Mission Trails Regional Park

HIKING & WALKING | This park 8 miles northeast of Downtown encompasses more than 7,000 acres of wooded hillsides, grasslands, chaparral, and streams. Trails range from easy to difficult; they include one with an impressive view of the city from Cowles Mountain and another along a historic missionary path. The park is also a popular place for rock climbing and camping (the Kumeyaay Lake Campground is open on weekends). Lake Murray is at the southern edge of the park, off Highway 8. ⊠ *1 Father Junípero Serra Trail, Mission Valley* ☎ *619/668–3281* ⊕ *www.mtrp.org.*

University Heights, Adams Avenue, and Normal Heights

Tucked between Hillcrest and North Park, the small but charming neighborhood of University Heights is centered on Park Boulevard. The tree-lined street is home to several notable bars and restaurants, as well as the acclaimed LGBTQ Diversionary Theatre. Kids love the playgrounds at Trolley Barn Park, just around the corner on Adams Avenue. The thriving nightlife and dining scene continues down Adams Avenue and into neighboring Normal Heights.

University Heights, Adams Avenue, and Normal Heights, North Park, South Park and Golden Hill

KEY

● Exploring Sights

● Restaurants

● Quick Bites

● Hotels

👁 Sights

Trolley Barn Park

CITY PARK | FAMILY | Kids will love the playgrounds at Trolley Barn Park, just around the corner on Adams Avenue. The park is also home to free family concerts in the summer. ✉ *Adams Ave., between Georgia and Alabama Sts., University Heights.*

🍴 Restaurants

On the mesas overlooking Mission Valley, these historic neighborhoods are experiencing a culinary renaissance with new, casual, ethnic dining and an array of wine bars and brewpubs, many with nightly entertainment.

★ Blind Lady Ale House

$ | PIZZA | FAMILY | There's almost no combination on earth as satisfying as pizza and beer—which just happen to be Blind Lady's specialties. The old-world-style pizzas are topped with organic ingredients, like house-made chorizo and avocado, which offer an excellent complement to their extensive beer selection, which is updated on their chalkboard daily. Just be patient waiting for a seat at the popular neighborhood spot, which is decorated with upcycled materials such as reclaimed wood floors and glass cases of vintage beer cans. **Known for:** spicy chorizo pizza with avocado; crispy Belgian frites; house-brewed craft beer. ⑤ *Average main: $18* ✉ *3416 Adams Ave., Normal Heights* ☎ *619/255–2491* ⊕ *www.blindladyalehouse.com* ⊘ *No lunch Mon.–Wed.*

El Zarape

$ | MEXICAN | Don't be fooled by the humble facade—this tiny Mexican taqueria serves up some of the best seafood-focused border food in town. There's almost always a crowd of Uptown locals and savvy travelers here, but orders for burritos, tacos, and combination plates almost fly out of the kitchen. **Known for:** 99¢ fish tacos; seafood dishes; extensive menu. ⑤ *Average main: $8* ✉ *4642 Park Blvd., University Heights* ☎ *619/692–1652* ⊕ *www.elzarapesandiego.com.*

Madi

$ | AMERICAN | A bright and bustling A.M.-hours counterpart to its sibling restaurant Madison, Madi is a haven for the Sunday brunch crowd. With colorful decor and no fewer than six different variations of mimosa on the menu, it's youthful and indulgent, but not exclusive to weekends—Madi serves its gooey morning treats like peanut butter and banana pancakes and chilaquiles every day starting at 8. **Known for:** Cool Cat Cakes (peanut butter, banana and bacon); six varieites of mimosa; waffle churro sticks with jalapeno-blackberry sauce and maple cream cheese. ⑤ *Average main: $16* ✉ *3737 Adams Ave., Normal Heights* ☎ *619/915–5522* ⊕ *brunchlikemadi.com* ⊘ *No dinner.*

Madison

$$ | MEDITERRANEAN | The award-winning design of this restaurant and bar is the definition of Southern California chic, as are its patrons. The vaulted wood-clad ceiling and indoor-outdoor space creates a stunning yet inviting backdrop for the inspired cocktails—mixologists incorporate ingredients such as matcha and hemp oil into their featured libations—and SoCal Mediterranean cuisine. **Known for:** dramatic interior design; innovative cocktails; weekend brunch. ⑤ *Average main: $20* ✉ *4622 Park Blvd., University Heights* ☎ *619/269–6566* ⊕ *www.madisononpark.com* ⊘ *Closed Mon. No lunch weekdays.*

Pop Pie Co.

$ | INTERNATIONAL | FAMILY | The atmosphere at Pop Pie Co. is fast-casual, but its menu is nothing less than rich, stick-to-your-ribs comfort food. With a menu full of internationally inspired meat and dessert pies and open-air seating at communal tables, the eatery offers either a quick dessert or the satisfaction of a hearty meal without the dining room dress code. **Known for:** classic chicken potpie; salted caramel-apple crumble; espresso with house-made sweeteners. $ *Average main: $9* ✉ *4404 Park Blvd., University Heights* ☎ *619/501–4440* ⊕ *www.poppieco.com.*

☕ Coffee and Quick Bites

Blackmarket Bakery SD
$ | **BAKERY** | **FAMILY** | Employing the motto "If your grandmother wouldn't bake with it, we won't either," Blackmarket Bakery emphasizes that all its creations are made from scratch, and the proof is in the tasting. Its pastry case is full of buttercream-frosted cakes, drop cookies, and other fresh-baked goodies, in addition to breakfast sandwiches and vegan pastries. **Known for:** vegan cookies; Cookie Monster bread pudding; handmade marshmallows. $ *Average main: $6* ✉ *4686 30th St., University Heights* ☎ *619/641–0081* ⊕ *www.blackmarketbakery.com.*

Lestat's Coffee Shop
$ | **CAFÉ** | One of the few San Diego coffee shops that's open 24 hours a day, this Normal Heights mainstay also has a great selection of baked goods and a neighboring music venue that stages acoustic and comedy acts seven days a week. Lestat's also has locations in University Heights and Hillcrest. **Known for:** Milky Way mocha with caramel and vanilla; breakfast paninis; funky, bohemian atmosphere. $ *Average main: $5* ✉ *3343 Adams Ave., Normal Heights* ☎ *619/282–0437* ⊕ *www.lestats.com.*

White Rice Bodega
$ | **FILIPINO** | With window service from its colorful, street-art-adorned kitchen and outdoor seat-yourself tables, this is an ideal spot for a quick bite, but that doesn't mean it's not substantial. The outdoor eatery serves savory and delicious abundant plates of traditional Filipino pork, sausage, and chicken dishes, along with signature snacks like *lumpia* (Filipino spring rolls) and their head-turning purple ube *pandesal* (bread rolls). **Known for:** crispy (Filipino spring rolls); Pork sisilog (fried egg and rice); fluffy, purple Ube pandesal (bread rolls). $ *Average main: $16* ✉ *3586 Adams Ave., Suite 100, Normal Heights* ☎ *619/289–9240.*

Nightlife

These low-key Uptown neighborhoods house some of San Diego's favorite local watering holes.

BARS
Cantina Mayahuel
BARS | The well-respected Cantina Mayahuel carries San Diego's largest collection of agave-based Mexican spirits—with tequila flights to boot—and is regularly frequented by local service industry pros. ✉ *2934 Adams Ave., University Heights* ☎ *619/283–6292* ⊕ *cantinamayahuelsd.com.*

Park and Rec
COCKTAIL LOUNGES | Craft cocktails and local beers are served up with a side of fun in this indoor-outdoor bungalow complex featuring live music and classic games from Ping-Pong to pinball. ✉ *4612 Park Blvd., University Heights* ☎ *619/795–9700* ⊕ *www.parkandrecsd.com.*

Sycamore Den
COCKTAIL LOUNGES | The heavy use of wood and stone, and accents like banjos and rifles, might give Sycamore Den a masculine vibe, but it's a highly specific and kitschy one: '70s dads. Though the hipster-pop concept might seem like it was plucked right out of a Tumblr meme, the drinks here are worth the irony, and the calendar is typically filled with great local, acoustic live bands. ✉ *3391 Adams Ave., Normal Heights* ☎ *619/563–9019* ⊕ *www.sycamoreden.com.*

Performing Arts

Diversionary Theatre

THEATER | San Diego's premier gay and lesbian company presents a range of original works that focus on LGBTQ themes. ✉ *4545 Park Blvd., Suite 101, University Heights* ☎ *619/220–0097* ⊕ *www.diversionary.org.*

🛍 Shopping

University Avenue is good for furniture, gift, and specialty stores appealing to college students, singles, and young families.

North Park

Named for its location north of Balboa Park, this evolving neighborhood is home to an exciting array of restaurants, bars, and shops. The stretch of Ray Street near University Avenue is home to several small galleries and boutiques. Just around the corner on University Avenue lies the stunning 1920s-era North Park Theatre (now known as Observatory North Park). With a steady stream of new openings in the neighborhood, North Park is one of San Diego's top dining and nightlife destinations. Beer enthusiasts won't want to miss the breweries and tasting rooms along the 30th Street Beer Corridor, dubbed "Beer Boulevard," for a chance to sample San Diego's famous ales.

👁 Sights

North Park Farmers' Market

MARKET | Held rain or shine every Thursday 3–7:30 pm, this weekly market features more than 50 vendors selling everything from locally grown produce and fresh flowers to arts and crafts and an impressive selection of gourmet foods. There are also activities for kids and live music. ✉ *N. Park Way, between Ray St. and Granada Ave., North Park* ☎ *619/294–2501* ⊕ *www.northparkfarmersmarket.com.*

Restaurants

City Tacos

$ | **MEXICAN** | This small space in North Park elevates the traditional taco shop experience with superior ingredients and unique toppings. Several vegan and paleo tacos are offered alongside their seafood and meat selections. **Known for:** unique toppings on traditional tacos; specialty aioli and salsa bar; vegan and paleo tacos. ⑤ *Average main: $8* ✉ *3028 University Ave., North Park* ☎ *619/296–2303* ⊕ *citytacossd.com.*

Grand Ole BBQ Y Asado

$ | **BARBECUE** | **FAMILY** | Reopened after a recent remodel, this North Park spot is an authentic and eclectic stop for barbecue—both Texas-style and Argentine—with patio dining to preserve the feeling of a backyard fete, even if someone else is cooking. Meat is served by the pound (or half- or quarter-pound—there's no minimum order when you're selecting between brisket, hot links, smoked turkey or ribs) or available as a sandwich, for those who prefer some carbs with their protein. **Known for:** smoked, grilled meats by the pound; Sunday Argentine BBQ dinner; casual backyard BBQ vibe with long, communal picnic tables. ⑤ *Average main: $14* ✉ *3302 32nd St., North Park* ☎ *619/213–3765* ⊕ *northpark.grandolebbq.com* 🕐 *Closed Mon. and Tues.*

Tribute Pizza

$ | **PIZZA** | **FAMILY** | The concept behind Tribute Pizza initially seems like a gimmick—each wood-fired oven baked pizza is a "tribute" to one at another famous pizzeria, whether in Brooklyn, Texas, or even Costco. But however campy in their presentation, the "Neo-Neapolitan" pizzas at the spacious, modern restaurant—which is housed in a converted former post office—are among the best in town, whether made from all-vegan ingredients or smothered in spicy salami. **Known for:** the Bees Mode—topped with soppresatta and spicy honey; fried Brussels sprouts with garlic and pecorino romano cheese; Miller High Life served in champagne buckets. $ *Average main: $19* 3077 N. Park Way, North Park 619/450–4505 *www.tributepizza. com* Closed Mon.

URBN North Park

$ | PIZZA | FAMILY | A 5,000-square-foot brick-and-wood industrial-style dining room and bar attracts hip young locals who chow down on thin-crust New Haven–style pies, fresh salads, cheese boards, and chicken wings. It can get loud and crowded at times, but is always festive for groups—first dates, not so much. **Known for:** mashed-potato pizza; local craft beer selection; desserts cooked in the coal-fired oven. $ *Average main: $19* 3085 University Ave., North Park 619/255–7300 *www.urbnnorth-park.com.*

Coffee and Quick Bites

Caffè Calabria

$ | ITALIAN | This long-standing North Park coffee roaster and café expands its evening offerings to include local beer, wine, and Italian-style cocktails. **Known for:** Neapolitan pizzas; house-roasted espresso; Campari cocktails. $ *Average main: $13* 3933 30th St., North Park 619/683–7787 *www.caffecalabria. com* No credit cards Closed Mon. and Tues. evening.

Communal Coffee

$ | CAFÉ | The exterior of Communal Coffee reads "Coffee + Flowers," and though that's not the name of the café, it's also not inaccurate—you actually can pick up a bouquet while you're there. But while there's plenty to keep patrons occupied—including a curated selection of housewares, books, and chocolates—the main attraction is still the fresh-brewed coffee and flaky, buttery pastries. **Known for:** French press coffee; buttery chocolate croissants; fresh-cut flowers. $ *Average main: $6* 2335 University Ave., North Park 619/363–7737 *www.communalcof-fee.com.*

★ Nomad Donuts

$ | CAFÉ | FAMILY | The doughnuts at Nomad are big, fluffy, colorful, and would make Homer Simpson drool. Its rotating menu of internationally inspired doughnut flavors is made with natural ingredients, like real fruit, and almost all of them have a vegan counterpart as well. Just make sure to show up early—doughnuts this good don't stick around for long. **Known for:** cinnamon-sugar cruller; pomegranate with Meyer lemon drizzle doughnut; Panther milk breve, iced with sweet-ened condensed milk. $ *Average main: $4* 3102 University Ave., North Park 619/431–5000 *nomaddonuts.com.*

Hotels

The Lafayette Hotel, Swim Club & Bungalows

$$ | HOTEL | Originally opened in the 1940s, the Lafayette was once frequent-ed by stars like Ava Gardner and Bob Hope; it eventually became something of a budget hipster stay, but since its $31 million renovation by local restaurant group CH Projects, the Lafayette has been given a makeover for the 21st cen-tury. **Pros:** eight different dining options; newly renovated; within walking distance to other restaurants and attractions. **Cons:** party vibe not particularly condu-cive to relaxing stay; not family-friendly; a little pretentious. $ *Rooms from: $299* 2223 El Cajon Blvd., North Park 619/296–2101 *www.lafayetteho-telsd.com* 139 rooms No Meals.

⛾ Nightlife

Young, hip artist types gather to sip craft beer along the 30th Street corridor.

BARS
Part Time Lover

COCKTAIL LOUNGES | A more laid-back counterpoint to nightclubs where DJs spin bass-heavy EDM, Part Time Lover is a haven for those who prefer their vinyl listening experience paired with a good cocktail. Inspired by listening bars in Japan, the stylish, Stevie Wonder-referencing lounge features a rotating cast behind the turntables every night, spinning jazz-funk, classic soul and other eclectic sounds, with a cocktail menu that features both refreshing and spirit forward options. And if you like what you hear, there's no need to vacate the bar to go shopping—Folk Arts Records is housed inside. ✉ *3829 30th St., North Park* ☎ *619/932–4434* ⊕ *parttimeloverhifi. com.*

Red Fox Steak House

PIANO BARS | Referred to as Red Fox Room by those in the know, this dimly lit lounge is dearly loved by locals, and not just the seniors who flock here to sing Sinatra tunes to tickled ivories and the occasional impromptu horn section. The bar opened in 1959, but much of the bar's features—including its ornately detailed fireplace—date back to 16th- and 1/th-century England. Though relocated just across the street, its charm and potent cocktails came along for the ride. ✉ *2220 El Cajon Blvd., North Park* ☎ *619/297–1313* ⊕ *www.redfoxsd.com.*

Seven Grand

PIANO BARS | This whiskey lounge is a swanky addition to an already thriving North Park nightlife scene and a welcome alternative to the neighboring dives and dance clubs. Live jazz, a tranquil atmosphere, and a bourbon-loving craft cocktail list keep locals flocking. ✉ *3054 University Ave., North Park* ☎ *619/269– 8820* ⊕ *www.sevengrandsd.com.*

BREWPUBS
Bivouac Ciderworks

BREWPUBS | In a town dominated by beer, craft ciders offer a refreshing alternative to the typical IPA. True to its name, Bivouac's design incorporates an open front and an interior seemingly held together by ropes—the rear table with suspended bench seating is a favorite of larger parties. Cider aficionados and newcomers alike can sample a wide range of styles through customizable flights, while skeptics can stick to the selection of wine, craft beer, and fruit-based cocktails (think brandy). The Filipino-influenced menu, much of it gluten-free and vegan, is as big a draw as the cider. ✉ *3986 30th St., North Park* ☎ *619/725–0844* ⊕ *www. bivouaccider.com* ⊘ *Closed Mon.*

Modern Times Flavordome

BREWPUBS | A lively spot along North Park's bustling 30th Street, Modern Times's tasting room balances tasteful kitsch with a no-nonsense approach to good beer. Decorated with '80s-era VHS boxes and a Yoda mosaic made from old floppy disks, Modern Times boasts 20 taps of rotating standard and seasonal brews, from their palate-pleasing Ice pilsner to more adventurous brews like their tropical cucumber-guava-lime gose. ✉ *3000 Upas St., North Park* ☎ *619/269– 5222* ⊕ *www.moderntimesbeer.com.*

🎭 Performing Arts

Observatory North Park

CONCERTS | Formerly North Park Theatre, the Observatory North Park has 90 years of history inside its ornate and beautiful walls. It's a top-tier destination for touring musical acts, hosting shows several nights a week. ✉ *2891 University Ave., North Park* ☎ *619/239–8836* ⊕ *www. observatorysd.com.*

🛍 Shopping

North Park, east of Hillcrest, is a hipster's paradise, with resale shops, trendy boutiques, and stores that sell mostly handcrafted items.

BOOKS

★ Verbatim Books

BOOKS | Visible from blocks away, thanks to its large mural paying homage to Stephen King, Verbatim Books boasts an inventory of more than 35,000 books in its wide-open wonderland of the printed word. Visually stunning inside and out—decked with chandeliers and the store's name spelled out in books on its back wall (which also has a mysterious, colorful door)—the shop carries everything from classics to cookbooks to supernatural and metaphysical volumes, in addition to maintaining a zine library for those interested in DIY publishers. ✉ *3793 30th St., North Park* ☎ *619/501–7466* ⊕ *verbatimbooks.com* ⊗ *Closed Tues.*

CLOTHING AND ACCESSORIES

Overload

MIXED CLOTHING | Get the latest brands of footwear, streetwear, skateboards, and accessories at this edgy skate shop. ✉ *3827 30th St., North Park* ☎ *619/819–6143* ⊕ *www.shopoverload.com.*

HOME ACCESSORIES AND GIFTS

★ Artelexia

SOUVENIRS | Browse the colorful selection of Mexican gifts, cooking supplies, and decor at this inviting local boutique. ✉ *3803 Ray St., North Park* ☎ *619/501–6381* ⊕ *www.artelexia.com.*

★ Pigment

SOUVENIRS | This beautifully styled shop carries a wide variety of design-conscious goods for the home, including geometric print pillows, outdoor bistro chairs, and home bar accessories. In Pigment's plant lab, you can build your own terrariums, which make great souvenirs. ✉ *3801 30th St., North Park* ☎ *619/501–6318* ⊕ *www.shoppigment.com.*

South Park and Golden Hill

The South Park neighborhood is actually on the east side of Balboa Park (it makes a backward L shape around the park's southeast corner), but it's south of North Park, hence the name. The tree-lined neighborhood is largely residential but its collection of interesting galleries, boutiques, and restaurants makes for a nice stroll.

Located below Balboa Park, Golden Hill is at the bottom of the aforementioned backward L shape. Within easy walking distance of both downtown and Balboa Park, it's one of the city's most architecturally diverse neighborhoods with Victorian, Craftsman, and colonial revival homes lining its streets.

🍴 Restaurants

★ Buona Forchetta

$ | **ITALIAN** | **FAMILY** | A golden-domed pizza oven, named Sofia after the owner's daughter, delivers authentic Neapolitan-style pizza to fans who often line up for patio tables at this dog- and kid-friendly Italian restaurant in South Park. Pizzas make a meal or can be shared, but don't miss the equally delicious appetizers, heaping salads, or fresh pastas, and be sure to save room for some *dolci.* **Known for:** house-made sangria; bubbly Neapolitan-style pizzas; bustling patio. ⑤ *Average main: $17* ✉ *3001 Beech St., South Park* ☎ *619/381–4844* ⊕ *buonaforchettasd.com.*

Eclipse Chocolate Bar & Bistro

$ | **AMERICAN** | This local bistro and chocolatier sells flavored bars, truffles, cupcakes, and many other confections, as well as breakfast favorites (buttermilk pancakes or avocado Benedict) and mains that are good at any point in the day—pulled pork and grits or mascarpone-stuffed meatballs—plus beer and wine. The owner of this popular brunch spot won a special chocolate episode of Food Network's *Guy's Grocery Games* in 2017. **Known for:** build-your-own chocolate bar nights; there's a little bit of vanilla, caramel, or cacao worked into every dish; add a chocolate pairing to your glass of wine for $1. ⑤ *Average main: $16* ✉ *2145 Fern St., South Park* ☎ *619/578–2984* ⊕ *www.eclipsechocolate.com* ⊘ *No dinner Sun.*

Kindred

$ | **VEGETARIAN** | Pink paisley wallpaper and marble-topped tables stand among skull prints, Gothic art, a heavy metal soundtrack and a giant ram's head in this busy restaurant-bar—emphasis on the bar. The vegan menu is not what you might expect, and the bold flavors and satisfying portions will please both herbivores and carnivores alike. **Known for:** Memphis barbecue jackfruit sandwich; potent tiki drinks; weekend brunch. ⑤ *Average main: $15* ✉ *1503 30th St., South Park* ☎ *619/546–9653* ⊕ *www. barkindred.com* ⊘ *No lunch weekdays.*

Kingfisher

$$$ | **VIETNAMESE** | Stepping into Kingfisher for the first time is a surefire way to stimulate the senses, from the elegantly kitschy green, tropical decor with gold trim to the rush of herbaceous scents that come wafting your way. The restaurant's menu of sharable items features both protein-heavy dishes (smoked duck, striped seabass) to vegetarian-friendly options with an abundance of umami flavors (mushroom congee, smoked eggplant), all of which pair nicely with a menu of cocktails that range from light and refreshing to spirit-heavy and bold—if you prefer to skip the booze altogether, don't hesitate to ask. **Known for:** potent, refreshing cocktails with a Southeast Asian twist; wild mushroom congee; smoked dry aged duck. ⑤ *Average main: $37* ✉ *2469 Broadway, Golden Hill* ☎ *619/432–1014* ⊕ *kingfishersd.com* ⊘ *Closed Tues. No lunch.*

Piacere Mio

$ | **ITALIAN** | Fresh homemade pasta served as the diner wants it is the mantra at this cozy Italian restaurant. Opt for indoor seating, which offers a charming, old-world feel, with warm lighting, wood beam ceilings, and exposed brick. **Known for:** make-it-your-own pasta menu; sizable portions; traditional antipasti plates. ⑤ *Average main: $17* ✉ *1947 Fern St., South Park* ☎ *619/794–2543* ⊕ *www. piaceremiosd.com.*

Coffee and Quick Bites

Dark Horse Coffee Roasters

$ | **AMERICAN** | There are six spots across San Diego including this one on the corner of Juniper and Fern in the heart of South Park. Open daily, this is the place to come for coffee, hot or iced, and a special treat—a scoop of one of the innovative flavors from Mutual Friend Ice Cream like lemon almond cake with a raspberry swirl or haupia haole pie. **Known for:** vegan mini-doughnuts; Mutual Friend Ice Cream; full coffee service until 5:30 pm daily. ⑤ *Average main: $4* ✉ *3004 Juniper St., South Park* ☎ *619/230–5307* ⊕ *www.darkhorsecoffeeroasters.com.*

Nightlife

★ Mothership

COCKTAIL LOUNGES | Launched by the team behind Kindred, Mothership is a cocktail experience right out of the most fantastical science fiction. Its interior has to be seen to be believed, half of it resembling a cinematic spaceship and the other half looking like the alien worlds it landed on, while the drinks they serve—with names referencing the likes of *Alien* and *Star Trek*—are dazzling and delicious tiki concoctions. Reservations open up 21 days in advance but fill up fast, but bar seating is first-come, first-served. ✉ *2310 30th St., South Park* ☎ *619/630–2187* ⊕ *mothershiptrip.com.*

Shopping

South Park's tree-lined 30th, Juniper, and Fern Streets are wonderful for a shopping stroll. Local boutiques have everything from eco-friendly fashions to craft supplies and home decor.

★ The Book Catapult

BOOKS | FAMILY | This exceptional bookstore offers well-curated local interest materials, best sellers, and an excellent children's section. Puzzle enthusiasts will appreciate the unique jigsaw selection, guaranteed to keep you challenged. Don't miss the back room with its selection of local clothing and gifts. ⊠ *3010-B Juniper St., South Park* ☎ *619/795–3780* ⊕ *thebookcatapult.com.*

★ Gold Leaf

HOUSEWARES | This home-decor shop is run by a husband-and-wife duo. There's furniture, kitchenware, jewelry, greeting cards, and a kids' section. ⊠ *2225 30th St., South Park* ☎ *619/738–8120* ⊕ *www. goldleafsouthpark.com.*

Thread and Seed

WOMEN'S CLOTHING | This indie boutique in South Park's historic 30th & Fern building is filled with quirky art, jewelry, gifts, and clothing from emerging designers and artists using recycled or repurposed materials. This is a great place to pick up souvenirs if you're into supporting local: 75% of the designers are from California. ⊠ *2220 Fern St., South Park* ☎ *858/433–0950* ⊕ *www.threadandseed.com.*

Vinyl Junkies Record Shack

MUSIC | A converted Craftsman house in a mixed residential and business area of South Park, Vinyl Junkies Record Shack is easy to spot, due to its bright orange walls inside and colorful murals outside. Spun off of a seasonal pop-up record swap event, Vinyl Junkies' brick-and-mortar shop is an appealing visit for both diehard record collectors and casual browsers alike. Its selection is well curated, and its walls are lined with an impressive array of eye candy, from classic show posters to vintage record players. DJs regularly spin during shopping hours, and on weekends the store hosts live performances outside.

■**TIP→ Spend a little time in the adjacent Digger's Den, where every record is priced $5 or under.** ⊠ *2235 Fern St., South Park* ☎ *619/794–2399* ⊕ *www.vinyljunkies.net.*

Chapter 6

MISSION BAY AND THE BEACHES

Updated by
Claire Deeks van der Lee

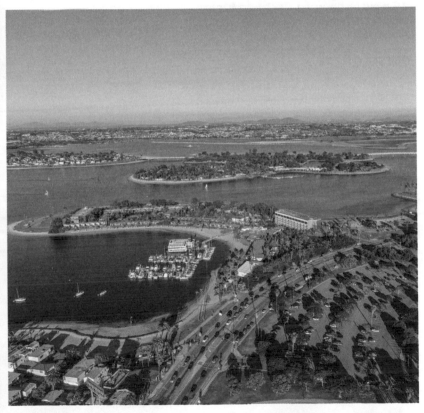

👁 Sights	🍴 Restaurants	🛏 Hotels	👜 Shopping	🍸 Nightlife
★★★★★	★★★☆☆	★★★★☆	★☆☆☆☆	★★★☆☆

NEIGHBORHOOD SNAPSHOT

TOP EXPERIENCES

■ **Sun and sand:** With sand stretching as far as the eye can see, Mission and Pacific beaches represent the classic Southern California beach experience.

■ **Bustling boardwalk:** Twentysomethings partying at the bars, families grilling in front of their vacation homes, and kids playing in the sand—take in the scene with a stroll along the Mission Beach boardwalk.

■ **Bay-side delights:** A quiet respite from the nearby beaches, Mission Bay is ringed with peaceful pathways, playgrounds, and parks.

■ **Get out on the water:** Catch a wave, paddle a kayak, or rev a Jet Ski at this irresistible water-sports playground.

GETTING HERE

SeaWorld, Mission Bay, and Mission and Pacific beaches are all served by public bus routes 8 and 9. Many local hotels offer shuttle service to and from SeaWorld. There is a free parking lot at Belmont Park, although it can quickly fill during busy times.

PLANNING YOUR TIME

You may not find a visit to SeaWorld fulfilling unless you spend at least half a day; a full day is recommended.

Belmont Park is open daily, but not all its rides are open year-round.

The Mission Beach boardwalk and the miles of trails around Mission Bay are great for a leisurely bike ride.

On foggy days, particularly in late spring or early summer, the beaches can be overcast in the morning with the fog burning off as the day wears on.

THE BEACHES

■ The long expanse of sand running from **Mission Beach** to **Pacific Beach** is some of the city's most popular. There is an energetic atmosphere among the throngs of beachgoers—the boardwalks bustle with activity, and surf culture reigns supreme.

■ The 2-mile stretch of sand that makes up Mission Beach extends north to Belmont Park and draws huge crowds on summer weekends. The boardwalk and volleyball courts are great for people-watching.

■ Pacific Beach picks up where Mission Beach leaves off and extends north to Crystal Pier. Parking is tough, but the scene on Ocean Front Walk and the party atmosphere may just be worth it. Technically part of Pacific Beach, a portion of **Tourmaline Surfing Park** is designated for surfing only. If you're looking for post-beach drinks, Garnet Street is home to the neighborhood's liveliest bars.

MISSION BAY WARNINGS

Swimmers at Mission Bay should note signs warning about water pollution; on occasions when heavy rains or other events cause pollution, swimming is strongly discouraged.

Mission Bay and the surrounding beaches are the aquatic playground of San Diego. The choice of activities available is astonishing, and the perfect weather makes you want to get out there and play. If you're craving downtime after all the activity, there are plenty of peaceful spots to relax and simply soak up the sunshine.

Mission Bay welcomes visitors with its protected waters and countless opportunities for fun. The 4,600-acre Mission Bay Park is the place for water sports like sailing, stand-up paddleboarding, and waterskiing. With 19 miles of beaches and grassy areas, it's also a great place for a picnic. And if you have kids, don't miss SeaWorld, one of San Diego's most popular attractions.

Heading west on Mission Bay Drive to the ocean, the Giant Dipper roller coaster rises into view, welcoming visitors to the Belmont Park amusement park and to Mission Beach. Mission Boulevard runs north along a two-block-wide strip embraced by the Pacific Ocean on the west and the bay on the east. Mission Beach is a famous and lively fun zone for families and young people both; if it isn't party time at the moment, it will be five minutes from now. The pathways in this area are lined with vacation homes, many for rent by the week or month. Those fortunate enough to live here year-round have the bay as their front yard, with wide sandy beaches, volleyball courts, and—less of an advantage—an endless stream of sightseers on the sidewalk.

North of Mission Beach is the college-packed party town of Pacific Beach, or "PB" as locals call it. The laid-back vibe of this surfer's mecca draws in free-spirited locals who roam the streets on skateboards and beach cruisers, in the local uniform of board shorts, bikinis, and baseball caps. Lining the main strip of Grand and Garnet Avenues are tattoo parlors, smoke shops, vintage stores, and coffeehouses. The energy level peaks during happy hour, when PB's cluster of nightclubs, bars, and restaurants open their doors to those ready to party.

Sights

Bahia Belle Cruises

OTHER ATTRACTION | Board this restored historic stern-wheeler for a scenic cruise of Mission Bay, with alternating departure days from the Bahia or the Catamaran Resort Hotels. There are two sailings per evening—the earlier Sightseeing Cruise is all ages while the later After Dark Sailing is strictly for those over 21. Enjoy music on board as well as *Belle*'s full bar during the 45-minute round-trip tour. ⊠ *998 W. Mission Bay Dr., Mission Bay* ⊕ *www.bahiahotel.com/bahia-belle*

Belmont Park, an amusement park between the bay and Mission Beach boardwalk, is home to lovely sunsets and the Giant Dipper Roller Coaster.

⌨ *$25; $15 for guests of Bahia and Catamaran hotels ⊗ Closed Dec.–Feb.*

★ Belmont Park
AMUSEMENT PARK/CARNIVAL | FAMILY |
The once-abandoned amusement park between the bay and Mission Beach boardwalk is now a shopping, dining, and recreation complex. Twinkling lights outline the Giant Dipper, an antique wooden roller coaster on which screaming thrill seekers ride more than 2,600 feet of track and 13 hills (riders must be at least 4 feet, 2 inches tall). Created in 1925 and listed on the National Register of Historic Places, this is one of the few old-time roller coasters left in the United States.

Other Belmont Park attractions include miniature golf, a laser maze, video arcade, bumper cars, a tilt-a-whirl, and an antique carousel. The zipline thrills as it soars over the crowds below, while the rock wall challenges both junior climbers and their elders.

The **Plunge** indoor swimming pool was the largest—60 feet by 125 feet—saltwater pool in the world when it opened in 1925; it's had freshwater since 1951. Johnny Weismuller and Esther Williams are among the stars who were captured on celluloid swimming here. After an extensive renovation, the pool now features expansive windows and a retractable glass ceiling, and is once again a San Diego landmark. Open to the public, its many lap lanes and a large inflatable obstacle course make the Plunge a popular choice for athletes and recreational swimmers alike. ✉ *3146 Mission Blvd., Mission Bay* ☎ *858/488–1549 for rides* ⊕ *www.belmontpark.com* ⌨ *Unlimited ride day package from $60, individual ride tickets available from $10; Plunge pass from $15.*

★ Crystal Pier
BEACH | Stretching out into the ocean from the end of Garnet Avenue, Crystal Pier is Pacific Beach's landmark. In the 1920s, it was a classic amusement park complete with ballroom. Today, it's mainly comprised of a series of quaint cottages that are all a part of the Crystal Pier

Planning a Day at the Beaches and Bay

A day spent at Mission Bay or the surrounding beaches can be as active or leisurely as you like.

If you want to play in the water, the bay is a great place to kayak, sail, or try some stand-up paddleboarding. If you're into surfing, be sure to check out the waves at **Crystal Pier** in Pacific Beach.

If you want to keep active on land, the Bayside Walk and Bike Path is a great place to jog or ride along the bay. Beach Cruiser bike rentals are widely available. For a more leisurely stroll and some people-watching, head to the **Mission Beach boardwalk**. At the south end of Mission Beach try your hand at some typically Californian beach volleyball.

If you'd rather take it easy, just find a spot to lay out your towel anywhere along Mission or Pacific Beach and soak up the sun. If you tire of the sand, enjoy a picnic at one of the many grassy spots throughout **Mission Bay Park** or enjoy the view from one of the restaurants at Paradise Point Resort and Spa. As the day winds down, the happy-hour crowd is just heating up along Garnet Avenue in Pacific Beach. Alternatively, head to the Bahia Resort Hotel, where you can catch the *Bahia Belle* for a cruise around the bay.

If you are traveling with kids, a day at **SeaWorld** should be high on your list. There is plenty of family fun beyond SeaWorld, too. The protected beaches of the bay are popular spots for youngsters. The well-paved, peaceful Bayside Walk and Bike Path winds past picnic tables, grassy areas, and playgrounds, making it an ideal family spot. For a more lively contrast, cross the street to reach the Mission Beach Boardwalk, a classic boardwalk popular with young, hip surfers. At the south end lies **Belmont Park**, which includes an amusement park, restaurants, and the Giant Dipper wooden roller coaster.

Hotel. Guests have access to fishing, as well as the intersecting Mission Beach boardwalk. For those that aren't hotel guests, you may access the pier through a side gate from 8 am to sunset. ✉ *Pacific Beach ✛ At end of Garnet Ave.*

Fiesta Island
BEACH | FAMILY | The most undeveloped area of Mission Bay Park, this is popular with bird-watchers (there's a large protected nesting site for the California tern at the northern tip of the island) as well as with dog owners, because it's the only place in the park where pets can run free. Firepits are scattered across the island for public use. In July the annual Over-the-Line Tournament, a competition involving a unique local version of

softball, attracts thousands of players and oglers. ✉ *Access from East Mission Bay Dr., Mission Bay.*

★ Mission Bay Park
BEACH | San Diego's monument to sports and fitness, this 4,600-acre aquatic park has 27 miles of shoreline including 19 miles of sandy beaches. Playgrounds and picnic areas abound on the beaches and low, grassy hills. On weekday evenings, joggers, bikers, and skaters take over. In the daytime, swimmers, water-skiers, paddleboarders, anglers, and boaters—some in single-person kayaks, others in crowded powerboats—vie for space in the water. ✉ *2688 E. Mission Bay Dr., Mission Bay ✛ Off I–5 at Exit 22, E. Mission Bay Dr.* ☎ *858/581–7602 park*

Mission Bay
and the Beaches

PACIFIC OCEAN

Tourmalin Surfing Park
Tourmaline Surfing Beach

Palisades Park

Pacific Beach Park

Pacific Beach/
North Pacific Beach

Mission Beach

MISSION BEACH

Giant Dipper Roller Coaster

Bonita Bay

Mariners Basin

Entrance Channel

Ocean Beach
Ocean Beach Park

Dog Beach

Kate O Sessions Memorial Park

PACIFIC BEACH

Pacific Beach Community Park

La Jolla Blvd
Mission Blvd

Archer St.
Agate St.
Sapphire St.
Tourmaline St.
Davies St.
Opal St.
Loring St.
Cass St.
Wilbur Ave.
Beryl St.
Law St.
Chalcedony St.
Missouri St.
Diamond St.
Emerald St.
Felspar St.
Garnet Ave.
Hornblend St.
Grand Ave.
Thomas Ave.
Reed Ave.
Olivet Ave.
Pacific Beach Dr.

Bayard St.
Everts St.
Fanuel St.
Gresham St.
Haines St.
Ingraham St.
Lamont St.
Jewell St.
Kendall St.
Lamont St.
Morrell St.
Olney St.
Everts St.
Gresham St.
Haines St.
Ingraham St.
Shasta St.
Sequoia St.
Riviera Dr.

Fanuel Street Park
Sail Bay
La Playa Ave.
Moorland Dr.

CROWN POINT

EAST SKI ISLAND
WEST SKI ISLAND

Santa Clara Cove
San Juan Cove
Santa Barbara Cove

Ocean Front Boardwalk
Mission Blvd

MISSION BAY

Model Yacht Pond

Mission Bay

W Mission Bay Dr.
Quivira Rd.
Quivira Basin
Quivira Way

Ingraham St.
Sunset Cliffs Blvd
South Shores Rd.
W Mission Bay

San Diego River Floodway

Dusty Rhodes Park

MIDWAY

W Point Loma Blvd
Abbott St.
Voltaire St.
Muir Ave.
Long Branch Ave.
Brighton Ave.
Cape May Ave.
Saratoga Ave.
Lotus
Newport Ave.
Soto St.
Colvier Park

Nimitz Blvd
Mientone St.
Montalo Ave.
Valeta St.
Bernard

Cleator Community Park

0   1,500ft
0   500m

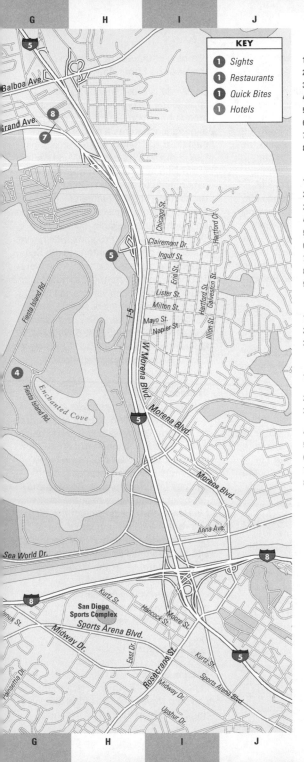

Sights ▼

1	*Bahia Belle* Cruises	**D6**
2	Belmont Park	**C6**
3	Crystal Pier	**B3**
4	Fiesta Island	**G5**
5	Mission Bay Park	**H3**
6	Mission Beach Boardwalk	**C7**
7	SeaWorld San Diego	**F7**
8	Vacation Isle	**E5**

Restaurants ▼

1	Cannonball	**C6**
2	Draft at Belmont Park	**C6**
3	The Fishery	**C1**
4	JRDN	**B3**
5	Moe's	**C4**
6	Pacific Beach Fish Shop	**E2**
7	Rubio's Coastal Grill	**G2**
8	Sushi Ota	**G2**
9	Waterbar	**B3**

Quick Bites ▼

1	The Baked Bear	**B3**
2	Kono's Café	**B3**
3	Mission + Garnet Food Hall	**C3**

Hotels ▼

1	Catamaran Resort Hotel and Spa	**C3**
2	Crystal Pier Hotel & Cottages	**B3**
3	Hyatt Regency Mission Bay Spa and Marina	**E7**
4	Pacific Terrace Hotel	**B2**
5	Paradise Point Resort & Spa	**E5**
6	Surfer Beach Hotel	**C3**
7	TOWER23	**B3**
8	The Wayfarer	**C3**

ranger's office ⊕ www.sandiego.gov/ park-and-recreation ✉ Free.

★ Mission Beach Boardwalk

BEACH | The cement pathway lining the sand from the southern end of Mission Beach north to Pacific Beach is always bustling with activity. Cyclists ping the bells on their beach cruisers to pass walkers out for a stroll alongside the oceanfront homes. Vacationers kick back on their patios, while friends play volleyball in the sand. The activity picks up alongside Belmont Park, where people stop to check out the action at the amusement park and beach bars. ⊠ *Mission Beach ⊹ Alongside sand from Mission Beach Park to Pacific Beach.*

SeaWorld San Diego

THEME PARK | **FAMILY** | Spread over 189 tropically landscaped bay-front acres, SeaWorld is one of the world's largest marine-life amusement parks. The majority of its exhibits are walk-through marine environments like Shark Encounter, where guests walk through a 57-foot acrylic tube and come face-to-face with a variety of sharks that call the 280,000-gallon habitat home. Turtle Reef offers an incredible up-close encounter with the green sea turtle, while the moving sidewalk at Penguin Encounter whisks you through a colony of nearly 300 penguins.

The park also wows with its recent heavy investment in adventure rides like the Electric Eel, a shocking multi-launch coaster that sends riders twisting forward and backward 150 feet in the air at speeds reaching 60 mph, and the Emperor, a floorless dive coaster with a 14-story face-down vertical drop. The newest addition is Arctic Rescue, a straddle coaster simulating a perilous animal rescue mission aboard a snowmobile at speeds of 40 mph. For a comparatively milder thrill, Journey to Atlantis water coaster splashes down a 60-foot plunge. Younger children will enjoy the rides,

climbing structures, and splash pads at the Sesame Street Bay of Play.

SeaWorld is most famous for its large-arena entertainments, but this is an area in transition. The park's latest orca experience features a nature-inspired backdrop and demonstrates orca behaviors in the wild, part of SeaWorld's efforts to refocus its orca program toward education and conservation. Other live-entertainment shows feature dolphins, sea lions and otters. Several upgraded animal encounters are available including the Dolphin Interaction Program, which gives guests the chance to interact with SeaWorld's bottlenose dolphins in the water. The hour-long program (20 minutes in the water), during which visitors can feed, touch, and give behavior signals, costs $215. ⊠ *500 SeaWorld Dr., near west end of I–8, Mission Bay ☎ 619/222–4732 ⊕ www.seaworld.com ✉ $110; advanced purchase discounts available online; parking $30.*

Vacation Isle

BEACH | Ingraham Street bisects this island, providing two distinct experiences for visitors. The west side is taken up by the Paradise Point Resort & Spa, but you don't have to be a guest to enjoy the hotel's lushly landscaped grounds and bay-front restaurants. Boaters and Jet-Skiers congregate near the launch at Ski Beach on the east side of the island, where there's a parking lot as well as picnic areas and restrooms. Ski Beach is the site of the annual Bayfair boat races held every September. At the model yacht pond on the south side of the island, children and young-at-heart adults take part year-round in motorized miniature boat races. ⊠ *Mission Bay.*

 Beaches

Mission Beach

BEACH | **FAMILY** | With an amusement park and rows of eclectic local shops, this 2-mile-long beach has a carnival vibe and is the closest thing you'll find to Coney Island on the West Coast. It's lively year-round but draws a huge crowd on hot summer days. A wide boardwalk paralleling the beach is popular with walkers, joggers, skateboarders, and bicyclists. To escape the crowds, head to South Mission Beach. It attracts surfers, swimmers, and volleyball players, who often play competitive pickup games on the courts near the north jetty. The water near the Belmont Park roller coaster can be a bit rough but makes for good body-boarding and bodysurfing. For free parking, you can try for a spot on the street, but your best bets are the two big lots at Belmont Park. **Amenities:** lifeguards; parking (no fee); showers; toilets. **Best for:** swimming; surfing; walking. ⊠ *3000 Mission Blvd., Mission Bay ✛ Parking near roller coaster at West Mission Bay Dr.* ⊕ *www.sandiego.gov/lifeguards/ beaches/mb.*

Pacific Beach/North Pacific Beach

BEACH | This beach, known for attracting a young college-age crowd and surfers, runs from the northern end of Mission Beach to Crystal Pier. The scene here is lively on weekends, with nearby restaurants, beach bars, and nightclubs providing a party atmosphere. In PB (as the locals call it) Sundays are known as "Sunday Funday," and pub crawls can last all day, although drinking is no longer allowed on the beach. The mood changes just north of the pier at North Pacific Beach, which attracts families and surfers. Although not quite pillowy, the sand at both beaches is nice and soft, which makes for great sunbathing and sandcastle building.

■ TIP➔ **Kelp and flies can be a problem on this stretch, so choose your spot wisely.**

Parking at Pacific Beach can also be a challenge. A few coveted free angle parking spaces are available along the boardwalk, but you'll most likely have to look for spots in the surrounding neighborhood.

Beach Bonfires

Just because the sun went down doesn't mean it's time to go home. Nothing compares to sitting around a crackling fire as the evening breeze ushers in whiffs of the sea. Fires are allowed only in portable propane fueled fire devices or in city-provided fire rings, which you can find at Mission Beach and Pacific Beach; they are also available in Ocean Beach and Coronado Beach. Revelers snap up ring slots quickly in summer; stake your claim early by filling one with wood and setting your gear nearby.

Amenities: food and drink; lifeguards; parking (no fee); showers, toilets. **Best for:** partiers; swimming; surfing. ⊠ *4500 Ocean Blvd., Pacific Beach* ⊕ *www.sand-iego.gov/lifeguards/beaches/pb.*

Tourmaline Surfing Park

BEACH | Offering slow waves and frequent winds, this is one of the most popular beaches for surfers. For windsurfing and kiteboarding, it's only sailable with northwest winds. The 175-space parking lot at the foot of Tourmaline Street normally fills to capacity by midday. Just like Pacific Beach, Tourmaline has soft, tawny-color sand, but when the tide is in the beach becomes quite narrow, making finding a good sunbathing spot a bit of a challenge. Parking will be difficult on evenings and weekends. **Amenities:** seasonal lifeguards; parking (no fee); showers; toilets. **Best for:** windsurfing; surfing. ⊠ *600 Tourmaline St., Pacific Beach.*

🍴 Restaurants

This sprawling area is all about great views of the water, sandy beaches, and relaxation. Most of the restaurants here are casual spots that diners can visit in T-shirts, shorts, and flip-flops. Food is

Talking Tacos

Even though terms like taco, burrito, enchilada, and tostada are as common as macaroni and cheese to San Diegans, don't count on any residents to agree on where to find the best ones. That's because tacos are as individual as spaghetti sauce and come in endless variations from small, authentic Mexico City–style tacos to Cal-Mex versions in crunchy shells topped with cheddar cheese.

The most traditional style of taco features a small soft corn tortilla pressed from corn masa dough and filled with shredded beef, carne asada (roasted beef), braised tongue in green sauce, spicy marinated pork, or deep-fried fish or seafood. Tortillas made from white flour are out there, too, but they're not nearly as tasty.

Garnishes usually include a drizzle of salsa and a squeeze of tart Mexican lime (a small citrus similar to the key lime that's juicier than the large lime commonly found in the United States), along with chopped cilantro and onion. Whole radishes topped with lime juice and a sprinkle of salt are served on the side.

---

similarly laid-back. Burgers and tacos are easy to find, but so are sushi, Mexican, and Thai food. Many of the restaurants here are bars at heart.

Streets closest to the ocean in Pacific Beach, San Diego's largest beach community, can be party central for visitors and locals who jam-pack a wide range of restaurants and bars reflecting the casual surf and beach culture.

Cannonball
$$ | **SUSHI** | While the panoramic ocean view is the star attraction at this rooftop restaurant next to Belmont Park, the tasty sushi and share plates are a pleasant surprise for such a touristy locale. Lunch and dinner service bookend a popular afternoon happy hour. **Known for:** incredible ocean views; large specialty sushi rolls; summer crowds. $ *Average main: $22* ⊠ *3105 Ocean Front Walk, Mission Beach* ☎ *858/228–9304* ⊕ *www. cannonballsd.com* ☯ *No lunch weekdays*.

Draft at Belmont Park
$ | **AMERICAN** | Patrons can have expansive seaside views and choose from over 68 craft beer selections, too, at this spacious Belmont Park bar and restaurant.

The relaxed, boardwalk atmosphere—and giant wall-size television screen—makes it a perfect spot for lounging after riding some waves at Mission Beach, or to cool down after soaking in some sun. **Known for:** all-day dining with Sunday brunch; huge draft beer selection; people-watching on the boardwalk. $ *Average main: $19* ⊠ *3105 Ocean Front Walk, Mission Beach* ☎ *858/228–9305* ⊕ *www. draftsandiego.com*.

The Fishery
$$$$ | **SEAFOOD** | Nestled in a quieter, less-touristy section of Pacific Beach, The Fishery is a local favorite for high-end, sustainable seafood. With a fish market incorporated into the restaurant's design, the freshness of their ingredients is proudly on display, and the extensive, albeit pricey, menu offers tartare, sushi rolls, and other raw bar favorites alongside excellently cooked preparations of spot prawns, crusted halibut, and a delicious bouillabaisse. **Known for:** the impressive Grand Seafood Tower; sustainably sourced menu; engaging wine list and cocktail selection. $ *Average main: $52* ⊠ *5040 Cass St., Pacific Beach*

☎ 858/272–9985 ⊕ www.thefishery.com ⊗ Closed Mon. and Tues.

JRDN

$$$ | ECLECTIC | This chic ocean-facing restaurant (pronounced Jordan), in the boutique TOWER23 Hotel, offers a diverse menu including a sushi and raw bar, and inspired California cuisine. Lunch and weekend brunch are very popular, and on Friday and Saturday the bar is jammed with under-thirty types eager to see and be seen. **Known for:** boozy weekend brunch and lunch with a view; smaller shared plates and family-style sides; upscale option on the beach boardwalk. ⑤ Average main: $36 ⊠ TOWER23 Hotel, 723 Felspar St., Pacific Beach ☎ 858/270–5736 ⊕ www.t23hotel.com/jrdn.

★ Moe's

$$$$ | STEAKHOUSE | An unexpected oasis of elegance among an often too casual Mission Beach, Moe's delivers an unpretentious but classic steak-house experience. Splurge-worthy treats such as Japanese A5 Wagyu or the Bone-In Ribeye are tempered by lighter and more wallet-friendly dishes marked as "Entree Alternatives." Classic cocktail fans will appreciate the extensive martini menu and other tried and true favorites. **Known for:** classic steak-house atmosphere; generous hand-cut steak selections; elegant bar and cocktail service. ⑤ Average main: $48 ⊠ 3768 Mission Blvd., Mission Beach ☎ 858/488–7311 ⊕ www.moesmissionbeach.com ⊗ No lunch.

Pacific Beach Fish Shop

$ | SEAFOOD | FAMILY | Also known as the Fish Shop, this is a favorite among locals. Peruse the customizable menu that lets diners select a type of fish, marinade, and preparation style (grilled or fried, and taco, sandwich, salad, or plate) that suits their tastes. **Known for:** serves local beer; daily fresh fish; fish tacos like the TKO Taco. ⑤ Average main: $17 ⊠ 1775 Garnet Ave., Pacific Beach ☎ 858/483–4746 ⊕ thefishshops.com.

Rubio's Coastal Grill

$ | SEAFOOD | Credited with popularizing fish tacos in the United States, Ralph Rubio brought the Mexican staple to San Diego, opening his first restaurant in Pacific Beach where it still stands today. The original beer-battered fish tacos have fried pollock topped with white sauce, salsa, and cabbage atop a corn tortilla. **Known for:** the original fish taco; Taco Tuesday deals—$1.99 fish taco; $8 lunch specials. ⑤ Average main: $10 ⊠ 4504 E. Mission Bay Dr., Pacific Beach ☎ 858/272–2801 ⊕ www.rubios.com.

★ Sushi Ota

$$ | SUSHI | One fan called it "a notch above amazing"—an accolade not expected for a Japanese eatery wedged in a strip mall in Pacific Beach. But it's a destination for lovers of high-quality, superfresh raw fish from around San Diego and abroad; reservations strongly encouraged. **Known for:** velvety hamachi belly; sea urchin specials; chef's omakase tasting menu. ⑤ Average main: $25 ⊠ 4529 Mission Bay Dr., Pacific Beach ☎ 858/880–8778 ⊕ www.sushi-ota.com ⊗ Closed Mon. No lunch weekends.

★ Waterbar

$$ | SEAFOOD | Occupying a prime ocean-front lot just south of Crystal Pier, the views from the raised dining room are impressive. Throw in an excellent raw bar, a wide selection of shared plates, and a buzzy bar scene and you get Waterbar's "social seafood" concept. **Known for:** "Boardwalk hour" oyster specials; boozy weekend brunch; ocean views. ⑤ Average main: $29 ⊠ 4325 Ocean Blvd., Pacific Beach ☎ 858/888–4343 ⊕ www.waterbarsd.com.

☕ Coffee and Quick Bites

The Baked Bear

$ | BAKERY | FAMILY | This build-your-own ice-cream-sandwich shop a block from Pacific Beach is a local favorite thanks to its homemade cookies and diverse array of ice-cream flavors, from birthday cake to peanut butter fudge. Don't miss out on their hot pressed ice-cream sandwiches! **Known for:** Bear Bowls made of cookies; doughnut ice-cream sandwiches; long lines on summer evenings. ⑤ *Average main: $7 ✉ 4516 Mission Blvd., Suite C, Pacific Beach ☎ 858/886–7433 ⊕ www. thebakedbear.com.*

Kono's Café

$ | **AMERICAN** | **FAMILY** | Surfers, bicyclists, and sun worshippers visiting or living in Pacific Beach line up at the counter of this casual seaside café for hearty breakfasts and lunches. Some chow down inside surrounded by surfing decor, while others watch waves crash from the outdoor patio. **Known for:** huge breakfast portions; local favorite for breakfast burritos; great people-watching along the boardwalk. ⑤ *Average main: $9 ✉ 704 Garnet Ave., Pacific Beach ☎ 858/483–1669 ⊕ www.konoscafe.com ⊘ No dinner.*

Mission + Garnet Food Hall

$ | **ECLECTIC** | On an iconic corner in the heart of Pacific Beach, this former Denny's site has been transformed into a multiconcept quick-serve food collective. Breakfast burritos, custom salad bowls, and churro waffles are just some of the tasty selections available at this highly anticipated spot with more in the pipeline. **Known for:** churro waffles—enough said; nearly round-the-clock food offerings; ultraconvenient location. ⑤ *Average main: $16 ✉ 4505 Mission Blvd., Pacific Beach ⊕ missiongarnet.com ⊘ Hrs vary by establishment but range from early morning to very late at night.*

Hotels

Mission Bay, with its beaches, bike trails, boat-launching ramps, and grassy parks—not to mention SeaWorld—is home to several hotels and resorts that take advantage of the calm waters and (relatively) quiet stretches of sand.

Staying here is a great way to experience the essence of San Diego's "Endless Summer" vibe without sacrificing a fairly central location, but be prepared to pay a premium for the privilege and don't arrive expecting solitude.

Smaller hotels, motels, and hostels can be found nearby in Pacific Beach, many of them directly on the boardwalk; expect few frills beyond the first-rate location.

Mission Beach has fewer hotels but is San Diego's top neighborhood for vacation rentals—both houses and apartments—and can be a great value for families or groups. Staying along this narrow stretch provides easy access to both the ocean and the bay.

Catamaran Resort Hotel and Spa

$$$$ | **RESORT** | **FAMILY** | Tiki torches light the way through grounds thick with tropical foliage to the six two-story buildings and the 14-story high-rise on Mission Bay known for its bayfront location and activities. **Pros:** superb bay-front location; some rooms have bay views; many activities for kids. **Cons:** common areas and some rooms in need of renovating; inconsistency in room quality between renovated versus outdated rooms; popular wedding and event venue can get busy. ⑤ *Rooms from: $530 ✉ 3999 Mission Blvd., Mission Beach ☎ 858/488–1081 ⊕ www.catamaran-resort.com ⇄ 310 rooms ⦿ No Meals ⊘ $36 resort fee.*

Crystal Pier Hotel & Cottages

$$$ | **HOTEL** | **FAMILY** | Rustic little oases with a charm all their own, the beachy cottages may lack some of the amenities of comparably priced hotels, but you're paying for character and proximity to the ocean—these lodgings are literally on the pier. **Pros:** ocean views everywhere you look; historic lodgings; free parking. **Cons:** few amenities; reservations fill up fast; busy foot traffic on pier. ⑤ *Rooms from: $380 ✉ 4500 Ocean Blvd., Pacific Beach*

☎ *800/748–5894* ⊕ *www.crystalpier.com* 🛏 *30 rooms* ⦿ *No Meals.*

Hyatt Regency Mission Bay Spa and Marina

$$$ | **RESORT** | **FAMILY** | This bayside property has many desirable amenities, including balconies with excellent views of the garden, bay, ocean, or swimming pool courtyard. **Pros:** proximity to water sports; 120-foot waterslides in pools, plus kiddie slide; several suite configurations good for families. **Cons:** daily resort fee; not centrally located; some common areas and bay building rooms are in need of updates. ⑤ *Rooms from: $409* ✉ *1441 Quivira Rd., Mission Bay* ☎ *619/224–1234, 800/233–1234* ⊕ *www.hyatt.com* 🛏 *429 rooms* ⦿ *No Meals* ☞ *$35 resort fee.*

Pacific Terrace Hotel

$$$$ | **HOTEL** | Travelers love this terrific beachfront hotel and the ocean views from most rooms as well as the pool; it's a perfect place for watching sunsets over the Pacific. **Pros:** beach views; large rooms; friendly service. **Cons:** busy and sometimes noisy area; expensive in peak season; resort fee. ⑤ *Rooms from: $699* ✉ *610 Diamond St., Pacific Beach* ☎ *858/581–3500, 800/344–3370* ⊕ *www.pacificterrace.com* 🛏 *73 rooms* ⦿ *No Meals* ☞ *$18 Resort Fee.*

Paradise Point Resort & Spa

$$$ | **RESORT** | **FAMILY** | Minutes from SeaWorld but hidden in a quiet part of Mission Bay, the beautiful landscape of this 44-acre resort offers plenty of space for families to play and relax. **Pros:** water views; five pools; sprawling grounds. **Cons:** not centrally located; motel-thin walls; parking and resort fees. ⑤ *Rooms from: $474* ✉ *1404 Vacation Rd., Mission Bay* ☎ *858/240–4913* ⊕ *www.paradisepoint.com* 🛏 *462 rooms* ⦿ *No Meals* ☞ *$39 Resort Fee.*

Surfer Beach Hotel

$$$ | **HOTEL** | Choose this place for its great location—right on bustling Pacific Beach—rather than for the amenities.

Pros: beach location; ocean-view rooms; courtyard pool. **Cons:** simple, somewhat dated rooms; no a/c; busy location near bars can get noisy at night. ⑤ *Rooms from: $415* ✉ *711 Pacific Beach Dr., Pacific Beach* ☎ *800/820–5772* ⊕ *www.surferbeachhotel.com* 🛏 *69 rooms* ⦿ *No Meals.*

TOWER23

$$$$ | **HOTEL** | Neo-modern with a beachy vibe, this boutique hotel is a favorite of the young and young-at-heart. **Pros:** beach views; central location; hip decor. **Cons:** no pool; busy area; on-site restaurant and bar often crowded. ⑤ *Rooms from: $569* ✉ *723 Felspar St., Pacific Beach* ☎ *858/270–2323* ⊕ *www.t23hotel.com* 🛏 *44 rooms* ⦿ *No Meals.*

The Wayfarer

$$$$ | **MOTEL** | **FAMILY** | A modern take on the beachfront motel, the Wayfarer hotel (formerly the Blue Sea Beach hotel) has Pacific Beach's best oceanfront pool and a wide choice of room configurations. **Pros:** variety of room and bedding configurations, many newly renovated; oceanfront pool deck; direct beach access. **Cons:** renovations ongoing, some rooms not yet updated; can be expensive in peak season; busy location along boardwalk. ⑤ *Rooms from: $607* ✉ *707 Pacific Beach Dr., Pacific Beach* ☎ *858/488–4700* ⊕ *www.wayfarersd.com* 🛏 *126 rooms* ⦿ *No Meals.*

Nightlife

Outside of Downtown, some of the most vibrant nightlife activity takes place alongside the coast. It's a great place to glug some suds by the boardwalk after a splash in the Pacific.

Pacific Beach's Garnet Street is home to the neighborhood's liveliest bars. It teems with activity from happy hour to last call, thanks to a healthy mix of casual hangouts for college students and recent, upscale upgrades to the otherwise dated beach-bum style of the neighborhood. Surfers meet here for happy hour and college students converge to spend their lost weekends.

BARS

★ The Grass Skirt and Captain's Quarters

COCKTAIL LOUNGES | This pair of speakeasies delights guests with high-theme decor and engaging menus. Entering the nondescript storefront, a sign above the desk in the seemingly cluttered travel agency reads "Other World Travel," but the working kitchen behind offers a hint that all is not as it seems. Accessed through a false freezer door on the left, the Grass Skirt tiki bar serves a wide selection of rum-based tropical cocktails and a menu of shareable pupus in delightfully kitsch surroundings. Venturing through the hidden door to the right transports travelers to the refined Captain's Quarters of a 17th-century sailing vessel where small bites are served alongside a gin-centric cocktail menu. Be sure to reserve a table through the website—these hidden gems are no secret! ✉ *910 Grand Ave., Pacific Beach* ☎ *858/412–5237* ⊕ *www.thegrassskirt. com.*

JRDN

BARS | This contemporary lounge (pronounced "Jordan") occupies the ground floor of Pacific Beach's chicest boutique hotel, TOWER23, and offers a more party-happy neighborhood. Sleek walls of windows and an expansive patio overlook the boardwalk. ✉ *723 Felspar St., Pacific Beach* ☎ *858/270–2323* ⊕ *www.t23hotel. com.*

BREWPUBS

Amplified Ale Works

BREWPUBS | Pacific Beach often veers between the trendy and the tawdry, so this genuine craft brewhouse offers a more casual middle ground. Amplified serves more than a dozen in-house-brewed beers and healthy, vegan-friendly Mediterranean/Californian food at its scenic outdoor beer garden with breathtaking ocean views. ✉ *4150 Mission Blvd., No. 208, Pacific Beach* ☎ *858/270–5222* ⊕ *www.amplifiedales. com.*

🛍 Shopping

Mission Boulevard and Grand and Garnet Avenues are the big shopping thoroughfares in the beach towns. Souvenir shops are scattered up and down the boardwalk, and along Mission Boulevard there are surf, skate, and bike shops, bikini boutiques, and stores selling hip T-shirts, jeans, sandals, and casual apparel. Garnet Avenue is the hot spot for resale boutiques, thrift stores, and pawn shops.

Gone Bananas Beachwear

SWIMWEAR | This store can be a bit overwhelming with thousands of pieces of swimwear lining the walls from floor to ceiling. To make shopping a bit easier, swimsuits have been arranged by color. Browse through mix-and-match pieces from the most fashion-forward swimwear designers like Luli Fama and Indah. It's worth taking the time to peruse what is simply San Diego's best swimwear selection. ✉ *3785 Mission Blvd., Mission Beach* ☎ *858/488–4900* ⊕ *www.gonebananasbeachwear.com.*

★ Pangaea Outpost

SOUVENIRS | This collective houses dozens of local shops under one roof and is a great place to pick up beachy clothing and decor or unique gifts for everyone on your list. ✉ *909 Garnet Ave., Pacific Beach* ☎ *858/581–0555* ⊕ *www.pangaeaoutpost.com.*

Activities

BIKING

A ride along the Mission Beach boardwalk is a great way to take in a classic California scene. Keep in mind this route is more for cruising than hard-core cycling, as the gawkers and crowds often slow foot and bike traffic to a crawl. For a leisurely ride, try Mission Bay. It has a 10-mile loop of cement bike/walking paths around Mission Bay and Fiesta Island bordering big green lawns, children's playgrounds, and picnic spots.

Cheap Rentals (⇨ *see the Surfing section*) has bike rentals, including beach cruisers, tandems, hybrids, and two-wheeled baby carriers. Kids bikes are also available. Demand is high during the busy season (May through September), so call to reserve equipment ahead of time.

DIVING AND SNORKELING
The kelp forests and protected marine areas off the San Diego coast are easily accessible and offer divers ample opportunities to explore. Classes are available for beginners, while experienced divers will appreciate the challenges of local wreck and canyon dives. Water temperatures can be chilly, so check with a local outfitter for the appropriate gear before setting out.

GOLF
Mission Bay Golf Course and Practice Center
GOLF | Making sure people have fun is the number one goal at this city-run golf course. San Diego's only night-lighted course, the final tee time is at 8 pm for 9 holes, and the executive course with par 3 and 4 holes isn't too challenging. The golf course's scenic and breezy location next to Mission Bay helps keep it comfortably cool. They also have a foot golf course, in which a player kicks a soccer ball into a cup in as few shots as possible. ⊠ *2702 N. Mission Bay Dr., Mission Bay* ☏ *858/581–7880* ⊕ *www.sandiego. gov/golf* ⛳ *From $35* ⅃ *18 holes, 2719 yards, par 58.*

SURFING
If you're a beginner, consider paddling in the waves off Mission Beach, Pacific Beach, and Tourmaline Surfing Park. Several outfitters offer year-round surf lessons as well as surf camp in the summer months and during spring break.

Over-the-Line

A giant beach party as much as a sport, Over-the-Line is a form of beach softball played with two teams of just three people each. Every July, over two weekends that include wild beer drinking and partying, the world championships are held on Fiesta Island. Admission is free, but parking is impossible (shuttle buses are available). Check the Old Mission Beach Athletic Club's website (⊕ *www.ombac.org*) for more information.

Cheap Rentals
SURFING | One block from the boardwalk, this place has good daily and weekly prices for surfboards, paddleboards, kayaks, snorkel gear, skateboards, coolers, umbrellas, chairs, and bike rentals, including beach cruisers, tandems, hybrids, and two-wheeled baby carriers. Kids' bikes are also available. Demand is high during the busy season (May through September) so call to reserve equipment ahead of time. ⊠ *3689 Mission Blvd., Mission Beach* ☏ *858/488–9070* ⊕ *www.cheap-rentals. com* ⛳ *Season passes $350, unlimited daytime pass $40, unlimited weekend pass $60.*

WATER SPORTS
Mission Bay and the surrounding beaches provide great access to a variety of water sports, both motorized and nonmotorized. The protected waters of the bay are great for beginners, while the open ocean awaits the adventurous. Rental outfitters are abundant and provide everything from skippered boats to single-person kayaks. Mission Bay has designated open speed areas that are popular with motorboats and Jet Skis, while sailboats and kayakers appreciate the no-wake zones. If you are new to an activity, or just in need of a refresher,

consider taking a lesson through the Mission Bay Aquatic Center.

The popularity of stand-up paddleboarding, or SUP, has grown tremendously in recent years. Devotees love the excellent core workout it provides, while newcomers appreciate how much quicker it is to master than traditional surfing. You can paddleboard pretty much anywhere and many local surf breaks are popular for those with experience, but the calmer waters of Mission Bay offer more stability for beginners.

Jet Skis can be launched from most ocean beaches, although you must ride beyond surf lines, and some beaches have special regulations governing their use. In addition to the open speed areas, Mission Bay has two specially designated areas for personal watercraft or Jet Skis. Take note of the speed limit markers when exiting these zones as enforcement is strict and ticketing is common.

Generally speaking, the western portion of Mission Bay is ideal for sailing and kayaking. The aptly named Sail Bay near the Catamaran Resort has seasonal speed restrictions to reduce summertime motorized use of this popular portion of the bay.

Action Sport Rentals
BOATING | From its facility at Catamaran Resort Hotel and six other sister locations, Action Sport Rentals has paddleboats, kayaks, powerboats, and sailboats from 14 to 22 feet. Thanks to their location on the calm waters of Mission Bay, both are great places for beginners to try paddleboarding. ⊠ *3981 Mission Blvd., Mission Bay* ☎ *619/241–4794* ⊕ *www. actionsportrentals.com.*

Mission Bay Aquatic Center
BOATING | FAMILY | One of the world's largest instructional waterfront facilities offers lessons in wakeboarding, sailing, surfing, waterskiing, rowing, kayaking,

and windsurfing. Equipment rental is also available, but the emphasis is on instruction, and most rentals require a minimum two-hour orientation lesson before you can set out on your own. Reservations are recommended, particularly during the summer. Skippered keelboats and boats for waterskiing or wakeboarding can be hired with reservations. Free parking is available but keep an eye out for signage—not all the parking spots are free or overnight. ⊠ *1001 Santa Clara Pl., Mission Beach* ☎ *858/488–1000* ⊕ *www. mbaquaticcenter.com.*

★ Mission Bay Sportscenter
BOATING | FAMILY | From its location on Santa Clara point, MBSC is a one-stop shop for all types of water-sports fun. This bustling facility rents a large selection of sailboats, motorboats, pedal boats, and kayaks as well as floating water trampolines for the kids, or the kids at heart. For something unique, experience the thrills of hydroflight with a jet board session or test your balance in a paddleboard yoga class. ⊠ *1010 Santa Clara Pl., Mission Bay* ☎ *858/488–1004* ⊕ *missionbaysportcenter.com.*

★ Seaforth Boat Rentals
BOATING | The Mission Bay outpost of this popular rental company offers a wide variety of motorized and nonmotorized craft. Jet Skis, SUPs, kayaks, and fishing skiffs are available alongside sailboats and powerboats of all sizes. For added relaxation, charter a skippered pontoon party boat, some with waterslides for added fun. ⊠ *1641 Quivira Rd., Mission Bay* ☎ *888/834–2628* ⊕ *www.seaforth-boatrental.com.*

Chapter 7

LA JOLLA

WITH CLAIREMONT, KEARNY MESA, AND MIRAMAR

Updated by
Marlise Kast-Myers

 Sights
★★★★☆

 Restaurants
★★★★☆

 Hotels
★★★★☆

 Shopping
★★★☆☆

 Nightlife
★★☆☆☆

LA JOLLA'S BEACHES AND BEYOND

La Jolla is synonymous with beautiful vistas.

La Jolla (pronounced La Hoya) means "the jewel" in Spanish and appropriately describes this small, affluent village and its beaches. Some beautiful coastline can be found here, as well as an elegant upscale atmosphere.

Between North County and the Mission and South bays, La Jolla is easily accessible from Downtown San Diego and North County. It's worth renting a car so you can sample the different beaches along the coast. The town's trademark million-dollar homes won't disappoint either—their cliff-side locations make them an attractive backdrop to the brilliant views of the sea below. Downtown La Jolla is more commercialized, with high-end stores great for browsing. La Jolla Shores, a mile-long beach, lies in the more residential area to the north. Above all, the beach and cove are La Jolla's prime charms—the cove's seals and underwater kelp beds are big draws for kayakers and nature lovers.

THE CLIFFS AT TORREY PINES

The ocean views from the 300-foot-high sandstone cliffs atop Torrey Pines State Natural Reserve are vast and exquisite. To reach the cliffs, hike one of the short trails that leads from the visitor center. Perch along the sandy edge, and let your legs dangle. You may even see dolphins swimming along the shore or surfers riding a break.

BEST BEACHES

Framed in scenic coves and backed by dramatic cliffs, La Jolla's beaches are legendary. Challenging surf breaks, an underwater marine park, and expansive stretches of sand offer something for everyone. Look out over the sparkling waters to see seals frolicking in the surf, or lie back in the sand and watch hang gliders soar overhead.

BLACK'S BEACH

This secluded stretch of sand is considered one of the most beautiful beaches in San Diego. Black's Beach was clothing-optional for many years; although nudity is now prohibited by law, many people still shed their suits whenever the authorities are out of sight.

CHILDREN'S POOL

This shallow bay was once a great place to bring the kids to swim. Nowadays, it's the best place on the coast to view harbor seals. Good thing kids enjoy that almost as much as playing in the waves.

LA JOLLA COVE

Truly the jewel of La Jolla, "the Cove" is one of the prettiest spots on the west coast.

LA JOLLA SHORES

One of the most popular beaches in San Diego, La Jolla Shores features a wide sandy beach and calm waves perfect for swimming and beginner surf lessons.

TORREY PINES STATE BEACH

This popular beach is located just below the Torrey Pines State Reserve. Bring your picnic here after an invigorating hike in the reserve.

WINDANSEA BEACH

Incredible views, secluded spots, and world-class waves make this a favorite beach for couples and surfers.

The view from Coast Highway 101 in Carlsbad is spectacular.

LA JOLLA COVE WALK AND SHOP

If you're not keen on dipping your toes in the water (or even the sand, for that matter), head over to La Jolla Cove, an ideal spot for strolling and shopping with a view. Park at any of the available metered spaces on Girard and browse the boutiques and galleries. Make your way toward the cove by following the signs, or simply walk toward any patches of ocean you see.

WATER SPORTS

One of the most popular water activities is kayaking along the caves and snorkeling among the kelp beds near the cove at the Underwater Ecological Reserve. Kayak rental shops offer special outings that include moonlight kayaking and the chance to dive among the leopard sharks that roam La Jolla's waters. Don't worry: the sharks are harmless.

7

La Jolla LA JOLLA'S BEACHES AND BEYOND

SURFING SAN DIEGO

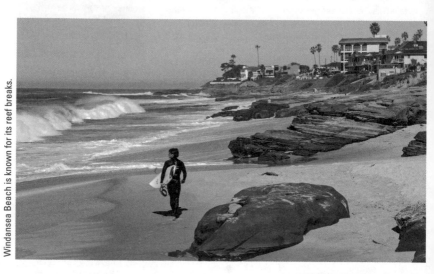

Windansea Beach is known for its reef breaks.

Head to a San Diego beach on any given day and chances are you'll see a group of surfers in the water, patiently waiting to catch a memorable wave.

Surfing may have originated in Hawaii, but modern surfing culture is inextricably linked to the Southern California lifestyle. From the Malibu setting of *Gidget* to the surf-city sounds of Jan and Dean and the Beach Boys, and TV's *Laguna Beach* and *The OC,* the entertainment industry brought a California version of surfing to the landlocked, and in the process created an enduring mystique.

San Diego surfing in particular is unique. Underwater kelp beds help keep waves intact, preventing the choppiness that surfers bemoan. Santa Ana winds that begin to arrive in fall and throughout early winter bring coveted offshore winds that contribute to morning and evening "glass" (the stillness of the water that encourages smooth waves).

BEST TIME TO GO

The biggest swells usually occur in winter, but good-size waves can form year-round. Generally, swells come from the north in winter and from the south in summer. Certain breaks are better on different swells. In winter, try beaches like Swami's or Black's Beach that can hold large swells without closing out. Summer spots are La Jolla's Windansea and nearby Tourmaline Surfing Park.

TYPES OF BREAKS

Beach break: Waves that break over sandbars and the seafloor and are usually tamer and consistently long, thus typically the best type for beginners, with the exception of Black's Beach, which is legendary for its uniquely large, fast, and punchy beach breaks. **La Jolla Shores, Mission Beach,** and **Pacific Beach** are destinations for gentler, more forgiving waves.

Point break: Created as waves that hit a point jutting into the ocean. Surfers then peel down the wave it creates. With the right conditions, this can create very consistent waves. **Swami's** has an excellent point break.

Reef break: Waves break as they hit a reef. It can create great (but dangerous) surf. There's a good chance of getting smashed and scraped over extremely sharp coral or rocks. Many of San Diego's best breaks are at **San Elijo, La Jolla Cove,** and **Windansea.**

SAN DIEGO SURF FINDER

Municipal piers, such as at **Oceanside, Pacific,** and **Mission beaches,** are great places to watch surfers. The high bluffs of **Black's Beach** is also a great spot.

Swami's: Famous for its point break and beautiful water.

Black's Beach: This strand below the cliffs is where to go for beach breaks. Serious surfers carry their boards down the narrow, steep trails to reach the beach.

Windansea Beach: Known for its reef breaks.

Tourmaline Surfing Park: Windsurfers and surfers share Tourmaline's smooth waves.

La Jolla Shores: First-timers head here for more modest waves.

Surfer hits the lip at a hollow beach break.

SURF SLANG

Barrel: The area created when a wave breaks onto itself in a curl.

Close out: When a wave breaks all at once, rather than breaking steadily in one direction.

Cutback: The most basic turn; executed to maintain position close to the barrel.

Dropping in: A severe breach of etiquette wherein a second surfer joins the wave later and cuts off the original rider.

Goofy foot: Having a right-foot-forward stance on the surfboard.

Grom: An affectionate term for those sun-bleached kids with tiny surfboards.

Hollow: Barrels big enough to create a tube that a surfer can ride within—also called the green room.

Lineup: A group of surfers waiting beyond the whitewash for waves.

Turtle roll: When a surfer rolls over on the surfboard, going underwater and holding the board upside down to bypass the crashing waves.

NEIGHBORHOOD SNAPSHOT

TOP EXPERIENCES

■ **Promenade above the cove:** The winding pathways above La Jolla Cove offer stunning views of the surf and sea lions.

■ **Shop 'til you drop:** La Jolla's chic boutiques and galleries are San Diego's answer to Rodeo Drive. Watch for celebrities as you browse on Prospect Street and Girard Avenue.

■ **Aquatic adventures:** Grab a kayak or scuba gear to explore the San Diego–La Jolla Underwater Park Ecological Preserve.

■ **Luxe living:** Visit top-notch spas and restaurants, or gawk at multimillion-dollar mansions and their denizens in Ferraris.

■ **Torrey Pines State Beach and Reserve:** Play the links, hike the trails, relax on the beach, or hang glide off the cliffs.

GETTING HERE

If you're traveling north, take the La Jolla Parkway exit off I–5, which veers into Torrey Pines Road, and turn right onto Prospect Street. If you're heading south, take La Jolla Village Drive exit, which also leads into Torrey Pines Road. For the scenic route, head north from Pacific Beach on La Jolla Boulevard and Camino de la Costa. Signs direct drivers and cyclists past many of La Jolla's famed vistas and coveted homes. As you approach the village, La Jolla Boulevard turns into Prospect Street.

PLANNING YOUR TIME

La Jolla's highlights can be seen in a few hours with a visit to La Jolla Village and the cove followed by a scenic drive along the coast and through Torrey Pines. A day allows for beach time, a hike in Torrey Pines, and some shopping.

The village and La Jolla Cove can be explored on foot, but it's a steep walk. Parking is tough, too.

GREAT DRIVE

The portion of **Coast Highway 101** that runs south from North County into La Jolla is one of San Diego's best drives. Start at South Carlsbad beach at Tamarack Avenue and continue through Leucadia, Encinitas, Cardiff, Solana Beach, Del Mar, and, finally, La Jolla. Any turn west will take you toward the beach. The drive offers intermittent glimpses of the sea; views from Carlsbad and Cardiff are especially beautiful. The grand finale is at Torrey Pines, where the waves roll into the misty, high-bluffed beach.

SUNSET VISTAS

Head to the shack-like hut that's nestled among the rocks at La Jolla's **Windansea Beach** for some great sunset viewing.

WITH KIDS

Despite its name, the **Children's Pool** isn't a great spot to take your kids to swim, but they'll love watching the seals and sea lions that populate its waters. **La Jolla Shores** is popular for the gentle waves in its swimmer's section.

La Jollans have long considered their village to be the Monte Carlo of California, and with good reason. Its coastline curves into natural coves backed by verdant hillsides covered with homes worth millions. La Jolla is both a natural and cultural treasure trove. The upscale shops, galleries, and restaurants of La Jolla Village satisfy the glitterati, while secluded trails, scenic overlooks, and abundant marine life provide balance and refuge.

Although La Jolla is a neighborhood of the city of San Diego, it has its own postal zone and a coveted sense of class; the ultrarich from around the globe own second homes here and old-money residents maintain friendships with the visiting film stars and royalty who frequent the area's exclusive luxury hotels and private clubs. Development has radically altered the once serene character of the village, but it has gained a cosmopolitan air that makes it a popular vacation resort.

Just off the coast, from La Jolla Cove to La Jolla Shores, lies the 533-acre, world-renowned San Diego–La Jolla Underwater Park Ecological Preserve.

Native Americans called the site Woholle, or "hole in the mountains," referring to the grottoes that dot the shoreline. The Spaniards changed the name to La Jolla (same pronunciation as La Hoya), "the jewel," which led to the nickname "Jewel City."

La Jolla

Sights

Birch Aquarium at Scripps
AQUARIUM | **FAMILY** | Affiliated with the world-renowned Scripps Institution of Oceanography, this excellent aquarium sits at the end of a signposted drive leading off North Torrey Pines Road and has sweeping views of La Jolla coast below. More than 60 tanks are filled with colorful saltwater fish, and a 70,000-gallon tank simulates a La Jolla kelp forest. A special exhibit on sea horses features several examples of the species, plus mesmerizing sea dragons and a sea horse nursery. Besides the fish themselves, attractions include interactive educational exhibits based on the institution's ocean-related research and a variety of environmental issues. ⊠ *2300 Expedition Way, La Jolla* ☎ *858/534–3474*

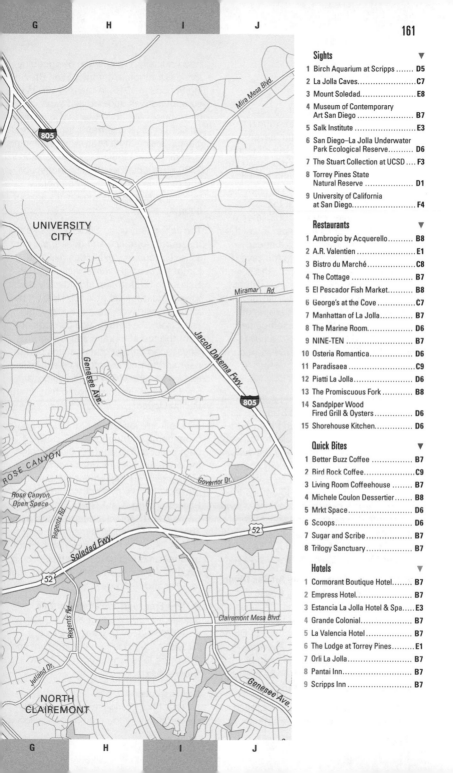

Sights ▼

Restaurants ▼

Quick Bites ▼

Hotels ▼

⊕ *www.aquarium.ucsd.edu* ✆ *$25*
☞ *Reservations required.*

La Jolla Caves

CAVE | **FAMILY** | It's a walk of 145 some-times slippery steps down a tunnel to Sunny Jim, the largest of the seven caves in La Jolla Cove and the only one reachable by land. This is a one-of-a-kind local attraction, and worth the time if you have a day or two to really enjoy La Jolla. The man-made tunnel took two years to dig, beginning in 1902; later, a shop was built at its entrance. Today the Cave Store, a throwback to that early shop, is still the entrance to the cave. The shop sells jewelry, postcards, shells, and watercolors by local artists. All visitors are required to sign a safety waiver at the entrance. Sturdy shoes are recom-mended for the 15-minute self-guided tour. ⊠ *1325 Coast Blvd. S, La Jolla* ☎ *858/459–0746* ⊕ *www.cavestore.com* ✆ *$10.*

Mount Soledad

MOUNTAIN | La Jolla's highest spot can be reached by taking Nautilus Street to La Jolla Scenic Drive South, and then turn-ing left. Proceed a few blocks to the park, where parking is plentiful and the views are astounding, unless the day is hazy. The top of the mountain is an excellent vantage point from which to get a sense of San Diego's geography: looking down from here you can see the coast from the county's northern border to the south far beyond Downtown. ⊠ *6905 La Jolla Scenic Dr. S, La Jolla* ✆ *Free.*

★ Museum of Contemporary Art San Diego

ART MUSEUM | Driving along Coast Boulevard, it is hard to miss the mass of watercraft jutting out from the rear of the Museum of Contemporary Art San Diego (MCASD) La Jolla location. *Pleasure Point* by Nancy Rubins is just one example of the mingling of art and locale at this spectacular oceanfront setting.

The oldest section of La Jolla's branch of San Diego's contemporary art museum

was originally a residence, designed by Irving Gill for philanthropist Ellen Brown-ing Scripps in 1916. In the mid-1990s the compound was updated and expanded by architect Robert Venturi, who respect-ed Gill's original geometric structure and clean Mission-style lines while adding his own distinctive touches. An expansion in 2020 quadrupled existing gallery space. The result is a striking contemporary building that looks as though it's always been here.

The light-filled Axline Court serves as the museum's entrance and does triple duty as reception area, exhibition hall, and forum for special events, including The Gala each September, attended by the town's most fashionable folk. Inside, the museum's artwork gets major compe-tition from the setting: you can look out from the top of a grand stairway onto a landscaped garden that contains perma-nent and temporary sculpture exhibits as well as rare 100-year-old California plant specimens and, beyond that, to the Pacific Ocean.

Artists from San Diego and Tijuana figure prominently in the museum's perma-nent collection of post-1950s art, but the museum also includes examples of every major art movement through the present—works by Andy Warhol, Robert Rauschenberg, Frank Stella, Joseph Cornell, and Jenny Holzer, to name a few. The museum also gets major visiting shows. Head to the museum's shop for unique cards and gifts. The street-facing plaza at the museum café is a great spot to relax and recharge.

■ **TIP➔ Free tours are offered at 2 on Sunday.** ⊠ *700 Prospect St., La Jolla* ☎ *858/454–3541* ⊕ *www.mcasd.org* ✆ *$25; MCASD is free on 2nd Sun. and 3rd Thurs. of every month* ⊙ *Closed Mon.–Wed.*

Salk Institute

COLLEGE | The world-famous biological research facility founded by polio vaccine developer Jonas Salk sits on 27 clifftop acres. The twin structures that modernist architect Louis I. Kahn designed in the 1960s in consultation with Dr. Salk used poured concrete and other low-maintenance materials to clever effect. The thrust of the laboratory–office complex is outward toward the Pacific Ocean, an orientation accentuated by a foot-wide "Stream of Life" that flows through the center of a travertine marble courtyard between the buildings. Architects-to-be and building buffs will enjoy the tours of the property; register online in advance. You can, however, stroll at will through the dramatic courtyard during the week—simultaneously monumental and eerie.

■TIP→ **Architectural docent-led tours lasting one hour are offered on Wednesday and Friday at 10 am. For groups of eight or more, private docent-led group tours may be requested on weekdays between 10 am and 4 pm (reservations required 10 days in advance, see website for details).** ✉ *10010 N. Torrey Pines Rd., La Jolla* ☎ *858/453–4100* ⊕ *www.salk.edu* ✆ *Public tour $20; private tours for minimum 8 people $200* ⊘ *Closed weekends.*

San Diego-La Jolla Underwater Park Ecological Reserve

REEF | Four habitats across 6,000 acres make up this underwater park and ecological reserve. When the water is clear, this is a diver's paradise with reefs, kelp beds, sand flats, and a submarine canyon reaching depths up to 600 feet. Plunge to see guitarfish rays, perch, sea bass, anchovies, squid, and hammerhead sharks. Snorkelers, kayakers, and stand-up paddleboarders are likely to spot sea lions, seals, and leopard sharks. The Seven La Jolla Sea Caves, 75-million-year-old sandstone caves, are at the park's edge.

■TIP→ **While the park can be explored on your own, the best way to view it is with a professional guide.** ✉ *La Jolla* ✚ *La Jolla Cove.*

The Stuart Collection at UCSD

PUBLIC ART | Less a gallery than an open-air scavenger hunt for some of the city's most impressive works of visual art, the Stuart Collection—located across the 1,200-acre UCSD campus—boasts over 20 must-see, and sometimes massive, pieces by some of the biggest names in contemporary art, including Jenny Holzer, John Baldessari, and Robert Irwin. A self-guided virtual tour can be accessed through their website. ✉ *UCSD, 9500 Gilman Dr., La Jolla* ⊕ *stuartcollection. ucsd.edu.*

★ Torrey Pines State Natural Reserve

NATURE PRESERVE | *Pinus torreyana,* the rarest native pine tree in the United States, enjoys a 1,500-acre sanctuary at the northern edge of La Jolla. About 6,000 of these unusual trees, some as tall as 60 feet, grow on the cliffs here. The park is one of only two places in the world (the other is Santa Rosa Island, off Santa Barbara) where the Torrey pine grows naturally. The reserve has several hiking trails leading to the cliffs, 300 feet above the ocean; trail maps are available at the park station. Wildflowers grow profusely in spring, and the ocean panoramas are always spectacular. From December to March, whales can be spotted from the bluffs. When in this upper part of the park, respect the restrictions. Not permitted: picnicking, camping, drones, smoking, leaving the trails, dogs, alcohol, or collecting plant specimens.

You can unwrap your sandwiches, however, at Torrey Pines State Beach, just below the reserve. When the tide is out, it's possible to walk south all the way past the lifeguard towers to Black's Beach over rocky promontories carved by the waves (avoid the bluffs, however; they're unstable). **Los Peñasquitos Lagoon** at the north end of the reserve is one of the many natural estuaries that flow inland between Del Mar and Oceanside. It's a good place to watch shorebirds. Volunteers lead guided nature walks

at 10 on most weekends and holidays. ✉ *12600 N. Torrey Pines Rd., La Jolla* ✛ *N. Torrey Pines Rd. exit off I–5 onto Carmel Valley Rd. going west, then turn left (south) on Coast Hwy. 101* ☎ *858/755–2063* ⊕ *www.torreypine.org* 🅿 *Parking from $20.*

University of California at San Diego

COLLEGE | The campus of one of the country's most prestigious research universities spreads over 1,200 acres of coastal canyons and eucalyptus groves, where students and faculty jog, bike, and skateboard to class. If you're interested in contemporary art, check out the Stuart Collection of Sculpture—18 thought-provoking, site-specific works by artists such as Nam June Paik, William Wegman, Niki de St. Phalle, Jenny Holzer, and others arrayed around the campus. UCSD's Price Center has a well-stocked, two-level bookstore—the largest in San Diego. Look for the postmodern Geisel Library, named for longtime La Jolla residents Theodor "Dr. Seuss" Geisel and his wife, Audrey. Bring cash or a credit card for the kiosks and park in lot P704, because free parking is only available on Sundays.

■ **TIP**→ **There are free outdoor walking tours offered at various times for the public. For scheduled tours, visit** ⊕ *www. admissions.ucsd.edu.* ✉ *La Jolla* ✛ *Exit I–5 onto La Jolla Village Dr. going west; take Gilman Dr. off-ramp to right and continue to information kiosk at campus entrance on Gilman Dr.* ☎ *858/534–2230 campus tour information* ⊕ *www.ucsd.edu.*

 Beaches

Black's Beach

BEACH | The powerful waves at this beach attract world-class surfers, and the strand's relative isolation appeals to nudist nature lovers (although by law nudity is prohibited). Backed by 300-foot-tall cliffs whose colors change with the sun's angle, Black's can be accessed from Torrey Pines State Beach to the north, or by a narrow path descending the cliffs from Torrey Pines Glider Port. Be aware that the city has posted a "do not use" sign there because the cliff trails are unmaintained and highly dangerous, so use at your own risk. If you plan to access Black's from the beaches to the north or south, do so at low tide. High tide and waves can restrict access. Strong rip currents are common—only experienced swimmers should take the plunge. Lifeguards patrol the area only between spring break and mid-October. Also keep your eyes peeled for the hang gliders and paragliders who ascend from atop the cliffs. Parking is available at the Glider Port and Torrey Pines State Beach. **Amenities:** none. **Best for:** solitude; nudists; surfing. ✉ *Between Torrey Pines State Beach and La Jolla Shores, La Jolla* ✛ *2 miles south of Torrey Pines State Beach parking lot* ⊕ *www.sandiego.gov/lifeguards/beaches/blacks.*

Children's Pool

BEACH | **FAMILY** | Due to the groups of harbor seals that have claimed it as their own, this shallow cove, protected by a seawall, is closed to the public for the winter pupping season, December 15 through May 15. People may access its calm, protected waters the other seven months of the year, however, and the beach's small waves make it an ideal place for children to splash and play. Adults will appreciate the view. Because of its location at the tip of La Jolla Peninsula, you can actually look east to get unmatched panoramic views of the coastline and ocean. The area just outside the pool is popular with scuba divers, who explore the offshore reef when the surf is calm. Although you may not be able to go down on the beach during the winter months, it's still worth a peek. It's fun to watch the seals and their pups from above.

■ **TIP**→ **Limited free parking is available along Coast Boulevard.**

The grassy palm-lined park above La Jolla Cove is great for picnics.

Amenities: lifeguards; showers; toilets; parking (no fee). **Best for:** walking; scuba diving. ⊠ *850 Coast Blvd., La Jolla* ⊕ *www.sandiego.gov/lifeguards/beaches/pool.*

★ La Jolla Cove

BEACH | FAMILY | This shimmering blue-green inlet surrounded by cliffs is what first attracted everyone to La Jolla, from Native Americans to the glitterati. "The Cove," as locals refer to it, beyond where Girard Avenue dead-ends into Coast Boulevard, is marked by towering palms that line a promenade where people strolling in designer clothes are as common as Frisbee throwers. Ellen Browning Scripps Park sits atop cliffs formed by the incessant pounding of the waves and offers a great spot for picnics with a view. The Cove has beautiful white sand that is a bit coarse near the water's edge, but the beach is still a great place for sunbathing and lounging. At low tide, the pools and cliff caves are a destination for explorers. With visibility at 30-plus feet, this is the best place in San Diego for snorkeling, where bright-orange garibaldi fish and other marine life populate the waters of the San Diego–La Jolla Underwater Park Ecological Reserve. From above water, it's not uncommon to spot sea lions and birds basking on the rocks, or dolphin fins just offshore. The cove is also a favorite of rough-water swimmers, while the area just north is best for kayakers wanting to explore the Seven La Jolla Sea Caves. **Amenities:** lifeguards; showers; toilets. **Best for:** snorkeling; swimming; walking. ⊠ *1100 Coast Blvd., east of Ellen Browning Scripps Park, La Jolla* ⊕ *www.sandiego.gov/lifeguards/beaches/cove.*

La Jolla Shores

BEACH | FAMILY | This is one of San Diego's most popular beaches due to its wide sandy shore, gentle waves, and incredible views of La Jolla Peninsula. There's also a large grassy park, and adjacent to La Jolla Shores lies the San Diego–La Jolla Underwater Park Ecological Reserve, 6,000 acres of protected ocean bottom and tide lands, bordered by the Seven La

Jolla Sea Caves. The white powdery sand at La Jolla Sands is some of San Diego's best, and several surf and scuba schools teach here. Kayaks can also be rented nearby. A concrete boardwalk parallels the beach, and a boat launch for small vessels lies 300 yards south of the lifeguard station at Avenida de Playa. Arrive early to get a parking spot in the lot near Kellogg Park at the foot of Calle Frescota. Street parking is limited to one or two hours. **Amenities:** lifeguards; parking (no fee); showers; toilets. **Best for:** surfing; swimming; walking. ⊠ *8200 Camino del Oro, in front of Kellogg Park, La Jolla* ⊕ *2 miles north of downtown La Jolla* ⊕ *www.sandiego.gov/lifeguards/beaches/shores.shtml.*

Marine Street Beach

BEACH | This wide expanse of white sand is famous for bodysurfing due to its powerful shorebreak, but it also teems with sunbathers, swimmers, walkers, joggers, and folks just out for the incredible views. The sand is soft and fluffy and feels wonderful as it squishes through your toes. Swimmers need to beware; waves break in extremely shallow water and you need to watch out for riptides. The beach sits just between Children's Pool Beach to the north and Windansea Beach to the south. There are no amenities at the beach, but picnic tables, showers, and toilets are available at the nearby cove. **Amenities:** lifeguards. **Best for:** solitude; swimming; walking. ⊠ *Marine St. at Vista Del Mar Ave., La Jolla* ⊕ *3 blocks west of La Jolla Blvd.*

Shell Beach

BEACH | The small cove north of the Children's Pool remains remarkably under the radar and is typically less crowded than nearby beaches like La Jolla Cove and La Jolla Shores. The secluded beach is accessible by stairs at the south end of Ellen Browning Scripps Park and has clear water and tide pools. The reef comes all the way up to the shore, making it a less-than-ideal spot for swimming, but children love to wade in the shallow water. Step with caution, as rocks can be extremely slippery. As the name would imply, tiny shells make up the sand near the water's edge. It's beautiful but coarse and can be hard on people's feet. Your visit is better spent exploring than sunning. The exposed rocks off the coast have been designated a protected habitat for sea lions; you can watch them frolic in the water. Picnic tables, showers, and toilets are available near the cove. **Amenities:** none. **Best for:** solitude. ⊠ *Coast Blvd., La Jolla* ⊕ *North of Children's Pool and south of Ellen Browning Scripps Park.*

★ Torrey Pines State Beach and Reserve

BEACH | With sandstone cliffs and hiking trails adjacent to the beach rather than urban development, Torrey Pines State Beach feels far away from the SoCal sprawl. The beach and reserve encompass 1,500 acres of sandstone cliffs and deep ravines, and a network of meandering trails lead to the wide, pristine beach below. Along the way enjoy the rare Torrey pine trees, found only here and on Santa Rosa Island, offshore. Guides conduct free tours of the nature preserve on weekends and holidays. Torrey Pines tends to get crowded in summer, but you'll find more isolated spots heading south under the cliffs leading to Black's Beach. Smooth rocks often wash up on stretches of the beach making it a challenge, at times, to go barefoot. If you can find a patch that is clear of debris, you'll encounter the nice soft, golden sand San Diego is known for. There is a paid parking lot at the entrance to the park but also look for free angle parking along North Torrey Pines Road. **Amenities:** lifeguards; parking (fee); showers; toilets. **Best for:** swimming; surfing; walking. ⊠ *12600 N. Torrey Pines Rd., La Jolla* ☎ *858/755–2063* ⊕ *www.torreypine.org* ⊠ *Parking from $20.*

When the Grunions Run

A generations-old San Diego tradition is heading to the beach during certain high tides—preferably when the moon is full—to hunt grunion. These small, barely edible fish come ashore to spawn and "run" on the beach, causing great excitement among spectators. As the fish flop across the sand in search of adventure (as it were), bold individuals chase them down and scoop up a few with their hands—catching them by any other means is illegal. Beach-area businesses and eateries often know the date of the next run, with peak spawning season from late March to early June. Oceanside, Del Mar, La Jolla, Mission Beach, and Coronado are the best beaches to watch the grunions run.

★ Windansea Beach

BEACH | With its rocky shoreline and strong shore break, Windansea stands out among San Diego beaches for its dramatic natural beauty. It's one of the best surf spots in San Diego County. Professional surfers love the unusual A-frame waves the reef break here creates. Although the large sandstone rocks that dot the beach might sound like a hindrance, they actually serve as protective barriers from the wind, making this one of the best beaches in San Diego for sunbathing. The beach's palm-covered surf shack built in 1946 is a protected historical landmark, and a seat here at sunset may just be one of the most romantic spots on the West Coast. The name Windansea comes from a hotel that burned down in the late 1940s. You can usually find nearby street parking. **Amenities:** seasonal lifeguards; toilets. **Best for:** sunset; surfing; solitude. ✉ *Neptune Pl. at Nautilus St., La Jolla* ⊕ *www.sandiego.gov/lifeguards/beaches/windan.shtml.*

🍴 Restaurants

This tony enclave that hugs the ocean from the Bird Rock area to Torrey Pines draws diners from around the world to experience an amazing collection of relaxed fine and casual dining establishments, ranging from classic French bistro fare to California modern cuisine. Ocean-view restaurants along Prospect Street are very popular, but there are many affordable neighborhood favorites that serve tasty food in attractive settings like La Jolla Cove.

★ Ambrogio by Acquerello

$$$$ | **ITALIAN** | Elegant yet unpretentious, this fine dining restaurant by chefs Choi Cheolhyeok and Silvio Salmoiraghi, integrate elements of Italy, France, Korea, Japan, and California to build masterpieces in an eight-course tasting menu. Both chefs have an impressive pedigree, formerly at the helm of Michelin Star restaurants in Tokyo and Italy, but at Ambrogio, they have joined forces to redefine modern Italian cuisine in San Diego. **Known for:** seabass with taggiasca olives; beautifully plated dishes; innovative new Italian cuisine. ⑤ *Average main: $150* ✉ *7556 Fay Ave., La Jolla* ☎ *858/412–3432* ⊕ *www.ambrogiobyacquerello.com* ⊗ *Closed Sun. and Mon. No lunch.*

A.R. Valentien

$$$$ | **AMERICAN** | Champions of in-season, fresh-today produce, the chefs at this cozy room in the luxurious, Craftsman-style Lodge at Torrey Pines have made A.R. Valentien one of San Diego's top fine dining destinations. Be prepared for food combinations that are simultaneously simple and delightfully

inventive—crispy skin sablefish; duck confit; prime rib with bordelaise, and an impressive collection of California wines. **Known for:** charcuterie platter; roasted duck; 280 wine selections. $ *Average main: $55* ⊠ *The Lodge at Torrey Pines, 11480 N. Torrey Pines Rd., La Jolla* ☎ *858/777–6635* ⊕ *www.arvalentien. com.*

Bistro du Marché

$$$ | **MODERN FRENCH** | Bringing Paris to La Jolla, acclaimed chef Jean Michel Diot unveils bistronomie cuisine, a culinary concept that blends bistro favorites with gastronomie techniques. The airy dining room, lined with black-and-white photos of France, is comfortable, if not romantic, an ideal setting for the ever-changing menu that emphasizes fresh ingredients sourced from the Sunday farmers' market that holds court in front of the restaurant. **Known for:** French classics like duck confit; poutine; crème brûlée with seasonal berries. $ *Average main: $38* ⊠ *7437 Girard Ave., La Jolla* ☎ *858/551– 7500* ⊕ *www.bistrodumarche.net* ⊘ *Closed Sun. and Mon. No lunch.*

The Cottage

$ | **AMERICAN** | **FAMILY** | A cozy beach cottage sets the stage for American comfort food with a California twist at this La Jolla staple. The restaurant serves lunch, but it's the well-loved daily breakfast that has locals and visitors happily queuing—sometimes up to two hours on weekends. **Known for:** daily breakfast that people line up for; substantial portions to keep you satisfied; great patio seating. $ *Average main: $17* ⊠ *7702 Fay Ave., La Jolla* ☎ *858/454–8409* ⊕ *www.cottagela-jolla.com* ⊘ *No dinner.*

El Pescador Fish Market

$ | **SEAFOOD** | This bustling café first opened as a full-service fish market in 1974, and has been popular with locals ever since. Order the char-grilled, locally caught halibut, swordfish, or yellowtail on a toasted torta roll to enjoy in-house or to go for an oceanfront picnic at nearby La Jolla Cove. **Known for:** clam chowder; bustling on-site fish market; daily-caught cuts to go. $ *Average main: $17* ⊠ *634 Pearl St., La Jolla* ☎ *858/456–2526* ⊕ *www. elpescadorfishmarket.com.*

George's at the Cove

$$$ | **AMERICAN** | La Jolla's ocean-view destination restaurant is like two dining experiences in one with Level2 bar and the roof-top Ocean Terrace. Prepare for spectacular views and an innovative menu featuring maple leaf duck with tangerine marmalade and salmon with braised lentils at the outdoor-only Ocean Terrace, while the Level2 lounge has unique craft cocktails like "Spa Day" with cucumber-mint infused vodka and elderflower. **Known for:** outstanding California coastal cuisine; excellent ocean views; attention to detail for special occasion dinners. $ *Average main: $37* ⊠ *1250 Prospect St., La Jolla* ☎ *858/454–4244* ⊕ *www.georgesatthecove.com.*

Manhattan of La Jolla

$$$ | **STEAKHOUSE** | Step into this swanky New York–style Italian chophouse that takes you back in time with its piano bar, paintings of Sinatra, and dirty martinis to match. The menu is as rich as the atmosphere with the taste of olive oil, garlic, and lemon in every bite. **Known for:** live jazz; veal chop; old-school vibes. $ *Average main: $35* ⊠ *Empress Hotel, 7766 Fay Ave., La Jolla* ✛ *Corner of Silverado St.* ☎ *858/459–0700* ⊕ *www. manhattanoflajolla.com* ⊘ *Closed Mon. No breakfast or lunch.*

The Marine Room

$$$ | **MODERN AMERICAN** | It's hard to dine closer to the Pacific than at this venerable La Jolla Shores mainstay whose two-story-tall windows capture beachgoers, kayakers, snorkelers, and swooping gulls; if the tide is high, waves race across the sand and crash against the glass. The Maine lobster bisque comes coated in Meyer lemon cream, while the bluefin tuna is dressed in a togarashi aioli and the truffle yuca fries are topped with shaved Parmesan. **Known for:** well-priced happy hours; produce, meats, fish sourced from local purveyors; a fine-dining menu that's sophisticated yet playful. ⑤ *Average main: $38 ☒ 2000 Spindrift Dr., La Jolla ☎ 866/644–2351 ⊕ www. marineroom.com ⊙ Closed Mon. and Tues. No breakfast and lunch.*

NINE-TEN

$$$ | AMERICAN | Accolades continue to roll in for executive chef Jason Knibb—winner of an award of excellence by *Wine Spectator* every year since 2002—whose seasonal menus are magnets for travelers and San Diegans seeking a memorable meal like pan-roasted Colorado lamb loin or duck breast with white asparagus and mustard greens. Located at La Jolla's Grande Colonial Hotel, the space encompasses a cozy ground-floor dining room, bar, and ocean-glimpse covered patio. **Known for:** juicy Jamaican jerk pork belly; half-off wine on Wednesday; half-baked chocolate cake with ice cream of the season. ⑤ *Average main: $40 ☒ Grande Colonial Hotel, 910 Prospect St., La Jolla ☎ 858/964–5400 ⊕ www.nine-ten.com ⊙ Bar service only Mon. and Tues.*

Osteria Romantica

$ | ITALIAN | Between music by Pavarotti, the checkered tablecloths, and the sight of homemade pasta and free-flowing vino, you'll swear you've died and gone to Italy. At this cozy La Jolla Shores eatery, northern and southwestern Italian flavors have fused into culinary magic—house-made breads, sauces, gnocchi, and pastas like pappardelle with braised lamb, and linguine with mussels—since 2004. **Known for:** tender lamb pappardelle; cozy Italian vibe; homemade pasta, breads, and sauces. ⑤ *Average main: $20 ☒ 2151 Av. de la Playa, La Jolla ☎ 858/551–1221 ⊕ www.osteriaromantica.com ⊙ No lunch Mon.*

Paradisaea

$$$$ | MODERN AMERICAN | This trendy La Jolla restaurant "plays" tribute to the past with its location inside William Kesling's historic piano showroom where live music still plays during cocktail hour. The casual yet refined menu features dry-aged cheeseburgers, pan-roasted chicken, and unconventional Caesar salads topped with jalapeño rings and Parmesan shavings; be sure to request a side of the creamy coconut rice pilaf. **Known for:** modern-Cali cuisine; live music during cocktail hour; dry-aged beef hamburger with sauce au poivre. ⑤ *Average main: $50 ☒ 5680 La Jolla Blvd., La Jolla ☎ 858/255–8011 ⊕ www.paradisaea.com ⊙ No lunch. Closed Mon. and Tues.*

Piatti La Jolla

$$ | MODERN ITALIAN | FAMILY | Blocks from the beach in La Jolla Shores, this comfortably modern dining room and shaded patio hits all the right notes—affordable, polished, and family-friendly. From lunch through close, it bustles with regulars from the neighborhood and visitors from around the world who are guided through the extensive Italian menu by the professional staff, some of whom have worked here for over three decades. **Known for:** stone-hearth oven pizza; gluten-free and vegan options; weekend brunch. ⑤ *Average main: $22 ☒ 2182 Av. de la Playa, La Jolla ☎ 858/454–1589 ⊕ www.piatti.com.*

The Promiscuous Fork

$ | AMERICAN | FAMILY | This 500-square-foot restaurant serves up heaping portions of tacos, burgers, bowls, and "sammiches" inspired by the owner's international travels. American classics have an Asian twist, like the smoked pork belly street tacos with kimchi aioli and ginger slaw or the Cajun spice-dusted lamb lollipops with coconut-jalapeño rice. **Known for:** unpretentious local hangout; weekdays 3–6 pm $2 off beer and wine; lamb lollipops and Kailua pork quesadillas. ⑤ *Average main: $15 ☒ 6984 La Jolla Blvd., La Jolla ☎ 858/454–3663 ⊕ www. thepromiscuousfork.com ⊙ Closed Sun.*

Sandpiper Wood Fired Grill & Oysters

$$ | **MODERN AMERICAN** | As the sister restaurant of La Jolla's Georges at the Cove, this laid-back restaurant is the perfect spot to chill with friends after a day in the sand and share oysters from the raw bar or rosemary Parmesan fries dipped in jalapeño ranch. Grab a seat on the dog-friendly patio or head indoors for grilled favorites including octopus, prime rib, and cast-iron focaccia with honey ricotta. **Known for:** shareable plates like skillet corn cake; no-fuss neighborhood vibe; $4 off select items during happy hour. ⑤ *Average main: $30* ⊠ *2259 Av. de la Playa, La Jolla* ☎ *858/228–5655* ⊕ *www.sandpipersd.com* ☺ *Closed Mon. and Tues.*

Shorehouse Kitchen

$ | **AMERICAN** | This casual indoor-outdoor eatery in La Jolla Shores has a sprawling outdoor patio perfect for leisurely lunches with friends and family. Surfers and well-heeled locals populate the 50-seat patio while enjoying made-to-order organic smoothies and fresh salads, as well as scrumptious breakfast and creative lunch entrées that include flatbreads, soups, sandwiches, and the popular cheeseburger and prime steak frites. **Known for:** mango pancakes; vanilla bean French toast; California K-9 breakfast off the doggie menu. ⑤ *Average main: $15* ⊠ *2236 Av. de la Playa, La Jolla* ☎ *858/459–3300* ⊕ *www.shorehousekitchen.com* ☺ *No dinner.*

☕ Coffee and Quick Bites

Better Buzz Coffee

$ | **CAFÉ** | With locations across San Diego County, this happening hot spot is ready to get you buzzed with honey lattes, "Killer Bee" triple espressos, pour overs, and nitro cold brews. The sandwiches, smoothies, pastries, and acai bowls are ideal grab-and-gos for those who would rather munch at the beach. **Known for:** Americano with creamy vanilla; breakfast sandwiches; rosewater latte. ⑤ *Average main: $10* ⊠ *909 Prospect St., #100 a, La Jolla* ☎ *858/255–8019* ⊕ *www.better-buzzcoffee.com.*

Bird Rock Coffee

$ | **AMERICAN** | For coffee with a view, the La Jolla branch of Bird Rock is the best spot to kickstart your day with fresh brewed artisan coffees and summer specials like the dirty Horchata iced coffee. Grab a table on the patio with the beach in the distance and take your pick from a comprehensive selection of morning brews and pastries. **Known for:** ethically sourced coffee; pull-apart cinnamon rolls; great ambience with friendly staff. ⑤ *Average main: $8* ⊠ *5627 La Jolla Blvd., La Jolla* ☎ *619/272–0203* ⊕ *www.birdrock-coffee.com* ☺ *No dinner.*

Living Room Coffeehouse

$ | **CAFÉ** | La Jolla's outpost of this local coffee chain is open until 11 pm and sports a full bar, which means that customers can spend a pleasant evening sipping a true-blue Irish coffee complete with whiskey at one of the many tables or couches. On those foggy marine-layer days, request one of their homemade soups and watch the waves roll in from the second floor. **Known for:** Milky Way mocha; acai bowl with homemade granola; quiche lorraine. ⑤ *Average main: $5* ⊠ *1010 Prospect St., La Jolla* ☎ *858/459–1187* ⊕ *livingroomcafe.com.*

★ Michele Coulon Dessertier

$ | **CAFÉ** | **FAMILY** | The desserts are magnificent at this small, charming shop in operation for nearly 50 years, where dessertier Michele Coulon confects wonders, using organic produce and imported chocolate. Snack on cookies, cupcakes, brownies, chocolate-dipped strawberries, and mini-desserts. **Known for:** Instagram-worthy presentation; the buttercream- and berry-filled Gateau Aileen; gluten-free items usually are available. ⑤ *Average main: $12* ⊠ *7556 Fay Ave., Suite D, La Jolla* ☎ *858/456–5098*

⊕ *www.dessertier.com* ⊙ *Closed Sun. and Mon. No dinner.*

Mrkt Space

$ | CAFÉ | A popular meeting place for casual connections and grab-and-go goodness, this café–bar–market is a great place to start your day with an energy boost like avocado egg cups on toasted sourdough or smoked salmon toast with jalapeño and micro greens. Later in the day, place your order at the counter for "not an ordinary sandwich" like the prosciutto with stracciatella and pesto, afternoon nibbles like smoothies and charcuterie boards, or cocktails and wines by the glass. **Known for:** 75% of wine is organic; espresso martini; avocado egg cups. ⑤ *Average main: $18 ⊠ 2202 Av. de la Playa, La Jolla ⊕ www. mrktspace.com.*

Scoops

$ | ICE CREAM | FAMILY | Homemade crepes and fresh-brewed coffee come second to the artisanal ice cream made with just a handful of ingredients. Even vegans can get their scoop on, with flavors like strawberry shortcake, mint, cookie dough, and chocolate made with cashew milk, cocoa butter, organic carob beans, and other natural goodness. **Known for:** vegan ice cream and sorbet; sweet crepes; flavors like honeycomb and brown sugar cookie dough chunk. ⑤ *Average main: $6 ⊠ 2179 Av. de la Playa, La Jolla ☎ 858/246–6321 ⊕ www. scoopslajolla.com.*

Sugar and Scribe

$ | BAKERY | If the chef at this La Jolla bakery looks familiar, it's because she won Food Network's Holiday Baking Championship in 2015. Since that win, chef Maeve Rochford has made a name for herself as a celebrity chef and owner of Sugar and Scribe offering baked goods like delicious scones as well as sit-down options like lobster Benedict, Irish sausage rolls, and irresistible blueberry pancakes with fresh-plucked berries, edible flowers, and vanilla whipped cream. **Known for:** house-made granola; traditional Irish favorites; award-winning bakery with fresh treats. ⑤ *Average main: $18 ⊠ 7660 Fay Ave., Unit I, La Jolla ☎ 858/274–1733 ⊕ www.sugarand-scribe.com* ⊙ *No dinner.*

Trilogy Sanctuary

$ | VEGETARIAN | Perched on a rooftop in La Jolla, this café features a mindful menu of bowls, tacos, and other creative entrées that are all 100% organic, vegan, gluten-free, dairy-free, and soy-free. There's also a boutique with sustainable products and a yoga studio with aerial yoga, sound healing, and training workshops. **Known for:** plentiful vegetarian and vegan options; Kombucha on tap; indoor and outdoor yoga studio. ⑤ *Average main: $17 ⊠ 7650 Girard Ave., La Jolla ☎ 858/633–3893 ⊕ www.trilogysanctu-ary.com.*

 Hotels

Multimillion-dollar homes line the beaches and hillsides of beautiful and prestigious La Jolla, a community about 20 minutes north of Downtown. La Jolla Shores is a mile-long sandy beach that gets crowded in summer with kayakers, sunbathers, and students in scuba-diving classes. The village—the heart of La Jolla—is chockablock with expensive boutiques, art galleries, restaurants, and a grassy beachfront park that's popular for picnics and weddings.

Cormorant Boutique Hotel

$$ | HOTEL | It's the view and location that will grab you at this new boutique hotel with plenty of perks including a rooftop restaurant, the 24-hour Prospect Market, and Tesla charging stations. **Pros:** wide range of amenities; guest discounts on kayak rentals and at the rooftop bar; outstanding location in center of town near the beach. **Cons:** $50 day parking fee; no elevator in four-story hotel; not all rooms have ocean view. ⑤ *Rooms from: $350 ⊠ 1110 Prospect St., La Jolla*

☎ 858/203–3565 ⊕ www.cormorantlajol-la.com ⇱ 26 rooms ⊙ No Meals.

Empress Hotel

$ | **HOTEL** | A few blocks from the ocean and Girard Avenue's upscale shops, this five-story hotel blends Southern California beach style with a touch of European flair, making it one of the more affordable and convenient options in La Jolla. **Pros:** near shops, restaurants, and beach; free coffee and muffins in the lobby; friendly staff. **Cons:** not exciting for kids; $35 pet fee; small bathrooms. ⑤ Rooms from: $149 ✉ 7766 Fay Ave., La Jolla ☎ 858/454–3001 ⊕ www.empress-hotel.com ⇱ 73 rooms ⊙ No Meals.

Estancia La Jolla Hotel & Spa

$$ | **RESORT** | With its rambling California mission–style architecture and brilliant gardens, this resort on what once was a famous equestrian ranch exudes rustic elegance. **Pros:** online offers and discount packages; grab-and-go items from Trading Post café; quiet courtyards with adobe fireplaces. **Cons:** mandatory $40 resort fees; not centrally located; sound of heavy doors echoes between rooms. ⑤ Rooms from: $279 ✉ 9700 N. Torrey Pines Rd., La Jolla ☎ 858/550–1000 ⊕ www.estancialajolla.com ⇱ 210 rooms ⊙ No Meals.

★ Grande Colonial

$$$ | **HOTEL** | This white-wedding-cake-style hotel in the heart of La Jolla Village has ocean views and charming European details that include chandeliers, mahogany railings, a wooden elevator, crystal doorknobs, and French doors. **Pros:** the Village's only four-diamond hotel; superb restaurant; hospitality extras included in rate. **Cons:** small pool; no fitness center; valet parking only. ⑤ Rooms from: $369 ✉ 910 Prospect St., La Jolla ☎ 888/828–5498 ⊕ www.thegrandecolonial.com ⇱ 97 rooms ⊙ No Meals.

La Valencia Hotel

$$$ | **HOTEL** | This elegant "Pink Lady" drew Hollywood film stars in the 1930s and '40s with its setting and views of La Jolla Cove; now it draws the Kardashians. **Pros:** comp bikes and golf cart service to explore La Jolla; poolside cabana service; 1920s charm. **Cons:** standard rooms are tiny; lots of traffic outside; valet $25 and pet fee $50 per day. ⑤ Rooms from: $449 ✉ 1132 Prospect St., La Jolla ☎ 858/454–0771 ⊕ www.lavalencia.com ⇱ 114 rooms ⊙ No Meals.

The Lodge at Torrey Pines

$$$ | **RESORT** | Best known for its location adjacent to two 18-hole championship golf courses, this beautiful Craftsman-style lodge sits on a bluff between La Jolla and Del Mar with commanding coastal views, excellent service, a blissful spa, and the upscale A. R. Valentien restaurant (named after a San Diego artist of the early 1900s), which serves farm-to-table California cuisine. **Pros:** spacious upscale rooms; remarkable service; adjacent to the famed Torrey Pines Golf Course; warm decor with Craftsman accents and hardwoods. **Cons:** not centrally located; expensive; $40 daily parking fee. ⑤ Rooms from: $452 ✉ 11480 N. Torrey Pines Rd., La Jolla ☎ 858/529–5641 ⊕ www.lodgetorreypines.com ⇱ 170 rooms ⊙ No Meals.

★ Orli La Jolla

$$ | **B&B/INN** | Since its unveiling in 2023, this historic estate-turned-boutique hotel has lured travelers from afar with its romantic courtyard, sophisticated lounge, and deco-modern suites just blocks from the beach. **Pros:** contactless on-demand services; boutique hotel with convenience of home; quiet street with intimate feel. **Cons:** sound carries between rooms; often booked; parking garage $25 per day. ⑤ Rooms from: $350 ✉ 7753 Draper Ave., La Jolla ☎ 858/727–2776 ⊕ www.stayorli.com ⇱ 13 rooms ⊙ No Meals.

Pantai Inn

$$$ | **HOTEL** | Located along La Jolla coastline with ocean views from almost every corner, this sophisticated, Bali-inspired inn offers a mix of studios, one- and

two-bedroom suites, and cottages. **Pros:** spacious rooms; ocean views; no resort fee. **Cons:** no pool, fitness center, or elevator; not pet-friendly; daily parking $25. ⑤ *Rooms from: $380* ⊠ *1003 Coast Blvd., La Jolla* ☎ *858/224–7600, 855/287–2682* ⊕ *www.pantai.com* ⌐ *29 rooms* ⦿ *Free Breakfast.*

Scripps Inn

$$$ | B&B/INN | You'd be wise to make reservations well in advance for this small, quiet inn tucked away on Coast Boulevard atop Whale Watch Point; its popularity with repeat visitors ensures that it's booked year-round. **Pros:** intimate feel with beach access; across from Museum of Contemporary Art; rooms spacious and clean. **Cons:** ground-level rooms face the parking lot; pricey hotel; daily parking fee $18. ⑤ *Rooms from: $355* ⊠ *555 S. Coast Blvd., La Jolla* ☎ *858/454–3391, 888/976–2912* ⊕ *www.scrippsinn.com* ⌐ *14 rooms* ⦿ *No Meals.*

ⓨ Nightlife

Just a little north of Pacific Beach, the bar tab increases considerably in the chichi clime of La Jolla, home to many of San Diego's wealthiest residents, and for that matter, the bars with the best ocean views. It's not all bank-breaking martini lounges, however; there's enough diversity in the options here to appease both the day-trippers and the residents alike.

BARS
Cusp

BARS | The stone walls and modern metal accents along the bar give the impression of Cusp being a dark, intimate lounge, but the panoramic views of La Jolla shores brighten up this chic spot on the 11th floor of Hotel La Jolla. Sip on one of their signature cocktails during their daily happy hour from 2 to 6. Live music sets the scene 8–8 on Thursday and most weekends. ⊠ *Hotel La Jolla, 7955 La Jolla Shores Dr., 11th fl., La Jolla* ☎ *858/551–3620* ⊕ *www.cusprestaurant.com.*

George's Level2

BARS | Located on the middle level of George's at the Cove, this hip, casual, and somewhat more affordable hangout is always buzzing with activity—especially on weekends. Stop in for craft cocktails or bar snacks that rank among La Jolla's best, and with gorgeous ocean views to boot. Enjoy discounts on beverages weekdays 2–6 pm. ⊠ *At George's at the Cove, 1250 Prospect St., La Jolla* ☎ *858/454–4244* ⊕ *www.georgesatthe-cove.com/level2.*

Manhattan of La Jolla

PIANO BARS | Lovingly referred to as the "Manhattan Lounge" by locals, this underrated and largely undiscovered bar neighbors the Italian steak house inside the Empress Hotel. The dark, old-school interior is perfect for sipping martinis and listening to live music Wednesday through Sunday. ⊠ *7766 Fay Ave., La Jolla* ☎ *858/459–0700* ⊕ *www.manhattano-flajolla.com* ⌐ *Jazz Wed., Thurs.–Sun. piano or guest musicians.*

The Spot

BARS | Nightlife can be kind of sleepy in affluent La Jolla, but in-the-know locals keep this sports bar buzzing on any given night thanks to powerful cocktails like the Killer Old Fashioned and the bar grub that's served late into the evening—one of the few spots that's open in La Jolla in the wee hours. ⊠ *1005 Prospect St., La Jolla* ☎ *858/459–0800* ⊕ *www.thespo-tonline.com.*

COMEDY AND CABARET
The Comedy Store La Jolla

CABARET | Like its sister establishment in Hollywood, this club hosts some of the best national touring and local talent. Cover charges range from nothing (with a two-drink minimum) to $50 or more for national acts. Seating is at bistro-style tables, and all shows are 21 and older. ⊠ *916 Pearl St., La Jolla* ☎ *858/454–9176* ⊕ *www.thecomedystore.com/la-jolla* ⌐ *Closed Mon. and Tues.*

⊚ Performing Arts

MUSIC

La Jolla Athenaeum Music & Arts Library

MUSIC | The Athenaeum is a membership-supported, nonprofit library with an exceptional collection of books, periodicals, CDs, and other media related to arts and music. It also hosts classes, exhibits, lectures, and intimate jazz, chamber music, and the occasional folk concert throughout the year. ⊠ *1008 Wall St., La Jolla* ☎ *858/454–5872* ⊕ *ljathenaeum.org* ☞ *Closed Sun. and Mon.*

The Loft at UCSD

CONCERTS | This quaint, comfortable performance space inside the Price Center on the University of California San Diego campus hosts intimate music concerts, spoken-word programs, film screenings, and culinary events. ⊠ *Price Center East, 9500 Gilman Dr., 4th fl., La Jolla* ☎ *858/678–0922* ⊕ *theloft.ucsd. edu* ☞ *Closed weekdays at 5 pm. Closed weekends.*

THEATER

More than a few Tony-winning Broadway productions have been launched at San Diego theaters; La Jolla Playhouse is one of the stars in the city's large ensemble.

The Conrad Prebys Performing Arts Center
(*The Conrad*)

MUSIC | With roots in classical and chamber music, the permanent home of the La Jolla Music Society features a range of performances from piano and jazz, to mariachi, dance, and world music. The venue's four spaces host concerts, performances, educational programs, and SummerFest—a four-week music festival featuring more than 80 world-class artists and ensembles. For the season schedule, visit their website. ⊠ *7600 Fay Ave., La Jolla* ☎ *858/459–3728* ⊕ *www. theconrad.org.*

★ La Jolla Playhouse

THEATER | Under the artistic direction of Christopher Ashley, the playhouse presents exciting and innovative plays and musicals on three stages. Many Broadway shows—among them *Memphis, Come From Away, Tommy,* and *Jersey Boys*—have previewed here before their East Coast premieres. Its Without Walls program also ensures that the productions aren't limited to the playhouse, having put on site-specific shows in places like outdoor art spaces, cars, and even the ocean. ⊠ *University of California at San Diego, 2910 La Jolla Village Dr., La Jolla* ☎ *858/550–1010* ⊕ *www.lajollaplayhouse.org* ⊠ *From $70* ⊙ *Closed Mon.*

⊚ Shopping

San Diego's answer to Rodeo Drive in Beverly Hills, La Jolla has chic boutiques, art galleries, and gift shops lining narrow streets that attract well-heeled shoppers and celebrities. Prospect Street and Girard Avenue are the primary shopping stretches, and North Prospect is packed with art galleries.

The Upper Girard Design District stocks home decor accessories and luxury furnishings. Store hours vary widely so it's wise to call in advance, though most shops on Prospect Street stay open until 10 pm on weeknights to accommodate evening strollers. If you're driving, there's free parking in the La Jolla Cove or garages along Prospect Street, between Wall and Silverado, or along Herschel, Girard, and Fay. Rates range from $1.50 for 20 minutes to a flat $20 per day. After 4 pm, there's a flat rate of $10.

La Jolla's chic boutiques offer a more intimate shopping experience, along with some of the classiest clothes, jewelry, and shoes in the county. La Plaza La Jolla is an open-air shopping center with boutiques and galleries in a Spanish-style building overlooking the cove.

BOOKS
Warwick's

BOOKS | This family-owned-and-operated bookstore has been a La Jolla fixture since 1939, and often hosts big-name author signings. They also carry stationery, calendars, and other gifts. ✉ *7812 Girard Ave., La Jolla* ☎ *858/454–0347* ⊕ *www.warwicks.com.*

CLOTHING AND ACCESSORIES
Ascot Shop

MEN'S CLOTHING | The classic Ivy League look is king in this traditional haberdashery that sells menswear by Saxx, Hagen, and Peter Miller. In-house same-day tailoring is available. ✉ *7750 Girard Ave., La Jolla* ☎ *858/454–4222* ⊕ *www.ascotshop.com.*

La Jolla Surf Systems

OTHER SPECIALTY STORE | One block from La Jolla Shores beach, this local institution stocks hip beach and resort wear, plus top-brand surfboards, bodyboards, and wet suits. The shop also rents surf and stand-up paddleboards, beach chairs, umbrellas, kayaks, and snorkel gear. ✉ *2132 Av. de la Playa, La Jolla* ☎ *858/456–2777* ⊕ *www.lajollasurfsystem.com* ☞ *Surfboards $9/hr; kayaks $70 for 2 hrs.*

Rangoni Firenze

SHOES | The shoe shop carries its own house brand of Valentina Rangoni footwear, as well as handbags. ✉ *7870 Girard Ave., La Jolla* ☎ *858/459–4469* ⊕ *www.rangonistore.com.*

GALLERIES
Thumbprint Gallery

ART GALLERIES | This quaint little gallery brings a little edge to otherwise sleepy La Jolla, showing off some of the best lowbrow and street artists in the city. This is a great place to purchase something truly unique for a low price. ✉ *920 Kline St., La Jolla* ☎ *858/354–6294* ⊕ *www.thumbprintgallery.com* ☞ *Closed Sun.–Fri.*

JEWELRY
CJ Charles

JEWELRY & WATCHES | An exquisitely appointed shop selling designer and estate jewelry, CJ Charles specializes in Bulgari watches, Cartier, and Patek Philippe, along with stunning fine jewelry, Baccarat crystal, and gift items. ✉ *1135 Prospect St., La Jolla* ☎ *858/454–5390* ⊕ *www.cjcharles.com.*

MARKETS
La Jolla Open Aire Market

MARKET | **FAMILY** | With a county-fair atmosphere and proceeds benefiting La Jolla Elementary, this large market features not only fresh produce and flowers, but also paintings from local artists, handmade clothing and jewelry, and a tempting food court serving everything from crepes and tacos to gyros and roasted corn on the cob. The market is open Sunday 9–1 pm. ✉ *La Jolla Elementary School playground, at corner of Girard St. and Genter St., 7335 Girard St., La Jolla* ☎ *858/454–1699* ⊕ *www.lajollamarket.com.*

SHOPPING MALLS
Westfield UTC

SHOPPING CENTER | **FAMILY** | This popular outdoor mall on the east side of I–5 has more than 150 shops and 40 eateries, plus an ArcLight Cinemas and a children's play area. Nordstrom and Macy's anchor the center, and specialty stores of note include Madewell (☎ *858/458–0012*) for high-quality basics; Pottery Barn Kids (☎ *858/824–9079*) for children's bedding and accessories; Crate & Barrel (☎ *858/558–4545*) for kitchenware, china, and furniture; and an Apple Store (☎ *858/795–6870*) for the latest gadgets. One of the country's greenest shopping centers, UTC has lush gardens, open-air plazas, and pedestrian-friendly walkways. Additional eco-friendly cred: Tesla Motors shows off its latest electric vehicles here. ✉ *4545 La Jolla Village Dr., between I–5 and I–805, La Jolla* ☎ *858/546–8858* ⊕ *www.westfield.com/utc.*

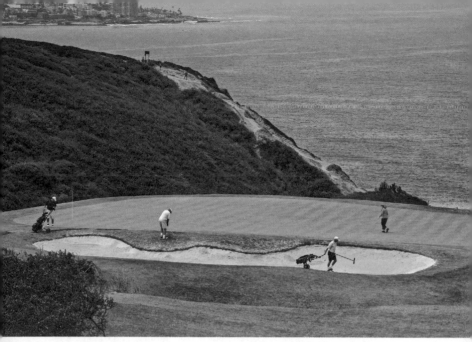

Torrey Pines Golf Course has fantastic views to go along with its challenging holes.

TOYS

Geppetto's Toys

TOYS | FAMILY | This family-run toy shop has been in business for more than 40 years. With nine locations throughout San Diego, the store offers classic toys and games as well as the newest must-haves. It's a great place to wander with kids or pick up something to take home. ✉ *7850 Girard Ave., La Jolla* ☎ *858/456–4441* ⊕ *www.geppettostoys.com.*

 Activities

BIKING

On many summer days, Route S21, more commonly known as "the 101," from La Jolla to Oceanside looks like a freeway for cyclists. About 24 miles long, it's easily the most popular and scenic bike route around, never straying far from the beach. Although the terrain is fairly easy, the long, steep Torrey Pines grade is famous for weeding out the weak. Another Darwinian challenge is dodging slow-moving pedestrians and cars pulling over to park in towns like Encinitas and Del Mar.

Hike Bike Kayak Adventures

BIKING | This outfitter offers two-hour guided eBike tours along La Jolla's coast. The company also rents kayaks, surfboards, paddleboards, and snorkel gear. ✉ *2222 Av. de la Playa, La Jolla* ☎ *858/551–9510* ⊕ *www.hikebikekayak. com* ✐ *From $49.*

DIVING

Scuba San Diego

SCUBA DIVING | This center is well regarded for its top-notch instruction and certification programs, as well as for guided dive tours. Scuba Adventure classes for noncertified divers are held daily in Mission Bay, meeting near Mission Point. Trips for certified divers depart from La Jolla and include dives to kelp reefs in La Jolla Cove, ship wrecks, and night diving at La Jolla Canyon. They also have snorkeling tours to La Jolla's Sea Caves. ✉ *8008 Girard St., La Jolla* ☎ *619/260–1880* ⊕ *www.scubasandiego. com* ✐ *From $80* ☞ *Scuba Adventure* *meeting point is 2615 Bayside La. in South Mission Bay, near Mission Point.*

GOLF

★ Torrey Pines Golf Course

GOLF | Due to its cliff-top location overlooking the Pacific and its classic championship holes, Torrey Pines is one of the best public golf courses in the United States. The course was the site of the 2008 and 2021 U.S. Open and has been the home of the Farmers Insurance Open since 1968. The par-72 South Course, redesigned by Rees Jones in 2001, receives rave reviews from touring pros; it is longer, more challenging, and more expensive than the North Course. Tee times may be booked up to 90 days in advance and are subject to an advance booking fee ($47). ⊠ *11480 N. Torrey Pines Rd., La Jolla* ☎ *858/452–3226, 800/985–4653* ⊕ *www.torreypinesgolf-course.com* ⊠ *South: from $278. North: from $176; $45 for golf cart* ⚎ *South: 18 holes, 7707 yards, par 72. North: 18 holes, 7258 yards, par 72.*

HANG GLIDING AND PARAGLIDING

Torrey Pines Gliderport

HANG GLIDING & PARAGLIDING | Perched on the cliffs overlooking the ocean north of La Jolla, this is one of the most spectacular spots to hang glide in the world. It's for experienced pilots only, but hang-gliding and paragliding lessons and tandem rides for inexperienced gliders are available. Those who'd rather just watch can grab a bite at the Cliffhanger Cafe, which offers incredible views of the Pacific and of the paragliders taking off. During the summer, there's live music 1–4 on weekends. ⊠ *2800 Torrey Pines Scenic Dr., La Jolla* ☎ *858/452–9858* ⊕ *www.flytorrey.com* ⊠ *Paragliding from $175; hang gliding from $225 (cash discounts).*

HIKING

Los Peñasquitos Canyon Preserve

HIKING & WALKING | Twelve miles of trails at this inland park north of Mira Mesa accommodate equestrians, runners,

walkers, and cyclists as well as leashed dogs. Look at maps for trails specific to bikes and horses. The trail parallels Los Peñasquitos and is marked by a small waterfall at the 3.5 mile marker. Hikers can cross the creek and loop back among large rock boulders—it's an unexpected oasis amid the arid valley landscape. ⊠ *12020 Black Mountain Rd., La Jolla* ✛ *From I–15, exit Mercy Rd., and head west to Black Mountain Rd.; turn right then left at first light; follow road to Ranch House parking lot* ☎ *858/484–7504* ⊕ *www.sdparks.org* ☞ *Parking $3.*

Torrey Pines State Natural Reserve

HIKING & WALKING | **FAMILY** | Hikers and runners will appreciate this park's many winning features: switchback trails that descend to the sea, an unparalleled view of the Pacific, and a chance to see the Torrey pine tree, one of the rarest pine breeds in the United States. The reserve hosts guided nature walks as well. Dogs and food are prohibited at the reserve. Parking is $20–$25, depending on day and season. ⊠ *12600 N. Torrey Pines Rd., La Jolla* ✛ *Exit I–5 at Carmel Valley Rd. and head west toward Coast Hwy. 101 until you reach N. Torrey Pines Rd.; turn left.* ☎ *858/755–2063* ⊕ *www.torreypine.org* ⊠ *Parking from $20.*

KAYAKING

There are several places to kayak throughout San Diego. You can spend an especially memorable afternoon exploring the Seven Caves off La Jolla Cove, where you can often see seals, sea lions, and even dolphins, or the Underwater Park and Ecological Reserve at the cove.

Everyday California

KAYAKING | This action-on-the-water sports company also has its own clothing line offering beach-casual styles inspired by La Jolla. Tours with expert guides include a sunset kayak tour, where wildlife to see includes sea lions, seals, pelicans, and dolphins; the tour combines kayaking and snorkeling. Leopard shark migration tours are offered May–August, and whale-watching tours December–March. Surf and stand-up paddleboard lessons are also available. If you'd rather go out on your own, Everyday California rents kayaks, stand-up paddleboards, surfboards, snorkel equipment, and bodyboards. ✉ *2261 Av. de la Playa, La Jolla* ☎ *858/454–6195* ⊕ *www.everydaycalifornia.com* ✆ *From $89*.

Hike Bike Kayak Adventures

KAYAKING | This shop offers several kayak tours, from easy excursions in La Jolla Cove that are well suited to families and beginners to more advanced jaunts. Tours include kayaking the caves off La Jolla coast, and whale-watching (from a safe distance) December through February. Tours last 90 minutes to two hours and require a minimum of four people. ✉ *2222 Av. de la Playa, La Jolla* ☎ *858/551–9510* ⊕ *www.hikebikekayak.com* ✆ *From $50*.

La Jolla Kayak

KAYAKING | This family-owned company offers kayak tours of the Seven Caves of La Jolla as well as snorkel and biking adventures. Several guides have extensive backgrounds in marine biology and ecology. ✉ *2199 Av. de la Playa, La Jolla* ☎ *858/459–1114* ⊕ *www.lajollakayak.com* ✆ *From $49*.

SURFING

Menehune Surf School

SURFING | This surf school provides surf lessons as well as paddleboard and surfboard rentals. Private or family lessons can be arranged ($105 per person for 90 minutes, minimum 4 people). Menehune Surf also offers popular surf camps for kids every summer from June through August at La Jolla Shores and Del Mar. ✉ *La Jolla Shores Beach, La Jolla* ✛ *Blue canopy at La Jolla Shores Beach located north of parking lot at Kellogg Park in front of 4th–5th house on sand as you walk toward Scripps Pier* ☎ *858/663–7299* ⊕ *www.menehunesurf.com* ✆ *From $105*.

★ Surf Diva Surf School

SURFING | Check out clinics, surf camps, and private lessons especially formulated for girls and women. Most clinics and trips are for women only, but there are some coed options. Guys can also book group or private lessons from the nationally recognized staff. Surf Diva is also home to a boutique that sells surf and stand-up paddleboard equipment. They also offer surf retreats in Costa Rica. ✉ *2160 Av. de la Playa, La Jolla* ☎ *858/454–8273* ⊕ *www.surfdiva.com* ✆ *Group lessons $105 per person; private lessons $150*.

Northern San Diego: Clairemont, Kearny Mesa, and Miramar

Located inland from La Jolla and north of Mission Valley, the neighborhoods of Clairemont and Kearny Mesa often fly under the radar of most visitors to San Diego. The shopping centers and restaurants of this area serve as a hub for San Diego's sizeable and diverse Asian population, especially along Convoy Street between Clairemont Mesa Boulevard and Aero Drive. Though these neighborhoods aren't traditional tourist destinations, those who do venture here will be rewarded as they dine at myriad authentic Asian restaurants, relax with a reflexology foot massage, or peruse the aisles of specialty grocery stores.

Clairemont

Centered on Tecolote Canyon, this suburban neighborhood occupies a series of mesas, many with views of Mission Bay. Heading inland, Balboa Avenue serves as the area's commercial hub.

The annual three-day Miramar Air Show is the country's largest military air show.

Restaurants

This postwar bedroom community offers adventurous diners numerous affordable and authentic mom-and-pop ethnic restaurants and grocery stores. The setting may be simple, and the service minimal, but the food can be unforgettable.

Zab Linda

$ | **THAI** | Zab Linda may be a bit out of the way and lacking in ambience, but the northeastern Thai dishes featured on the menu—noodles, curry, and the spicy larb (think meat salad), which comes with pork, chicken, beef, catfish, or duck—make the trip worth it. Pick your spicy level, from 1 to 10 to add extra heat to your dish. **Known for:** drunken noodles; spicy shrimp; authentic northeastern Thai cuisine. ⑤ *Average main: $15* ✉ *6925 Linda Vista Rd., Clairemont* ☎ *858/650–6868* ⊕ *www.zablinda.com* ⊙ *No breakfast.*

Kearny Mesa

Farther inland, Kearny Mesa is less residential than neighboring Clairemont. The bustling shopping centers lining Convoy Street are home to many popular Asian restaurants, supermarkets, and probably the best ramen you'll have outside of Japan.

◉ Sights

Societe Brewing Company

BREWERY | Societe's tasting room offers a prime view of their adjacent barrel room and brewing facility. While you can't go wrong with The Pupil IPA, wine lovers shouldn't miss The Thief feral ale, made with Grenache blanc grapes. The Harlot Belgian blonde ale is used to marinate the juicy carnitas served at their on-site food truck, Chachos Tacos. ✉ *8262 Clairemont Mesa Blvd., Kearny Mesa* ☎ *858/598–5409* ⊕ *www.societebrewing.com.*

Northern San Diego: Clairemont, Kearny Mesa, and Miramar

🍴 Restaurants

Kearny Mesa, considered the city's "Asian Restaurant Row," is definitely off the tourist radar but offers a host of small family-owned eateries serving superb authentic Chinese, Vietnamese, Thai, Japanese, Korean, and Filipino food—all within a stone's throw of one another.

Dumpling Inn

$ | CHINESE | Since 1994, this family-owned restaurant has been serving fans of traditional northern Chinese food who drive hours to sample dumplings made by hand every morning with fresh dough and filling; top sellers include the signature *xiao long bao*, the pork pot sticker, and the deep-fried beef curry. After dumplings, move on to house specialties like sea bass with black bean sauce, salt-and-pepper calamari, and pork shank Shanghai style. **Known for:** authentic mainland-style Chinese cuisine; spicy chow mein; handmade dumplings. $ *Average main: $15* ⊠ *4625 Convoy St., Kearny Mesa* ☎ *858/268-9638* ⊕ *www. dumplinginn.com* � *Closed Mon. and Tues. No lunch Wed.–Thurs.*

Phuong Trang

$ | VIETNAMESE | This much-praised, popular Vietnamese restaurant offers over 200 dishes that choosing a meal here can be difficult. Waiters steer diners to familiar tasty offerings like traditional pho, kung pao chicken, garlic-butter fried chicken wings, and fresh pork or shrimp spring rolls. **Known for:** garlic-butter chicken wings; fried spring rolls; oven-roasted catfish. $ *Average main: $12* ⊠ *Convoy Plaza, 4170 Convoy St., Kearny Mesa* ☎ *858/565-6750* ⊕ *www.phuongtrangrestaurant.com* ☻ *Closed Mon. and Tues.*

★ RakiRaki

$ | JAPANESE | The line out the door is the first sign you're at San Diego's best ramen spot, and the sight of thick organic mochi noodles soaking in deep pots of tonkotsu broth and garlic oil is sure to seal the deal. Original, red, or black-edition ramen are local go-tos, each topped with cabbage, bean sprouts, pickled egg, wakame seaweed, garlic chips, and crushed sesame. **Known for:** black-edition ramen; lunch specials; sake and beer. $ *Average main: $15* ⊠ *4646 Convoy St, #102-A, Kearny Mesa* ☎ *858/771-7254* ⊕ *www.rakirakiramen.com.*

Spicy City Chinese

$$ | SICHUAN | Get bold Sichuan flavors with loads of chili peppers at this restaurant, where food is served family style, and "mild" is not an option. If you speak Mandarin, you're in luck, but if you don't, simply point at the menu with full color photos of every dish, including the top selections like deep-fried chicken cubes with hot pepper, or the fish fillet with chili. **Known for:** affordable prices; extremely quick service; authentic Sichuan cuisine. $ *Average main: $20* ⊠ *4690 Convoy St., Kearny Mesa* ☎ *858/278-1818* ⊕ *www. spicycitycatogo.com.*

★ Tajima

$ | JAPANESE | Opened in 2001, this Japanese restaurant helped pioneer San Diego's ramen movement as the first noodle house on Convoy to set down roots without compromising the purity of Japanese cuisine. All ramens are made from scratch, and you can taste it with every slurp of the flavorful broth. **Known for:** Japanese craft beer; homemade fresh and springy ramen noodles; authentic Japanese cuisine. $ *Average main: $12* ⊠ *4681 Convoy St,, Suite I, Kearny Mesa* ☎ *858/576-7244* ⊕ *www. tajimasandiego.com.*

Nightlife

Beer-snob heaven is situated between ramen houses and car dealerships.

Common Theory

BREWPUBS | More than 30 craft beers on tap, elevated pub-style food, and a killer weekday happy hour (3–6 pm) make this Kearny Mesa brewery a magnet for beer aficionados. Depending on the day of the week, last call hits between 11 pm and 1 am, meaning you can curl up in the unique living-room setting and make yourself right at home for the night. ⊠ *4805 Convoy St., Kearny Mesa* ☎ *619/780–6689* ⊕ *www.commontheorysd.com.*

Miramar

In the past, Miramar was generally associated with the annual Miramar Air Show, the largest military air show in the country. Today, Miramar is better known as the epicenter of San Diego's ever-growing beer scene. More than a dozen breweries call this zone between the 805 and 15 freeways their brewing headquarters, or, more commonly, "Beeramar." This sprawling industrial district won't win any awards for its warehouse facilities, but it certainly delivers when it comes to brewing, tasting, and on occasion, feeding the multitudes with elevated pub food. Don't expect a stacking of hands between neighbors; they fly solo. One brewery might offer tours, another might have a barrel-aged tasting room, another might have a food truck, and they all have their own operating hours. Far from your ordinary pub crawl, you'll need a designated driver to chauffeur you between isolated breweries.

◉ Sights

AleSmith Brewing Co.

BREWERY | With one of the largest tasting rooms in San Diego, this artisanal microbrewery offers tastings at its out-of-the-way locale in the Miramar area. Try the special edition of AleSmith's popular Speedway Stout brewed with Madagascar vanilla and a dark espresso. The tasting room is open to visitors daily 11 am–10 pm. ⊠ *9990 Alesmith Ct., Miramar* ☎ *858/549–9888* ⊕ *www.alesmith.com* ⌖ *Closed Mon.–Wed.*

Cutwater Spirits

DISTILLERY | Cutwater Spirits is best known for its 19 flavors of canned cocktails, including a tequila margarita, vodka mule, and rum mint mojito. Their Tasting Room & Kitchen in Miramar is a full-service restaurant and bar with mixed drinks, neat pours, and tasting flights. ⊠ *9750 Distribution Ave., Miramar* ☎ *858/564–2140* ⊕ *www.cutwaterspirits.com* ⊙ *Closed Mon.*

Miramar Air Show

TRANSPORTATION | Considered the nation's largest air show, this annual event features aerial acts, military demonstrations, immersive experiences, and static displays. You can even tour vintage aircraft and get the experience of soaring high in one of the on-site simulators. The event is usually held in September or October. ⊠ *Marine Corps Air Station Miramar, La Jolla* ⊕ *www.miramarairshow.com.*

Chapter 8

POINT LOMA PENINSULA

WITH HARBOR AND SHELTER ISLANDS, OCEAN BEACH, AND LIBERTY STATION

Updated by
Marlise Kast-Myers

8

 Sights
★★★☆☆

 Restaurants
★★★☆☆

 Hotels
★★★☆☆

 Shopping
★★★☆☆

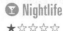 **Nightlife**
★☆☆☆☆

CABRILLO NATIONAL MONUMENT

The cliffs in front of Cabrillo National Monument are prime whale-watching territory.

Cabrillo National Monument marks the site of the first European visit to San Diego, made by 16th-century Spanish explorer Juan Rodríguez Cabrillo on September 15, 1542. Cabrillo called the spot San Miguel. Today the 166-acre preserve is one of the most frequently visited national monuments.

Catching sight of a whale from the cliffs of Cabrillo National Monument can be a highlight of a wintertime visit to San Diego. More accessible sea creatures can be seen in the tide pools at the foot of the monument's western cliffs.

Trails lead down the hillside through sagebrush and cactus, and overlook points at 430 feet offer unobstructed views of the desert mountains, Downtown, and beyond.

■TIP→ **Restrooms and water fountains are plentiful, but, except for the Visitor Center's vending machines, there's no food. Exploring the grounds consumes time and calories; pack a picnic to enjoy with the views.**

SERVICE INFORMATION

The informative visitor center, located next to the statue of Cabrillo, and the lighthouse give a historical perspective to this once-remote promontory. The center presents films and lectures about Cabrillo's voyage, the sea-level tide pools, and migrating gray whales.

✉ *1800 Cabrillo Memorial Dr., Point Loma* ☎ *619/523–4285* 🎫 *$20 per car, $10 per person entering on foot or by bicycle, admission good for 7 days* ◷ *Park daily 9–5.*

A HALF DAY AT CABRILLO NATIONAL MONUMENT

A **statue of Cabrillo** overlooks Downtown from a windy promontory, where people gather to admire the stunning panorama over the bay, from the snowcapped San Bernardino Mountains, 130 miles north, to the hills surrounding Tijuana to the south. The stone figure standing on the bluff looks rugged and dashing, but he is a creation of an artist's imagination—no portraits of Cabrillo are known to exist.

The moderately steep **Bayside Trail,** 2½ miles round-trip, winds through coastal sage scrub, curving under the cliff-top lookouts and taking you ever closer to the bayfront scenery. You cannot reach the beach from this trail and must stick to the path to protect the cliffs from erosion and yourself from thorny plants and snakes—including rattlers. You'll see prickly pear cactus and yucca, fragrant sage, and maybe a lizard, rabbit, or hummingbird. The climb back is long but gradual, leading up to the old lighthouse.

Old Point Loma Lighthouse's oil lamp was first lighted in 1855 and was visible from the sea for 25 miles. Unfortunately, it was too high above the cliffs to guide navigators trapped in Southern California's thick offshore fog. In 1891 a new lighthouse was built 400 feet below. The restored old lighthouse is open to visitors. An exhibit in the Assistant Keepers Quarters next door tells the story of the Old Lighthouse, the daily lives of the keepers, how lighthouses work, and the role they played in the development of early maritime commerce along the West Coast. On the edge of the hill near the old lighthouse sits a refurbished radio room containing displays of U.S. harbor defenses at Point Loma used during World War II.

8

Point Loma Peninsula CABRILLO NATIONAL MONUMENT

WHALE-WATCHING

The western and southern cliffs of Cabrillo National Monument are prime whale-watching territory. A sheltered **viewing station** has wayside exhibits describing the great gray whales' yearly migration from Baja California to the Bering and Chukchi seas near Alaska. High-powered telescopes and binoculars—available from the visitor center—help you focus on the whales' waterspouts. Whales are visible on clear days from late December through early March, with the highest concentration in January and February. Note that when the whales return north in spring, they are too far out in the ocean to be seen from the monument.

TIDE POOLS

When the tide is low you can walk on the rocks around saltwater pools filled with starfish, crabs, anemones, octopuses, and hundreds of other sea creatures and plants. Tide pooling is best when the tide is at its lowest, so call ahead or check tide charts online before your visit.

NEIGHBORHOOD SNAPSHOT

TOP EXPERIENCES

■ **Boating paradise:** San Diego's picturesque marinas are filled with sportfishing charters and ultraluxe yachts.

■ **Military might:** From the endless rows of white headstones at Fort Rosecrans National Cemetery to the roar of fighter jets over North Island Naval Air Station, San Diego's strong military ties are palpable.

■ **Peninsula hopping:** The thin strips of land that make up Harbor and Shelter islands pack in restaurants, hotels, marinas, and parks, all with water views.

■ **Taste of Liberty:** Point Loma's Liberty Station is home to galleries, museums, restaurants, breweries, and the bustling culinary hub, Liberty Public Market.

GETTING HERE

West of Downtown San Diego, you'll find Point Loma Peninsula accessible from the I–5 at Sea World Drive. Take Exit 21 and continue on Sea World Drive to Nimitz Boulevard. This thoroughfare splits to Harbor Island, Shelter Island, and Point Loma by way of Catalina Boulevard. Bus 84 has routes that pass near Point Loma.

PLANNING YOUR TIME

The best way to take in the entire peninsula is by car or bike, with afternoon excursions set aside for strolling Liberty Station, Harbor Island, Shelter Island, Sunset Cliffs, the Old Point Loma Lighthouse, and a few other noteworthy sites in between. Active travelers can spend a day biking the trails that run along the marinas to America's Cup Harbor. For a challenging climb, the views from Cabrillo National Monument often reward with an occasional whale-spotting. If museums, galleries, and theaters are on your itinerary, add in an extra day. Generally, two to three days are enough to soak in the Point Loma attractions and still have time for an afternoon on the water followed by fresh seafood at a local market.

POINT LOMA'S BEST BEACHES

On Point Loma's beaches surfers and even dogs join in on the fun. Humans head to the southern **Ocean Beach** to swim and sunbathe and surfers congregate around the Ocean Beach Pier. The small beach to the north, known as **Dog Beach**, is one of the few beaches in the county where dogs can play leash-free.

VIEWFINDER

Popular with surfers and sunbathers seeking privacy among the small coves, **Sunset Cliffs** makes for a better viewpoint than a swimming beach. The views are dramatic and heart-achingly beautiful. Look for the few picnic tables that are positioned near the edge of the cliffs to sit a spell and soak it all in.

Point Loma protects the San Diego Bay from the Pacific's tides and waves. Here you'll find sandy beaches, private marinas, and prominent military installations. Nestled between Coronado and Point Loma, Harbor and Shelter islands owe their existence to dredging in the bay.

Point Loma is a low-key community that caters to sailing enthusiasts, trading the bar-hopping culture of Pacific Beach for a few select locales, like the industrial-warehouse look of Modern Times Brewing, or the mid-century cool of the Pearl. Yet in neighboring Ocean Beach, it's a different world, where an inescapable hippie culture bleeds into the kitschy and earnestly earthy dives along Newport Avenue, allowing it to retain its bohemian beach-town vibe void of chain businesses. Shelter Island's best watering holes boast campy tiki-theme decor; it's also home to revered concert destination Humphrey's Concerts by the Bay, which is famous for its great sound, scenic location, and kayaking passersby.

Bays, beaches, and cliffs are the stars of these diverse coastal communities, where low-key seafood spots mingle with romantic eateries, quaint bistros, and lively beer bars. The bars and restaurants of Harbor and Shelter islands are great places to take in the views of Downtown across the bay. Although the water view is always lovely during the day, the lights of the city make the scene come alive at night. Every December, more than 80 boats are lavishly illuminated for the festive San Diego Bay Parade of Lights.

Point Loma

The hilly peninsula of **Point Loma** curves west and south into the Pacific and provides protection for San Diego Bay. Its high elevations and sandy cliffs provide incredible views, and make Point Loma a visible local landmark. Its maritime roots are evident, from its longtime ties to the U.S. Navy to its bustling sportfishing and sailing marinas. The funky community of **Ocean Beach** coexists alongside the stately homes of **Sunset Cliffs** and the honored graves at **Fort Rosecrans National Cemetery.**

Sights

★ **Cabrillo National Monument**
VIEWPOINT | FAMILY | This 166-acre preserve marks the site of the first European visit to San Diego, made by 16th-century Spanish explorer Juan Rodríguez Cabrillo when he landed at this spot on September 15, 1542. Today the site, with its rugged cliffs and shores and outstanding overlooks, is one of the most frequently visited of all the national monuments. There's a good visitor center and useful interpretive stations along the cliff-side walkways. Highlights include the moderately difficult Bayside Trail, the

Point Loma Peninsula

Sights ▼

1 ARTS DISTRICT
Liberty Station............E3

2 Cabrillo
National Monument.....C9

3 Eppig Brewing
Waterfront
Biergarten D4

4 Fort Rosecrans
National Cemetery........C7

5 Nautical History
Gallery and Museum....E3

6 Ocean Beach Pier......B2

7 San Diego Watercolor
Society....................E3

8 Shoreline Park E5

9 Visions Museum of
Textile Art.................F3

Restaurants ▼

1 Bali Hai Restaurant......E5

2 Blue Water Seafood
Ocean Beach B2

3 Breakfast Republic C2

4 Cesarina D2

5 Coasterra G4

6 Hodad's B2

7 Humphreys
Restaurant................E5

8 Island Prime and
C Level G4

9 Jimmy's Famous
American Tavern E4

10 Ketch Grill & Tapas.....D4

11 Little Lion Cafe B3

12 Mike's Taco Club........B2

13 Mitch's Seafood D4

14 Pizza Port C2

15 Point Loma Seafoods...D4

16 Raglan Public House ...B2

17 Slater's 50/50 ....F3

18 South Beach
Bar & Grille B2

19 Stone Brewing
World Bistro & Gardens –
Liberty Station............F3

20 3rd Corner Wine
Shop and Bistro..........C2

21 Tom Ham's
Lighthouse................F4

22 The Venetian
Point Loma..............D3

Quick Bites ▼

1 Azucar C2

2 Con Pane Rustic
Breads & Cafe F3

3 The Cravory E1

4 Liberty Public Market ...F3

Hotels ▼

1 Best Western Plus
Island Palms
Hotel & Marina..........D5

2 Courtyard by Marriott
San Diego Airport
Liberty Station............E3

3 Hampton Inn & Suites
San Diego Airport
Liberty Station............F4

4 Holiday Inn San Diego
Bayside E4

5 Homewood Suites by
Hilton San Diego
Airport
Liberty Station............E4

6 Inn at
Sunset Cliffs.............B3

7 Kona Kai
Resort & Spa.............D5

8 The Monsaraz...........D4

9 The Pearl Hotel D4

A Point Loma-Harbor Island Tour

Take Catalina Boulevard all the way south to the tip of Point Loma to reach **Cabrillo National Monument**. North of the monument, as you head back into the neighborhoods of Point Loma, you'll see the white headstones of **Fort Rosecrans National Cemetery**. Continue north on Catalina Boulevard to Hill Street and turn left to reach the dramatic **Sunset Cliffs**, at the western side of Point Loma near Ocean Beach. Park to tour the dramatic cliff tops and the boiling seas below, but be cautious because the cliffs can be unstable. Signs generally warn you where not to go. Head north on Sunset Cliffs Boulevard until you reach Newport Avenue, where you will make a left to enter the heart of **Ocean Beach**. If you have your dog with you,

head north to **Ocean Beach's Dog Beach** or check out surfers from the **Ocean Beach Pier** off Niagara Avenue. Just before the pier, turn left onto Newport Avenue, OB's main drag.

Return to Sunset Cliffs Boulevard and backtrack south to take a left on Point Loma Avenue. Turn left at Canon Street, which leads toward the peninsula's eastern (bay) side. Almost at the shore you'll see Scott Street, Point Loma's main commercial drag. Scott Street is bisected by Shelter Island Drive, which leads to **Shelter Island**. For another example of what can be done with tons of material dredged from a bay, go back up Shelter Island Drive, turn right on Rosecrans Street, another right on North Harbor Drive, and a final right onto **Harbor Island**.

Old Point Loma Lighthouse, and the tide pools (at low tide only). There's also a sheltered viewing station where you can watch the gray whales' yearly migration (December–February) from Baja California to Alaska (including high-powered telescopes). ⊠ *1800 Cabrillo Memorial Dr., Point Loma* ☎ *619/523–4285* ⊕ *www.nps.gov/cabr* ⊠ *$20 per car, $10 per person on foot/bicycle, entry good for 7 days.*

Eppig Brewing Waterfront Biergarten

BREWERY | Overlooking the San Diego Bay and a nearby marina, this German-inspired brewery is quite possibly one of San Diego's most scenic. Expect a diverse spread of lagers, pilsners, ales, sours, and stouts that can be sampled as a draft or taster flight. Time your visit so you can watch the sunset over the water with a beer in hand. ⊠ *2817 Dickens St., Point Loma* ☎ *619/756–6825* ⊕ *www.eppigbrewing.com.*

Fort Rosecrans National Cemetery

CEMETERY | In 1934, eight of the 1,000 acres set aside for a military reserve in 1852 were designated as a burial site. More than 100,000 people are now interred here; it's moving to see the rows upon rows of white headstones that overlook both sides of Point Loma just north of the Cabrillo National Monument. Some of those laid to rest here were killed in battles that predate California's statehood; the graves of the 17 soldiers and one civilian who died in the 1874 Battle of San Pasqual between troops from Mexico and the United States are marked by a large bronze plaque. The 75-foot granite obelisk, the Bennington Monument, commemorates the 66 crew members who died in a boiler explosion and fire on board the USS *Bennington* in 1905. ⊠ *Cabrillo Memorial Dr., Point Loma* ☎ *619/553–2084* ⊕ *www.cem.va.gov.*

🔱 Beaches

Sunset Cliffs

BEACH | As the name would suggest, this natural park near Point Loma Nazerene University is one of the best places in San Diego to watch the sunset thanks to its cliff-top location and expansive ocean views. Some limited beach access is accessible via an extremely steep stairway at the foot of Ladera Street. Beware of the treacherous cliff trails and pay attention to warning signs since the cliffs are very unstable. If you're going to make your way to the narrow beach below, it's best to go at low tide when the southern end, near Cabrillo Point, reveals tide pools teeming with small sea creatures. Farther north the waves lure surfers, and Osprey Point offers good fishing off the rocks. Keep your eyes peeled for migrating California gray whales during the winter months. Check WaveCast (⊕ *www.wavecast.com/socal/*) for tide schedules. **Amenities:** parking (no fee). **Best for:** solitude; sunset; surfing. ⊠ *Sunset Cliffs Blvd., between Ladera St. and Adair St., Point Loma* ⊕ *www.sunsetcliffs.info.*

🍴 Restaurants

Once a neighborhood of tuna-fishing families, this famous peninsula is now a wealthy enclave where residents enjoy charming neighborhood restaurants and new upscale dining spots clustered in walkable Liberty Station, and Harbor and Shelter islands. Although there's some fine dining here, most eateries are casual and cater to laid-back locals, sun-loving tourists, and sailing enthusiasts.

★ Cesarina

$$ | **ITALIAN** | A wall of mason jars with pickled vegetables and brined olives transports you to an Italian market in Rome where the owner's mother perfected generations of recipes that have made their way into this Point Loma eatery. Since its 2019 opening, customers have lined up for generous portions of homemade Italian staples including pasta, gnocchi, meatballs, sausage, bread, and decadent desserts. **Known for:** nearly everything made from scratch; authentic Italian cuisine; excellent vegan options. ⑤ *Average main: $25* ⊠ *4161 Voltaire St., Point Loma* ☎ *619/226–6222* ⊕ *www.cesarinarestaurant.com.*

Jimmy's Famous American Tavern

$$ | **AMERICAN** | Tucked bay-side between Harbor and Shelter islands, Jimmy's (JFAT for short) draws hungry boaters and sea lovers with its marina views and elevated backyard-barbecue faves like the Cowboy burger with crispy onion rings and pecanwood bacon. The interior blends varnished wood with industrial-chic I beams and garage-style doors, plus there's a patio facing the water. **Known for:** Bloody Marys during weekend brunch; seven types of burgers; happy hour specials ($9 cocktails and $12 burgers). ⑤ *Average main: $21* ⊠ *4990 N. Harbor Dr., Point Loma* ☎ *619/226–2103* ⊕ *www.j-fat.com.*

Mitch's Seafood

$ | **SEAFOOD** | Three local families—with a fishing history—joined nets in 2008 to provide the best catch in Point Loma; a chalkboard menu showcases sustainable seafood caught mostly by them, off the shores of San Diego and Baja. The fisherman's stew and fish tacos are on point, loaded with swordfish, octopus, calamari, and rock fish, while the tuna melt and breaded shrimp beckon a cold brew to wash it all down. **Known for:** big fish sandwiches; great seafood without the fine dining price; seafood combo with chips. ⑤ *Average main: $17* ⊠ *1403 Scott St., Point Loma* ☎ *619/222–8787* ⊕ *www.mitchsseafood.com.*

Point Loma Seafoods

$ | **SEAFOOD** | **FAMILY** | When fishing boats unload their catch on-site, a seafood restaurant and market earns the right to boast that they offer "the freshest thing in town." In the late 1950's, mostly sportfishermen came here, but word got out about the just-caught fried fish on San Francisco–style sourdough bread, and now locals and visitors come to enjoy bay views, sunshine, and a greatly expanded menu of seafood dishes. A friendly, efficient crew takes orders for food and drinks at the counter, keeping the wait down even on the busiest days. **Known for:** San Francisco–style seafood on sourdough; dockside bay views; hickory-wood smoked fish. $ *Average main: $20* ⊠ *2805 Emerson St., Point Loma* ☎ *619/223–1109* ⊕ *www.pointlomaseafoods.com.*

The Venetian Point Loma

$$ | **ITALIAN** | **FAMILY** | Two sons carry on the tradition of Italian home cooking begun by their father more than 55 years ago at this neighborhood favorite. House specialties like shrimp puttanesca, and bow-tie pasta tossed with prosciutto, peas, and mushrooms in a rose-tinted cream sauce reflect the family's origins in Southern Italy. **Known for:** huge portions; some of the best pizza in Point Loma; quaint and cozy setting. $ *Average main: $22* ⊠ *3663 Voltaire St., Point Loma* ☎ *619/223–8197* ⊕ *www.thevenetianrestaurantpointloma.com.*

😃 Coffee and Quick Bites

The Cravory

$ | **BAKERY** | San Diego's best cookies come in crowd-pleasing flavors such as birthday cake, red velvet, and pancakes and bacon. There's also craft sodas, Cravory flavored milks, edible cookie dough, ice cream, and cold brew to round out your snack. **Known for:** amazing cookies; cookie-of-the-month club; ships anywhere. $ *Average main: $5* ⊠ *3960 W. Point Loma Blvd., Suite M, Point Loma* ⊹ *Next to King Crab* ☎ *619/795–9077* ⊕ *www.thecravory.com.*

 Hotels

Point Loma is a hilly community that's home to Cabrillo National Monument, a naval base, and a growing destination for shopping, dining, and art called Liberty Station. The central location near the San Diego airport has made Point Loma a popular spot for chain hotels.

Holiday Inn San Diego Bayside

$$ | **HOTEL** | **FAMILY** | The swanky lobby, central location, and hotel rates will appeal to parents, while the outdoor activities—a pool, a Jacuzzi, a nine-hole putting green, shuffleboard, and Ping-Pong—will surely have the kids worn out by bedtime. **Pros:** great for kids; free airport shuttle; happy hour at the on-site Bayside Bar. **Cons:** not centrally located; confusing layout; might be too kid-friendly for some. $ *Rooms from: $216* ⊠ *4875 N. Harbor Dr., Point Loma* ☎ *619/224–3621, 800/662–8899* ⊕ *www.holinnbayside.com* 🛏 *291 rooms* ⫶◉⫶ *No Meals.*

★ The Monsaraz

$$ | **HOTEL** | This new Hilton property pays tribute to the Portuguese fisherman who discovered Point Loma in the 16th century, as evident in the mosaic tiles, basket lamps, and roped pillars. **Pros:** centrally located, 5 minutes from the airport; small market for grab n' go snacks; outstanding restaurant and bar. **Cons:** courtyard often booked for private events; smallish rooms; no pool. $ *Rooms from: $299* ⊠ *1451 Rosecrans St, Point Loma* ☎ *619/790–5700* ⊕ *www.themonsaraz.com* 🛏 *92 rooms* ⫶◉⫶ *No Meals.*

The Pearl Hotel

$$ | **HOTEL** | This 1960s Sportsman's Lodge received a mid-century modern makeover in 2007, turning it into a retro-chic hangout decorated with kitschy lamps and original, in-room photographs of pearl divers. **Pros:** near marina; hip bar/restaurant on-site (dinner only, except for summer Sunday brunch and seasonal specials); "Oysters and Bubbles" Thursdays with $2 oysters and half-off bubbly. **Cons:** not centrally located; one bed in rooms; noise on movie night. $ *Rooms from: $249* ⊠ *1410 Rosecrans St., Point Loma* ☎ *619/226–6100* ⊕ *www.thepearlsd.com* ⇲ *23 rooms* ♦| *No Meals.*

Nightlife

Point Loma is a low-key community, trading the bar-hopping culture of Pacific Beach for a few select locales, like the clean and artsy look of the Lomaland Fermentorium, or the mid-century cool of the Pearl Hotel.

BARS

Charles and Dinorah

PIANO BARS | Paying tribute to Charles and Dinorah, the property's original owners, this hotel bar is like stepping back into late '60s Palm Springs, with a modular orange leather sofa, clean lines, and wood accents. The lobby bar is almost as fabulous as the outdoor pool area, where inflatable balls bob in illuminated water and vintage flicks show on a huge screen. Check their website for the line up. ⊠ *The Pearl Hotel, 1410 Rosecrans St., Point Loma* ☎ *619/226–6100* ⊕ *www. thepearlsd.com.*

BREWPUBS

Lomaland Fermentorium (*Modern Times Beer Tasting Room*)

BREWPUBS | Fondly referred to as the Lomaland Fermentorium, this Modern Times tap house is California's first employee-owned brewery. The popular warehouse tasting room lives up to its name with innovative design—including a mural made entirely of Post-It notes—simple and stylish take-home six-packs, and a rotating cast of beers on tap with the diversity to please every palate. ⊠ *3725 Greenwood St., Point Loma* 🖷 *010/646–9694* ⊕ *www.moderntimes-beer.com.*

Activities

FISHING

Pier fishing doesn't offer as much excitement, but it's the cheapest ocean fishing option available. No license is required to fish from a public pier, which includes those at Ocean Beach.

Fisherman's Landing

FISHING | You can book space on a fleet of luxury vessels from 57 feet to 124 feet long and embark on multiday trips in search of yellowfin tuna, yellowtail, and other deep-water fish. Half-day fishing is also available. ⊠ *2838 Garrison St., Point Loma* ☎ *619/221–8500* ⊕ *www.fishermanslanding.com* 🖾 *From $65.*

H&M Landing

FISHING | Join the West's oldest sportfishing company for year-round fishing trips in search of rockfish, bass, white fish, and tuna. ⊠ *2803 Emerson St., Point Loma* ☎ *619/222–1144* ⊕ *www.hmlanding.com* 🖾 *From $70.*

HIKING

★ Bayside Trail at Cabrillo National Monument

HIKING & WALKING | Driving here is a treat in itself, as a vast view of the Pacific unfolds before you. The view is equally enjoyable on Bayside Trail (2½ miles round-trip), which is home to the same coastal sagebrush that Juan Rodriguez Cabrillo saw when he first discovered the California coast in the 16th century. After the hike, you can explore nearby tide pools, the monument statue, and the Old Point Loma Lighthouse. Don't worry if you don't see everything on your first visit; your entrance receipt ($20 per car) is good for seven days. ⊠ *1800 Cabrillo Memorial Dr., Point Loma* ✛ *From I–5, take Rosecrans exit and turn right on Canon St. then left on Catalina Blvd. (also known as Cabrillo Memorial Dr.); follow until end* ☎ *619/523–4285* ⊕ *www.nps. gov/cabr* 🖾 *Parking $20* ☞ *No restrooms or water along the trail; Pets and bikes are not allowed.*

Liberty Station

From 1923 to 1997, Liberty Station served as the Naval Training Center (NTC) where 1.75 million Navy recruits and 1 million A and C school sailors were trained. Following its 70 years of operation, Liberty Station was transformed into a 361-acre center for dining, shopping, art, entertainment, and history. Since its rebirth in 2000, Liberty Station never lost touch with its historic roots, demonstrated in the architecture and barracks repurposed for modern-day use. The center of the action is Liberty Public Market, once used as the Naval Training Center mess hall. In 2023 Liberty Station celebrated its 100-year impact on San Diego.

 Sights

ARTS DISTRICT Liberty Station

ARTS CENTER | Ever since the renovation of the former Naval Training Center, Liberty Station has championed local artists by transforming the space into a hub for culture and arts. This thriving ARTS DISTRICT showcases murals, sculptures, and other mediums by local artists whose pieces are commissioned for approximately one year. To get a closer look, a Public Art Scavenger Hunt invites visitors to tour the public art by scanning a QR code at any work of art. Once the self-guided tour is launched, the art adventure begins. Those who complete the full route can receive discounts from participating vendors. Some of the most notable pieces include Victor Ving's mural "Greetings from the U.S. Naval Training Station," an interpretation of a 1940s military postcard; Jonathan Allen's wooden boat "USS Brave" that honors the navy heritage; and Mary Buckman's terra cotta sculpture "Sisterhood," representing the bond between Kumeyaay and western women. ⌧ *2820 Roosevelt Rd., Liberty Station* ☎ *619/573–9300* ⊕ *www.ntcfoundation.org. Murals and Installations of Liberty Station*

Nautical History Gallery and Museum

HISTORY MUSEUM | **FAMILY** | Curated by Joe Frangiosa, this 800-square-foot exhibit is dedicated to depicting the history of the U.S. Navy, its ships, and their evolution from the Revolutionary War period to World War II. In addition to constructed model ships, the exhibit includes artifacts, photographs, uniforms, and toys detailing the Navy's history. ⌧ *2640 Historic Decatur Rd., Bldg. 200, Suite 108, Liberty Station* ⊹ *Dick Laub NTC Command Center* ☎ *619/366–2469* ⊕ *www.nhgallery.org* ⌧ *Free* ⊙ *Closed Mon.*

The San Diego Watercolor Society

ARTS CENTER | Founded in 1965, this nonprofit promotes water-based media through workshops, exhibitions, and an impressive collection of work by talented plein air painters. ⌧ *2825 Dewey Rd., Suite 105, Bldg. 202, Liberty Station* ☎ *619/876–4550* ⊕ *www.sdws.org* ⊙ *Closed Mon. and Tues.*

Visions Museum of Textile Art

OTHER MUSEUM | This three-room museum pays tribute to textile artists and the quilting community with impressive fabric works on display. An on-site shop is stocked with jewelry, baskets, books, textile hangings, and other items related to fabric art. Monthly workshops are hosted regularly. ⌧ *2825 Dewey Rd., Suite 100, Liberty Station* ☎ *619/546–4872* ⊕ *www.visionsartmuseum.org* ⌧ *Free (donations welcome)* ⊙ *Closed Sun.–Tues.*

 Restaurants

Slater's 50/50

$ | **BURGER** | **FAMILY** | Bacon is king at this lively burger, beer, and sports bar in Liberty Station. Founder Scott Slater's signature "designer" patty, half beef and half ground bacon, is topped with a fried egg and cheese, and sauced with chipotle adobo mayonnaise. **Known for:** weekend brunch; extensive craft beer selection; pet-friendly patio with dog menu.

$ *Average main: $15* ⊠ *2750 Dewey Rd., Liberty Station* ☎ *619/398–2600* ⊕ *www. slaters5050.com.*

Stone Brewing World Bistro & Gardens— Liberty Station

$$ | ECLECTIC | FAMILY | This 50,000-square-foot monument to beer and good food is a crowd-pleaser, especially for fans of San Diego's nationally known craft beer scene. The global menu features dishes like the Bavarian pretzel and Brewmaster's Beef Dip that pair perfectly with on-tap and bottled beers from around the world and Stone's famous IPAs. **Known for:** massive outdoor patio; brew-friendly eats; artisanal burgers. $ *Average main: $22* ⊠ *2816 Historic Decatur Rd., Liberty Station* ☎ *619/269–2100* ⊕ *www.stone-libertystation.com.*

☕ Coffee and Quick Bites

Con Pane Rustic Breads & Cafe

$ | CAFÉ | FAMILY | The scent of fresh-baked bread whets the appetite of customers at this Liberty Station bakery and café seeking rustic scones or raisin brioche cinnamon rolls for breakfast, or one of the hearty lunch sandwiches like almost-grilled cheese with melted Brie and Gorgonzola on warm rosemary–olive oil bread. All can be enjoyed inside or on the sunny patio with hot or cold drinks including the house-made lemonade. **Known for:** fluffy raisin brioche cinnamon rolls; sandwiches served in half portions; box lunches to go. $ *Average main: $9* ⊠ *2750 Dewey Rd., Liberty Station* ☎ *619/224–4344* ⊕ *www.conpanesd.com* ☉ *Closed Tues. and Wed.*

★ Liberty Public Market

$ | INTERNATIONAL | FAMILY | The city's former Naval Training Center is home to more than 30 vendors so even the pickiest of diners will be pleased. Options include tacos and quesadillas at Cecilia's Taqueria; fried rice, pad Thai, and curries at Mama Made Thai; lavender lattes from Westbean Coffee Roasters; fried chicken and fries from Fluster Cluck; sweet and savory crepes from Olala; more than a dozen Argentinean empanadas at Paraná; and croissants, éclairs, and macarons at Le Parfait Paris. **Known for:** cuisines from around the world; lively kid- and dog-friendly patio; the best regional foods under one roof. $ *Average main: $10* ⊠ *2820 Historic Decatur Rd., Liberty Station* ☎ *619/487–9346* ⊕ *www.liberty-publicmarket.com.*

🛏 Hotels

Courtyard Marriott San Diego Airport Liberty Station

$$$ | HOTEL | FAMILY | Close to the restaurants and shops of Liberty Station, this family-friendly hotel spares travelers the extra fees charged by most Downtown and coastal lodgings. **Pros:** accommodating staff; free airport shuttle; no resort fees. **Cons:** limited views; not much charm or personality; family-friendly might not appeal to you. $ *Rooms from: $279* ⊠ *2592 Laning Rd., Liberty Station* ☎ *619/221–1900, 888/236–2427* ⊕ *www. marriott.com/sanal* ⇥ *200 rooms* ⦿ *No Meals.*

Hampton Inn & Suites San Diego Airport Liberty Station

$$ | HOTEL | FAMILY | Modern decor, spacious rooms, convenient location, and endless amenities make this 2019 property the best bet for travelers wanting a little bit of everything in one hotel. **Pros:** close to the airport and Liberty Station; spotless hotel; free airport shuttle. **Cons:** sparse rooms; no tubs; $15 daily parking fee. $ *Rooms from: $199* ⊠ *2211 Lee Ct., Liberty Station* ☎ *619/881–2710* ⊕ *www.hilton.com* ⇥ *181 rooms* ⦿ *Free Breakfast.*

★ Homewood Suites San Diego Airport Liberty Station

$$$ | HOTEL | FAMILY | With amenities like kitchens and a business center, most guests stay at least four nights, turning this all-suites hotel into a home.

Pros: outstanding central location near attractions; close to paths for joggers and bikers; complimentary airport shuttle. **Cons:** breakfast area can get crowded; $19 parking fee and $75 pet fee; far from nightlife. ⑤ *Rooms from: $249* ✉ *2576 Laning Rd., Liberty Station* ☎ *619/222–0500* ⊕ *www.homewoodsuites.com* ⇨ *150 suites* ⦿ *Free Breakfast.*

🎭 Performing Arts

Arts District Liberty Station
ARTS CENTERS | FAMILY | The former Naval Training Center at Liberty Station is a hub for arts and culture with over 120 tenants, including artists, galleries, museums, and nonprofits. ✉ *2750 Historic Decatur Rd., Liberty Station* ☎ *619/573–9300* ⊕ *www.LibertyStation.com.*

Malashock Dance
MODERN DANCE | The city's esteemed modern dance company presents edgy, intriguing works at venues throughout the city; Malashock has often collaborated on performances with the San Diego Opera, the San Diego Symphony, and other major cultural institutions. ✉ *2650 Truxtun Rd., Suite 104, Liberty Station* ☎ *619/260–1622* ⊕ *www.malashock-dance.org.*

San Diego Dance Theater
THEATER | The company has earned serious kudos for its diverse company and provocative programming, including Mexican waltzes and its annual "Trolley Dances," which take place at various trolley stops throughout San Diego. Other performances are held at venues around the city. ✉ *2650 Truxtun Rd., Suite 108, Liberty Station* ☎ *619/225–1803* ⊕ *www.sandiegodancetheater.org.*

San Diego Ballet
BALLET | The ballet brings a vast repertory of classic and contemporary ballets to several venues countywide, as well as in-studio performances. ✉ *2650 Truxtun Rd., Suite 102, Liberty Station* ☎ *619/294–7378* ⊕ *www.sandiegoballet.org.*

Shopping

The laid-back Point Loma Peninsula offers incredible views of Downtown San Diego, and some great shopping away from the large crowds often seen in Downtown and at Fashion Valley. In the former Naval Training Center, the Liberty Station shopping area has art galleries, restaurants, and home stores. If you're in town on the first Friday of the month, check out Liberty Station's **Friday Night Liberty** (5 to 9 pm), a free art walk featuring refreshments and entertainment.

Moniker General
MIXED CLOTHING | Grab your hipster plaid flannels, cleverly named candles, linen jumpsuits, plant-dyed bandanas, and canvas backpacks at this Instagram-worthy shop where you can stock up on clothing, home goods, and accessories, all while sipping on a craft cocktail or coffee. ✉ *2860 Sims Rd., Liberty Station* ☎ *619/255–8772* ⊕ *www.monikergeneral.com.*

Ocean Beach

At the northern end of Point Loma lies the chilled-out, hippie-esque town of Ocean Beach, commonly referred to as "OB." The main thoroughfare of this funky neighborhood is dotted with dive bars, coffeehouses, surf shops, and 1960s diners. OB is a magnet for everyone from surfers to musicians and artists. Newport Avenue, generally known for its boisterous bars, is also home to San Diego's largest antiques district. Fans of OB applaud its resistance to "selling out" to upscale development, whereas detractors lament its somewhat scruffy edges, so don't expect any chain restaurants.

Historic Walking Tour

A self-guided walking tour, "A Walk Back Through Time" (⊕ *libertystation. com*) highlights Liberty Station's rich past as a Naval Training Center (NTC) from 1923 to 1997. Of the 50 buildings at Liberty Station, only six are new construction. All others have been repurposed as offices, retail space, restaurants, fitness centers, and services. You can retrace the steps of the past by scanning the QR codes posted on placards around Liberty Station. Each one offers an audio summary, photos, and a synopsis of the structure's original use.

Begin at **Sellers Plaza and Gate One**, the oldest area of NTC where recruits and visitors entered the main gates and only entrance past curfew. During the earliest days of the base, the **Sail Ho Golf Course** provided a recreational outlet for officers to hit the greens. Today it operates as a 9-hole golf course under the name The Loma Club. The **WAVES** building—now a spin cycling studio—offered housing for women who worked as emergency service volunteers, reporting for duty for medical and communication needs. Built in 1922, the **Commissary and Mess Hall** in Building 1 was the first construction at NTC. Despite the passing of time, it's still being used to feed the masses with eateries, bars, and specialty food vendors all under one roof at Liberty Public Market. The *USS Brave* 12-man rowboat, is a work of art by artist Jonathan Allen, made to honor the sailors who gave their lives to service. The **Enlisted Club** was built in 1941 to encourage sailors to relax and be at ease. Once housing a bowling alley, pool tables, and theater, today it has three restaurants, office space, and several stores. Now operating as event space, the **Library** in Building 177 opened as a quiet place for recruits to study and read. **Preble Field** highlights the 50-caliber dual-purpose guns used on support vessels. Honoring the lives of more than 3,500 American submariners is the **52 Boats Memorial.** In the 1920s, **Ingram Plaza** became an acclimatization place where small-town recruits could adjust to their new environment. The **Gymnasium** in Building 210 functioned as the fitness center with a basketball court and swimming pool. It still functions as a fitness center today. When collecting their paychecks, recruits would head to **Building 202**, directly next to the Command Center in **Building 200** where highest-ranking officers resided. These buildings are now designated for dining and office space. Gracing **Luce Auditorium** in Building 35 were big bands and performers like Nat King Cole, Bob Hope, and Lawrence Welk. This space has been repurposed as a theater with multiple screens and a restaurant. Unlike the barracks, the **North Chapel in Building 208** stood as the only white structure on the premises where religious services were held. Today it is reserved for private events. Now retail and office space, **Buildings 27–30** were designated as housing and services for over 100 men. During the first three months of training, recruits underwent basic training in the **Schools,** which are slated to become office space. Commissioned in 1949, the **USS** *Recruit* trained over 50,000 recruits in basic naval procedures on a land-bound ship; it now houses an exhibit with historic photos and renderings.

Sights

Ocean Beach Pier

MARINA/PIER | Constructed in 1966, this T-shape pier is the West Coast's longest concrete pier. It's the perfect place to take in views of the harbor, the surfers, the ocean, and Point Loma Peninsula. It's also a popular fishing spot and home to the Walking On Water Cafe and a small tackle shop; however, a winter storm in 2023 caused severe damage to the pier, resulting in its closure (as well as that of the café and shop) until at least 2026 when construction is expected to start. Surfers flock to the waves that break just below. ✉ *1950 Abbott St., Ocean Beach.*

Beaches

Ocean Beach

BEACH | This mile-long beach south of Mission Bay's channel is the place to get a slice of vintage SoCal beach culture. It's likely you'll see VW vans in the parking lot near the Ocean Beach Pier. The wide beach is popular with volleyball players, sunbathers, and surfers. The municipal pier at the southern end extends a ½ mile out to sea. Major storm damage in January 2023 resulted in the pier being closed until full reconstruction, slated for 2026. Until then, the pier and the historic café about halfway out, are both closed. Taco shops, bars, and restaurants can be found on the streets near the beach. Swimmers should beware of strong rip currents around the main lifeguard tower, where lifeguards are on duty year-round. One of Ocean Beach's most popular features is the Dog Beach at the northern end, where canines can run freely and splash in the waves 24 hours a day. For shade, picnic areas with barbecues, and a paved path, check out Robb Field, across from Dog Beach. **Amenities:** lifeguards; parking (no fee); showers; toilets. **Best for:** surfing; swimming; walking. ✉ *Newport Ave. at Abbott St., Ocean Beach* ✛ *7 miles from Downtown San Diego* ⊕ *www.sandiego.gov.*

Restaurants

One of the last "real" California beach towns, OB, as locals know it, has one foot in its hippie past and another in gentrified coastal living, which explains why it's home to an eclectic group of bars and restaurants, everything from charming wine bars and bistros to Cuban cafés and burger joints.

Blue Water Seafood

$ | **SEAFOOD** | **FAMILY** | Portions and prices are on point at this OB seafood hole-in-the-wall where dining is a three-step process—choose your fish, pick your marinade, and decide how you want it prepared (sandwich, plate, salad, taco, or à la carte). There's an on-site market serving wild, organic, and local seafood ranging from snapper and calamari to shrimp and scallops, and all the soups are from scratch including the New England clam chowder served in a bread bowl. **Known for:** fish served five ways; locally sourced seafood; beer-battered fish tacos. ⑤ *Average main: $9* ✉ *5083 Santa Monica Ave., #1b, Ocean Beach* ☎ *619/255–8497* ⊕ *www.bluewaterseafoodsandiego.com.*

Breakfast Republic

$ | **AMERICAN** | Creeping toward 20 locations, this breakfast chain is spreading like wildfire thanks to the owner, Johan Engman's obsession with the first meal for the day. Served out of an Airstream kitchen, hot breakfast plates hit your table within 20 minutes and nearly every dish puts a spin on a standard like the tres leches vegan pancakes, the gouda shrimp and grits, and the breakfast burrito with Jurassic pork. **Known for:** fluffy pancakes; both classic and innovative breakfast dishes; unique coffee creations and morning cocktails. ⑤ *Average main: $13* ✉ *4839 Newport Ave., Ocean Beach*

☎ 619/255–7255 ⊕ www.breakfastrepublic.com ☾ No dinner.

★ **Hodad's**

$ | **BURGER** | **FAMILY** | Surfers with big appetites, and fans of Food Network's *Diners, Drive-ins and Dives,* chow down on huge, messy burgers, fries, onion rings, and shakes at this funky, hippie beach joint adorned with beat-up surfboards, stickers, and license plates from almost every state. Don't be put off by lines out the door—they move quickly and the wait is worth it, especially for the Guido Burger; inspired by Guy Fieri, it's topped with pastrami, onions, pickles, and Swiss cheese. **Known for:** legendary bacon cheeseburgers and thick-cut onion rings; surf-shack vibe; a little sass with your burger. $ *Average main: $12* ✉ *5010 Newport Ave., Ocean Beach* ☎ *619/224–4623* ⊕ *www.hodadies.com.*

★ **Little Lion Cafe**

$$ | **MODERN AMERICAN** | Amid surf shacks and hippie beach bars, this restaurant perched on stunning Sunset Cliffs feels like a hidden European bistro. The sisters who run the show come from a long line of successful local restaurateurs and have brought their passed-down expertise to the thoughtful service and simple, healthy menu that features entrées like plant-based tacos, quinoa bowls, and the Bistro Burger with Hatch Chile cheddar on a brioche bun. **Known for:** eggs Benedict; cozy bistro setting; chocolate hazelnut scone. $ *Average main: $20* ✉ *1424 Sunset Cliffs Blvd., Ocean Beach* ☎ *619/756–6921* ⊕ *www.thelittlelioncafe.com* ☾ *Closed Tues. No dinner.*

Mike's Taco Club

$ | **MEXICAN** | Tucked away on the bottom floor of a tattoo parlor, this funky little taco shop has a drink menu larger than the Mexican food lineup (but don't let that dissuade you). Place your order next to the wall of bottle caps, and then head to the pet-friendly street-side patio that draws a crowd for the hearty burritos wrapped in warm, soft tortillas and

authentic salsas that range from tradi-tional red salsa to chipotle cream. **Known for:** carne asada fries; battered fish tacos; no-skimp burritos. $ *Average main: $8* ✉ *5060 Newport Ave., between Bacon St. and Abbott St., Ocean Beach* ⊕ *www.mikestacoclub.com.*

Pizza Port

$ | **PIZZA** | Rows of picnic tables, surf-board decor, and beer-brewing on-site have made this funky, friendly brewpub a block from the beach a locals' favorite. The nearly 40 brews on tap include a namesake pour and other craft beers that have made San Diego a beer-drinkers destination. **Known for:** namesake Pizza Port beer; beer-friendly menu items; one of most awarded breweries in the country. $ *Average main: $20* ✉ *1956 Bacon St., Ocean Beach* ☎ *619/224–4700* ⊕ *www.pizzaport.com.*

★ **Raglan Public House**

$ | **BURGER** | Inspired by the grass-fed burgers they sampled in New Zealand, the founders of this convivial eatery set out to replicate those same high-quality flavors in their Ocean Beach spot. The interior nods to the outdoor-oriented Kiwi country, with surfboards turned into light fixtures, rugby photos, and bodyboards as wall art. **Known for:** grass-fed beef burgers; exceptional handmade cock-tails and great daily specials; great local craft beer. $ *Average main: $20* ✉ *1851 Bacon St., Ocean Beach* ☎ *619/794–2304* ⊕ *www.raglanpublichouse.com.*

South Beach Bar & Grille

$ | **SEAFOOD** | This two-story-tall restau-rant and bar in Ocean Beach looks like a typical sports bar from the outside, but inside is the place to eat what many consider to be the best fish tacos in San Diego. Grab a seat at the bar and choose from an ever-changing array of fresh grilled fish from lobster to mahi. **Known for:** mahimahi fish tacos; great sunset and ocean views; Taco Tuesday $4 specials. $ *Average main: $13* ✉ *5059 Newport Ave. #104, Ocean Beach*

☎ *619/226–4577* ⊕ *www.southbeachob. com.*

3rd Corner Wine Shop and Bistro

$$ | **WINE BAR** | Enthusiasts from around the world laud this combined wine shop, bar, and cozy California bistro. Available from lunch until 10 pm, the American bistro fare starts with baked Brie or chick-en-liver mousse, moves on to savory short-rib sliders and seafood risotto, and ends with flourless chocolate marquise or goat's milk cheesecake. **Known for:** more than 1,000 bottles of wine; consistently top-notch; knowledgeable staff who can offer bottle recommendations. ⑤ *Average main: $27* ⊠ *2265 Bacon St., Ocean Beach* ☎ *619/223–2700* ⊕ *www. the3rdcorner.com* ⊗ *Closed Mon.*

☕ Coffee and Quick Bites

Azucar

$ | **CUBAN** | For a taste of Cuba in San Diego, head to this Ocean Beach bakery where owner Vivian Hernandez Jackson combines her Cuban heritage, Miami childhood, and London culinary training in breakfast and lunch offerings. Morning specialties like raspberry scones with passion fruit icing, a traditional guava-and-cheese puff pastry, and ham-and-Manchego quiche can be savored with café con leche, a sweet Cuban espresso with hot milk. **Known for:** tangy, citrus-centric desserts; traditional Cuban pastries; a quick bite before shopping or hitting the beach. ⑤ *Average main: $7* ⊠ *4820 Newport Ave., Ocean Beach* ☎ *619/523–2020* ⊕ *www.iloveazucar.com* ⊗ *No dinner.*

🛏 Hotels

Inn at Sunset Cliffs

$$ | **HOTEL** | At this 1950s former apartment complex, every room at the U-shape hotel gets a glimpse of the ocean, meaning you can fall asleep to the sound of the crashing waves and wake up to the sight of surfers paddling just in front of the hotel. **Pros:** midweek rates from $175; rooms remodeled in 2022; Rooms 114, 201, and 214 have full ocean views. **Cons:** rooms are tiny; no elevator; thin walls. ⑤ *Rooms from: $315* ⊠ *1370 Sunset Cliffs Blvd., Ocean Beach* ☎ *619/222–7901, 866/786–2543* ⊕ *www. innatsunsetcliffs.com* ⇨ *24 rooms* ⑩ *No Meals.*

🍸 Nightlife

Ocean Beach's nightlife is a world away from Point Loma. There's not a dress code in sight, and an inescapable hippie culture bleeds into the kitschy and earnestly earthy dives along Newport Avenue.

OB Brewery

BREWPUBS | Grab a seat on the rooftop deck of this brewpub where ocean views and a dozen craft beers are on tap. During happy hour, locals head to this dog-friendly pub for shuffleboard, foosball, fire pits, and some of the best sunset views San Diego has to offer. Check their website for upcoming events. ⊠ *5041 Newport Ave., Ocean Beach* ☎ *619/955–8053* ⊕ *www.obbrewingco.com.*

🛍 Shopping

Ocean Beach Farmers' Market

MARKET | **FAMILY** | Every Wednesday from 4 to 8 pm, this bustling market features fresh produce, samples from local restaurants, crafts, and more. Other popular offerings include handmade apparel and accessories, holistic products, and fresh flowers. ⊠ *4900 Newport Ave., between Cable and Bacon Sts., Ocean Beach* ☎ *619/279–0032* ⊕ *oceanbeachsandiego.com/attractions/annual-events/farmers-market-wednesdays.*

Ocean Gifts & Shells

SOUVENIRS | This huge beach-theme store is filled with seashells of every size and shape, nautical decor items, wind chimes, T-shirts, swimwear, accessories, and toys. For the ultimate "OB" souvenir, grab a sticker or shirt featuring the OB seagull logo, representing the notorious beach town for nearly 50 years. ✉ *4934 Newport Ave., Ocean Beach* ☎ *619/224–6702* ⊕ *www.oceangiftsandshells.com.*

★ **Vignettes**

ANTIQUES & COLLECTIBLES | Expect a pleasant culture shock when you step from the bohemian Newport Avenue into this French-inspired antiques shop with time-worn pieces with a rich history. More than 30 vendors showcase vintage and antique collectibles and fascinating oddities. ✉ *4828 Newport Ave., Ocean Beach* ☎ *619/222–9244* ⊕ *www.vignettesdecor. com.*

Shelter Island

In 1950 San Diego's port director decided to raise the shoal that lay off the eastern shore of Point Loma above sea level with the sand and mud dredged up during the course of deepening a ship channel in the 1930s and '40s. The resulting peninsula, **Shelter Island,** became home to several marinas and resorts, many with Polynesian details that still exist today, giving them a retro flair. Shelter Island is the center of San Diego's yacht-building industry, and boats in every stage of construction are visible in its yacht yards. A long sidewalk runs past boat brokerages to the hotels and marinas that line the inner shore, facing Point Loma. On the bay side, fishermen launch their boats and families relax at picnic tables along the grass, where there are fire rings and permanent barbecue grills. Within walking distance is the huge Friendship Bell, given to San Diegans by the people of Yokohama, Japan, in 1958 and the Tunaman's Memorial, a statue commemorating San Diego's once-flourishing fishing industry.

Sights

Shoreline Park (*Shelter Island Art Walking Tour*)

PUBLIC ART | Immerse yourself in art and history with a 2-mile walk along Shelter Island through Shoreline Park. This self-guided tour highlights seven public works of art starting at the tip of the island with the **Yokohoma Friendship Bell**. Dating back to 1958, the bell was gifted to San Diego by sister city, Yokohama, as a symbol of the post-World War II friendship. Weighing over two tons, the bronze bell designed by artist Masahiko Katori is suspended from a small pagoda. At the foot of the bell stands *The Girl in Red Shoes,* a sculpture by Japanese artist Munehiro Komeno. Representing the compassion between the two nations, it tells the story of Kimi, a Japanese orphan adopted by an American couple in the 1920s. Nearby is *Pearl of the Pacific,* created in 1998 by architectural students from four cities—Yantai, China; Tijuana, Mexico; Vladivostok, Russia; and San Diego. It's comprised of a fountain, walls, and tile work representing the four quadrants of the Pacific Rim. Built over the course of a month, this symbol of unity depicts the beauty that can be created when countries are united in friendship. Along the water's edge is *Pacific Spirit,* a bronze sculpture by James Hubbell. Standing 6 feet tall, the plaque below the female statue reads, "The waves echo behind me. Patience-Faith-Openness, is what the sea has to teach." Near the west end of Shelter Island stands the impressive *Tunaman's Memorial* created by Franco Vianello in 1988. At an impressive 15 feet tall, the work pays tribute to San Diego's fishermen lost at sea. Located at the Children's Playground, the bronze sculpture, *Bubble Bath* by Dan Hill was erected as a memorial to a little girl. In striking contrast, the massive arched *Pacific Portal* is a concrete and mosaic structure created by James Hubbell. Commonly referred to as the Shelter

Shelter Island is home to several marinas and resorts like Kona Kai Resort & Spa, as well as the Polynesian-themed restaurant Bali Hai.

Island Gazebo, this gathering place is reflective of ocean waves and billowing sails. ⊠ *Shelter Island Dr., Shelter Island* ⊕ *www.portofsandiego.org* 🖼 *Free.*

🍴 Restaurants

Countless yachts and sailboats are berthed at marinas and hotels along this bayfront spit of land where visitors and locals come to picnic, enjoy concerts, and dine at a variety of casual bay-side restaurants specializing in fresh seafood.

Bali Hai

$$ | HAWAIIAN | For more than 50 years, generations of San Diegans and visitors have enjoyed this Polynesian-theme icon with its stunning bay and city skyline views. The menu is a fusion of Hawaiian and Asian cuisines with standouts like the crispy ahi tuna, wok-fried bass, and pan-seared scallops with macadamia nut butter. **Known for:** potent Bali Hai mai tais; Sunday brunch buffet with a DIY sundae bar; Happy hours Monday–Thursday 3–5.

$ *Average main: $25* ⊠ *2230 Shelter Island Dr., Shelter Island* ☎ *619/222–1181* ⊕ *www.balihairestaurant.com* ⊗ *No lunch Sun.*

Humphreys Restaurant

$$$ | MODERN AMERICAN | Step inside this restaurant, part of a tropic-style hotel complex and concert venue on Shelter Island, and discover a dining room that's contemporary in look and outlook with amazing vistas of bobbing sailboats, seabirds, and sunsets. Hotel guests, concertgoers, yachties, and a few locals enjoy the contemporary menu featuring classic American fare like crab cakes, lobster mac and cheese, and skirt steak (regulars request the macadamia-crusted halibut). **Known for:** macadamia-crusted halibut; unique concert venue setting; bay-side views. $ *Average main: $29* ⊠ *2241 Shelter Island Dr., Shelter Island* ☎ *619/224–3577* ⊕ *www.humphreysrestaurant.com.*

Ketch Grill & Tapas

$$ | **AMERICAN** | This outcrop of the Brigantine chain brings a modern vibe to Shelter Island with a beer-friendly menu as impressive as the harbor view. For a true San Diego dining experience, try the California tuna bowls, surf n' turf fondue, or chili-glazed salmon with kale hash. **Known for:** fried calamari; outdoor patio overlooking the harbor; heaping surf n' turf. $ *Average main: $23* ✉ *2614 Shelter Island Dr., Shelter Island* ☎ *619/814–8080* ⊕ *www.ketchgrillandtaps.com.*

 ## Hotels

One of two man-made peninsulas between Downtown and Point Loma, Shelter Island has grassy parks, tree-lined paths, and views of Downtown.

Best Western Plus Island Palms Hotel & Marina

$ | **HOTEL** | **FAMILY** | With tennis courts, two pools, jogging paths, fitness center, and complimentary bike rentals, this waterfront hotel is a natural fit for healthy travelers. **Pros:** excellent value; great water views; private marina and outdoor firepits. **Cons:** confusing layout; can be noisy; $25 daily parking fee. $ *Rooms from: $200* ✉ *2051 Shelter Island Dr., Shelter Island* ☎ *619/222–0561, 800/922–2336* ⊕ *www.islandpalms.com* ⌨ *227 rooms* ⦿I *No Meals.*

★ Kona Kai Resort & Spa

$$ | **RESORT** | A $30-million renovation took this Shelter Island resort up a notch, with remodeled rooms, a new pool, spa, gym, and lobby—making the marina view an added bonus rather than the main focus. **Pros:** private beach with firepits; near marina with water view; on-site sports rental equipment. **Cons:** not centrally located; resort fees; popular for business meetings and weddings. $ *Rooms from: $269* ✉ *1551 Shelter Island Dr., Shelter Island* ☎ *619/221–8000, 800/566–2524* ⊕ *www.resortkonakai.com* ⌨ *170 rooms* ⦿I *No Meals.*

 ## Nightlife

Shelter Island's best watering holes boast campy tiki-theme decor; it's also home to revered concert destination Humphrey's Concerts by the Bay, which is famous for its great sound, scenic location, and kayaking passersby.

Humphrey's Concerts by the Bay

LIVE MUSIC | From June through September, this dining and drinking oasis surrounded by water hosts the city's best outdoor jazz, folk, and light-rock concert series and is the stomping ground of such musicians as the Cowboy Junkies, Kenny G, Dolly Parton, Jimmy Buffett, and Chris Isaak. The rest of the year the music moves indoors for first-rate jazz (on Sunday), blues, classic rock, and more. ✉ *2241 Shelter Island Dr., Shelter Island* ☎ *619/224–3577* ⊕ *www. humphreysconcerts.com* ⌨ *Cover charge from $5.*

Harbor Island

Following the successful creation of Shelter Island, in 1961 the U.S. Navy used the residue from digging berths deep enough to accommodate aircraft carriers to build **Harbor Island**, a 1½-mile-long peninsula adjacent to the airport. Restaurants and high-rise hotels dot the inner shore while the bay's shore is lined with pathways, gardens, and scenic picnic spots. On the west point, the restaurant **Tom Ham's Lighthouse** has a U.S. Coast Guard–approved beacon shining from its tower and a sweeping view of San Diego's bay front.

Restaurants

The man-made peninsula across from the airport, with its bay-side parks, marinas, and hotels, is a popular dining destination for lunches and dinners served with stunning views of San Diego Bay and the city skyline.

Coasterra

$$$ | **MODERN MEXICAN** | Swathed in murals, intricate light fixtures, breezy outdoor seating, and a cushy interior, this massive waterfront destination has one of the best skyline views in the city, making it a top spot for Mexican craft cocktails and bayfront dining. The menu veers toward modern Mexican with starters like tableside guacamole, tuna tostadas, and crispy calamari; be sure to try their organic margaritas or various agave-based libations. **Known for:** extraordinary skyline views; happy hour appetizers; crispy ahi tuna tostadas. $ *Average main: $33* ✉ *880 Harbor Island Dr., Harbor Island* ☎ *619/814–1300* ⊕ *www.cohnrestaurants.com/coasterra.*

Island Prime and C Level

$$$$ | **MODERN AMERICAN** | Two restaurants in one share this enviable spot on the shore of Harbor Island: the splurge-worthy Island Prime steak house and the relaxed C Level with a choice terrace. Both venues tempt with unrivaled views of Downtown San Diego's skyline. **Known for:** sunset views; popovers served with jalapeño jelly butter; waterfront dining. $ *Average main: $44* ✉ *880 Harbor Island Dr., Harbor Island* ☎ *619/298–6802* ⊕ *www.cohnrestaurants.com/island-prime* ⊗ *Closed Mon. No lunch at Island Prime.*

Tom Ham's Lighthouse

$$ | **SEAFOOD** | It's hard to top this longtime Harbor Island restaurant's incredible views across San Diego Bay to the Downtown skyline and Coronado Bridge. An alfresco dining deck and a contemporary seafood-focused menu ensure the dining experience at this working lighthouse doesn't take a back seat to the scenery. **Known for:** Sunday brunch; alfresco dining deck with skyline and Coronado bridge views; fresh seafood and beer-battered cod. $ *Average main: $30* ✉ *2150 Harbor Island Dr., Harbor Island* ☎ *619/291–9110* ⊕ *www.tomhamslighthouse.com.*

 Activities

Harbor Sailboats

BOATING | You can rent sailboats from 22- to 45-feet-long here for open-ocean adventures. The company also offers sailing lessons and bareboat charters. ✉ *2040 Harbor Island Dr., Harbor Island* ☎ *619/291–9568* ⊕ *www.harborsailboats.com* 🎫 *From $75.*

Chapter 9

CORONADO

Updated by
Jeff Terich

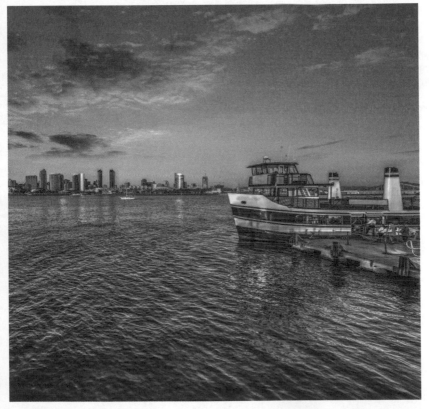

👁 **Sights**
★★★☆☆

🍴 **Restaurants**
★★★★☆

🛏 **Hotels**
★★★★☆

🛍 **Shopping**
★★★☆☆

🍸 **Nightlife**
★★☆☆☆

NEIGHBORHOOD SNAPSHOT

TOP EXPERIENCES

■ **The Hotel del Coronado:** As the grande dame of San Diego, the historic Hotel del Coronado charms visitors with her graceful architecture and oceanfront setting.

■ **Sandy beaches:** The long stretches of sand on Coronado are family-friendly.

■ **Small-town charm:** Though just across the bay from San Diego, Coronado has the quaint charm of a more intimate seaside small town.

■ **History:** From the classic Hollywood connections at the Del and *Wizard of Oz* creator L. Frank Baum to the island's naval history, including an actual sunken ship, there's a lot to discover in Coronado's past.

GETTING HERE

Coronado is accessible via the arching blue 2.2-mile-long San Diego–Coronado Bay Bridge, which offers breathtaking views of the harbor and Downtown. Alternatively, pedestrians and bikes can reach Coronado via the popular ferry service. Bus 904 meets the ferry and travels as far as Silver Strand State Beach. Bus 901 runs daily between the Gaslamp Quarter and Coronado.

PLANNING YOUR TIME

A leisurely stroll through Coronado takes at least an hour, more if you stop to shop or walk along the family-friendly beaches. If you're a history buff, you might want to visit on Tuesday, Thursday, or Saturday, when you can combine the tour of the historic homes that departs from the Glorietta Bay Inn at 11 am with a visit to the Coronado Museum of History and Art, open daily. Whenever you come, if you're not staying overnight, remember to get back to the dock in time to catch the final ferry out at 9:30 (10:30 on weekends).

BEST BEACHES

Coronado's wide beaches and gentle waves have been entertaining families for well over a century. The north end of **Coronado Beach,** nearest the Naval Air Station, is the widest expanse of beach in San Diego County and is great for families. **Silver Strand State Beach,** the stretch of sand that runs along Silver Strand Boulevard from the Hotel del Coronado to Imperial Beach, is a perfect family gathering spot, with restrooms and lifeguards. The shallow shoreline and minimal crowds also make it a popular spot for kitesurfing.

TAKING THE FERRY DOWNTOWN

While many travelers prefer to take the Coronado bridge between the peninsula and the city, the Coronado Ferry (coronado-ferrylanding.com/ferry-info/) is convenient and direct. Starting at 9:30 am, ferries leave from Coronado for Broadway Pier every half hour until 9 pm, and at 9:10 they begin service to 5th Avenue (Convention Center), continuing every hour until 9:55 pm. Service is extended an hour later on Friday and Saturday. Round-trip service is $14, or $7 for one-way.

Although Coronado is actually an isthmus, easily reached from the mainland if you head north from Imperial Beach, it has always seemed like an island and is often referred to as such. Coronado has stately homes, sandy beaches, private marinas, and prominent military installations.

As if freeze-framed in the 1950s, Coronado's quaint appeal is captured in its old-fashioned storefronts, well-manicured gardens, and charming **Ferry Landing Marketplace.** The streets of Coronado are wide, quiet, and friendly, and many of today's residents live in grand Victorian homes handed down for generations. Naval Air Station North Island was established in 1911 on Coronado's north end, across from Point Loma, and was the site of Charles Lindbergh's departure on the transcontinental flight that preceded his famous solo flight across the Atlantic. Coronado's long relationship with the U.S. Navy has made it an enclave for military personnel; it's said to have more retired admirals per capita than anywhere else in the United States.

 Sights

Coronado Ferry Landing
STORE/MALL | FAMILY | This collection of shops at Ferry Landing is on a smaller scale than the Embarcadero's Seaport Village, but you do get a great view of the Downtown San Diego skyline. The little bay-side shops and restaurants resemble the gingerbread domes of the Hotel del Coronado. ✉ *1201 1st St., at B Ave., Coronado* ⊕ *www.coronadoferrylanding. com.*

Coronado Museum of History and Art
HISTORY MUSEUM | The neoclassical First Bank of Commerce building, constructed in 1910, holds the headquarters and archives of the Coronado Historical Association, a museum, the Coronado Visitor Center, and the Coronado Museum Store. The museum's collection celebrates Coronado's history with photographs and displays of its formative events and major sights. A guided tour of the area's architecturally and historically significant buildings departs from the museum lobby on Sunday morning at 11 and Tuesday afternoon at 1 and costs $20 (reservations required). Alternatively, pick up a self-guided tour in the museum's shop. ✉ *1100 Orange Ave., at Park Pl., Coronado* ☎ *619/435–7242* ⊕ *www. coronadohistory.org* ✉ *Free.*

★ **Hotel del Coronado**
HOTEL | The Del's distinctive red-tile roofs and Victorian gingerbread architecture have served as a set for many movies, political meetings, and extravagant social happenings. It's speculated that the

Early-morning fog occasionally meets surfers off the waters of Coronado.

Duke of Windsor may have first met the Duchess of Windsor Wallis Simpson here. Eleven presidents have been guests of the Del, and the film *Some Like It Hot*—starring Marilyn Monroe, Jack Lemmon, and Tony Curtis—used the hotel as a backdrop.

The Hotel Del, as locals call it, was the brainchild of financiers Elisha Spurr Babcock Jr. and H. L. Story, who saw the potential of Coronado's virgin beaches and its view of San Diego's emerging harbor. It opened in 1888 and has been a National Historic Landmark since 1977. The History Gallery displays photos from the Del's early days, and books elaborating on its history are sold, along with logo apparel and gifts, in the hotel's 15-plus shops.

Although the pool area is reserved for hotel guests, several surrounding dining patios make great places to sit back and imagine the scene during the 1920s, when the hotel rocked with good times.

Behind the pool area, an attractive shopping arcade features a classic candy shop as well as several fine clothing and accessories stores. A lavish Sunday brunch is served in the Crown Room. During the holidays, the hotel hosts Skating by the Sea, an outdoor beachfront ice-skating rink open to the public.

■ TIP→ **Whether or not you're staying at the Del, enjoy a drink at the Sun Deck Bar and Grill in order to gaze out over the ocean—it makes for a great escape.**

Tours of the Del are $40 per person and take place daily at 10 am. Tours are free for children ages five and under. ✉ *1500 Orange Ave., at Glorietta Blvd., Coronado* ☎ *619/435–6611* ⊕ *www.hoteldel.com.*

★ **Orange Avenue**

TOWN | Comprising Coronado's business district and its village-like heart, this avenue is one of the most charming spots in Southern California. Slow-paced and very "local" (the city fights against chain stores), it's a blast from the past, although entirely up-to-date in other respects. The military presence—Coronado is home to the U.S. Navy Sea, Air, and Land (SEAL) forces—is reflected in shops selling military gear and places like McP's Irish Pub, at No. 1107. A family-friendly stop for a good, all-American meal, it's the unofficial SEALs headquarters. Many clothing boutiques, home-furnishings stores, and upscale restaurants cater to visitors with deep pockets, but you can buy plumbing supplies, too, or get a genuine military haircut at Crown Barber Shop, at No. 947. If you need a break, stop for a latte at the sidewalk café of Bay Books, San Diego's largest independent bookstore, at No. 1007. ⊠ *Orange Ave., near 9th St., Coronado.*

Beaches

★ Coronado Beach

BEACH | FAMILY | This wide beach is one of San Diego's most picturesque thanks to its soft white sand and sparkly blue water. The historic Hotel del Coronado serves as a backdrop, and it's perfect for sunbathing, people-watching, and Frisbee tossing. The beach has limited surf, but it's great for bodyboarding and swimming. Exercisers might include Navy SEAL teams or other military units that conduct training runs on beaches in and around Coronado. There are picnic tables, grills, and popular fire rings, but don't bring lacquered wood or pallets. Only natural wood is allowed for burning. There's also a dog beach on the north end. There's free parking along Ocean Boulevard, though it's often hard to snag a space. **Amenities:** food and drink; lifeguards; showers; toilets. **Best for:** walking; swimming. ⊠ *Ocean Blvd., between S. O St. and Orange Ave., Coronado* ✢ *From San Diego–Coronado bridge, turn left on Orange Ave. and follow signs.*

Silver Strand State Beach

BEACH | FAMILY | This quiet beach on a narrow sand spit allows visitors a unique opportunity to experience both the Pacific Ocean and San Diego Bay. The 2½ miles of the ocean side is great for surfing and other water sports while the bay side, accessible via foot tunnel under Highway 75, has calmer, warmer water and great views of the San Diego skyline. Lifeguards and rangers are on duty year-round, and there are places for biking, volleyball, and fishing. Picnic tables, grills, and firepits are available in summer, and the Silver Strand Beach Cafe is open Memorial Day through Labor Day. The beach is close to Loews Coronado Bay Resort and the Coronado Cays, an exclusive community popular with yacht owners. You can reserve RV sites ($65 beach; $50 inland) online. Three day-use parking lots provide room for 800 cars. **Amenities:** food and drink; lifeguards; parking (fee); showers; toilets. **Best for:** walking; swimming; surfing. ⊠ *5000 Hwy. 75, Coronado* ✢ *4½ miles south of city of Coronado* ☎ *619/435–5184* ⊕ *www.parks.ca.gov/ silverstrand* ⌂ *Parking from $10.*

Restaurants

The home of charming, but pricey, vintage houses, the famous Hotel del Coronado, and historic North Island Naval Station offers visitors a great variety of tourist-oriented bars and eateries—a few of them very good. While most of the dining options are recommended for the view (it's hard to beat), there are a number of excellent restaurants that range from family-friendly and casual to glamorous and upscale.

Chez Loma

$$ | FRENCH | French meets Southern Californian cuisine at this charming historic Victorian home in the heart of Coronado. A favorite of locals and guests at the nearby Hotel del Coronado, the

Coronado

KEY

- ① Sights
- ① Restaurants
- ① Quick Bites
- ① Hotels

Mexico's Napa Valley

Responsible for some 90% of the Mexico's wine production, Valle de Guadalupe is a gorgeous valley covered with sprawling vineyards, farm-to-table restaurants, and boutique hotels.

Why Go Now

For the past few years, wine experts, including *Wine Enthusiast*, who recently named the region one of the 10 best wine destinations, have been calling Valle de Guadalupe the next Napa. Get there while it's still relatively undiscovered and experience winemaker Phil Gregory's wine cave made from recycled fishing boats, sample vintages from Mexican wine legend, Hugo D'Acosta, and dine in the growing number of restaurants in the middle of farms, where chefs harvest vegetables and then bring them directly to the cutting board.

Insider Tip

A private car is essential for touring the wine country as you will need to drive from one winery to the next. Or you can arrange half- or full-day tours with many of the taxi drivers in Ensenada.

When to Go

The climate is pleasant year-round, but the region's best event is the Harvest Festival in August. This 21-day celebration brings in thousands of wine lovers who commemorate the harvest with wine tastings, cultural blessings, live music, and elaborate feasts. Be sure to make hotel reservations well in advance.

romantic bistro offers French favorites like boeuf bourguignon and moules marinière as well as California standbys like rockfish ceviche in tomatillo sauce. **Known for:** eclectic Sunday brunch; solid dessert selection; romantic atmosphere. $ *Average main: $25* ⊠ *1132 Loma Ave., Coronado* ☎ *619/435–0661* ⊕ *chezloma. net* ⊘ *No lunch.*

Coronado Brewing Company

$ | AMERICAN | FAMILY | Perfect for beer lovers with kids, this popular, laid-back Coronado brewpub offers a menu that features large portions of basic bar food like burgers, sandwiches, pizza, and salads. Enjoy a brew at a pair of sidewalk terraces or belly up to the bar and a new batch being made such as the Islander Pale Ale (IPA) or Mermaid's Red Ale. **Known for:** a good selection of house-crafted beers; kids' menu; more strollers than bar stools. $ *Average main: $12* ⊠ *170 Orange Ave., Coronado* ☎ *619/437–4452* ⊕ *www.coronadobrewing.com.*

The Henry

$$ | FUSION | A recent addition to the landscape of Orange Avenue, The Henry brings a more modern and spacious dining option to the small-town feel of Coronado Island. Though part of a small chain, the restaurant's cuisine is eclectic and inspired, with a menu full of both contemporary American staples and more innovative fusion offerings, including Korean prime skirt steak and a charred avocado salad with bok choy and ginger miso vinaigrette. **Known for:** house-made pretzels and provolone fondue; braised short rib; simple, potent, and delicious cocktails. $ *Average main: $29* ⊠ *1031 Orange Ave., Coronado* ☎ *619/762–1022* ⊕ *thehenryrestaurant.com.*

★ Serẽa

$$$$ | **SEAFOOD** | Adjacent to the Hotel Del Coronado's more casual, family-friendly Shorewater is its more dazzling upscale restaurant, Serẽa. With tables featuring stunning views of the Pacific Ocean and a menu of sustainable, market-fresh seafood, Serẽa puts full emphasis on its seaside location. **Known for:** breathtaking ocean view; tableside wood-grilled or flash-fried fish; the "Pearl Diver" dessert, served in a white chocolate shell. $ *Average main: $48* ⊠ *1500 Orange Ave., Coronado* ☎ *619/435–6611* ⊕ *sereasandiego.com* ◔ *Closed Mon.–Wed.*

Stake Chophouse

$$$$ | **STEAKHOUSE** | A recent addition to the Orange Avenue dining scene, this chophouse is a more modern alternative to the vintage steak house. Stake features high-quality cuts of beef along with fresh seafood, oysters, hand-cut fries, and an award-winning wine list. **Known for:** Australian Wagyu rib eye; extensive wine offerings; the "Baked California" dessert. $ *Average main: $42* ⊠ *1309 Orange Ave., Coronado* ☎ *619/522–0077* ⊕ *www.stakechophousesd.com.*

Tartine

$ | **FRENCH** | **FAMILY** | Dine any time of day at this French-inspired café a block from San Diego Bay, as breakfast commences at 6 am with house-made granola, quiche, and just-baked coffee cakes and croissants. Sandwiches, salads, and soups round out the daytime menu, while dinner highlights include the catch of the day; just be sure be sure to save room for the Paris-pretty desserts. **Known for:** Coronado's best bet for casual but satisfying fare; in-house pastries and desserts; quiche any time of the day. $ *Average main: $15* ⊠ *1106 1st St., Coronado* ☎ *619/435–4323* ⊕ *www.tartinecoronado.com.*

☕ Coffee and Quick Bites

Clayton's Coffee Shop

$ | **AMERICAN** | **FAMILY** | A classic diner with bar seating in a circle, Clayton's is a great lunch or breakfast spot with a menu that ranges from classic American fare to Mexican-inspired dishes like the popular breakfast burrito. Just don't forget dessert! **Known for:** bottomless coffee; breakfast burrito; gooey cinnamon roll sundae. $ *Average main: $10* ⊠ *979 Orange Ave., Coronado* ☎ *619/435–5425* ⊕ *www.claytonscoffeeshop.com.*

High Tide Bottle Shop & Kitchen

$ | **PIZZA** | While it carries an extensive selection of craft beers, wine, and spirits, High Tide Bottle Shop is a lot more than a liquor store. The extensive menu of signature pizzas, wraps, sandwiches, wings, and more are worth savoring at one of its outdoor tables or carrying out for a picnic on the beach. **Known for:** more than 20 different signature pizzas; dry-rub wings; an extensive collection of bottled local craft beers. $ *Average main: $11* ⊠ *933 Orange Ave., Coronado* ☎ *619/435–1480* ⊕ *www.hightidecoronado.com.*

Mootime Creamery

$ | **CAFÉ** | **FAMILY** | For a deliciously sweet pick-me-up, check out the rich ice cream, frozen yogurt, and sorbet made fresh daily on the premises. Dessert nachos made from waffle-cone chips are an unusual addition to an extensive sundae menu. Just look for the statue of Elvis on the sidewalk in front. **Known for:** daily house-made ice cream, yogurt, and sorbet; dessert nachos; "moopies" sandwiches, with ice cream between two cereal bars. $ *Average main: $5* ⊠ *1025 Orange Ave., Coronado* ☎ *619/435–2422* ⊕ *www.mootimecreamerysd.com* ▭ *No credit cards.*

Hotel Del Coronado's iconic red-roof building houses the resort's ballroom, which can accommodate 600 people.

Night & Day Cafe

$ | MEXICAN | FAMILY | Easy to spot from its red neon sign perched above the front door, Night & Day Cafe offers simple, hearty Mexican food with counter service and ample portions. The café closes at 2 pm most days, but the hearty breakfast burritos, bacon cheeseburgers, and fish tacos provide more than enough sustenance for two meals. **Known for:** Coronado breakfast burrito (with hash browns inside); the iconic red sign; friendly service. ⑤ *Average main: $13 ⊠ 847 Orange Ave., Coronado ☎ 619/435–9776 ⊕ www. coronadondcafe.com ⊗ No dinner.*

Hotels

Occupying its own strip of land across the bay from San Diego, Coronado doesn't boast the overwhelming number of hotels as its neighboring city, but most of the properties on the island offer luxurious accommodations. None more

so than the iconic Hotel del Coronado, a historic beachside hotel with more than 100 years of history that attracts a large number of tourists, if only sometimes for a beachside drink. At Loews Coronado, visitors can expect more modern upscale accommodations, while the 1906 Lodge offers more of an intimate, yet very comfortable, bed-and-breakfast-type stay.

★ Coronado Island Marriott Resort & Spa

$$ | RESORT | FAMILY | Near San Diego Bay, this snazzy hotel has rooms with great Downtown skyline views. **Pros:** spectacular views; on-site spa; close to water taxis. **Cons:** not in downtown Coronado; resort fee; expensive self-parking. ⑤ *Rooms from: $329 ⊠ 2000 2nd St., Coronado ☎ 619/435–3000 ⊕ www. marriott.com/hotels/travel/sanci-corona-do-island-marriott-resort-and-spa ⇆ 300 rooms ⑩ No Meals.*

Glorietta Bay Inn

$ | **HOTEL** | **FAMILY** | The main building on this property is an Edwardian-style mansion built in 1908 for sugar baron John D. Spreckels, who once owned much of Downtown San Diego. **Pros:** great views; friendly staff; close to beach. **Cons:** mansion rooms are small; lots of traffic nearby; due for a renovation. ⑤ *Rooms from: $179* ⊠ *1630 Glorietta Blvd., Coronado* ☎ *619/435–3101, 800/283–9383* ⊕ *www.gloriettabayinn.com* ⇨ *100 rooms* ❙◎❙ *Free Breakfast.*

★ Hotel del Coronado

$$$ | **RESORT** | **FAMILY** | As much of a draw today as it was when it opened in 1888, the Victorian-style "Hotel Del" is always alive with activity, as guests—including U.S. presidents and celebrities—and tourists marvel at the fanciful architecture and ocean views. **Pros:** 17 on-site shops; on the beach; well-rounded spa. **Cons:** some rooms are small; expensive dining; hectic public areas. ⑤ *Rooms from: $500* ⊠ *1500 Orange Ave., Coronado* ☎ *800/468–3533, 619/435–6611* ⊕ *www.hoteldel.com* ⇨ *757 rooms* ❙◎❙ *No Meals.*

Loews Coronado Bay Resort

$$ | **RESORT** | **FAMILY** | You can park your boat at the 80-slip marina of this romantic retreat set on a secluded 15-acre peninsula on the Silver Strand. **Pros:** great restaurants; lots of activities; all rooms have furnished balconies with water views. **Cons:** far from anything; confusing layout; not ideal for couples. ⑤ *Rooms from: $349* ⊠ *4000 Coronado Bay Rd., Coronado* ☎ *619/424–4000, 877/872–8559* ⊕ *www.loewshotels.com/coronado-bay-resort* ⇨ *439 rooms* ❙◎❙ *No Meals.*

★ 1906 Lodge at Coronado Beach

$$ | **B&B/INN** | Smaller but no less luxurious than the sprawling beach resorts of Coronado, this lodge—whose name alludes to the main building's former life as a boardinghouse built in 1906—welcomes couples for romantic retreats two blocks from the ocean. **Pros:** most suites feature Jacuzzi tubs, fireplaces, and porches; historic property; free underground parking. **Cons:** too quiet for families; no pool; limited on-site dining options. ⑤ *Rooms from: $329* ⊠ *1060 Adella Ave., Coronado* ☎ *619/437–1900, 866/435–1906* ⊕ *www.1906lodge.com* ⇨ *17 rooms* ❙◎❙ *Free Breakfast.*

Performing Arts

Coronado Playhouse

THEATER | This cabaret-type theater near the Hotel del Coronado stages regular dramatic and musical performances. ⊠ *1835 Strand Way, Coronado* ☎ *619/435–4856* ⊕ *www.coronadoplayhouse.org.*

Lamb's Players Theatre

THEATER | **FAMILY** | The theater's regular season of four to five mostly uplifting productions runs from February through November. It also stages an original musical, *Festival of Christmas,* in December. The company has two performance spaces: the one used for most productions in Coronado, and the Horton Grand Theatre in the Gaslamp Quarter. ⊠ *1142 Orange Ave., Coronado* ☎ *619/437–6000* ⊕ *www.lambsplayers.org.*

🛍 Shopping

Coronado's resort hotels attract tourists in droves, but somehow the town has managed to avoid being overtaken by chain stores. Instead, shoppers can browse through family-owned shops, dine at sidewalk cafés along Orange Avenue, stroll through the historic Hotel del Coronado, and take in the specialty shops at Coronado Ferry Landing. Friendly shopkeepers make the boutiques lining Orange Avenue, Coronado's main drag, a good place to browse for clothes, home decor, gift items, and gourmet foods.

Day Trip to Tijuana

Just 18 miles south of San Diego, Tijuana is an easy day trip, but gone are the days when Americans could cross into Mexico and return by simply showing their driver's license. For the last 15 years, U.S. Customs and Border Protection has required Americans to show a valid passport (or passport card) to return to the United States.

Getting to the Border

There are several options for getting to the border at San Ysidro, but the easiest is via the trolley. Check the CBP Border Wait Times mobile app for estimated wait times.

The trip on I–5 takes a half hour (no traffic) to an hour or more (rush hour). Leave your car on the U.S. side at one of the border parking lots ($8–$15 per day), and then cross on foot or by bus. Border Station Parking (⊕ *borderstationparking.com*), a 24-hour guarded lot at Camino de la Plaza, next to the Las Americas Premium Outlets, is a reliable choice; they also have shuttle service to and from Tijuana. To get there, take the last U.S. exit off I–5 (marked "Last US Exit, Camino de la Plaza"), turn right at the stoplight, and follow the signs for the lot.

A taxi ride from Downtown San Diego to the border at San Ysidro will cost about $60. Uber and Lyft are also options; expect to pay about $45.

The San Diego Trolley travels from the Santa Fe Depot in San Diego, at Kettner Boulevard and Broadway. Take the blue line to the last stop, San Ysidro/Tijuana, which is within 100 feet of the border. The blue line runs approximately every 15 minutes from 5 am to 1 am. The 45-minute trip costs $6.

Crossing the Border

The most common way to cross the border is on foot, and the experience—going through a metal turnstile amid the throngs of people—is a memorable one. Don't expect much of a hassle when crossing into Mexico, but allow extra time on your return and expect random inspections. To reach the border from the San Ysidro trolley stop (a five-minute walk) or any of the border parking garages, follow the crowds.

Once you've crossed the border, you'll be inundated with taxi drivers, who will take you to downtown Tijuana for about $10. However, it's an easy ½-mile walk to downtown (follow the crowds).

You can avoid the turnstile congestion by taking the bus. If you arrive by trolley, take a shuttle from the San Ysidro trolley terminal to the Tijuana Tourist Terminal on Avenida Revolución between 6th and 7th Streets.

When You're There

Avenida Revolución is lined with restaurants, bars, cafés, and stores selling everything from tequila to Tiffany-style lamps. The shopping area spreads across Calle 2 to a pedestrian walkway leading from the border. Beware of fake goods, and above all, beware of higher prices offered to gringos. The best bargains can be closer to the border; pick up your piñatas and serapes on your way out of town. Between Calles 1 and 8, Avenida Revolución is lined with crafts and curios.

Playas de Tijuana is Tijuana's beach neighborhood; Rosarito and Ensenada are thought to be the best.

BOOKS

Bay Books

BOOKS | FAMILY | This independent bookstore is the spot to sit, read, and sip coffee on an overcast day by the sea. Great for international travelers, there's a large selection of foreign-language magazines and newspapers, and for youngsters, there's a section in the back devoted to children's books and games. Because of its close proximity to the Navy bases on Coronado, the shop has a large stock of books dedicated to military history. Bay Books also has hosted regular book-signing events; it has hosted a wide array of authors, from Newt Gingrich to Captain Chesley "Sully" Sullenberger. While you're there, grab an espresso or a pastry from the sidewalk-facing **Buona Forchetta** café within the bookstore. ⊠ *1007 Orange Ave., Coronado* ☎ *619/435–0070* ⊕ *www.baybookscoronado.com.*

CLOTHING AND ACCESSORIES

Emerald City Surf Shop

MIXED CLOTHING | FAMILY | For more than 30 years, Emerald City has provided Orange Avenue shoppers with a broad selection of swimwear, clothing, sunglasses, and hats from beachy brands like Billabong, Roxy, Vans, and O'Neill. The shop also offers surfboard, bodyboard, and swim fin rentals. ⊠ *1118 Orange Ave., Coronado* ☎ *619/435–6677* ⊕ *www.emeraldcitysurf.com.*

Wild Dove Boutique

WOMEN'S CLOTHING | Presenting a more chic, yet still casual alternative to the beach attire available throughout the island, Wild Dove offers a selection of fashion-forward apparel appropriate for both work and play. ⊠ *1029 Orange Ave., #B, Coronado* ☎ *619/316–1969* ⊕ *shop-wilddove.com.*

FOOD AND WINE

Coronado Taste of Oils

FOOD | The walls are lined, front to back, with countless flavors of olive oils and balsamic vinegars, from more standard fare to creative infusions. Some of the varied choices include lemon and lime, chilies, currants, garlic, harissa (hot chili pepper paste), chipotle, and herbes de Provence, all of which are available to sample with bread inside the shop. ⊠ *954 Orange Ave., Coronado* ☎ *619/522–0098* ⊕ *www.coronadotasteofoils.com.*

Wine A Bit

SOUVENIRS | Part store and part wine bar, the popular Wine A Bit carries hundreds of boutique wines, along with craft beers, appetizers, and decadent desserts. Cigars, gifts, and wine-related accessories are also for sale. ⊠ *928 Orange Ave., Coronado* ☎ *619/365–4953* ⊕ *www.wineabitcoronado.com.*

HOME ACCESSORIES AND GIFTS

Française

HOUSEWARES | A sleek new boutique on Orange Avenue, Française offers a selection of housewares in a modern industrial motif with a touch of class imported from France itself. The shop is stocked with attractive items for every room in the house, including cookware and serving utensils, posters and stationery, and even a variety of kids' toys. Before departing, make sure to peruse the backroom, which is stocked with edible treats like honey, hot sauce, chocolate bars, and floral salts. ⊠ *1037 Orange Ave., Coronado* ☎ *619/319–5318* ⊕ *www.francaise-shop.com.*

★ Seaside Papery

STATIONERY | Customize your correspondence with products from Seaside Papery, including high-end wedding invitations, greeting cards, luxury personal stationery, and wrapping papers. ⊠ *1162 Orange Ave., Coronado* ☎ *619/435–5565* ⊕ *www.seasidepapery.com.*

SHOPPING CENTERS

Coronado Ferry Landing

SHOPPING CENTER | A staggering view of San Diego's Downtown skyline across the bay and a dozen boutiques make this a delightful place to shop while waiting for a ferry. La Camisa (☎ 619/319–5826) is a fun place to pick up kitschy souvenirs, T-shirts, fleece jackets, and postcards. Lisa's Boutique (☎ 619/550–7366) specializes in comfy women's shoes and affordable casual wear. Vom Fass (☎ 619/534–5034) is a shop and tasting room full of olive oils, vinegars, spices, and other foodie essentials. There's a farmers' market every Tuesday 2:30–6, and some restaurants offer a daily late-afternoon happy hour. ✉ 1201 1st St., Coronado ☎ 619/435–8895 ⊕ www. coronadoferrylanding.com.

★ Hotel del Coronado

SHOPPING CENTER | At the gift shops within the peninsula's main historic attraction, you can purchase sportswear, designer handbags, jewelry, and antiques. **Spreckels Sweets & Treats** offers old-time candies, freshly made fudge, and decadent truffles. **Monroe** has designer fashions and accessories, inspired by its Hollywood namesake, while **Brady's for Men**, with its shirts and sport coats, caters to well-dressed men. **S.R.F.** is the spot to hit up for outdoor and action sports accessories. **En Route** is a haven for travelers, offering a selection of top-quality luggage and leather goods. ✉ 1500 Orange Ave., Coronado ☎ 619/435–6611 ⊕ www. hoteldel.com/coronado-shopping.

Activities

BIKING
Holland's Bicycles

BIKING | This is a great bike rental source on Coronado Island, so you can ride the Silver Strand Bike Path on an electric bike, beach cruiser, road bike, or tandem. ✉ 977 Orange Ave., Coronado ☎ 619/435–3153 ⊕ www.hollandsbicycles.com ⊠ From $10.

CRUISES
California Cruisin'

BOATING | Contact California Cruisin' for sailboat or powerboat charter excursions and dinner cruises. The company also

provides dockside accommodations aboard a private luxury yacht or houseboat on San Diego Bay. ✉ 1450 Harbor Island Dr., Coronado ☎ 619/296–8000 ⊠ From $350.

The Gondola Company

BOATING | You don't have to travel to Venice to be serenaded by a gondolier. This company features authentic Venetian gondola rides that depart daily from the picturesque Coronado Cays. ✉ 503 Grand Caribe Causeway, Suite C, Coronado ☎ 619/429–6317 ⊕ www.gondolacompany.com ⊠ From $129 for 2 people.

GOLF
★ Coronado Municipal Golf Course

GOLF | Spectacular views of Downtown San Diego and the Coronado Bridge as well as affordable prices make this public course one of the busiest in the world. Bordered by the bay, the trick is to keep your ball out of the water. Wind can add some difficulty, but otherwise this is a leisurely course and a good one to walk. It's difficult to get on unless you reserve a tee time 3 to 14 days in advance. The course's Bayside Grill restaurant is well-known for its Thursday and Sunday night prime rib dinner. Reservations are recommended. ✉ 2000 Visalia Row, Coronado ☎ 619/522–6590 ⊕ www.golfcoronado. com ⊠ From $42 ⚐ 18 holes, 6590 yards, par 72.

JET SKIING
Seaforth Boat Rentals

JET SKIING | You can rent Yamaha WaveRunners and explore San Diego Bay or Mission Bay from Seaforth Boat Rentals' four different San Diego locations. On most Fridays and weekends you can join a two-hour WaveRunner tour of La Jolla's coast, departing from the Mission Bay location (April–September only). ✉ 1715 Strand Way, Coronado ☎ 888/834–2628 ⊕ www.seaforthboatrental.com ⊠ From $95.

KAYAKING
SUP & Saddle
KAYAKING | While La Jolla's Bike & Kayak Tours, under the same ownership, offers a Leopard Shark Encounter snorkeling tour ($59 per person), where adventuresome travelers can see the shy spotted creatures up close, the Coronado location has you embarking on a kayak tour ($40 per person) underneath the Coronado Bridge at dusk to enjoy incredible views of Downtown San Diego. The Coronado branch also offers stand-up paddleboards for as little as $39 per person. ⊠ *1201 1st St., #215, Coronado* ☎ *619/880–6236* ⊕ *www.supandsaddle.com* ⊠ *From $39.*

SAILING AND BOATING
Seaforth Boat Rentals
BOATING | You can book charter tours and rent kayaks, Jet Skis, fishing skiffs, powerboats, and sailboats at Seaforth's five locations around town. The outfitter also can hook you up with a skipper for a deep-sea fishing trip. Seaforth also rents paddleboards at their Mission Bay and Coronado locations. ⊠ *1715 Strand Way, Coronado* ☎ *888/834–2628* ⊕ *www. seaforthboatrental.com* ⊠ *From $25.*

Chapter 10

NORTH COUNTY AND AROUND

Updated by
Marlise Kast-Myers

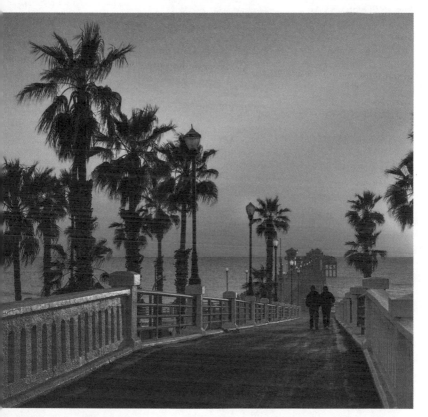

👁 **Sights**
★★★★☆

🍴 **Restaurants**
★★★☆☆

🛏 **Hotels**
★★★☆☆

🛍 **Shopping**
★★☆☆☆

🍸 **Nightlife**
★★☆☆☆

WELCOME TO NORTH COUNTY AND AROUND

TOP REASONS TO GO

★ **Talk to the animals:** Get almost nose to nose with giraffes, lions, tigers, and rhinos at the San Diego Zoo Safari Park in Escondido.

★ **Build a dream at LEGOLAND California Resort:** Explore model cities built with LEGO bricks, including New Orleans, Washington, D.C., and New York City.

★ **Be a beach bum:** Surf Swami's for towering blue-water breaks, tip-toe through the sand at Moonlight Beach, cruise the coast in a sailboat, or spot a whale spouting.

★ **Tour SoCal-style wineries:** Savor the red and white wines while touring in Temecula, home to nearly 50 wineries as well as boutique lodging and elegant restaurants.

★ **Step back in time:** Sink your teeth into sweet apple pie in the historic mining town of Julian where the Cuyamuca Mountains meet the Colorado Desert.

1 Del Mar. The coastal town is the location of the Del Mar Fairgrounds and the famed Del Mar Thoroughbred Club.

2 Solana Beach. Adjacent to Del Mar and Encinitas, the area is known for shopping—antiques, collectibles, and contemporary artwork—and the Cedros Design District.

3 Rancho Santa Fe. An affluent town east of I–5 where you'll find the Inn at Rancho Santa Fe and the Rancho Valencia Resort & Spa.

4 Encinitas. The surfer town encompasses Cardiff-by-the-Sea, Leucadia, and Olivenhain. It's one of the largest flower-producing areas in the world, and is home to the longboarding favorite, Swami's Beach.

5 Carlsbad. Famous for LEGOLAND, the Carlsbad Outlets, and the Flower Fields at Carlsbad Ranch.

6 Oceanside. Surf shops, casual dining options, a museum, a great boardwalk, and some of the best surfing beaches.

7 Rancho Bernardo. Straddling I–15 between San Diego and Escondido, the town is home to Rancho Bernardo Inn and Bernardo Winery.

8 Escondido. Home to the San Diego Zoo Safari Park and the California Center for the Arts.

9 Temecula. A darling Old Town and the center of the wine-making industry in Temecula Valley.

10 Julian. The historic mining town of Julian is famous for its apple pies, B&Bs, and July 4 parade.

11 Ramona. Golf at two highly rated courses (Barona Creek Golf Club and Mount Woodson Golf Club), the Barona casino, and a budding winery scene.

12 Anza-Borrego Desert State Park. This is desert at its best: vast, mostly untracked wilderness where you can wander and camp; a huge repository of prehistoric beasts, illustrated by a large collection of life-size sculptures along desert roadsides; and the best wildflower display in Southern California in the springtime.

13 Borrego Springs. Set in the heart of the Anza-Borrego Desert State Park, this is an emerging destination for desert lovers.

A whole world of scenic grandeur, fascinating history, and scientific wonder lies just beyond San Diego's city limits. If you travel north along the coast, you'll encounter the great beaches for which the region is famous, along with some sophisticated towns, fine restaurants, great galleries, and museums.

What these towns shared was at least a half-century's worth of Southern California beach culture—think Woodies (wood-bodied cars), surfing, the Beach Boys, alternate lifestyles—and the road that connected them. That was U.S. Highway 101, which nearly passed into oblivion when I–5 was extended from Los Angeles to the Mexican border. If you venture off the freeway and head for the ocean, you can discover remnants of the old beach culture surviving in the sophisticated towns of Del Mar, Solana Beach, Cardiff-by-the-Sea, Encinitas, Leucadia, Carlsbad, and Oceanside, where the arts, fine dining, and elegant lodgings also now rule. As suburbanization continues, the towns are reinventing themselves—Carlsbad, for instance, has morphed from a farming community into a tourist destination with such attractions as LEGOLAND California, several museums, and an upscale outlet shopping complex.

If you travel east, you'll find art hubs and organic farms in Escondido, the San Diego Zoo Safari Park, a pair of world-class destination spas, a selection of challenging golf courses, and nightlife in bucolic settings. Inspiring mountain scenery plus beautiful places to picnic and hike can be found in the Cuyamaca Mountains and in the surrounding areas near the historic gold-rush-era town of Julian, known for its apple pies. Just beyond the county limits in Temecula you can savor Southern California's only developed wine country, where dozens of wineries offer tastings and tours.

MAJOR REGIONS

San Diego's North County, encompassing the portion of San Diego County that lies north of the metro area from the ocean to the desert, has some of the same attractions of the city to the south: perpetual sunshine, great beaches, and entertainment, including LEGOLAND and the San Diego Zoo's Safari Park. A visit to North County offers a chance to escape the metro area and find a little quiet in the backcountry, serious wine tasting and good eating in Temecula, several luxury resorts and golf courses, some world-class destination spas, art and historic centers, a bit of gold rush–era history, and a more laid-back lifestyle.

Once upon a time, to say that the **North Coast** of San Diego County was different from the city of San Diego would have been an understatement. From the northern tip of La Jolla up to Oceanside, a half-dozen small communities developed separately from urban San Diego—and from one another. **Del Mar,** because of its 2 miles of wide beaches, splendid views, and Thoroughbred horse-racing complex, was the playground of the rich and famous. The affluent town of **Rancho Santa Fe** was also a haunt of Old Hollywood with the likes of Bette Davis and Bing Crosby hanging out at the Inn at Rancho Santa Fe. Up the road, agriculture played a major role in the development of **Solana Beach** and **Encinitas.**

Carlsbad, too, rooted in the old Mexican rancheros, has agriculture in its past, as well as the entrepreneurial instinct of a late-19th-century resident, John Frazier, who promoted the area's water as a cure for common ailments and constructed a replica of a European mineral-springs resort. **Oceanside** was a beachside getaway for inland families in the 19th century; today it's home to one of the longest wooden piers on the West Coast (its first pier was built in the 1880s), and the city promotes its beach culture with a yacht harbor and beachside resort hotels. It's also the location of Camp Pendleton, a Marine Corps training base during World War II that's still in use today.

Long regarded as San Diego's beautiful backyard, replete with green hills, quiet lakes, and citrus and avocado groves, **Inland North County** is home to some of Southern California's fastest growing areas. Subdivisions, many containing palatial homes, now fill the hills and canyons around **Escondido** and **Rancho Bernardo.** Hot on their heels are Vista and San Marcos (between coastal Oceanside and inland Escondido), both growing rapidly with gentrification and an influx of businesses due to Cal State San Marcos and proximity to the coast. For farm life and a small-town vibe, nearby Valley Center is where San Diegans are heading for land and potential. Growth notwithstanding, the area still has such natural settings

as the San Diego Zoo Safari Park and the destination spas like the renowned Golden Door Spa and Cal-a-Vie Health Spa.

As the premium wine-making region of Southern California, **Temecula** produces award-winning blends, ideal for those who want to tour local vineyards after a stroll through historic Old Town center or a round of golf on any one of Temecula's championship courses.

The area known as **The Backcountry** contains the Cuyamaca and Laguna mountains to the east of Escondido, which are favorite weekend destinations for hikers, bikers, nature lovers, stargazers, and apple-pie fanatics. Most of the latter group head to **Julian,** a historic mining town now better known for apple pie than for the gold once extracted from its hills. But golfers will want to head to **Ramona** for two courses (Barona Creek Golf Club and Mount Woodson Golf Club), and there's also the Barona casino, and a budding winery scene.

In most spring seasons the stark desert landscape east of the Cuyamaca Mountains explodes with colorful wildflowers. The beauty of this spectacle, as well as the natural quiet and blazing climate, lures many tourists and natives each year to **Anza-Borrego Desert State Park,** about a two-hour drive from central San Diego. There are 110 miles of trails that allow you to explore canyons, capture scenic vistas, and possibly see wildlife. The desert town of **Borrego Springs** is a great base for exploring the park by day and stargazing by night. It's best visited from October through May to avoid the extreme summer temperatures. Winter temperatures are comfortable, but nights (and sometimes days) are cold, so bring a warm jacket.

Planning

Getting Here and Around

BUS AND TRAIN

The Metropolitan Transit System covers the city of San Diego up to Del Mar.

Buses and trains operated by North County Transit District (NCTD) serve all coastal communities in San Diego County, going as far east as Escondido; the NCTD Sprinter runs a commuter service between Oceanside and Escondido. Routes are coordinated with other transit agencies serving San Diego County. Amtrak stops in Oceanside, Solana Beach, Old Town, and Downtown San Diego.

Coaster operates commuter rail service between San Diego and Oceanside, stopping en route in Old Town, Sorrento Valley, Solana Beach, Encinitas, and Carlsbad. The last Coaster train leaves San Diego at about 7 each night. NCTD's bus system, Breeze, serves North County; for on-demand service they offer Flex, and door-to-door paratransit service on LIFT.

BUS AND TRAIN CONTACTS Amtrak.

✉ *235 S. Tremont St., Oceanside*
☎ *760/722–4622 in Oceanside, 800/872–7245* ⊕ *www.amtrak.com.* **Coaster.**
☎ *760/966–6500* ⊕ *www.gonctd.com.*
Metropolitan Transit System. ☎ *619/233–3004* ⊕ *www.sdmts.com.* **North County Transit District.** ☎ *760/966–6500* ⊕ *www.gonctd.com.*

CAR

Interstate 5 is the main freeway artery connecting San Diego to Los Angeles, passing just east of the beach cities from Oceanside south to Del Mar. Running parallel west of I–5 is Route S21, also known and sometimes indicated as historic Highway 101, Old Highway 101, or Coast Highway 101, which never strays too far from the ocean. An alternate, especially from Orange and Riverside counties, is I–15, the inland route through Temecula, Escondido, and eastern San Diego County.

A loop drive beginning and ending in San Diego is a good way to explore the backcountry and Julian area. You can take the S1, the Sunrise National Scenic Byway (sometimes icy in winter) from I–8 to Route 79 and return through Cuyamaca Rancho State Park (also sometimes icy in winter). If you're only going to Julian (a 75-minute trip from San Diego in light traffic), take either the Sunrise Byway or Route 79, and return to San Diego via Route 78 past Santa Ysabel to Route 67; from here I–8 heads west to Downtown.

Escondido sits at the intersection of Route 78, which heads east from Oceanside, and I–15, the inland freeway connecting San Diego to Riverside, which is 30 minutes north of Escondido. Route 76, which connects with I–15 north of Escondido, veers east to Palomar Mountain. Interstate 15 continues north to Temecula.

Restaurants

Dining in North County tends to reflect the land where the restaurant is located. Along the coast, for example, there is one fine-dining spot after another. Most have dramatic water views and offer platters of exquisite fare created by graduates of the best culinary schools. Right next door you can wander into a typical beach shack or diner for the juiciest hamburger you've ever tasted. Locally sourced food and farm-to-table cuisine can be found at restaurants throughout the area. Backcountry cooking east of Escondido toward Julian is generally served in huge portions and tends toward home-style steak and potatoes, burgers, and anything fried. Several casinos near Temecula and Valley Center are famous for their all-you-can-eat seafood buffets.

Hotels

Like the restaurants, hotels in the North County reflect the geography and attractions where they are set. There are a number of luxury resorts that offer golf, tennis, entertainment, and classy service. For those who want the ultimate pampered vacation, North County holds two world-class spas: Cal-a-Vie and the Golden Door. Along the beach, there are quite a few stand-alone lodgings that attract the beach crowd; while some lack in appeal and service, they still charge a big price in summer. Lodgings in the Carlsbad area are family-friendly, and close to beaches and LEGOLAND. In Temecula, some of the best and most delightful lodgings are tied to wineries; they offer a whole experience: accommodations, spa, dining, and wine. One-of-a-kind bed-and-breakfasts are the rule in the Julian area. Some hotels charge resort fees up to $60 per night.

Flowers

The North County is a prolific flower-growing region. Nurseries, some open to the public, line the hillsides on both sides of I–5 in Encinitas, Leucadia, and Carlsbad. Most of the poinsettias sold in the United States get their start here. If you're visiting in spring, don't miss the ranunculus bloom at the Flower Fields at Carlsbad Ranch.

San Diego Botanic Gardens in Encinitas displays native and exotic plants year-round. The gardens at the San Diego Zoo Safari Park attract nearly as many people as the animals do.

VISITOR INFORMATION San Diego Tourism Authority. ☎ *619/232–3101* ⊕ *www. sandiego.org.*

Del Mar

23 miles north of Downtown San Diego on I–5, 9 miles north of La Jolla on Rte. S21.

Del Mar comprises two sections: the small historic village adjacent to the beach west of I–5 and a growing business center surrounded by multi-million-dollar tract housing east of the freeway. Del Mar village, the smallest incorporated city in San Diego County, holds a population of 4,500 tucked into a 2.1-square-mile beachfront. It's known for its quaint half-timbered Tudor-style architecture, 2 miles of accessible beaches, and the Del Mar racetrack and San Diego County Fairgrounds complex. The village attracted rich and famous visitors from the beginning; they still come for seclusion and to watch the horses run. Inland you'll find a business complex, high-rise hotels, and fast-food outlets east of the interstate at the entrance to Carmel Valley. Both Del Mars, old and new, hold expensive homes belonging to staff and scientists who work in the biotech industry and at UC San Diego in adjacent La Jolla. Access to Del Mar's beaches is from the streets that run east–west off Coast Boulevard; access to the business complex is via Highway 56.

TOURS
Civic Helicopters
AIR EXCURSIONS | Civic Helicopters gives whirlybird tours of the area along the beaches, starting at $335 for 30 minutes aboard a Robinson R-44. ⊠ *2206 Palomar Airport Rd., Suite H, Carlsbad* ☎ *760/438–8424.*

◉ Sights

Del Mar Fairgrounds (*Del Mar Racetrack*)
FAIRGROUND | FAMILY | The Spanish Mission–style fairground is the home of the Del Mar Thoroughbred Club (⊕ *www. dmtc.com*). Crooner Bing Crosby and his Hollywood buddies—Pat O'Brien,

Del Mar to Oceanside

Gary Cooper, and Oliver Hardy, among others—organized the club in the 1930s, and the racing here (usually July through September, Wednesday through Monday, post time 2 pm) remains a fashionable affair. Del Mar Fairgrounds hosts more than 500 different events each year, including the San Diego County Fair and the Del Mar National Horse Show. ⊠ 2260 Jimmy Durante Blvd., Del Mar ☎ 858/755–1161 ⊕ www.delmarfairgrounds.com.

Free Flight Exotic Bird Sanctuary
WILDLIFE REFUGE | FAMILY | This small exotic-bird aviary adjacent to the Del Mar Fairgrounds houses a collection of parrots and other exotic birds—a guaranteed child pleaser. Visits are by reservation only. ⊠ 2132 Jimmy Durante Blvd., Del Mar ☎ 858/481–3148 ⊕ www.freeflightbirds.org ⊠ $8.

Seagrove Park (*Powerhouse Park*)
CITY PARK | Picnics and weddings make this coastal park popular on weekends. For free summer evening concerts (Tuesday 6–9 pm) and beach access, head to Powerhouse Park at the north end of this small stretch of grass overlooking the ocean. ⊠ 15th St. and Coast Blvd., Del Mar ☎ 858/755–1524 ⊕ www.delmar. ca.us ⌔ Metered parking $3 per hr or $15 per day.

Beaches

Del Mar Beach
BEACH | FAMILY | This famously clean 2-mile-long beach is the perfect place for long barefoot walks and sunbathing due to its extremely fine, soft sand and lack of seaweed and other debris. Del Mar Beach is also a great place for families. It has year-round lifeguards and areas

clearly marked for swimming and surfing. Depending on the swell, you may see surfers at the 15th Street surf break, right below two coastal parks, Powerhouse and Seagrove; volleyball players love the courts at the beach's far north end. The section of beach south of 15th is lined with cliffs and tends to be less crowded than Main Beach, which extends from 15th north to 29th. Leashed dogs are permitted on most sections of the beach, except Main Beach, where they are prohibited from June 15 through the Tuesday after Labor Day. For the rest of the year, dogs may run off leash at North Beach, just north of the River Mouth, also known locally as Dog Beach. Food, shopping, and hotels including L'Auberge Del Mar, are near Del Mar Beach. Parking costs $3 per hour or $15 per day at meters and pay lots on Coast Boulevard and along Camino Del Mar. **Amenities:** food and drink; lifeguards; parking (fee); showers; toilets. **Best for:** swimming; walking. ⊠ *Main Beach, 1700 Coast Blvd., North Beach 3200–3300 Camino Del Mar, Del Mar* ☎ *858/755–1556* ⊕ *www.delmar. ca.us/203/Beaches-Parks.*

🍴 Restaurants

The neighborhood just north of La Jolla is well-known for its posh, ocean-view homes and the famed Del Mar racetrack. It's also known for the numerous restaurants that line the main drag of Camino Del Mar; there's even a few worthwhile spots tucked into upscale shopping centers and beachside locales.

★ Addison

$$$$ | **FRENCH** | Indulge in the finer things in life at this AAA 5-Diamond, three-star Michelin restaurant by acclaimed chef William Bradley who serves up haute French flavors in his 10-course prix-fixe dinners that feature dishes like Kumamoto oysters or Osetra caviar with gold leaf, coffee-roasted duck or tender *calotte de boeuf* with escargot. Beyond the swanky

Did You Know?

bar and wine cave is a sophisticated Tuscan-style dining room with intricately carved dark woods, marble pillars, and arched windows draped in red velvet. **Known for:** decadent tasting menus; impeccable service; San Diego's first Michelin-starred restaurant. ⑤ *Average main: $355* ⊠ *5200 Grand Del Mar Way, Del Mar* ☎ *858/314–1900* ⊕ *www.addisondelmar.com* ⊘ *Closed Sun. and Mon. No lunch.*

CUCINA enoteca

$$ | **MODERN ITALIAN** | An offshoot of Bankers Hill's Cucina Urbana, enoteca occupies a grand two-story space in the Flower Hill Promenade shopping center and is as notable for its whimsical decor—antler chandeliers, burlap-wrapped chairs, and more than 400 horse figurines honor the restaurant's proximity to the Thoroughbred Club—as it is for its beloved Italian food. There are many familiar favorites like the creamy polenta board and pizzas, as well as unique enoteca plates, including short-rib pappardelle, and chicken fra diavolo. **Known for:** wines at retail; Tuesday–Friday deals 4–6 pm; gardenlike second-floor seating area. ⑤ *Average main: $25* ⊠ *Flower Hill Promenade, 2730 Via de la Valle, Del Mar* ☎ *858/704–4500* ⊕ *www.cucinaenoteca.com* ⊘ *No lunch. Closed Mon.*

Flower Child

$ | MODERN AMERICAN | FAMILY | Fast-casual takes a healthy spin at this cheery spot—think Technicolor peace sign, floral wallpaper in the bathroom, and power-boosting juices. The menu evokes the same colorful vibe with bowls like the Mother Earth (ancient grains and sweet potato) or the glow bowl (sweet potato noodles, bok choy, shiitake mushroom, and coconut milk); soups; mix-and-match sides; wraps; and salads mixed with fresh ingredients like organic kale, ginger miso vinaigrette, and proteins that include sustainable salmon, grass-fed steak, and organic, non-GMO tofu. **Known for:** kid-friendly ambience; house-made lemonades; mix-and-match healthy sides. $ Average main: $16 ✉ Flower Hill Promenade, 2690 Via De La Valle, Del Mar ☎ 858/314–6818 ⊕ www.iamaflowerchild.com.

Jake's Del Mar

$$$ | AMERICAN | Situated next to grassy Powerhouse Park, Jake's feels like Southern Californian dining at its best—a beachfront location coupled with beautiful ocean views and the freshest ingredients. In a true aloha spirit, friendly servers are ready to tempt with cucumber margaritas and starters like macadamia-crusted calamari as well as items from the main menu, which is split "by garden," "by sea," and "by land," with options like the seafood pot, the chef's burger, and the barbecued ribs. Just steps from the sand, this is one of San Diego's best restaurants for mai tai sunsets. **Known for:** prime beachfront location; iconic Hula Pie dessert, a thick wedge of macadamia nut ice cream on a chocolate cookie crust that's topped with chocolate fudge, whipped cream, and more macadamia nuts; Sunday brunch. $ Average main: $32 ✉ 1660 Coast Blvd., Del Mar ☎ 858/755–2002 ⊕ www.jakesdelmar.com ۞ No lunch on Mon.

Market Restaurant + Bar

$$$$ | AMERICAN | Carl Schroeder, one of California's hottest young chefs, draws well-heeled foodies to his creative and locally sourced California fare, much of it with an Asian influence from his time in Japan. The three-course tasting menu changes regularly depending upon what's fresh, but Schroeder's seasonally inspired dishes have a playful spirit, whether it's a gorgonzola soufflé with strawberry-rhubarb compote, a grapefruit-avocado salad, or miso-glazed cod with ramen noodles and snap pea tempura. **Known for:** Cabernet-braised prime beef short rib; award-winning chef; well-edited wine list. $ Average main: $79 ✉ 3702 Via de la Valle, Del Mar ☎ 858/523–0007 ⊕ www.marketdelmar.com ۞ Closed Sun. and Mon. No lunch.

Monarch Ocean Pub

$$ | MODERN AMERICAN | Over the past decade, this coveted ocean-view spot in Del Mar has seen restaurants come and go, but finally Monarch did it right by transforming an 8,000-square-foot facility into dining space, an entertainment venue, and a sundeck for patrons and their pups. Inside, the California coastal menu itself is as cool as the 1970s decor, with rattan furniture and a poster of Tom Selleck greeting you at the door; outside a bridge connects the restaurant to "Monarch Park" where grab-'n'-go goodies can be enjoyed with live music Thursday–Sunday. **Known for:** happy hour $6 deals weekdays 4–6 pm; dragonfruit margaritas; community-centric place to connect. $ Average main: $24 ✉ 1555 Camino Del Mar, Del Mar ☎ 858/925–6047 ⊕ www.monarchdelmar.com.

Pacifica Del Mar

$$$ | SEAFOOD | The view of the shimmering Pacific from this lovely restaurant perched atop Del Mar Plaza is one of the best along the coast, and complements the simply prepared, beautifully presented seafood. The highly innovative menu is frequently rewritten to show off such

creations as barbecue sugar-spice salmon with mustard sauce and soy-glazed halibut. **Known for:** incredible views of the Pacific; ever-changing, creative seafood menu; Sunday brunch. $ *Average main: $35* ✉ *Del Mar Plaza, 1555 Camino Del Mar, Del Mar* ☎ *858/792–0476* ⊕ *www. pacificadelmar.com.*

Sbicca

$$$ | **AMERICAN** | The menu at this American bistro changes quarterly but the clientele is here to stay, especially during summer months when people-watching becomes a sport. Grab a seat on the terrace if you're lucky to enjoy such magical cocktails like a cucumber crush of grapefruit, vodka, and elderflower, and menu mainstays such as buttermilk-fried Jidori chicken, braised short ribs, and seared ahi tuna. **Known for:** half-off wine Tuesday and Thursday; truffle fettuccine; no cork fee on Monday. $ *Average main: $32* ✉ *215 15th St., Del Mar* ☎ *858/481–1001* ⊕ *www.sbiccadelmar.com.*

 ## Hotels

★ Fairmont Grand Del Mar

$$$$ | **RESORT** | **FAMILY** | Mind-blowing indulgence in serene surroundings, from drop-dead-gorgeous guest accommodations to myriad outdoor adventures, sets the opulent Mediterranean-style Fairmont Grand Del Mar apart from any other luxury hotel in San Diego. **Pros:** ultimate luxury; secluded, on-site golf course; enormous rooms; has most acclaimed fine-dining restaurant in San Diego. **Cons:** floor plan may be confusing; 6 miles from the coast; $150 pet fee per stay. $ *Rooms from: $800* ✉ *5200 Grand Del Mar Ct., Del Mar* ☎ *858/314–2000, 855/314–2030* ⊕ *www.fairmont.com/ san-diego* ⇥ *249 rooms* ℗ *No Meals.*

L'Auberge Del Mar

$$$$ | **HOTEL** | An $11 million remodel in 2021 revamped this oceanfront luxury hotel, taking it from beach cottage to coastal modern with subdued colors, contemporary pieces, and an elevated vibe reminding you that you're in Del Mar. From the lobby reminiscent of a chic living room, to the guest rooms in warm hues of tan, ivory, and gray, the hotel spared no expense in comfort or design. **Pros:** tennis courts, a fitness center, and shuttle service to neighboring beaches, shops, and restaurants; excellent service; dogs welcomed with gift bags. **Cons:** occasional train noise; adult atmosphere; $50 resort fee and $200 per stay pet fee. $ *Rooms from: $600* ✉ *1540 Camino Del Mar, Del Mar* ☎ *858/259–1515, 800/245–9757* ⊕ *www.laubergedelmar.com* ⇥ *121 rooms* ℗ *No Meals.*

 ## Shopping

Browse the cute boutiques in Del Mar Plaza or head to Flower Hill Promenade, an outdoor shopping center that has become one of San Diego's most thriving retail destinations with an eclectic mix of locally owned retailers. If you're headed to the Del Mar Racetrack, be sure to pick up a glamorous hat to wear while cheering on the ponies—a racetrack tradition.

Del Mar Plaza

MALL | Developed in 1989 by Del Mar residents Ivan Gayler and David Winkler, this plaza is worth a side trip if you're visiting the racetrack. Along with its collection of high-end shops, the tiered plaza contains outstanding restaurants and fountain courtyards with Pacific views. Some businesses validate parking, which is underground. ✉ *1555 Camino Del Mar, Del Mar* ⊕ *www.delmarplaza.com.*

Flower Hill Promenade

SHOPPING CENTER | At first glance, this open-air shopping center anchored by a Whole Foods Market (☎ *858/436–9800*) might look like your typical upscale SoCal mall, but take a closer look, because there's way more to it than meets the eye. There's not only some great shopping—much of it locally owned and eco-minded—but also some of San

Diego's best restaurateurs like Tracy Borkum and Steven Molina have opened restaurants here (CUCINA enoteca and Flower Child, respectively). Sweetpea (☎ 858/481–0683) stocks children's clothing from brands like Magnetic Me and Petit Bateau. Van de Vort (☎ 858/925–7676) sells the latest curated fashion from around the world. ☒ 2720 Via De La Valle, Del Mar ☎ 858/481–2904.

Activities

HORSE RACING
Del Mar Racetrack (*Del Mar Thoroughbred Club*)
HORSE RACING | The racetrack attracts the best horses and jockeys in the country—Seabiscuit even won a much-talked-about race here in 1938. Spectators can enjoy 11 weeks of racing annually at the historic Del Mar Racetrack. The summer season starts in mid-July and runs through early September and includes a summer concert series and opening- and closing-day celebrations. The fall season lasts for a month starting in November. The track, which opened in 1937, was founded in part by singer and actor Bing Crosby. ☒ 2260 Jimmy Durante Blvd., Del Mar ⊹ Take I–5 north to Via de la Valle exit ☎ 858/755–1141 ⊕ www.dmtc.com ☑ From $10.

Solana Beach

1 mile north of Del Mar on Rte. S21, 25 miles north of Downtown San Diego on I–5 to Lomas Santa Fe Dr. west.

Once-quiet Solana Beach is *the* place to stroll with a latte and look for collectibles, artwork, and contemporary fashions. The Cedros Design District, occupying four blocks south of the Amtrak station, contains shops, galleries, designers' studios, restaurants, and a popular music venue, the Belly Up Tavern. The town is known for its excellent restaurants, but most area lodging is in adjacent Del Mar and Encinitas.

Beaches

Fletcher Cove
BEACH | FAMILY | Most of the beaches in the little city of Solana Beach are nestled under cliffs, and access is limited to private stairways. However, at the west end of Lomas Santa Fe Drive, where it turns into Plaza Street, there's an entrance to this small beach, along with parking lot, picnic area, playground, and restrooms. The softest sand can be found by the cliffs and it gets a bit coarser as you near the water's edge. During low tide it's an easy walk under the cliffs to nearby beaches, but high tide can make some of the beach impassable. At the northern end of town there are also restrooms, a pay lot, and easy beach access. The City of Solana Beach and the Belly Up Tavern often host free summer concerts at Fletcher Cove (⊕ www.cityofsolanabeach.org) and there are plenty of great restaurants nearby on Highway 101 and on Cedros Avenue. Tides and surf conditions are posted at a kiosk by this parking lot. **Amenities:** lifeguards; parking (no fee); showers; toilets. **Best for:** surfing; solitude; swimming; walking. ☒ Plaza St. at S. Sierra Ave., Solana Beach ⊹ Public access at the end of Lomas Santa Fe Blvd ⊕ www.cityofsolanabeach.org.

Restaurants

Claire's on Cedros
$ | BAKERY | FAMILY | Breakfast foodies religiously line up for a table at this cheerful A-frame restaurant for the chance to dig into wholesome food made from scratch like organic quinoa Benedict, multigrain pancakes, and French toast stuffed with fresh ricotta. Built from reclaimed wood and salvaged bricks, the eatery has a

green roof, solar panels, and is insulated with recycled denim—all of which helped it earn platinum LEED status. **Known for:** scratch kitchen; California-style comfort food; generous portions. $ *Average main: $17* ✉ *246 N. Cedros Ave., across from Solana Beach Transit Center, Solana Beach* ☎ *858/259–8597* ⊕ *www. clairesoncedros.com* ☾ *No dinner.*

The Fish Market

$$ | **SEAFOOD** | **FAMILY** | In 1976, a fisherman and captain teamed up to deliver fresh, quality seafood at a decent price. Today, they run four restaurants across California including this North County branch that lacks an ocean view but makes up for it with perfectly cooked fish and simple preparations from a menu that changes daily. **Known for:** delicious clam chowder and crisp fish-and-chips; crab cioppino; happy hour 3–6 on weekdays. $ *Average main: $25* ✉ *640 Via de la Valle, Solana Beach* ☎ *858/755–2277* ⊕ *www.thefishmarket.com.*

Pamplemousse Grille

$$$ | **FRENCH** | One of North County's best restaurants, across the street from the Del Mar Fairgrounds and racetrack, offers French cuisine with California flare. Chef-proprietor Jeffrey Strauss brings a caterer's sensibilities to the details, like a mix-or-match selection of sauces—such as wild mushroom, béarnaise, au jus, grain mustard, or peppercorn—to complement the simple but absolutely top-quality grilled meats and seafood. **Known for:** exceptional service; comprehensive wine list and great martinis; traditional French sauces to accompany entrées. $ *Average main: $36* ✉ *514 Via de la Valle, Suite 100, Solana Beach* ☎ *858/792–9090* ⊕ *www.pgrille.com* ☾ *Closed Mon. No lunch.*

Pizza Port

$$ | **PIZZA** | **FAMILY** | Local families flock here for great pizza and handcrafted brews, which started in 1987 when siblings, Gina and Vince Marsaglia, bought a struggling pizza place in Solana Beach. Following the success of this original location, they've opened branches in Carlsbad, San Clemente, Ocean Beach, Bressi Ranch, and Imperial Beach. **Known for:** handcrafted beer and whole-grain beer crust; popular postwork spot; family-friendly dining. $ *Average main: $25* ✉ *135 N. Hwy. 101, Solana Beach* ☎ *858/481–7332* ⊕ *www.pizzaport.com.*

Ranch 45 Local Provisions

$ | **BARBECUE** | Get ready for savory perfection with a concept built around locally sourced ingredients from ranchers, fishermen, and farmers who are dedicated to their harvest and sharing the beauty of their bounty. While the all-day breakfasts are a hit, it's what's between the bread that matters, like Brandt beef patty burgers, smoked tri trip sandwiches, and beef sliders with house-made chips. **Known for:** chef's daily Brand Beef Tasting menu; no corkage fee when purchasing wine from their shop; locally sourced everything. $ *Average main: $18* ✉ *512 Via de la Valle, #102, Solana Beach* ☎ *858/461–0092* ⊕ *www.ranch45.com* ☾ *No dinner Mon. and Tues.*

Red Tracton's

$$$$ | **STEAKHOUSE** | Across the street from the Del Mar racetrack, this classic old-fashioned, family-owned, steak and seafood house is a high-roller's heaven and a perennial favorite with jockeys celebrating their wins. The food is simple but good, and the menu highlights roasted prime rib in addition to filet mignon, panfried scallops, and such starters as lobster bisque and jumbo shrimp on ice. **Known for:** lively piano music; juicy steaks, prime rib, and shrimp; supper-club atmosphere. $ *Average main: $60* ✉ *550 Via de la Valle, Solana Beach* ☎ *858/755–6600* ⊕ *www.redtractons-steakhouse.com* ☾ *Closed Mon. No lunch Tues.–Thurs. and weekends.*

Coffee and Quick Bites

★ Grange Garden

$ | **CAFÉ** | **FAMILY** | Get ready for a true French garden experience, where you can sip espresso, pluck flowers from galvanized buckets, and even hold a bunny. This flower shop-meets-café experience has lite bites and pastries that will have you sinking your teeth into a flaky croissant and saying "merci!" **Known for:** French pastries; flower shop-meets-café; bunny experience for kids. $ *Average main: $10* ⊠ *240 S Cedros Ave., Solana Beach* ☎ *858/342–0565* ⊕ *www.grange-garden.com* ⊘ *No dinner.*

Ⓨ Nightlife

Belly Up

LIVE MUSIC | A fixture on local papers' "best of" lists, Belly Up has been drawing crowds since it opened in 1974. Its longevity attests to the quality of the eclectic entertainment on its stage. Within converted Quonset huts, critically acclaimed artists play everything from reggae and folk to—well, you name it. ⊠ *143 S. Cedros Ave., Solana Beach* ☎ *858/481–8140* ⊕ *www.bellyup.com.*

🎟 Performing Arts

North Coast Repertory Theatre (*North Coast Rep*)
THEATER | For over 40 years, a diverse mix of comic and dramatic works has shown in the 194-seat space. The emphasis is on contemporary productions, but the theater has been known to stage some classics, too. ⊠ *987 Lomas Santa Fe Dr., Suite D, Solana Beach* ☎ *858/481–1055* ⊕ *www.northcoastrep.org.*

🛍 Shopping

A collection of more than 85 shops, along a two-block stretch of South Cedros Avenue (⊕ *www.cedrosavenue. com*), this district specializes in interior design, apparel, jewelry, galleries, salons, and gifts. You won't find chain restaurants here, as they are not allowed, but you will find local chefs shopping at the Sunday Farmers' Market (noon–4). There's also free parking along this dog-friendly strip.

ART GALLERIES

Aaron Chang Ocean Art Gallery

ART GALLERIES | On the south end of Cedros Design District, the Ocean Art Gallery features works by award-winning surf photographer, Aaron Chang. On display are photographic prints with ocean themes and several striking surfboard sculptures. ⊠ *415 S. Cedros Ave., No. 110, Solana Beach* ☎ *858/345–1880* ⊕ *www.aaronchang.com* ⊘ *Closed Tues.*

BOOKS

★ Solo

ANTIQUES & COLLECTIBLES | Operated by seven creative women, this upscale collective is a highlight of Cedros. Shoppers are lured in by the restored warehouse and won over by antiques, artwork, home furnishings, greeting cards, and books on cooking, industrial design, and everything in between. ⊠ *309 S. Cedros Ave., Solana Beach* ☎ *858/794–9016* ⊕ *www. solocedros.com.*

CLOTHING

Cedros Soles

MIXED CLOTHING | Shoes, clothing, accessories, and plenty of cashmere and jewelry to boot are what make this well-curated boutique a Cedros Avenue favorite. ⊠ *143 S. Cedros Ave., Suite L, Solana Beach* ☎ *858/794–9911* ⊕ *www. socalboutiques.com.*

HOME ACCESSORIES AND GIFTS

Bixby & Ball

OTHER SPECIALTY STORE | Candles, quilts, cushions, cookbooks, and other cozy items to put the finishing touches on your home are available at this sweet cottage-turned-shop. They even offer interior design services if you happen to fall in love with San Diego and never want to leave. For even more treasures, walk across the street to their second location. ✉ *214 S. Cedros Ave., Solana Beach* ☎ *858/436–7214* ⊕ *www.bixbyandball.com.*

David Alan Collection

OTHER SPECIALTY STORE | Soak in the Balinese beauty of this gallery-like store where North County's wealthy come to shop for Indonesian art, wooden furniture, clothing, jewelry, pottery, antiques, artifacts, and other international imports. ✉ *241 S. Cedros Ave., Solana Beach* ☎ *858/481–8044* ⊕ *www.thedavidalancollection.com.*

DIY Headquarters

ANTIQUES & COLLECTIBLES | Inside this tiny 1920s cottage (open only on the weekends) are funky, handmade treasures including repurposed furniture and craft kits for DIY projects. The owner also hosts monthly on-site art classes like furniture painting 101 and DIY paint class. ✉ *315 S. Cedros Ave., Solana Beach* ☎ *858/222–2989* ⊕ *www.debisdesigndiary.com* ☺ *Closed Mon.–Fri.*

Activities

BIKING

Lomas Santa Fe Drive

BIKING | Experienced cyclists follow this route in Solana Beach east into Rancho Santa Fe, perhaps even continuing east on Del Dios Highway, past Lake Hodges, to Escondido. These roads can be narrow and winding in spots.

Rancho Santa Fe

4 miles east of Solana Beach on Rte. S8, Lomas Santa Fe Dr., 29 miles north of Downtown San Diego on I–5 to Rte. S8 east.

Groves of huge, drooping eucalyptus trees cover the hills and valleys of this affluent and exclusive town east of I–5. Rancho Santa Fe and the surrounding areas are primarily residential, where there are mansions at every turn. It's also common to see entire families riding horses on the many trails that crisscross the hillsides.

Modeled after a Spanish village, the town was designed by Lilian Rice, one of the first women to graduate with a degree in architecture from the University of California. Her first structure, a 12-room house built in 1922, evolved into the Inn at Rancho Santa Fe, which became a gathering spot for celebrities such as Bette Davis, Errol Flynn, and Bing Crosby in the 1930s and 1940s. The challenging Rancho Santa Fe Golf Course, the original site of the Bing Crosby Pro-Am, is considered one of the best courses in Southern California.

🍽 Restaurants

Mille Fleurs

$$$$ | **FRENCH** | Wealthy regulars who have dined at this elegant Rancho Santa Fe eatery since 1985 got a pleasant surprise when chef Brandon Jennings took over the kitchen in 2022, bringing a sophisticated take on their favorite comfort classics. Devotees can still enjoy Mille Fleurs favorites like Wiener schnitzel and lobster salad, but new highlights include seasonal dishes prepared with ingredients from neighboring Chino Farms like roasted dover sole with potato fondant, or veal porterhouse with roasted mushrooms. **Known for:** fresh produce from neighboring Chino Farms; authentic French desserts; soft jazz in the piano bar Wednesday–Saturday. ⑤ *Average main: $50* ✉ *Country Squire Courtyard, 6009 Paseo Delicias, Rancho Santa Fe* ☎ *858/756–3085* ⊕ *www.millefleurs.com* ☺ *No lunch. Closed Mon.*

☕ Coffee and Quick Bites

Thyme in the Ranch

$ | **CAFÉ** | Put your phone down and lose track of time—or thyme—at this darling cottage in the heart of Rancho Santa Fe.

Owner-chef Keely Barrera has created quite the spread with artisan-baked goods made with locally sourced ingredients like the homemade muffins that blend blueberry with bran or raspberry with mango. **Known for:** fruit muffins; savory brunch items; garden setting. $ *Average main: $16* ⊠ *16905 Av. de Acacias, Rancho Santa Fe* ☎ *858/759–0747* ⊕ *www.thymeintheranch.com* ⊘ *Closed Mon. No dinner.*

Hotels

The Inn at Rancho Santa Fe

$$$$ | HOTEL | As one of the country's first boutique hotels—it was designed in 1923 by Lilian Rice, who was known for her architectural works reflecting Spanish colonial style—The Inn's 17 individual cottages are spread around 22 lushly landscaped acres. **Pros:** charming historic hotel; excellent service; morning yoga classes. **Cons:** dim lighting in the rooms; cold pool; some rooms close to the road. $ *Rooms from: $550* ⊠ *5951 Linea del Cielo, Rancho Santa Fe* ☎ *858/756–1131, 800/843–4661* ⊕ *www.theinnatrsf.com* ⇥ *80 rooms* ⊠ *No Meals.*

★ Rancho Valencia Resort & Spa

$$$$ | RESORT | FAMILY | Elegant and luxurious two-level, hacienda-style casitas—appointed with corner fireplaces, luxurious bathrooms, and shuttered French doors leading to private patios—are nestled among 45 acres in one of Southern California's most affluent neighborhoods. **Pros:** one of the few properties in the United States with both five-star spa and resort; impeccable personalized service; use of minibar, fitness classes, Bentleys, and tennis clinic included in rate; one of nation's top tennis resorts. **Cons:** $65 daily resort fee; very expensive; far from San Diego attractions. $ *Rooms from: $999* ⊠ *5921 Valencia Circle, Rancho Santa Fe* ☎ *858/756–1123, 866/233–6708* ⊕ *www.ranchovalencia.com* ⇥ *49 suites* ⊠ *No Meals.*

Shopping

Chino Farm

FOOD | This is the place to buy the same premium (and very expensive) fruits, micro greens, edible flowers, and rare vegetables that the farm grows for many of San Diego's upscale restaurants, and for such famed California eateries as Chez Panisse in Berkeley and George's in La Jolla. ⊠ *6123 Calzada del Bosque, Rancho Santa Fe* ☎ *858/756–3184* ⊕ *www.chinofamilyfarm.com* ⊘ *Closed Mon. and Tues.*

The Country Friends

SOUVENIRS | Operated by a nonprofit foundation, the Country Friends carries collectibles, silver, furniture, and antiques donated or consigned by community residents. ⊠ *6030 El Tordo, Rancho Santa Fe* ☎ *858/756–1192* ⊕ *www.thecountryfriends.org* ⊘ *closed Sun. and Mon.*

Activities

SPAS

The Spa at Rancho Valencia

SPAS | The Spa at Rancho Valencia Resort invites couples (and everyone else) to relax, romance, and renew. Massages include relaxation, deep tissue, hot stone, and prenatal, but the Lovers Ritual begins with a couple's bath, followed by a Duet Massage in a cabana for two. Treatment rooms have private Jacuzzis, fireplaces, and outdoor showers. Day access to the spa amenities—plunge circuit, sauna, steam room, relaxation room, saline pool, fitness classes—is included when you book a treatment. Price: Massages from $250; manicures from $75; facials from $255; body therapies from $265; couples from $500. ⊠ *5921 Rancho Valencia Cir., Rancho Santa Fe* ☎ *858/759–6490* ⊕ *www. ranchovalencia.com.*

Encinitas

6 miles north of Solana Beach on Rte. S21, 7 miles west of Rancho Santa Fe on Rte. S9, 28 miles north of Downtown San Diego on I-5.

Flower breeding and growing has been the major industry in Encinitas since the early part of the 20th century. The city, which encompasses the coastal towns of Cardiff-by-the-Sea and Leucadia as well as inland Olivenhain, is home to Paul Ecke Poinsettias (open only to the trade), and today is the largest producer and breeder of the Christmas blossom in the world. The golden domes of the Self-Realization Fellowship Retreat mark famed Swami's Beach and the southern entrance to downtown Encinitas.

The vibe is laid-back, with surfing and yoga as top priorities for residents. Expect to see flip-flop-clad locals crossing the boulevard with surfboards in tow, and signs of historic California alive and well. Lining the main drag are plenty of cafés, bars, and restaurants to hold your attention, as well as the 1928 La Paloma Theater that still shows cult classics, foreign films, and music performances nightly.

GETTING HERE AND AROUND

From San Diego, head north on I-5. If you're already on the coast, drive along Route S21. Lodgings, restaurants, and the beach pop up along Route S21 (Old Highway 101) west of the freeway. The San Diego Botanic Gardens lie to the east of the freeway.

Sights

Nature Collective

TRAIL | FAMILY | Between Solana Beach and Encinitas, this is the most complex of the estuary systems in San Diego North County. A 7-mile network of trails surrounds the 979-acre reserve, where more than 700 species of plants, fish, and birds (many of them migratory) live. In 2021, Nature Collective began a $120 million restoration project that included new mudflats and tidal dredging in basins of San Elijo Lagoon Ecological Reserve. Their efforts have restored habitats for wildlife and waterfowl. Be sure to stop by the San Elijo Lagoon Nature Centre. The center, open 9 to 5 daily, offers museum-quality exhibits about the region and a viewing deck overlooking the estuary. ⊠ *2710 Manchester Ave., Cardiff-by-the-Sea* ☎ *760/436–3944 conservancy, 760/634–3026 nature center* ⊕ *www.naturecollective.org* ✉ *Free.*

San Diego Botanic Gardens

GARDEN | FAMILY | More than 5,300 rare, exotic, and endangered plants are on display on 37 landscaped acres. Displays include plants from Central America, Africa, Australia, the Middle East, the Mediterranean, the Himalayas, Madagascar, and more; the most diverse collection of bamboo in North America; California native plants; and subtropical fruits. The park contains the largest interactive children's garden on the West Coast, where kids can roll around in the Seeds of Wonder garden, explore a baby dinosaur forest, discover a secret garden, or play in a playhouse. An Undersea Garden displays rocks and succulents that uncannily mimic an underwater environment. ⊠ *230 Quail Gardens Dr., Encinitas* ☎ *760/436–3036* ⊕ *www.sdbgarden.org* ✉ *$18* ⊗ *Closed Tues.*

Self-Realization Fellowship Encinitas Temple

GARDEN | Founded in 1920 as a retreat and place of worship, the center also offers one of the best views along the Pacific Coast, a sweeping seascape extending north and south as far as the eye can see. Paramahansa Yogananda, author of the classic *Autobiography of a Yogi*, created two beautiful meditation gardens that are open to the public. The gardens are planted with flowering shrubs and trees and contain a series of koi ponds connected by miniature waterfalls. Swami's Point at the south end of the gardens is a popular surfer's break. ⊠ 215 W. K St., between 2nd and 3rd Sts., Encinitas ⊕ Off 1150 S. Coast Hwy. 101 ☎ 760/753–2888 ⊕ www.encinitas-temple.org ⊠ Free ⊘ Closed Mon.

Beaches

★ Moonlight State Beach

BEACH | FAMILY | Its large parking areas, many facilities, and proximity to the quaint coastal town of Encinitas make this beach tucked into a break in the cliffs a great getaway; it's perfect for families with young kids. The volleyball courts on the northern end attract many competent players, and professionals can be spotted surfing the break known locally as "D Street." Moonlight is easily accessible from the Encinitas Coaster train station and Coast Highway 101, which runs right through town and is lined with great shops, restaurants, and bars; there's a large free parking lot near the corner of 3rd and B Street. **Amenities:** food and drink; lifeguards; parking (no fee); showers; toilets. **Best for:** sunset; surfing; swimming. ⊠ 399 C St., Encinitas ⊕ To get to beach from I–5, take Encinitas Blvd. west until it ends ⊕ www.parks.ca.gov.

Swami's

BEACH | The palms and the golden lotus-flower domes of the nearby Self-Realization Fellowship temple and ashram earned this picturesque beach, also a top surfing spot (it's one of the few spots that can hold a massive winter swell), its name. Extreme low tides expose tide pools that harbor anemones, starfish, and other sea life. The only access is by a long stairway leading down from the cliff-top Swami's Seaside Park, where there's free parking. A shower is at the base of the steps. On big winter swells, the bluffs are lined with gawkers watching the area's best surfers take on—and be taken down by—some of the county's best big waves. The beach has flat, packed sand and can accumulate seaweed and some flies, so if lying out is your main objective, you might want to head north to Moonlight Beach. Offshore, divers do their thing at North County's underwater park, Encinitas Marine Life Refuge. The small park next to the Swami's parking lot offers shade trees, picnic tables, barbecues, and clean bathrooms. Across the street is the cheerful Swami's Cafe, where surfers refuel postsurf. **Amenities:** lifeguards; parking (no fee); showers; toilets. **Best for:** snorkeling; surfing; swimming. ⊠ 1298 S. Coast Hwy. 101 (Rte. S21), Encinitas ⊕ 1 mile north of Cardiff.

Restaurants

★ Buona Forchetta

$$ | ITALIAN | For authentic Italian cuisine, head to the "Good Fork" where you'll feel like you've stepped into the home of your long-lost Italian relatives, no matter where you're from. Nearly every dish—Neapolitan-style pies, eggplant Parmesan, lasagna Bolognese, vegetarian ravioli—is made from scratch, with many of the ingredients imported from Italy; even the star of the show, "Isabella," their golden-domed pizza oven, was handmade in Naples. **Known for:** Neapolitan-style pizza; homemade Italian desserts; vegan, vegetarian, gluten-free options. ⑤ Average main: $20 ⊠ 250 N. Coast Hwy. 101, Encinitas ☎ 760/704–8070 ⊕ www.buonaforchettanc.com.

Fish 101

$ | SEAFOOD | The line out the door—especially during happy hour—is a clear sign you're at the best place in North County to find locally sourced, sustainably caught fish at a great price. Owned by surfers-divers-fishermen, John Park and Ray Lowe, the vibe is SoCal at its best, with a chill staff serving fresh-shucked oysters, thick clam chowder, and fish sandwiches grilled to perfection; a chalkboard menu displays the day's catch and what's been shucked on ice. **Known for:** SoCal vibe with amazing fish tacos; fresh and healthy seafood; seasonal, sustainable ingredients. ⑤ *Average main: $15* ✉ *1468 N. Coast Hwy. 101, Encinitas* ☎ *760/943–6221* ⊕ *www.fish101restaurant.com* ☽ *Closed Mon.*

Ki's Restaurant

$$ | **VEGETARIAN** | Veggies with a view could be the subtitle for this venerable Cardiff restaurant that grew from a simple juice shack. Ki's is well known for heart-healthy, gluten-free, vegan, locally sourced, ovo-lacto, vegetarian-friendly dishes like huevos rancheros, filling tofu scrambles, taco plates, chopped salads with feta and nuts, seasonal juice, and carrot ice-cream smoothies. **Known for:** healthy vegan and gluten-free menu; yummy Asian-inspired dishes; popular postsurfing spot across from the beach. ⑤ *Average main: $20* ✉ *2591 S. Coast Hwy. 101, Cardiff-by-the-Sea* ☎ *760/436– 5236* ⊕ *www.kisrestaurant.com.*

Las Olas

$ | **MEXICAN** | **FAMILY** | In 1981, Señora Mendoza created a home-cooked menu that is still used today, making this one of North County's best Mexican restaurants. Across the street from Cardiff Beach— you can grab a margarita or some fish tacos before heading off to view surfers awaiting their next wave—expect big platters of fajitas, chiles rellenos, and chicken taquitos served with rice and beans. **Known for:** fish tacos; authentic Mexican food; local craft beers. ⑤ *Average main: $18* ✉ *2655 S. Coast Hwy. 101, Cardiff-by-the-Sea* ☎ *760/942–1860* ⊕ *www.lasolasrestaurant.com.*

Pacific Coast Grill

$$$ | **SEAFOOD** | This casual beachy-style eatery offers sweeping ocean views and seasonal Pacific Coast fare that reflects California's Mexican and Asian influences with dishes like seabass tacos and ahi poke bowl. Evenings are a scene, as attractive beachy types sip microbrews and well-priced wines along with morsels from the sushi bar; dinner in the spacious dining room or on the dog-friendly sunny patio brings porcini-crusted scallops with corn-truffle puree, or plum-ginger–braised short ribs washed down with a margarita that sings with fresh lime and lemon juice. **Known for:** romantic waterfront dining; fresh oysters and sushi rolls; stunning sunsets. ⑤ *Average main: $37* ✉ *2526 S. Hwy. 101, Cardiff-by-the-Sea* ☎ *760/479–0721* ⊕ *www.pacificcoastgrill. com.*

VAGA

$$$ | **AMERICAN** | Cleverly drawing inspiration from near and "farms," Chef Claudette Zepeda boldly colors outside the lines with a variety of dishes influenced by her travels to Mexico, Morocco, Philippines, and beyond. Grab a seat in the chic dining room where a crew of cooks in an open kitchen fire up a seasonally changing menu that features dishes like beef tartare topped with caviar, clams in a birria broth, or Brandt Farms rib eye with heavy marbling. **Known for:** menu by James Beard semifinalist, Claudette Zepeda; farm-fresh cuisine; ocean-view dining. ⑤ *Average main: $38* ✉ *At Alila Marea, 2100 N. Coast Hwy. 101, Encinitas* ☎ *760/452–3484* ⊕ *www.vagarestaurant.com.*

★ Valentina

$$ | **TAPAS** | It's lively, it's casual, and it's the coolest spot to share tapas with a date over a glass of wine. This Leucadia-based bistro turns heads with its black-and-white decor, as does the Spanish-meets-Mediterranean menu inspired by the owners' travels. **Known for:** ideal date spot; tapas menu great for sharing; weekend brunch 11–2:30. ⑤ *Average main: $20* ✉ *810 N Coast Hwy. 101, Encinitas* ☎ *760/943–6686* ⊕ *www. restaurantvalentina.com.*

Coffee and Quick Bites

Juanitas Taco Shop

$ | **MEXICAN** | Don't let the bars on the windows or the illuminated billboard covered in skate stickers deter you, as the line of hungry surfers-in-waiting is a sure sign you've found the best taco bar in town. Tacos are served on paper plates and burritos are rolled in parchment paper—you'll need both hands to hold these bad boys—at this no-frills hole-in-the-wall that's open until midnight, but that makes it easier to munch streetside, or better yet, take your feast to the beach and ride on. **Known for:** big portions at a great price; shredded chicken quesadillas; chorizo breakfast burrito. ⑤ *Average main: $10* ⊠ *290 N. Coast Hwy. 101, Encinitas* ☎ *760/943–9612* ⊕ *juanitas-taco-shop.business.site.*

🛏 Hotels

★ Alila Marea Beach Resort Encinitas

$$$$ | **RESORT** | Thirty years in the making, this striking hotel perched on the ocean bluffs has successfully captured the essence of SoCal's luxurious beach culture with sleek rooms and spaces that pay tribute to its environment. **Pros:** health-focused lifestyle resort with throughtful approach; breathtaking beachfront location; solar-powered, zero-plastic hotel. **Cons:** daily resort fee $55; parking fee $55; not child- or pet-friendly; small pool. ⑤ *Rooms from: $800* ⊠ *2100 N. Coast Hwy. 101, Encinitas* ☎ *760/452–3500* ⊕ *www.alilahotels.com* 🛏 *130 rooms* ⍟⊙ *No Meals.*

🛍 Shopping

Souvenir items are sold at shops along South Coast Highway 101 and in the Lumberyard Shopping Center.

Hansen's

SPORTING GOODS | One of San Diego's oldest surfboard manufacturers is owned by Don Hansen, surfboard shaper extraordinaire, who came here from Hawaii in 1962. The store stocks a full line of surf, snowboard, and ski gear and apparel. They also have entire departments dedicated to wet suits and footwear. Local "groms" love their Goods for Grades program that earns $4 store credit for every "A" on their school report card (max up to $24). ⊠ *1105 S. Coast Hwy. 101, Encinitas* ☎ *800/480–4754, 760/753–6596* ⊕ *www.hansensurf.com.*

Activities

GOLF

Encinitas Ranch Golf Course

GOLF | See the Pacific Ocean from virtually every vantage point at this course on bluffs in North County. Local golfers love it because low scores aren't that hard to come by. It's a forgiving course with wide-open fairways. Encinitas Ranch also has a 6,000-square-foot clubhouse with a bar and café. The adjoining patio has a stone fireplace and great ocean views. ⊠ *1275 Quail Gardens Dr., Encinitas* ☎ *760/944–1936* ⊕ *www.jcgolf.com* 🏷 *From $115* ⅄ *18 holes, 6587 yards, par 72.*

Carlsbad

6 miles from Encinitas on Rte. S21, 36 miles north of Downtown San Diego on I–5.

Once-sleepy Carlsbad, lying astride I–5 at the north end of a string of beach towns extending from San Diego to Oceanside, has long been popular with beachgoers, sunseekers, surfers, skaters, and cyclists. Carlsbad is home to the first skateboard park in the world, and has lured such local athletes as Tony Hawk and Shaun White.

On a clear day, you can take in sweeping ocean views that stretch from La Jolla to Oceanside along the 2-mile-long path between the Encina Power Station and

Pine Street. En route, you can get closer to the water via several stairways leading to the beach; quite a few benches are here as well.

East of I–5 is LEGOLAND California and other attractions like a discount shopping mall, golf courses, the cattle ranch built by movie star Leo Carrillo, and the colorful spring-blooming Flower Fields at Carlsbad Ranch. Closest to Encinitas is the upscale residential area of La Costa where you'll find plenty of shops, restaurants, wetlands, and two luxurious resort hotels. Until the mid-20th century, when suburban development began to sprout on the hillsides, farming was the main industry in Carlsbad, with truckloads of vegetables shipped out year-round. Some agriculture remains. Area farmers develop and grow new varieties of flowers, including the ranunculus that transform a hillside into a rainbow each spring. Carlsbad strawberries are among the sweetest in Southern California; in spring you can pick them yourself in fields on both sides of I–5.

GETTING HERE AND AROUND

LEGOLAND California Resort, off Cannon Road east of I–5, is surrounded by the Flower Fields, hotels, and the Museum of Making Music. On the west side of the freeway is beach access at several points and quaint Carlsbad village shops.

VISITOR INFORMATION

CONTACT Visit Carlsbad. ✉ *Carlsbad* ⊕ *visitcarlsbad.com.*

Sights

Batiquitos Lagoon

NATURE PRESERVE | While development destroyed many of the saltwater marsh wildlife habitats that once punctuated the North County coastline, this 610-acre lagoon was restored in 1997 to support fish and bird populations. Today, there are more than 200 species of birds here. A stroll along the 2-mile trail from the Batiquitos Lagoon Foundation Nature

> **Did You Know?**
>
> Carlsbad village owes its name to John Frazier, who dug a well for his farm here in the 1880s. The water bubbling from it was soon found to have the same properties as water from the mineral wells of Karlsbad, Bohemia (now Karlovy Vary, Czech Republic, but then under the sway of the Austro-Hungarian Empire). When Frazier and others went into the business of luring people to the area with talk of the healing powers of the local mineral water, they changed the name of the town from Frazier's Station to Carlsbad, to emphasize the similarity to the famous Bohemian spa.

Center along the north shore of the lagoon reveals nesting sites of the red-winged blackbird; lagoon birds such as the great blue heron, the great egret, and the snowy egret; and life in the mud flats. This wheelchair-accessible trail is a quiet spot for contemplation or a picnic. The Nature Center showcases exhibits on butterflies, moths, birds, and the Kumeyaay tribe who once fished on the lagoon. They spent half the year on the coast and half the year in the highlands of Julian to gather acorns—an important part of their diet. Today there are just 12 Kumeyaay reservations in California, predominately in East County San Diego. Within the Nature Center, you can view examples of the tribe's traditional clothing, fish traps, baskets, clay pots, bows and arrows, and more. Guided walking tours, lasting 1–2 hours, are offered monthly by appointment and can be arranged through the website. ✉ *7380 Gabbiano La., Carlsbad* ⊹ *Take Poinsettia La. exit off I–5, go east, and turn right onto Batiquitos Dr., then right again onto Gabbiano La.* ☎ *442/320–7009* ⊕ *www. batiquitoslagoon.org* 💲 *free.*

The spring blooms at the Flower Fields at Carlsbad Ranch are not to be missed.

★ Flower Fields at Carlsbad Ranch

GARDEN | FAMILY | The largest bulb-production farm in Southern California has hillsides abloom here each spring, when thousands of Giant Tecolote ranunculus produce a stunning 50-acre display of color against the backdrop of the blue Pacific Ocean. Other knockouts include the rose gardens—with examples of every All-American Rose Selection award-winner since 1940—and a historical display of Paul Ecke poinsettias. Peak flower season is mid-March through mid-April. Open to the public during this time, the farm offers family activities that include wagon rides, panning for gold, and a kids' playground. ⊠ *5704 Paseo del Norte, east of I–5, Carlsbad* ☎ *760/431–0352* ⊕ *www.theflowerfields.com* ✉ *$23* ⊙ *Closed mid-May–Feb.* ☞ *All tickets must be purchased online.*

★ LEGOLAND California Resort

AMUSEMENT PARK/CARNIVAL | FAMILY | The centerpiece of a development that includes resort hotels, a designer discount shopping mall, an aquarium, and a water park, LEGOLAND has rides and attractions geared to kids ages 2 to 12. THE LEGO MOVIE WORLD, which opened in 2021, has fans riding on Emmet's triple-decker flying couch on Emmet's Flying Adventure Ride, spinning on Unikitty's Disco Drop, and exploring Bricksburg. There's also Miniland U.S.A., which features a miniature, animated, interactive collection of iconic U.S. cities built from more than 24 million LEGO bricks, including the newest addition, MINILAND San Diego. You can test your ninja skills in LEGO NINJAGO WORLD.

If you're looking for rides, NINJAGO The Ride uses hand-gesture technology to throw fireballs, shock waves, ice, and lightning to defeat villains in this interactive 4-D experience. Be submerged underwater in a real submarine and partake in an interactive treasure hunt at LEGO City: Deep Sea Adventure. Journey through ancient Egyptian ruins in a desert roadster, scoring points as you hit targets with a laser blaster at Lost Kingdom Adventure. Or, jump on the Dragon

Coaster, an indoor-outdoor steel roller coaster that goes through a castle. Don't let the name frighten you—the motif is more humorous than scary. Kids ages 6 to 13 can stop by the Driving School to drive speed-controlled cars (not on rails) on a miniature road; driver's licenses are awarded after the course. Junior Driving School is the pint-size version for kids three to five.

You'll need your swimsuit for LEGO Chima Water Park, where an additional $30 gives you access to slides, rides, rafts, Soak-N-Sail, which has 60 interactive features, including a pirate shipwreck-theme area, and the CHIMA Water Park, as well as Surfer's Bay with competitive water raceways and a "spray ground" with water jets.

Be sure to try Granny's Apple Fries, Castle Burgers, and Pizza Mania for pizzas and salads. The Market near the entrance has excellent coffee, fresh fruit, and yogurt. The LEGOLAND Hotel is worth a visit even if you're not staying overnight. There are activities and a LEGO pit in the lobby that will entertain kids while parents recover with a cocktail.

■ TIP➔ The best value is one of the Hopper Tickets that give you one admission to LEGOLAND plus Sea Life Aquarium and/or the LEGOLAND Water Park from $104. These can be used on the same day or on different days. Purchase tickets online for discounted pricing. Go midweek to avoid the crowds. All guests are required to make advanced reservations to LEGOLAND California Theme Park. ⊠ 1 Legoland Dr., Carlsbad ⊹ Exit I–5 at Cannon Rd. and follow signs east ¼ mile 🕾 760/918–5346 ⊕ www. legoland.com/california 🖾 LEGOLAND Theme Park from $89; LEGOLAND and SEA LIFE Aquarium $104; LEGOLAND, SEA LIFE Aquarium and Waterpark $129 ⊗ Closed Tues. and Wed. Sept.–Feb.

Leo Carrillo Ranch Historic Park
HISTORIC SIGHT | This was a real working ranch with 600 head of cattle owned by actor Leo Carrillo, who played Pancho in the Cisco Kid television series in the 1950s. Before Carrillo bought the spread, known as Rancho de Los Kiotes, in 1937, the rancho was the home of a band of Luiseno Indians. Carrillo's hacienda and other buildings have been restored to reflect the life of the star when he hosted his Hollywood friends for long weekends in the country. Four miles of trails take visitors through colorful native gardens to the cantina, washhouse, pool and cabana, barn, and stable that Carrillo used. You can tour these buildings on weekends when guided tours are offered twice daily. After Carrillo's death in 1961, the ranch remained in the family until 1979, when part of the acreage was acquired by the city for a park. ⊠ 6200 Flying Leo Carrillo La., Carlsbad 🕾 442/339–5042 ⊕ www.carrillo-ranch. org 🖾 Free ⚲ Guided tours weekends at 10 am and 1 pm.

Museum of Making Music
OTHER MUSEUM | FAMILY | Take an interactive journey through 100 years of popular music with displays of more than 500 vintage instruments and samples of memorable tunes from the past century. Hands-on activities include playing a digital piano, drums, guitar, and more. ⊠ 5790 Armada Dr., east of I–5, Carlsbad 🕾 760/438—5996 ⊕ www.museumof-makingmusic.org 🖾 $15 ⊗ Closed Mon.

SEA LIFE Aquarium
AQUARIUM | FAMILY | Offering an educational and interactive underwater experience, the walk-through exhibits focus on creatures found in local waters including California lakes and streams and the cold-water marine animals that live along the California coast. Other exhibits include an underwater acrylic tunnel that affords a deep-sea (but dry) look at sharks, fish, and invertebrates. There's a seahorse kingdom, interactive tide pools, and jellyfish discovery. This park has a separate admission from LEGOLAND, although you can upgrade

LEGOLAND California's Miniland U.S.A. has scenes from San Francisco, Washington, D.C., New Orleans, New York, and Las Vegas.

your LEGOLAND ticket to include the aquarium. ⊠ *1 LEGOLAND Dr., Carlsbad* ☎ *760/918–5346* ⊕ *www.legoland.com/california* ⊠ *$25* ☞ *Strollers not permitted.*

Beaches

South Carlsbad State Beach/Carlsbad State Beach

BEACH | There are fine street- and beach-level promenades at Carlsbad State Beach, where people come to surf and swim at Ponto and Tamarack beaches. On the bluff, there's overnight camping for self-contained RVs (☎ *800/444–7275*) and tents (from $50 with $8 reservation fee). Farther north at the foot of Tamarack Avenue is Carlsbad State Beach. You can't camp here, but there's fishing and jogging trails and the beach has separate swimming and surfing sections. In summer, the south swell creates good surf when other San Diego beaches are bereft. The cement walkway that borders the beach continues into

downtown Carlsbad, which has plenty of restaurants. Carlsbad State Beach has a paid parking lot on Tamarack Avenue and at South Ponto. **Amenities:** lifeguards; parking (fee); showers; toilets. **Best for:** walking; swimming; surfing. ⊠ *South Carlsbad Beach, 7201 Carlsbad Blvd., Carlsbad Beach; Tamarack Ave. at Carlsbad Blvd., Carlsbad* ☎ *760/720–7001* ⊕ *www.parks.ca.gov* ⊠ *$15 per vehicle.*

Restaurants

Campfire

$$$ | **BARBECUE** | Paying tribute to community around the campfire, it's all about connecting here, both with the cool crowd and with the distinctive cocktail and dinner menus. Throughout the restaurant, subtle hints of the camping theme—canvas-backed booths, servers in flannels, leather menus branded with the Campfire logo—are visible, but it's the food that will leave you setting up camp, as chefs work their magic behind glass walls grilling, roasting, and smoking almost every dish including the oysters warmed over coals. **Known for:** smoky cocktails; wood-fired American fare; innovative seasonal menu. $ *Average main: $32* ✉ *2725 State St., Carlsbad* ☎ *760/637–5121* ⊕ *www.thisiscampfire.com* ⊘ *Closed Tues. No lunch.*

★ Jeune et Jolie

$$$ | FRENCH | Say "bonjour" to this delightful French restaurant with a *Breakfast at Tiffany's* vibe, where pink velvet booths and a center bar with an absinthe tower will leave you thinking you've died and gone to Paris. The French-inspired, four-course menu changes with the season, but expect labor-of-love cuisine like veal tartare, rabbit with spring peas, or duck with fig and black truffle; embrace the moment with ibérico ham and caviar or fresh-shucked oysters. **Known for:** cocktails inspired by the French Belle Epoque; raw oyster bar; four-course tasting menu. $ *Average main: $34* ✉ *2659 State St., Carlsbad* ☎ *760/637–5266* ⊕ *www.jeune-jolie.com* ⊘ *Closed Mon. and Tues.*

Vigilucci's Cucina Italiana

$$$ | ITALIAN | Restaurateur Roberto Vigilucci's fell in love with San Diego in the '80s and decided to bring Milan to North County with three eateries that are fine-dining experiences without the stuffiness. While each has its own character, Vigilucci's on historic State Street has an authenticity that's hard to beat, right down to its street-side patio, bustling servers with thick Italian accents, and wine list that will leave you appreciating *la bella vita*. Roasted artichokes are blanketed in melted mozzarella, and paper-thin carpaccio is topped with a mound of peppery arugula. **Known for:** classic Italian menu; bustling outdoor patio; extensive wine list. $ *Average main: $31* ✉ *2943 State St., Carlsbad* ☎ *760/434–2500* ⊕ *www.vigiluccis.com.*

The Wise Ox

$ | BARBECUE | Order any one of just seven menu items and then dig into mouth-stretching sandwiches on the small patio with communal picnic tables. The turkey with Swiss comes on perfectly toasted sourdough, while the Philly cheesesteak is heaping with shaved New York strip and pickled peppers; just about everything pairs well with their selection of beers on tap, and of course the beef-fat fries. **Known for:** beef-fat fries; homemade sauces and marinades; classic butcher shop and deli. $ *Average main: $12* ✉ *The Beacon La Costa, 7750 El Camino Real Suite P, Carlsbad* ☎ *760/477–0377* ⊕ *www.thewiseoxsd.com* ⊘ *No dinner* ☞ *Closes at 5 pm.*

Coffee and Quick Bites

Sweet Spot

$ | ICE CREAM | FAMILY | Willy Wonka would be impressed with this authentic candy shop with barrels and bins piled high with gummies, drops, jellybeans, sour candies, and other nostalgic treats. There's even ice cream to cool you down on a hot summer day. **Known for:** chocolates and gummies; ice cream; cotton candy. $ *Average main: $5* ✉ *3001 Carlsbad Blvd., #B, Carlsbad* ☎ *760/729–3005* ⊕ *www.sweetspotcarlsbad.com* ⊘ *Closed Mon.*

🛏 Hotels

Beach Terrace Inn

$$$ | HOTEL | One of only four SoCal hotels directly on the sand, this former 1960s Best Western was remodeled in 2011 as a boutique inn with plantation shutters, luxurious linens, and open floor plans. **Pros:** direct beach access; small onsite market; enormous rooms. **Cons:** lots of stairs; amenity fee $40 and parking fee $25; no restaurant or bar. $ *Rooms from: $309* ✉ *2775 Ocean St., Carlsbad* ☎ *760/729–5951* ⊕ *www.beach-terraceinn.com* ⇄ *48 rooms* ⦿ *Free Breakfast.*

Cape Rey Carlsbad

$$ | **HOTEL** | **FAMILY** | Sea and sand loom large at this Hilton property, where the fitness center has an ocean view and guest rooms have sitting areas so you can easily enjoy the sea views and breezes when you're not exploring South Carlsbad State Park nearby. **Pros:** beach toys for kids; 150 steps from the beach; shuttle service to nearby sites within 5 miles. **Cons:** on main highway; resort fee $35 and pet fee $75; some rooms face the parking lot. ⑤ *Rooms from: $229* ✉ *1 Ponto Rd., Carlsbad* ☎ *760/602–0800* ⊕ *www.caperey.com* ⊋ *215 rooms* ⦿ *No Meals.*

Carlsbad Inn Beach Resort

$$ | **HOTEL** | **FAMILY** | In the heart of Carlsbad village, this sprawling inn and time-share condominium complex is popular with families and has a variety of rooms, ranging from cramped to large, including many with ocean views, balconies, and kitchenettes, and some with fireplaces and Jacuzzis. **Pros:** near the beach; walking distance to shops and restaurants; warm ambience. **Cons:** lobby chaotic during check-in time; can be noisy; tiny pool. ⑤ *Rooms from: $266* ✉ *3075 Carlsbad Blvd., Carlsbad* ☎ *760/434–7020, 800/235–3939* ⊕ *www.carlsbadinn.com* ⊋ *61 rooms* ⦿ *No Meals.*

LEGOLAND Hotel

$$ | **HOTEL** | **FAMILY** | This is the place for the family that eats, sleeps, and lives LEGO; check out the neighboring LEGO-LAND Castle Hotel with rooms themed around knights, dragons, wizards, and royal princesses. **Pros:** guests get early admission to LEGOLAND; dive-in movies at the pool and nightly children's entertainment; tempting hands-on activities throughout the hotel. **Cons:** frequently sells out; no romance here; small rooms. ⑤ *Rooms from: $230* ✉ *5885 The Crossings Dr., Carlsbad* ☎ *888/690–5346* ⊕ *www.legoland.com/california* ⊋ *250 rooms* ⦿ *Free Breakfast.*

★ Ocean Palms Beach Resort

$$$ | **HOTEL** | **FAMILY** | Just 40 steps from the sand, bring your kids (furry or not) to this delightful pet- and family-friendly hotel where the staff go out of their way to please guests. **Pros:** no resort fees; helpful staff; full kitchens; near shops and restaurants. **Cons:** some rooms face the street; small parking lot with limited spaces; no refunds on cancelled reservations. ⑤ *Rooms from: $369* ✉ *2950 Ocean St., Carlsbad* ☎ *760/729–2493* ⊕ *www.oceanpalms.com* ⊋ *52 rooms* ⦿ *Free Breakfast.*

Omni La Costa Resort & Spa

$$$ | **RESORT** | **FAMILY** | This chic Spanish colonial oasis on 400 tree-shaded acres has ample guest rooms, two golf courses, and is known for being family-friendly, with plenty of kids' activities (including a kids' club, a game room, eight swimming pools, three waterslides, and a water play zone). **Pros:** adult-only pool; excellent kids' facilities; spa under the stars, and free fitness classes every hour. **Cons:** very spread out, making long walks necessary; lots of kids; $40 daily resort fee, and self parking is $35. ⑤ *Rooms from: $350* ✉ *2100 Costa del Mar Rd., Carlsbad* ☎ *760/438–9111, 800/439–9111* ⊕ *www.lacosta.com* ⊋ *655 rooms* ⦿ *No Meals.*

Park Hyatt Aviara Resort

$$$$ | **RESORT** | **FAMILY** | As one of the most luxurious hotels in San Diego, this retreat completed a $50 million resort-wide transformation in 2020, with redesigned rooms, a new lobby, family pool with water park, luxury cabanas, and three new restaurants including Ember & Rye by celebrity chef Richard Blais. **Pros:** coastal-chic resort with unbeatable location; best golf course in San Diego; surrounding nature trails. **Cons:** $45 resort fee and $65 parking; expensive; breakfast not included. ⑤ *Rooms from: $725* ✉ *7100 Aviara Resort Dr., Carlsbad* ☎ *800/233–1234, 760/448–1234* ⊕ *www.parkhyattaviara.com* ⊘ *Greens fee $275;*

18 holes, 7007 yards, par 72 🏌 327 rooms 🍽 No Meals.

West Inn and Suites

$$ | **B&B/INN** | **FAMILY** | Coastal luxury meets Cape Cod practicality at this warm and friendly inn near the beach. **Pros:** full buffet breakfast; great service; near beaches. **Cons:** adjacent to railroad tracks and freeway; no water views; no in-room dining. $ *Rooms from: $289* ✉ *4970 Av. Encinas, Carlsbad* ☎ *760/448–4500* ⊕ *www.westinnandsuites.com* 🏌 *86 rooms* 🍽 *Free Breakfast.*

Shopping

The Big Shop (☎ *760/918–5346*) at LEGOLAND is great for collectors and collectors-in-training, with the largest selection of LEGO sets in the nation. ⇨ *For more information about LEGOLAND, see the Carlsbad Sights section.*

Carlsbad Premium Outlets

OUTLET | **FAMILY** | This outdoor shopping center contains more than 90 outlet stores, including designer brands like Coach, Kate Spade, Marc Jacobs, Michael Kors, and Nike. ✉ *5620 Paseo del Norte, Carlsbad* ☎ *760/804–9000* ⊕ *www.premiumoutlets.com/carlsbad.*

Activities

GOLF

Omni La Costa Resort & Spa

GOLF | One of the premier golf resorts in Southern California, La Costa over the years has hosted many of the best professional golfers in the world as well as prominent politicians and Hollywood celebrities. The Dick Wilson–designed Champions course with fairways and bunkers was remodeled in 2023 as a PGA regulated course. The more spacious Legends Course has wide, paspalum-grass fairways and a challenging par-4 15th hole with tough shots around wetlands. After a day on the links

you can wind down with a massage, steam bath, and dinner at the resort. ✉ *2100 Costa del Mar Rd., Carlsbad* ☎ *760/438–9111* ⊕ *www.omnihotels. com* ✉ *$195 before 2 pm; $135 after 2 pm* 🏌 *Champions: 18 holes, 6747 yards, par 72. Legends: 18 holes, 6587 yards, par 72.*

★ Park Hyatt Aviara Golf Club

GOLF | This golf course consistently ranks as one of the best in California and is the only course in San Diego designed by Arnold Palmer. Blanketed with new grass in late 2022, the course features gently rolling hills dotted with native wildflowers and views of the protected adjacent Batiquitos Lagoon and the Pacific Ocean. There are plenty of bunkers and water features for those looking for a challenge, and the golf carts, included in the cost, come fitted with GPS systems that tell you the distance to the pin. TaylorMade golf clubs are available for rent. The two-story Spanish colonial clubhouse has full-size lockers, lounge areas, a bar, and a steak house. ✉ *7447 Batiquitos Dr., Carlsbad* ☎ *760/603–6900* ⊕ *www. golfaviara.com* ✉ *From $250* 🏌 *18 holes, 7007 yards, par 72.*

SPAS

Miraval Life in Balance Spa

SPAS | With its soothing sauna, steam room, Jacuzzi, and relaxation lounge, simple elegance defines the spa at Park Hyatt Aviara. In 2023, a $60 million dollar resort-wide renovation leaned heavily on the new Life in Balance Spa, offering everything from spa treatments to yoga classes. The healing sanctuary offers purposefully placed crystals, cairns, and mandalas to boost energy and create relaxation. The spa features 20 indoor and outdoor treatment rooms including a spa pool for the acclaimed sensory deprivation treatment, *Vasudhara,* and an expansive room with hanging yoga silks. Non-hotel guests who book treatments are given day access to the pool. ✉ *7100*

Aviara Resort Dr., Carlsbad ☎ *760/603–6902* ⊕ *www.hyatt.com/en-US/spas/Aviara-Spa/home.html* ☞ *Massages and facials from $180.*

WATER SPORTS
California Watersports
JET SKIING | FAMILY | Waveless Carlsbad Lagoon, east of the intersection of Tamarack Avenue and I–5, is easy to reach from this water recreation center, which has a private beach and landing ramp. You can rent ski boats, WaveRunners, Jet Skis, pontoon boats, kayaks, aqua cycles, and stand-up paddleboards. ⊠ *4215 Harrison St., Carlsbad* ☎ *760/434–3089* ⊕ *www.carlsbadlagoon.com* ⌑ *From $25.*

Oceanside

8 miles north of Carlsbad on Rte. S21, 37 miles north of Downtown San Diego on I–5.

The beach culture is alive and well in Oceanside with surf shops, casual restaurants, museums, and a boardwalk that leads to the pier and harbor where surfers line up to catch the next wave. In 2023, the city went through quite a renaissance—revamped with new businesses reflecting its rich past and booming present of surfing, dining, art, and culture. Numerous hotels are within walking distance of the city's best swimming and surfing beaches: Harbor Beach, brimming with beach activities and fun, and Buccaneer Beach, home to some of the best surfing in North County. Camp Pendleton, the sprawling U.S. Marine base, lies at the north end of the city.

■ **TIP→ If you'd like to see the base, visitors must be sponsored and vetted, with forms filled out four days in advance.**

Oceanside is also home to Mission San Luis Rey, the largest and one of the best-preserved California missions.

The town's history extends back to the 1700s, when the Spanish friars walked along the California coast founding missions as they went. Today it celebrates its historic culture with the regionally exciting Oceanside Museum of Art, which displays the works of San Diego area artists. Residents and visitors gather weekly at the farmers' market and Sunset Market on Main Street, where shopping for fresh-picked produce is a pleasant pastime.

GETTING HERE AND AROUND
The northernmost of the beach towns, Oceanside, lies 8 miles north of Carlsbad via I–5; exit the freeway on Mission Avenue. If you go west, you'll come to downtown and the harbor where you'll find most of the restaurants, lodgings, and attractions. Downtown Oceanside is quite walkable from the Transportation Center, where Amtrak, the Coaster, and Sprinter stop. Buses and taxis are also available at the Transportation Center.

VISITOR INFORMATION
CONTACT California Welcome Center, Oceanside. ⊠ *928 N. Coast Hwy., Suite A, Oceanside* ☎ *760/721–1101, 800/350–7873* ⊕ *www.visitoceanside.org.*

 Sights

California Surf Museum
OTHER MUSEUM | A large collection of surfing memorabilia, going back to the earliest days of the sport, is on display here, along with old black-and-white photos, vintage boards, apparel, and accessories. ⊠ *312 Pier View Way, Oceanside* ☎ *760/721–6876* ⊕ *www.surfmuseum.org* ⌑ *$7.*

Oceanside Harbor
MARINA/PIER | With 1,000 slips, this is North County's fishing, sailing, and water-sports center. On the south end of the harbor, the Oceanside Harbor Village has oyster bars, fish-and-chip shops, and an ice-cream parlor where you can

linger and watch the boats coming and going. If you fancy a day at sea, Helgren's Sportfishing can arrange whale-watching and harbor tours. ⊠ *1540 Harbor Dr. N, Oceanside* ☎ *760/435–4000* ⊕ *www. oceansideharborvillage.com.*

Oceanside Museum of Art

ART MUSEUM | Housed in side-by-side buildings designed by two Southern California modernist architects—Irving Gill and Frederick Fisher—the museum showcases contemporary art exhibitions including paintings, photography, sculptures, furniture, quilts, and architectural glass by SoCal area artists. ⊠ *704 Pier View Way, Oceanside* ☎ *760/435–3720* ⊕ *www.oma-online.org* ⊠ *$10; free for students and military* ⊙ *Closed Mon. and Tues.*

Oceanside Pier

MARINA/PIER | At 1,954 feet, this is one of the longest piers on the West Coast. The water surrounding it is known for its surf breaks and good fishing. A restaurant, Ruby's Diner, stands at the end of the wooden pier's long promenade. ⊠ *Pier View Way, Oceanside.*

Old Mission San Luis Rey

RELIGIOUS BUILDING | **FAMILY** | Known as the King of the Missions, the 18th, the largest, and the most prosperous of California's missions was built in 1798 by Franciscan friars under the direction of Father Fermin Lasuen to help educate and convert local Native Americans. The *sala* (parlor), the kitchen, a friar's bedroom, a weaving room, and a collection of religious art and old Spanish vestments convey much about early mission life. A special behind-the-scenes tour starts at 11 am on Saturday, and Mass is held at noon weekdays. ⊠ *4050 Mission Ave., Oceanside* ☎ *760/757–3651* ⊕ *www.sanluisrey.org* ⊠ *$8; audio tour available $3* ☞ *Almost every Sat., special Behind-the-Scenes Tour starts at 11 am.*

Beaches

Oceanside City Beach

BEACH | **FAMILY** | This long, straight beach is popular with swimmers, surfers, and U.S. Marines from nearby Camp Pendleton. The impressive wooden Oceanside Pier extends a quarter of a mile into the ocean, and there's a '50s-style diner called Ruby's at the end. The sand here is a bit coarse, and smaller rocks can be found in some sections, but due to its width (a quarter mile from street to surf near 1200 N. Pacific Street), nice patches can almost always be found. There is surfing around the pier, but the waves are faster and usually better just north at Oceanside Harbor, which gets a south swell in the summer. Pay lots and meters are located around the pier and also in the Oceanside Harbor area. A free two-hour lot can be found east of the pay lots on Harbor Drive South. There are plenty of shops and restaurants along Oceanside Harbor Village. Families love the kid-friendly Buccaneer Beach, just south of the pier across from Buccaneer Beach Park. This area has free parking, a café, restrooms, showers, and lifeguards on duty in summer. **Amenities:** seasonal lifeguards; food and drink; parking (fee); toilets; showers. **Best for:** surfing; swimming; walking. ⊠ *200 N. The Strand, Oceanside* ⊠ *$5 parking.*

Restaurants

Flying Pig Pub & Kitchen

$$ | **AMERICAN** | **FAMILY** | This meat-focused eatery fills bellies with farm-to-table artisanal cuisine like bacon mac and cheese, and a 12-ounce pork chop served over house grits. Add a sunny-side-up farm egg to your burger, chop, shank, or house-made pasta, and if you're into sauces, the chef is on point with lick-your-plate gravies with garlic, onions, and herbs. **Known for:** elevated comfort food with craft beers on tap; house-made pasta, bread, and bacon; natural prime-grade steaks seared in a cast-iron skillet. ⑤ *Average main: $25 ⌧ 509 Mission Ave., Oceanside ☎ 760/453–2940.*

Harbor Fish & Chips

$ | **SEAFOOD** | Pick up a basket of fresh-cooked fish-and-chips at this dive and you're in for a treat. The shop has been serving clam chowder, shrimp cocktail, and fish sandwiches since 1969. **Known for:** crunchy, battered fish tacos piled high with coleslaw and secret sauce; great prices; affordable daily specials. ⑤ *Average main: $12 ⌧ 276 S. Harbor Dr., Oceanside ☎ 760/722–4977 ⊕ www. harborfishandchips.net.*

Hello Betty

$ | **SEAFOOD** | **FAMILY** | Overlooking the water in Oceanside, this beachside restaurant serves oysters, clam chowder, fish tacos, and several fresh catch options, which can be enjoyed from their rooftop lounge. **Known for:** classic Baja SoCal food like margaritas and fish tacos; rooftop deck; Taco Tuesday 3–9 pm. ⑤ *Average main: $20 ⌧ 211 Mission Ave., Oceanside ☎ 760/722–1008 ⊕ www. hellobettyoceanside.com.*

101 Cafe

$ | **AMERICAN** | **FAMILY** | A diner dating back to 1928 is both a local hangout and the headquarters of the historic Highway 101 movement. Find all kinds of Highway 101 memorabilia here along with old-school ambience, prompt service, and great prices. **Known for:** headquarters of the historic Highway 101 movement; all-day breakfast; thick milkshakes. ⑤ *Average main: $12 ⌧ 631 S. Coast Hwy., Oceanside ☎ 760/722–5220 ⊕ www.101cafe-oceanside.com ⊘ No dinner.*

333 Pacific

$$$$ | **SEAFOOD** | Directly across from Oceanside Pier, Oceanside's most upscale restaurant specializes in seafood dishes and upscale comfort food in an elegant, art-deco setting; it's worth visiting for the ocean views and appetizers and sides like charred Brussels sprouts

and lamb lollipops. If you're thirsty, start with a drink from the menu of more than 120 vodkas that make up exotic cocktails like the Spicy Pineapple, Pear Blossom, and Cali Mango. **Known for:** martinis; weekly dinner specials; ocean views. ⑤ *Average main: $50 ⌧ 333 N. Pacific St., Oceanside ☎ 760/433–3333 ⊕ www.333pacific.com ⊘ Closed Tues. No lunch Mon.–Thurs.*

★ Valle

$$$$ | **MODERN MEXICAN** | Valle de Guadalupe has arrived in Oceanside thanks to executive chef Roberto Alcocer who brings the flavors of Baja directly to the beach. This Michelin-star chef prepares four- and eight-course tasting menus paired with the best of Valle's robust wines. **Known for:** seasonal menu influenced by Valle de Guadalupe; charcoal oven and wood-fire cooking; agave-based cocktails. ⑤ *Average main: $110 ⌧ 222 N. Pacific St., Oceanside ☎ 866/723–8906 ⊕ www.valleoceanside.com ⊘ Closed Mon. and Tues. No lunch.*

🍴 Coffee and Quick Bites

High Pie

$ | **BAKERY** | **FAMILY** | Fans of *Top Gun*—or the 2022 *Maverick* comeback—can get a taste of the historic house featured in the original 1986 film. In 2023, the 100-year-old home was moved to its current beachfront location, which operates as a pie shop serving hot hand-held pies in cherry, apple, blueberry, and seasonal favorites. **Known for:** seasonal selections; fresh hand-held pies; historic house. ⑤ *Average main: $9 ⌧ 250 N. Pacific St., Oceanside ⊕ www.famoushighpie.com ⊘ Closed Tues.*

Hotels

Courtyard by Marriott San Diego Oceanside

$$ | **HOTEL** | Close proximity to the beach and train, coupled with plenty of modern amenities, make this SoCal-style Marriott a great Oceanside option. **Pros:**

convenient location; two wheelchair-accessible rooms; helpful and friendly staff. **Cons:** breakfast not included; hotel could use an upgrade; 10-minute drive to the beach. $ *Rooms from: $309* ✉ *3501 Seagate Way, Oceanside* ☎ *760/966–1000* ⊕ *www.courtyardoceanside.com* 🚪 *142 rooms* ⏐◎⏐ *No Meals.*

Mission Pacific Hotel
$$$ | HOTEL | In 2021, Oceanside awakened with major redevelopment due in part to this beachfront boutique hotel across from the pier, which beckons young couples with perfect martinis, chill vibes, and sleek water-facing rooms. **Pros:** filtered alkaline water stations; prime location across from historic pier; complimentary beach concierge. **Cons:** no spa; daily $44 parking fee and $46 resort fee; small pool. $ *Rooms from: $394* ✉ *201 N. Myers St., Oceanside* ☎ *760/655–1332* ⊕ *www.missionpacifichotel.com* 🚪 *161 rooms* ⏐◎⏐ *No Meals.*

★ The Seabird
$$$ | HOTEL | FAMILY | As the star of Oceanside's renovation project, this oceanfront property is the epitome of coastal fresh with an inviting air reflective of a luxury beach house. **Pros:** relaxed local vibe; online dine and wine packages; family- and pet-friendly. **Cons:** can get busy; Piper restaurant lacks ambience; somewhat pricey. $ *Rooms from: $479* ✉ *101 Mission Ave., Oceanside* ☎ *760/655–1334* ⊕ *www.theseabirdresort.com* 🚪 *226 rooms* ⏐◎⏐ *No Meals.*

🛍 Shopping

Sunset Market
MARKET | Every Thursday night 5–9 pm, Oceanside's Main Street comes alive with food stalls, a farmers' market, live music, and an arts and crafts fair. ✉ *316 Mission Ave., Oceanside* ✛ *Corner of Pier View Way and S. Tremont St.* ☎ *760/754–4512* ⊕ *www.mainstreetoceanside.com.*

Activities

FISHING
Helgren's Sportfishing
FISHING | Your best bet in North County, Helgren's offers fishing and whale-watching trips from Oceanside Harbor. ✉ *1395½ N. Harbor Dr., Oceanside* ☎ *760/722–2133* ⊕ *www.helgrensportfishing.com* 🚤 *From $75.*

HIKING
San Luis Rey River Trail
BIKING | Paralleling the San Luis Rey River, this 7.2-mile (one-way) paved trail starts in Oceanside and ends at the beach near the Harbor. Void of traffic lights and motorized vehicles, the path is relatively flat and is a fun way to reach the coast for bikers, walkers, and in-line skaters. ✉ *N. Santa Fe Ave. and Hwy. 76, Oceanside.*

SPAS
Sunny's Spa and Beauty Lounge
SPAS | Set on the third floor of The Seabird hotel, this spa hits all five senses starting with the relaxation room overlooking the ocean. Book any spa treatment for access to the common spaces with hot-cold therapy stations, a radiant heat table, and an active relaxation room. Each spa ritual combines a dry warming space, cooling mist, and an aromatherapy sanarium. Prepare to fall asleep during the "Soul" treatment which includes a body scrub, healing wrap, sound bath, and full body massage. Open to the public, The Seabird invites locals to relax and get pampered with a 15% discount on all treatments. ✉ *The Seabird, 101 Mission Ave., Oceanside* ☎ *760/655–1338* ⊕ *www.sunnysspa.com.*

SURFING
San Diego Surfing Academy
SURFING | One-on-one instruction is available with surf coach, Pat Weber, who is known throughout the community for his dedication to coaching top contenders in the World Adaptive Surfing Championships. Instructional videos are also

available online. The academy, which has been running since 1995, is based near Oceanside Harbor and meets for lessons at the harbor parking lot 12 near the north jetty. ✉ *Oceanside ✛ Harbor Pay Lot 12 near the North Jetty* ☎ *760/230–1474* ⊕ *www.sandiegosurfingacademy.com* ✉ *Private half-day lesson $200.*

Rancho Bernardo

23 miles northeast of Downtown San Diego on I-15.

Rancho Bernardo straddles a stretch of I-15 between San Diego and Escondido and is technically a neighborhood of San Diego. Originally sheep- and cattle-grazing land, it was transformed in the early 1960s into a planned suburban community, one of the first, and a place where many wealthy retirees settled down. It's now home to a number of high-tech companies, the most notable of which is Sony. If you want to spend some time at the nearby San Diego Zoo Safari Park, this community, home of the Rancho Bernardo resort, makes a convenient and comfortable headquarters for a multiday visit.

Sights

Bernardo Winery

WINERY | A trip to the oldest operating winery in Southern California, founded in 1889 and run by the Rizzo family since 1928, feels like traveling back to early California days; some of the vines on the former Spanish land-grant property have been producing grapes for more than 100 years. Most of the grapes now come from other wine-growing regions. A collection of quaint shops surrounds the winery. Manzanita Roasting Company has coffee and fresh pastries, and The Kitchen serves lunch daily except Monday and Tuesday. Shops sell cold-pressed olive oil and other gourmet goodies,

as well as apparel, home-decor items, and arts and crafts. A farmers' market is held Friday 9 am–1 pm. ✉ *13330 Paseo del Verano N, Rancho Bernardo* ☎ *858/487–1866* ⊕ *www.bernardowinery.com* ✉ *Winery free, wine tasting $25* ⊗ *Closed Mon. and Tues.* ☞ *Pets not allowed.*

Restaurants

AVANT

$$$$ | **AMERICAN** | The appropriately named AVANT—meaning stylistically advanced and original—delivers contemporary California cuisine—duck, lobster, lamb, fish, or the pride of AVANT, Wagyu beef—in an upscale setting. Dark woods, leather chairs, and pillar-candle chandeliers adorn the mission-style dining room, and the upper-level bar shakes up handcrafted cocktails with their own double-barrel reposado tequila. **Known for:** local, sustainable, and seasonal ingredients; their own double-barrel reposado tequila; $10 wines by the glass during happy hour 4–5. ⑤ *Average main: $43* ✉ *Rancho Bernardo Inn, 17550 Bernardo Oaks Dr., Rancho Bernardo* ☎ *866/990–6845* ⊕ *www.avantrestaurant.com* ⊗ *Closed Sun. and Mon. No lunch.*

The Barrel Room

$$ | **EUROPEAN** | A wine bar ambience and a simple menu set the tone for the unpretentious creations of chef Trevor Chappell. Shareable plates and innovative sides complement an impressive new-world wine list that includes more than 250 blends, plus four of their own beers on tap from Mason Ale Works. **Known for:** flourless chocolate cake; plates to share; signature sandwiches. ⑤ *Average main: $30* ✉ *The Plaza, 16765 Bernardo Center Dr., Rancho Bernardo* ☎ *858/673–7512* ⊕ *www.lovethebarrelroom.com.*

Hotels

Rancho Bernardo Inn

$$$ | **RESORT** | **FAMILY** | The gorgeous, flower-decked 265-acre grounds draw a sophisticated clientele looking for a golf and spa getaway. **Pros:** excellent service; popular golf course; website offers great packages and specials. **Cons:** walking required in spacious grounds; sections of hotel are showing signs of age; $75 day use of spa amenities. ⑤ *Rooms from: $374* ✉ *17550 Bernardo Oaks Dr., Rancho Bernardo* ☎ *858/675–8500, 888/476–4417* ⊕ *www.ranchobernardoinn.com* ⇨ *287 rooms* ⦾ *No Meals.*

Activities

GOLF

Rancho Bernardo Inn Golf Course

GOLF | Designed by William Francis Bell in 1962, this 18-hole course has a traditional layout, but regular upgrades keep it feeling fresh and new. The course has hosted both PGA and LPGA events and offers an oasis in Rancho Bernardo, with its tree-lined fairways and various water features. A challenging 18th hole requires an approach shot over a creek. Located at the esteemed Rancho Bernardo Inn, the property offers great amenities like a spa and several restaurants, including AVANT, where gourmet mustards are served on tap. ✉ *17550 Bernardo Oaks Dr., Rancho Bernardo* ☎ *858/675–8470* ⊕ *www.ranchobernardoinn.com/golf* ⌛ *Mon.–Thurs. $120; Fri. $135; weekends $170* ⚐ *18 holes, 6631 yards, par 72.*

Escondido

8 miles north of Rancho Bernardo on I–15, 31 miles northeast of Downtown San Diego on I–15.

Escondido and the lovely rolling hills around it were originally a land grant bestowed by the governor of Mexico on Juan Bautista Alvarado in 1843. The Battle of San Pasqual, a bloody milestone in California's march to statehood, took place just east of the city. For a century and a half, these hills supported citrus and avocado trees, plus large vineyards. The rural character of the area began to change when the San Diego Zoo established its Safari Park in the San Pasqual Valley east of town in the 1970s. By the late 1990s suburban development had begun to transform the hills into housing tracts. The California Center for the Arts, opened in 1993, now stands as the downtown centerpiece of a burgeoning arts community that includes a collection of art galleries along Grand Avenue. On Friday nights (June–September), downtown is lined with pre-1970s vintage cars that slowly cruise Grand Avenue. Despite its urbanization, Escondido still supports several pristine open-space preserves that attract nature lovers, hikers, and mountain bikers. And, the area's abundant farms are slowly luring award-winning chefs who are taking the lead on opening farm-to-fork establishments.

VISITOR INFORMATION
CONTACT Visit Escondido. ⊠ *235 E. Grand Ave., Escondido* ☎ *760/839–4777* ⊕ *www.VisitEscondido.com.*

Sights

California Center for the Arts
ARTS CENTER | FAMILY | An entertainment complex with two theaters, an art museum, and a conference center, the center presents operas, musicals, plays, dance performances, and symphony and chamber-music concerts. Performers conduct free workshops for children; check the website for dates. The museum, which focuses on 20th-century art, occasionally presents blockbuster exhibits that make a side trip here worthwhile. ⊠ *340 N. Escondido Blvd., Escondido* ☎ *800/988–4253 box office, 760/839–4138 museum* ⊕ *www.artcenter.org* ⌨ *Museum $12* ⊙ *Closed Mon.*

Daley Ranch (*Dixon Lake*)
NATURE SIGHT | FAMILY | A 3,058-acre conservation area and historic ranch site is laced with more than 25 miles of multipurpose trails for hikers, mountain bikers, and equestrians. The 2.4-mile Boulder Loop affords sweeping views of Escondido, and the 2.5-mile Ranch House Loop passes two small ponds, the 1928 Daley family ranch house, and the site of the original log cabin. Private cars are prohibited on the ranch, but there's free parking just outside the entrance. From the main trailhead, you can access Dixon Lake, a popular fishing and camping spot. Free naturalist-guided hikes are offered on a regular basis; call for schedule. Leashed dogs permitted. ⊠ *3024 La Honda Dr., Escondido* ☎ *760/839–4680* ⊕ *www.daleyranch.org* ⌨ *Free.*

Escondido Arts Partnership Municipal Gallery
ART GALLERY | This gallery showcases works by local artists, with regular exhibitions and year-round special events. ⊠ *262 E. Grand Ave., Escondido* ☎ *760/480–4101* ⊕ *www.escondidoarts.org* ⌨ *Free* ⊙ *Closed Sun., Mon., and Wed.*

Escondido History Center
OTHER MUSEUM | This outdoor museum adjacent to the California Center for the Arts in Grape Day Park consists of several historic buildings moved here to illustrate local development from the late 1800s, when grape growing and gold mining supported the economy. Exhibits include the 1888 Santa

Fe Depot, Escondido's first library, the Bandy Blacksmith shop, a furnished 1890 Victorian house, and other 19th-century buildings. ⊠ *321 N. Broadway, Escondido* ☎ *760/743–8207* ⊕ *www.escondidohistory.org* 🖾 *$3 suggested donation* ☉ *Closed Fri., Sat., Mon.–Wed.*

Orfila Vineyards & Winery

WINERY | Visitors here can taste award-winning Syrah, Sangiovese, and Viognier produced from grapes harvested from the 10,000-acre vineyard. The Rose Arbor has a picnic area, and there's a gift shop with wine-related merchandise. There's also a tasting room on Cleveland Street in Oceanside. ⊠ *13455 San Pasqual Rd., Escondido* ☎ *760/738–6500* ⊕ *www.orfila.com* 🖾 *Tastings $25.*

Queen Califia's Magical Circle

PUBLIC ART | **FAMILY** | The last work by sculptor Niki de Saint Phalle (1930–2002), this sculpture garden designed for entertaining children consists of nine totemic figures up to 21 feet tall. Adorned with stylized monsters, animals, protective deities, geometric symbols, and crests, the pieces evoke ancient tales and legends. Youngsters can climb on the giant fanciful figures. ⊠ *Kit Carson Park, Bear Valley Pkwy. and Mary La., Escondido* ☎ *760/839–4000* 🖾 *Free* ☉ *Closed Wed. and Fri.–Mon.*

★ San Diego Zoo Safari Park

ZOO | **FAMILY** | A branch of the San Diego Zoo, 35 miles to the north, the 1,800-acre preserve in the San Pasqual Valley is designed to protect endangered species from around the world. Exhibit areas have been carved out of the dry, dusty canyons and mesas to represent the animals' natural habitats in various parts of Africa and Asia.

The best way to see these preserves is to take the 25-minute, 2½-mile Africa tram safari, included with admission. More than 3,500 animals of more than 400 species roam or fly above the expansive grounds. Predators are separated

from prey by deep moats, but only the elephants, tigers, lions, and cheetahs are kept in enclosures. Good viewpoints are at the Elephant Viewing Patio, African Plains Outlook, and Kilmia Point. The park's newest project is the Tull Family Tiger Trail, a Sumatran tiger habitat where you can get face-to-face (with a glass between) with the gorgeous cats. The 5-acre exhibit features a waterfall and swimming hole, and addresses poaching and other environmental threats to the species.

■ **TIP** → **In summer, when the park stays open late, the trip is especially enjoyable in the early evening, when the heat has subsided and the animals are active and feeding. When the tram travels through the park after dark, sodium-vapor lamps illuminate the active animals. Photographers with zoom lenses can get spectacular shots of zebras, gazelles, and rhinos.**

For a more focused view of the park, you can take one of several other safaris that are well worth the additional charge. You can choose from several behind-the-scenes safaris, fly above it all via the zipline safari, or get up close to giraffes and rhinos on a Caravan safari.

The park is as much a botanical garden as a zoo, serving as a "rescue center" for rare and endangered plants. Unique gardens include cacti and succulents from Baja California, a bonsai collection, a fuchsia display, native plants, and protea.

The gift shops are well worth a visit for their limited-edition items. There are lots of restaurants, snack bars, and some picnic areas. Rental lockers, strollers, and wheelchairs are available. ⊠ *15500 San Pasqual Valley Rd., Escondido* ⊕ *Take I–15 north to Via Rancho Pkwy. and follow signs for 6 miles* ☎ *760/747–8702* ⊕ *www.sdzsafaripark.org* 🖾 *$71 one-day pass including Africa tram ride; multipark and multiday passes are available; parking $20.*

San Dieguito River Park

TRAIL | FAMILY | The park maintains several hiking and walking trails in the Escondido area. These are part of an intended 70-mile-long Coast to Crest Trail that will eventually link the San Dieguito Lagoon near Del Mar with the river's source on Volcan Mountain, north of Julian. Among the existing trails are three that circle Lake Hodges: the **North Shore Lake Hodges Trail;** the **Piedras Pintadas Trail,** which informs about native American Kumeyaay lifestyles and uses for native plants; and the **Highland Valley Trail,** the first mile of which is the Ruth Merrill Children's Walk. Three trails in **Clevenger Canyon** lead to sweeping views of the San Pasqual Valley.

■ TIP→ **Visit the website for a list of upcoming free guided hikes and pay attention to signs warning against leaving valuables in your car.** ⊠ *18372 Sycamore Creek Rd., Escondido* ☎ *858/674–2270* ⊕ *www.sdrp. org* ☜ *Free.*

🍴 Restaurants

It might not have coastal views and ocean breezes, but don't be surprised to find an elegant French restaurant next to a hole-in-the-wall taco stand, along with a clientele as mixed as the area's cuisine. Despite the inland location, Grand Avenue has a string of charming downtown eateries, with local chefs serving farm-to-table dishes at a fraction of what you'd pay along the coast.

Bellamy's Restaurant

$$$$ | FRENCH FUSION | Live piano music, crystal chandeliers, and leather tufted chairs set the stage at this fine-dining restaurant for a delectable menu that includes market oysters, scallops with squash blossoms, free-range chicken with bourbon glaze, and braised beef short ribs. For a sweet conclusion, try the warm butter cake or the decadent chocolate torte. **Known for:** California-French cuisine; upscale dining; half off wine Wednesdays. ⑤ *Average main: $45* ⊠ *417 W. Grand Ave., Escondido* ☎ *760/747–5000* ⊕ *www.bellamysdining. com* ⊘ *Closed Sun. No lunch.*

★ Stone Brewing World Bistro & Gardens—Escondido

$$ | BISTRO | FAMILY | One of the fastest-growing companies in the United States, Stone staked out a hilltop overlooking Escondido to create, brew, and sell its beloved craft beer in a gorgeous, solar-run facility. Thirty-six craft and specialty beers are always on tap in the tasting bar and the bistro, which has indoor and garden seating for lunch and dinner, where you can dine on an ingenious menu that features honey-sriracha quail knots, hemp seed pretzels, and the plant-based Impossible Burger; save room for a real beer float. **Known for:** real beer floats; brewery tours offered twice daily at 2 and 4 pm.; farm-to-table bistro food. ⑤ *Average main: $25* ⊠ *1999 Citracado Pkwy., Escondido* ☎ *760/294–7866* ⊕ *www.stonebrewing.com.*

Vintana

$$ | MODERN AMERICAN | Don't let its location above the Lexus dealership dissuade you; this swanky restaurant is part of the Cohen Restaurant empire and it's designed as three restaurants in one: a formal glass-walled dining room; a lively patio with firepits and cabanas; and the lobby bar with leather couches and a wine shop. No matter where you dine, try the macadamia-crusted sea bass or the pork chop with maple bourbon sauce, followed with a cocktail using one of the more than 125 vodkas. **Known for:** Tuesday Date Night deals; nightly specials; large portions. ⑤ *Average main: $30* ⊠ *The Centre at Lexus Escondido, 1205 Auto Park Way, Escondido* ☎ *760/745–7777* ⊕ *www.dinevintana.com* ⊘ *Closed Mon.*

Hotels

With the exception of the Welk Resort, which is primarily a time-share property, Escondido has little to offer in the way of accommodations. The neighboring towns of Vista and San Marcos are home to two of the most luxurious destination spas in the nation.

Cal-a-Vie Health Spa

$$$$ | RESORT | At this destination spa—celebrities like Julia Roberts and Oprah Winfrey escape here for some serious R&R—you'll feel like you've died and gone to a pampering Provençal village heaven. **Pros:** exclusive spa haven; on 600 private acres; customized to health and fitness goals. **Cons:** no children under 16; three-day minimum stay; no TVs or alcohol might be an issue for some. ⑤ *Rooms from: $5750* ⊠ *29402 Spa Havens Way, Vista* ✢ *13 miles west of Escondido* ☎ *760/945–2055* ⊕ *www.cal-a-vie.com* ⤳ *32 rooms* ⦿ *Free Breakfast.*

★ Golden Door

$$$$ | RESORT | Considered by many to be the world's best destination spa, the venerable Golden Door takes you on a journey to tranquillity, transformation, and self-realization during a seven-night stay. **Pros:** peaceful sanctuary; four-to-one staff ratio; luxury camp forms sisterhood; largest collection of Japanese art in the country. **Cons:** no alcohol, sugar, or salt; mostly appeals to women; expensive; all stays Sunday arrival. ⑤ *Rooms from: $1575* ⊠ *777 Deer Springs Rd., San Marcos* ✢ *6½ miles west of Escondido* ☎ *760/744–5777* ⊕ *www.goldendoor.com* ⤳ *40 rooms* ⦿ *Free Breakfast.*

Lakehouse Resort

$$ | HOTEL | The slogan in the lobby, "Paddle your own canoe" sets the tone at this maritime-themed hotel reminiscent of a lake house with subtle nautical touches and private patios overlooking the marina or pool. **Pros:** unique lakefront location; central location; two pools. **Cons:** lots of weddings and parties; just 35% of rooms have lake views; sound carries between rooms. ⑤ *Rooms from: $339* ⊠ *1025 La Bonita Dr., San Marcos* ✢ *6½ miles west of Escondido* ☎ *760/744–0120* ⊕ *www.lakehousehotelandresort.com* ⤳ *144 rooms* ⦿ *No Meals.*

Shopping

Although farmland began to give way to suburbs in the 1990s, and the area's fruit, nut, and vegetable bounty has diminished, you can still find overflowing farm stands in the San Pasqual Valley and in Valley Center, just east of the city.

The San Diego Zoo Safari Park's Bazaar (☎ *760/738–5055*) sells authentic African artifacts, books, home-decor items, and apparel. ⇨ *For more information on the Safari Park, see the Escondido Sights Section.*

Bates Nut Farm

OTHER SPECIALTY STORE | FAMILY | Home of San Diego's largest pumpkin patch each fall, this family farm is where you might find a 200-pound pumpkin. It also sells locally grown pecans, macadamia nuts, and almonds. On the 100 acres, there's a farm zoo, a picnic area, and a gift shop. ⊠ *15954 Woods Valley Rd., Valley Center* ✢ *9 miles northeast of Escondido* ☎ *760/749–3333* ⊕ *www.batesnutfarm.biz* ☞ *$5 parking fee in Oct. on weekends.*

Brick n Barn

ANTIQUES & COLLECTIBLES | Dating back to 1872, this former homestead of baking legend Betty Crocker opens its gates monthly for antique shows hosted in a massive white barn. Step inside for theme events, unveiling a range of inventory including mid-century, industrial, vintage, rustic, primitive, and French country items. Ten local artisans, food trucks, craft workshops, and gardens with free-range birds make this a family-friendly outing. You'll often find homemade baked goods and gourmet coffee to enjoy on the manicured grounds. Check their website for show dates and other events. ✉ *29200 Miller Rd., Valley Center ✛ 9 miles northeast of Escondido* ☎ *760/651–2635* ⊕ *www.bricknbarn.com* ⊙ *Open 1 weekend a month, 9–5.*

Activities

FISHING

There are three freshwater lakes—Dixon, Hodges, and Wohlford—that surround the North County city of Escondido.

California Department of Fish and Game

FISHING | A fishing license, available at most bait-and-tackle and sporting-goods stores, is required for fishing from the shoreline. Nonresidents can purchase an annual license or a 10-day, 2-day, or 1-day short-term license. Licenses can also be purchased online through the department's website or at the San Diego headquarters. Children younger than 16 do not need a license. Note that some city reservoirs no longer sell snacks, drinks, bait, or fishing licenses, nor do they rent pedal boats or electric motors. They also accept payment by credit card or check (no cash) for day-use fees. Make sure to check updated concession availability for your specific destination, or obtain a fishing license in advance.

■TIP➜ **You do not need a license to fish from public piers. Any lobster or crab taken on hook and line must be returned to the water immediately.** ✉ *3883 Ruffin Rd., San Diego* ☎ *858/467–4201* ⊕ *www.wildlife. ca.gov* ◳ *Fishing license from $20.*

HIKING

San Dieguito River Park

HIKING & WALKING | This corridor begins at the mouth of the San Dieguito River in Del Mar and heads from the riparian lagoon area through coastal sage scrub and mountain terrain to end in the desert; eventually the Coast to Crest Trail will connect 70 miles to Volcan Mountain. It's open to hikers, bikers, and horses. The expansive park is also home to the Sikes Adobe Farmhouse,

Go Fish

The California Department of Fish and Game (⊕ *www.wildlife.ca.gov*) issues "Fishing Passports" showing 150 different species of fresh and saltwater fish and shellfish found throughout the state. In San Diego County fishing aficionados can catch (and, hopefully, release) many of the species listed, receiving a stamp for each species caught.

an 1880s farmstead that was almost completely destroyed by wildfire in 2007. After painstaking restoration it reopened in 2010 and is now home to a museum, open most Sundays for free tours (9:30 am to noon). The restored adobe creamery reopened in 2014. ✉ *18372 Sycamore Creek Rd., Escondido* ☎ *858/674–2270* ⊕ *www.sdrp.org.*

Temecula

29 miles from Escondido, 60 miles from San Diego on I–15 north to Rancho California Rd. east.

Once an important stop on the Butterfield Overland Stagecoach route and a market town for the huge cattle ranches surrounding it, Temecula (pronounced teh- *mec*-yoo-la) is now a developed wine region, designated the South Coast region, which also includes some wineries in San Diego County. Known for its gently rolling hills, the region is studded with ancient oak trees and vernal pools. French and Italian grapes thrive in the valley's hot climate, which has turned Temecula's wine route into a tourist attraction and weekend escape for San Diegans. Today there are nearly 50 wineries open to the pubic. Winemakers are creating luscious blended reds and whites that resemble rich Rhônes and Tuscan vintages. Because most of the wineries sell their bottles only at the wineries, it pays to stock up if you find something you especially enjoy.

Most of the wineries that line both sides of Rancho California Road offer tours (by reservation) and tastings (for a fee) daily and have creatively stocked boutiques, picnic facilities, and restaurants on the premises. Some wineries have opened luxury boutique lodgings and fine-dining restaurants. For shopping, restaurants, and museums, Old Town runs along historic Front Street on the west side of I–15. In addition to its visitor appeal, Temecula is also a suburban bedroom community for many who work in San Diego's North County. Between hot-air-balloon rides over vineyards and wine tours by horse-drawn carriage, this romantic destination has plenty to offer for the wine lover, and everyone else.

TOURS

Several companies offer individual and group tours of the Temecula wine country with departures from San Diego and Temecula. Some include lunch or refreshments as part of the package.

Destination Temecula

FOOD AND DRINK TOURS | Let someone else do the driving and enjoy this tour service that takes groups of up to 15 in a luxury Mercedes Sprinter van for tasting and touring Temecula wineries. They also offer a join-in tour to the public if you're looking to make friends along the way, or bring a group with you of up to 15 people. ☒ *28475 Old Town Front St., Suite F, Temecula* ☎ *951/695–1232, 800/584–8162* ⊕ *www.destem.com* 🖾 *$179 per person for 15 people.*

Grapeline Wine Tours

FOOD AND DRINK TOURS | Grapeline Wine Tours offers custom private tours, daily shared tours, and by-the-hour chauffeured service. ☒ *Temecula* ☎ *951/693–5755* ⊕ *www.gogrape.com* 🖾 *From $129.*

Temecula Carriage Company

FOOD AND DRINK TOURS | Special occasion winery tours, by reservation, include a two-hour ride and a picnic lunch ($295 for up to four people). A one-hour private carriage ride is $185 for four people max. For a memorable experience, get your feet moving with a two-hour grape stomping experience following a carriage tour ($495 for up to eight guests). ☒ *Temecula* ☎ *844/369–1852* ⊕ *www.temeculacarriageco.com* 🖾 *From $185.*

VISITOR INFORMATION

A good resource for information on Temecula's 35-some wineries, the Temecula Valley Winegrowers Association distributes brochures and sells tickets to special wine events. Ask about their SIP Temecula Wine Tasting Passport, which allows passport holders to taste award-winning wines at five wineries for $50, weekdays only.

CONTACTS Temecula Valley Winegrowers Association. ☒ *Temecula* ☎ *951/699–3626, 800/801–9463* ⊕ *www.temeculawines.org.* **Visit Temecula Valley.** ☒ *28690 Mercedes St., Suite A, Temecula* ☎ *951/491–6085* ⊕ *www.visittemeculavalley.com.*

Sights

Europa Village

GARDEN | You'll find three traditional styles of European wine reflecting French Cabernet Sauvignon; Spanish Tempranillo; and Italian Pinot Grigio. You can walk through lush gardens, grab a table under the pergola, and enjoy live music every Sunday 2–6 pm. ☒ *33475 La Serena Way, Temecula* ☎ *951/216–3380* ⊕ *www.europavillage.com* 🖾 *Tastings $25.*

Leoness Cellars

WINERY | Bordeaux and Rhône blends are the specialties of this 20-acre hilltop estate with magnificent views of Cabernet Sauvignon vines. If it's available, try the winemaker's pride and joy, the Mélange de Reves (Blend of Dreams),

With more than 40 wineries, most along Rancho California Road, Temecula is Southern California's premier wine-making region.

made from the traditional Rhône combo of Grenache, Syrah, and Mourvèdre. Winery tours take in the vineyards and the wine-making areas. The tours require a reservation, as do wine-and-food pairing sessions that might include fruits and cheeses or, in the case of dessert wines, chocolates. Leoness's popular French-inspired restaurant is open daily. ⊠ *38311 De Portola Rd., Temecula* ☎ *951/302–7601* ⊕ *www.leonesscellars. com* ⊠ *Tasting from $30; tours with tasting from $45.*

Miramonte Winery

WINERY | Temecula's hippest winery sits high on a hilltop. Rhône-style whites (including the Four Torch Blanc blend of Grenache Blanc) and reds like the estate Syrah and Opulente blend of Grenache, Syrah, and Mourvèdre are the strong suits, though the Tempranillo and rosé have their partisans. Taste inside at the casual bistro, outside on the deck, perhaps with an artisanal cheese plate. On Friday night from 5 to 8, the winery goes into party mode with tastings of wine and beer, music, and dancing that spills into the vineyards. ⊠ *33410 Rancho California Rd., Temecula* ☎ *951/506–5500* ⊕ *www.miramontewinery.com* ⊠ *Tastings from $30.*

Mount Palomar Winery

WINERY | One of the original Temecula Valley wineries, opened in 1969, Mount Palomar introduced Sangiovese, a varietal that has proven perfectly suited to the region's soil and climate. New owners have transformed the homey winery into a grand Mediterranean villa with acres of gardens and trees, turning it into an award-winning wedding and event venue. The Sangiovese is worth a try, as are the Solera Cream Sherry (ask how it's made) and the popular Cloudbreak, an inky red blend with a Petit Verdot base. The restaurant is open daily for lunch and dinner. ⊠ *33820 Rancho California Rd., Temecula* ☎ *951/676–5047* ⊕ *www.mountpalomar. com* ⊠ *Tastings from $20.*

★ Old Town Temecula

TOWN | Once a hangout for cowboys, Old Town is in full swing with boutique shops, good restaurants, a children's museum, and a theater, while retaining its Old West appearance. A walking tour put together by the Temecula Valley Historical Society, starting at the Temecula Valley Museum, covers some of the old buildings; most are identified with bronze plaques. Free maps can be downloaded from their website (⊕ *www. temeculahistoricalsociety.org*). A walking tour ($5) of Old Town Temecula is given every Saturday 10–11:30, departing from the Temecula Valley Museum, located in the Sam Hicks Monument Park directly across from the weekly Farmer's Market. ⊠ *Temecula* ⊕ *oldtowntemecula.org* ⊗ *Tours not held on 2nd Sat. of every month.*

Old Town Temecula Community Theater

PERFORMANCE VENUE | Within the landmark Mercantile Building from 1890 is Temecula's community theater composed of two performance venues showcasing music, dance, and theater. Musicals, comedy, and cabaret orchestra performances draw a crowd. ⊠ *42051 Main St, Temecula* ☎ *866/653–8696* ⊕ *www.temeculatheater.org* ☎ *From $20* ⊗ *Closed Mon. and Tues.*

Pennypickle's Workshop (*Temecula Children's Museum*)

CHILDREN'S MUSEUM | **FAMILY** | This is the imaginary home of Professor Phineas Pennypickle, where kids accompanied by parents enter a time machine that carries them through 11 rooms of interactive exhibits demonstrating perception and illusion, music making, flight and aviation, chemistry and physics, plus power and electricity. The shop stocks an array of educational toys, games, and books. Reservations are not taken, so be sure to get their early, especially during school vacations. ⊠ *42081 Main St., Temecula* ☎ *951/308–6376* ⊕ *www.pennypickles. org* ☎ *$10* ⊗ *Closed Mon.*

Santa Rosa Plateau Ecological Reserve

TRAIL | **FAMILY** | This 9,000-acre wooded preserve provides a glimpse of what this countryside was like back in the day, with bunch-grass prairies frequented by mule deer, golden eagles, and other wildlife. Trails wind through ancient oak forests and past seasonal, vernal pools and rolling grassland. A visitor and operations center has interpretive displays and maps; some of the reserve's hiking trails begin here. There are designated trails for leashed dogs, horses, and mountain bikers. ⊠ *39400 Clinton Keith Rd., Murrieta* ⊹ *Take I–15 south to Clinton Keith Rd. exit and head west 5 miles* ☎ *951/677–6951* ⊕ *www.rivcoparks.org/ srp* ☎ *$4 per person; $1 for each horse or dog* ⊗ *Visitor center closed Mon.*

South Coast Winery

WINERY | As one of the only local wineries to produce their wine on-site, South Coast is all about the experience with tastings and tours (by reservation) that start at the wall of awards and end with a wine-cheese pairing in the tasting room with a "wine tree" of five blends. The wine list here features estate-grown and-made Viognier, Merlot, Cabernet Sauvignon, and Black Jack Port. The award-winning Group Therapy has spicy notes of Grenache, earthy character of Zinfandel, and acidity of Sangiovese. Be sure to try their sparkling wines. The winery also operates a hotel, spa, and restaurant. ⊠ *34843 Rancho California Rd., Temecula* ☎ *951/587–9463, 866/994–6379* ⊕ *www.southcoastwinery.com* ☎ *Tastings $25; tours $55.*

Temecula Valley Museum

HISTORY MUSEUM | **FAMILY** | Adjacent to Sam Hicks Monument Park, this museum focuses on Temecula Valley history, including early Native American life, Butterfield stage routes, and the ranchero period. A hands-on interactive area for children holds a general store, photographer's studio, and ride-a-pony station. Outside there's a playground and picnic area. A walking tour ($5) of Old Town Temecula is given every Saturday 10–11:30, departing from the Temecula Valley Museum. ⊠ *28314 Mercedes St., Temecula* ☎ *951/694–6450* ⊕ *www. temeculavalleymuseum.org* ⊠ *$5 suggested donation* ⊘ *Closed Mon.*

Thornton Winery

WINERY | Known for his line of popular sparkling wines using the French méthode champenoise, winemaker Tom Stolzer also produces still wines made from Rhône- and Mediterranean-type varietals such as Nebbiolo and old-vine Zinfandels. Tastings are offered daily, and jazz concerts are presented weekends April through September. ⊠ *32575 Rancho California Rd., Temecula* ☎ *951/699–0099* ⊕ *www.thorntonwine.com* ⊠ *Tastings from $30.*

★ Wiens Family Cellars

WINERY | A visit to this family-owned winery can be an enlightenment with its combinations of Cabernet Sauvignon, Cabernet Franc, Petite Syrah, Zinfandel, and Pinot Noir. The winery is known for its big reds like Refugio Cabernet Sauvignon, as well as its Amour de L'Orange sparkling wine, which pairs well with breakfast dishes and hors d'oeuvres. There's live music Thursday through Sunday. ⊠ *35055 Via del Ponte, Temecula* ☎ *951/694–9892* ⊕ *www.wienscellars.com* ⊠ *Tastings $30.*

Wilson Creek Winery & Vineyards

WINERY | One of Temecula's busiest tasting rooms sits amid inviting, parklike grounds. Wilson is known for its Almond sparkling wine, but the winery also produces appealing still wines. Among these the Petite Sirah, Viognier, reserve Syrah, white Cabernet Sauvignon, and reserve Zinfandel all merit a taste. The on-site Creekside Grill Restaurant serves sandwiches, salads, seasonal seafood, and has an entire menu dedicated to those who are gluten-free. ⊠ *35960 Rancho California Rd., Temecula* ☎ *951/699–9463*

⊕ *www.wilsoncreekwinery.com* ⊠ *Tastings $30.*

Restaurants

Bushfire Kitchen

$ | **AMERICAN** | **FAMILY** | Void of GMOs, colorings, preservatives, or enhancers, this family-owned business taps into locally sourced ingredients to offer great food at a remarkable price. Located on the edge of Old Town Temecula, it's as simple as point, grab, and go with an online kitchen firing up bowls, burgers, sandwiches, and entrées like grass-fed tri-tip, free-range chicken, and sustainable salmon. **Known for:** antibiotic-free meat; food is made slow and served fast; vegan, vegetarian, and gluten-free dishes. ⑤ *Average main: $15* ⊠ *40665 Winchester Rd., Temecula* ☎ *951/296–0190* ⊕ *www. bushfirekitchen.com.*

Café Champagne

$$$ | **CONTEMPORARY** | With its flowering trellises and vineyard views, the spacious patio at Thornton Winery's café is the perfect place to lunch on a sunny day. The kitchen, which faces the French country–style dining room, turns out lobster ravioli, margarita flatbread, sandwiches, and other hearty fare. **Known for:** bacon cheeseburger; Sunday brunch; live music weekends April–Sept. ⑤ *Average main: $32* ⊠ *Thornton Winery, 32575 Rancho California Rd., Temecula* ☎ *951/699–0099* ⊕ *www.thorntonwine.com.*

★ The Goat & Vine

$ | **MEDITERRANEAN** | Every morning at 3 am, chefs are hard at work in this scratch, stone-hearth kitchen where nearly everything is produced in-house, including the sauces, dressings, and breads baked with a sourdough starter dating back 120 years. Handcrafted sandwiches range from steak-mushroom melts with smoked blue cheese to turkey with aged Brie and balsamic compote, and the pizzas are large enough to share, though most people find themselves walking out with a to-go box—especially if they start with "Mother's Meatballs," made with Kobe beef, bubbling in a cast-iron skillet. **Known for:** stone-hearth kitchen; house sangria; sourdough pretzels. $ *Average main: $20* ✉ *41923 2nd St., #102, Temecula* ☎ *951/695–5600* ⊕ *www.thegoatandvine.com* ⊙ *No breakfast.*

Trattoria Toscana

$$ | **TUSCAN** | California native Blythe Wilson and Sardinian-born chef Pietro Cinus met while Wilson was exploring the Tuscan countryside and together they brought all things Italian to Temecula. Grab a seat at a wooden table—built by the chef—and try gnocchi, ravioli, and soft breads all made by hand; the bustling scratch kitchen integrates spicy sausage and aged pecorino imported from Italy. **Known for:** dishes from Tuscany and Sardinia; special three-course dinners; tiramisu and panna cotta with citrus coulis made with lemons from chef's garden. $ *Average main: $30* ✉ *Creekside Center, 41789 Nicole La. B1, Temecula* ☎ *951/587–8030* ⊕ *www. trattoriatoscanaintemecula.com* ⊙ *Closed Tues. No lunch weekdays.*

Vineyard Rose

$$$ | **MODERN AMERICAN** | Step into South Coast Winery's dimly lit restaurant, where prices are high but wine pours are generous. Wooden pillars divide L-shape booths, and stained-glass windows of red roses that pay tribute to the name are the backdrop to a menu that delivers favorites like the charcuterie platter, Jidori chicken, and roasted salmon with heirloom tomato marmalade; hearty eaters will appreciate the selection of pork chop, Scottish salmon, and grilled filet mignon. **Known for:** generous portions; good service; steak and frites. $ *Average main: $40* ✉ *34843 Rancho California Rd., Temecula* ☎ *951/587–9463, 866/994–6379* ⊕ *www.southcoastwinery.com.*

☕ Coffee and Quick Bites

Old Town Sweet Shop

$ | **DESSERTS** | **FAMILY** | Don't count calories here, because you'll lose track at this old-fashioned sweet shop with 22 types of fudge, 43 flavors of ice cream, 15 different candy apples, and funnel cake sprinkled with powdered sugar and every naughty topping imaginable. Their retro candy will take you back in time. **Known for:** funnel cakes; old-fashioned candy; ice cream. $ *Average main: $12* ✉ *28545 Old Town Front St., Temecula* ☎ *951/693–1919* ⊕ *www.facebook.com/ oldtownsweetshop/.*

🛏 Hotels

Carter Estate Winery and Resort

$$ | **HOTEL** | Enter by way of a long driveway lined with olive trees, past the automatic gates, and suddenly you're in a Mediterranean-inspired neighborhood of freestanding bungalows that overlook the vineyards and mountains. **Pros:** all rooms have vineyard views with patio; complimentary in-room breakfast; use of facilities at South Coast Winery Resort. **Cons:** $150 pet fee; no on-site restaurant; rose gardens attract bees. $ *Rooms from: $300* ✉ *34450 Rancho California Rd., Temecula* ☎ *844/851–2138* ⊕ *www. carterestatewinery.com* 🛏 *60 rooms* 🍽 *Free Breakfast.*

★ Domaine Chardonnay

$$$$ | **B&B/INN** | Owners Laura and Mike opened the most romantic estate in Temecula to bring exclusivity, perfection, and a splash of Tuscany to the heart of San Diego's wine country. **Pros:** exceptional breakfast delivered to your room; double gold award, sulfate-free wines available exclusively to guests; friendly owners with attention to detail. **Cons:** usually booked solid; no children under 12, so not ideal for families; minibar and snacks somewhat limited. $ *Rooms from: $542* ✉ *33810 Madera de Playa*

Dr., Temecula ☎ *951/383–8989* ⊕ *www. domainechardonnay.com* ⇔ *3 rooms* ⦿ *Free Breakfast.*

The Inn at Europa Village
$$$ | B&B/INN | Offering a lovely hillside setting for an escape to the wine country, this B&B has additional lodging in the newer Spanish-style casitas at neighboring Bolero. **Pros:** privacy and scenery; delicious home-cooked breakfast; in-room tablets to access resort services. **Cons:** long walk to wineries; not pet-friendly; two-night minimum stay on weekends. ⓢ *Rooms from: $469* ⊠ *33350 La Serena Way, Temecula* ☎ *877/676–7047* ⊕ *www.europavillage. com* ⇔ *21 rooms* ⦿ *Free Breakfast.*

Ponte Vineyard Inn
$$$$ | HOTEL | Comfortable and relaxed digs offer vineyard and garden views and are modeled after the Carmel Mission with lots of dark wood, massive doors, leather furnishings, and open spaces. **Pros:** firepits in garden; excellent service; live music on weekends. **Cons:** $30 tastings not discounted for hotel guests; rather pricey; not pet-friendly; pool bar service only available May–October. ⓢ *Rooms from: $380* ⊠ *35001 Rancho California Rd., Temecula* ☎ *951/587–6688* ⊕ *www.pontevineyardinn.com* ⇔ *90 rooms* ⦿ *No Meals.*

South Coast Winery Resort & Spa
$ | RESORT | At Temecula's largest winery, this resort offers your choice of a private villa or hotel room in the tower building, all surrounded by 38 acres of vineyards. **Pros:** elegantly appointed rooms; one of Temecula's more affordable hotels; lovely pool and spa. **Cons:** spread-out property requires lots of walking; villas could use updating; $19 resort fee and no cleaning service. ⓢ *Rooms from: $199* ⊠ *34843 Rancho California Rd., Temecula* ☎ *951/587–9463, 866/994–6379* ⊕ *www. southcoastwinery.com* ⇔ *132 rooms* ⦿ *No Meals.*

Temecula Creek Inn
$$ | RESORT | This property sprawls over 360 acres, and rooms have private patios or balconies that overlook the resort's championship golf course. **Pros:** beautiful grounds; free shuttle to sister property, Pechanga Resort Casino; course views from most rooms. **Cons:** $100 pet fee; often busy; location away from Old Town and wineries. ⓢ *Rooms from: $209* ⊠ *44501 Rainbow Canyon Rd., Temecula* ☎ *833/267–2418, 888/976–3404* ⊕ *www. temeculacreekinn.com* ⇔ *127 rooms* ⦿ *No Meals.*

Shopping

Old Town Antique Faire
ANTIQUES & COLLECTIBLES | Reminiscent of a Wild West saloon, this antiques mall in the heart of Old Town Temecula has one-of-a-kind collectibles from 30 local vendors including jewelry, furniture, glassware, linens, tools, and books. ⊠ *28601 Front St., Temecula* ☎ *951/694–8786* ⊕ *www.facebook.com/ OldTownAntiqueFaire.*

Temecula Lavender Co.
OTHER HEALTH & BEAUTY | Owner Jan Schneider offers an inspiring collection of the herb that fosters peace, purification, sleep, and longevity. Bath salts, hand soaps, essential oil, even dryer bags to freshen up the laundry—she's got it all. ⊠ *28561 Old Town Front St., Temecula* ☎ *951/676–1931* ⊕ *www.temeculalavenderco.com.*

Temecula Olive Oil Company
MARKET | FAMILY | Ranch tours and complimentary tastings of locally pressed olive oil are offered at the Temecula Olive Oil Company, where you can find a selection of oils seasoned with garlic, herbs, and citrus. This Old Town shop has dipping and cooking oils, locally crafted oil-based soaps and bath products, a selection of preserved and stuffed olives, and

Hot-air ballooning is available daily, year-round, in Temecula and flights typically last 60–75 minutes.

house-made wines. ✉ *28653 Old Town Front St., Temecula* ☎ *951/693–4029* ⊕ *www.temeculaoliveoil.com* ☞ *Tours by reservation only at 10 am on 2nd and 4th Sat. of every month.*

 ## Activities

BALLOONING
California Dreamin'

BALLOONING | Head here for hot-air-balloon rides over Temecula's wine country. One-hour flights include a champagne toast. ✉ *33133 Vista del Monte Rd., Temecula* ☎ *800/373–3359* ⊕ *www.californiadream-in.com* ✉ *Weekdays $188; weekends $248.*

A Grape Escape Balloon Adventure

BALLOONING | Enjoy a sunrise hot-air-balloon liftoff from Europa Village Winery. ✉ *33475 La Serena Way, Temecula* ☎ *951/699–9987, 800/965–2122* ⊕ *www.hotairtours.com* ✉ *From $159.*

Julian

62 miles from San Diego to Julian, east on I–8 and north on Rte. 79.

Gold was discovered in the Julian area in 1869, and gold-bearing quartz a year later. More than $15 million worth of gold was taken from local mines in the 1870s. Many of the buildings along Julian's Main Street and the side streets today date back to the gold-rush period; others are reproductions.

When gold and quartz became scarce, the locals turned to growing apples and pears. During the fall harvest season you can buy fruit, sip apple cider (hard or soft), eat apple pie, and shop for local original art, antiques, and collectibles. But spring is equally enchanting (and less congested), as the hillsides explode with wildflowers—thousands of daffodils, lilacs, and peonies. More than 50 artists have studios tucked away in the hills surrounding Julian; they often show their work in local shops and galleries.

The Julian area comprises three small crossroads communities: Santa Ysabel, Wynola, and historic Julian. You can find bits of history, shops, and dining options in each community. Most visitors come to spend a day in town, especially after snowfall, but the hillsides support small B&B establishments for those who want to linger longer, read, rest, hike, bird-watch, and stargaze.

It's worth a side trip to Cuyamaca Rancho State Park, 15 miles south of Julian. Spread over more than 25,000 acres of meadows and forests, the park offers a beautiful outdoor experience with a lake, camps, picnic areas, and more than 100 hiking trails. For an inspirational desert view, stop at the lookout about 2 miles south of Julian on Route 79. The Sunrise Highway, passing through the Cleveland National Forest, is the most dramatic approach to Julian.

VISITOR INFORMATION
CONTACT Julian Chamber of Commerce.
✉ *Town Hall, 2129 Main St., Julian* ✛ *Corner of Washington and Main* ☎ *760/765–1857* ⊕ *www.visitjulian.com.*

 # Sights

Blue Door Winery
WINERY | Take one part historic stables and one part French-and-Italian reds, and you've got an urban winery with nothing but unfiltered goodness. You won't find sparkling, white, rosé, or anything sweet on the menu, just straight reds (and occasional sangria). Named for the servants' entrance at the Governor's Palace in Santa Fe, New Mexico, this boutique winery is captured in a painting of the blue door hung above the bar. With its flagship in Pacific Beach, this small tasting room is the only one of its kind in the heart of Julian. ✉ *2608 B St., Julian* ☎ *760/765–0361* ⊕ *www.thebluedoor-winery.com.*

Calico Cidery
BREWERY | Pull up a bale of hay in the orchard and sample a flight of refreshing hard cider made from the apple trees just steps from your table. On tap are four traditional dry ciders that rotate regularly. This warehouse tasting room on the outskirts of town is the ideal escape from the pie people. ✉ *4200 Hwy. 78, Julian* ☎ *858/586–0392* ⊕ *www.calicocidery.com* ✆ *Closed Mon.–Wed.*

California Wolf Center
WILDLIFE REFUGE | **FAMILY** | This center, just outside Julian, is one of the few places in North America where you can get an up-close view of the gray wolves that once roamed much of the continent. The center participates in breeding programs and houses several captive packs, including some rare Mexican grays, a subspecies of the North American gray wolf that came within seven individuals of extinction in the 1970s. The animals are kept secluded from public view in 3-acre pens, but some may be seen by visitors during conservation and behavioral enrichment tours, by advanced reservation only. The dirt road here is rough, so it's best to have a high-clearance vehicle. ✉ *Hwy. 79 at KQ Ranch Rd., Julian* ☎ *760/765–0030* ⊕ *www.californiawolfcenter.org* ✆ *$30, reservations required* ⊗ *Closed Tues.–Thurs.* ✆ *Tours Fri.–Mon. with advanced reservation.*

Julian Beer Company
BREWERY | **FAMILY** | Although lights are out by 10 pm, this brewery might be the closest thing to nightlife in Julian. On tap are craft farmhouse-style beers along with small plates and bar bites when you need to sober up. As the largest venue on Main Street, they have games, events, and plenty of indoor–outdoor seating for you and your crew. ✉ *2307 Main St., Julian* ☎ *760/765–3757* ⊕ *www.julianbeercompany.com.*

Julian Pioneer Museum

HISTORY MUSEUM | FAMILY | When the gold mines in Julian played out, the mobs of gold miners who had invaded it left, leaving behind discarded mining tools and empty houses. Today the Julian Pioneer Museum, a 19th-century brewery, displays remnants of that time, including pioneer clothing, a collection of old lace, mining tools, and original photographs of the town's historic buildings and mining structures. ⊠ *2811 Washington St., Julian* ☎ *760/765–0227* ⊕ *www. julianpioneermuseum.org* ✉ *$3* ⊘ *Closed Mon.–Thurs.*

★ Nickel Beer Company

BREWERY | Some of the best brew in San Diego is served at this little beer bar that occupies an old jail in Julian. Owner Tom Nickel is considered one of the most creative brewers in the region and is always cooking up new recipes that win accolades from judges and fans. There are 16 taps and contents change regularly. The Jalapeno Gold is peppery, the Nebula Red is summery, and the Stonewall Stout is like a meal in itself. For something Julian-memorable, try the apple pie beer. If you're having trouble making your pick, go for the flight of six beers for $15. The patio is dog-friendly. ⊠ *1485 Hollow Glen Rd., Julian* ☎ *760/765–2337* ⊕ *www. nickelbeerco.com.*

Santa Ysabel Preserve

NATURE PRESERVE | This valley looks pretty much the way the backcountry appeared a century ago, with sweeping meadows surrounded by oak-studded hillsides. The San Dieguito River (Santa Ysabel Creek) emerges from Volcan Mountain here and winds its way 65 miles to San Dieguito Lagoon at Del Mar along the Coast to Crest Trail. An 7-mile trail follows the river for the first mile, from Farmer Road in Julian to the East Entrance of Santa Ysabel Preserve. Legacy oak trees shade the trail, there are spectacular views along the way, and picnic tables abound. The

trail is best explored in the fall. ⊠ *Hwy. 79, Julian* ☎ *760/765–4098* ⊕ *www. sdparks.org.*

Volcan Mountain Wilderness Preserve

NATURE PRESERVE | San Diego County Parks and Recreation manages this 3,000-acre preserve, where hikes challenge your stamina and views are stunning. A 5-mile trail through the preserve passes through black-and-canyon oak forest, native manzanita, and rolling mountain meadows to a viewpoint where the panorama extends north all the way to Palomar Mountain. On a clear day you can see Point Loma in San Diego. At the entrance you pass through gates designed by James Hubbell, a local artist known for his ironwork, wood carving, and stained glass. You can see splendid views from the Volcan Summit. ⊠ *1209 Farmer Rd. (trailhead), north of Julian Town, Julian* ✛ *From Julian take Farmer Rd. to Wynola Rd., go east a few yards, and then north on continuation of Farmer Rd.* ☎ *760/765–4098* ⊕ *www. volcanmt.org* ✉ *Free.*

Julian's Black History

According to local history and old photos, the Julian area had a large population of African Americans in the years following the Civil War. Indeed, it was Fred Coleman, who discovered gold in Julian, and the Julian Hotel was founded and operated by Albert and Margaret Robinson, also Black. Headstones recognizing the contributions of Julian's Black pioneers continue to be placed in the old section of the Pioneer Cemetery.

🍴 Restaurants

Jeremy's on the Hill

$$ | **MODERN AMERICAN** | **FAMILY** | Julian's most upscale restaurant has gained a solid reputation thanks to the chef's commitment to quality cuisine reflected in the farm-to-table menu. Although the menu features grilled steak and locally grown pork and veggies, the stars are rack of lamb, bison meat loaf, and some of the best burgers around. **Known for:** live music weekend nights; flash-fried Brussels sprouts; on-site sommelier and full bar; family run. ⑤ *Average main: $27* ✉ *4354 Hwy. 78, Julian* ☎ *760/765–1587* ⊕ *www.bestrestaurantinjulian.com* ⊘ *Closed Wed.*

★ Moms Pie House

$ | **BAKERY** | **FAMILY** | In 1984, "Mom" (aka Anita Nichols) opened her first pie shop in the old Julian Café building. People lined the streets for a slice of the guilty pleasure, known for its buttery crust, not-too-sweet filling with local apples, and commitment to quality. **Known for:** pressed apple cider; cinnamon ice cream; baking classes. ⑤ *Average main: $9* ✉ *2119 Main St., Julian* ☎ *760/765–2472* ⊕ *www.momspiesjulian.com* ⊘ *No dinner.*

Quecho

$ | **MEXICAN** | The elevated Mexican cuisine, margaritas, mariachi, and Talavera pottery may transport you to central Mexico before you dip that first chip into homemade guacamole. Pull up a colorful barstool and watch Julian go by from a wraparound porch where street tacos, enchiladas, and organic carne served in a stone *molcajete* come out sizzling hot. **Known for:** classic guacamole; Julian apple margarita; street tacos. ⑤ *Average main: $14* ✉ *2603 B St., Julian* ☎ *760/765–1560* ⊕ *www.quechojulian.com* ⊘ *Closed Tues. and Wed.*

★ Romano's Restaurant

$ | **SICILIAN** | For four generations, recipes have been handed down the line of this Sicilian family who opened their first restaurant in 1920. From Milwaukee to Julian, they set down roots in the quaint pie capital in 1982 and never looked back, creating this casual, red-checked-table-cloth kind of place, where you can dine outside in good weather. **Known for:** thin-crust pizza; cozy setting; old-school Italian cooking. ⑤ *Average main: $20* ✉ *2718 B St., Julian* ☎ *760/765–1003* ⊕ *www.romanosrestaurantjulian.com.*

Soups & Such Cafe

$ | **CAFÉ** | It's worth the wait for breakfast or lunch at this cozy café, where everything is fresh and made to order. The breakfast standout is eggs Benedict, both classic and vegetarian. **Known for:** combo soup, salad, and sandwich for $15; fresh and fast food; homemade soups. ⑤ *Average main: $15* ✉ *2000 Main St., Julian* ☎ *760/765–4761* ⊕ *www.facebook.com/soupsandsuchcafe* ⊘ *Closed Tues. No dinner.*

☕ Coffee and Quick Bites

Apple Alley Bakery

$ | **BAKERY** | This bakery tucked down a narrow alley proves there's no such thing as too many pie shops in Julian. After mastering the apple-to-crust ratio, they took on lunch specials by offering a soup–sandwich–pie combo for $13. **Known for:** apple pie; lunch specials; gluten-free and vegan options. ⑤ *Average main: $13* ✉ *2122 Main St., Julian* ☎ *760/765–2532* ⊕ *www.julianapplealley.com.*

Julian Pie Company

$ | **CAFÉ** | The apple pies that made Julian famous come from the Smothers family bakery in a one-story house on Main Street. In pleasant weather you can sit on the front patio and watch the world go by while savoring a slice of hot pie—from Dutch apple to apple mountain berry crumb—topped with homemade cinnamon ice cream. **Known for:** sweet Dutch apple pie; frozen uncooked pies to go;

apple cider doughnuts. $ *Average main:* *$8* ⊠ *2225 Main St., Julian* ☎ *760/765–* *2449* ⊕ *www.julianpie.com* ⊘ *No dinner.*

Julian Tea & Cottage Arts

$$$ | **CAFÉ** | **FAMILY** | Sample finger sandwiches, scones topped with whipped cream, and lavish sweets, which are served during afternoon tea inside the Clarence King House, built by Will Bosnell in 1898. Regular sandwiches, soups, salads, and a children's tea are also available. **Known for:** homemade lemon curd and scones; bottomless tea; charming turn-of-the-century home. $ *Average main: $39* ⊠ *2124 3rd St., Julian* ☎ *760/765–0832, 866/765–0832* ⊕ *www. juliantea.com* ⊘ *Closed Tues. and Wed. No dinner* ⌕ *Reservations essential.*

 Hotels

Butterfield Bed & Breakfast

$ | **B&B/INN** | This beautifully landscaped inn on a 3-acre hilltop is cordial and romantic, with knotty-pine ceilings, Laura Ashley accents, and rooms with nice touches, such as fireplaces or wood stoves and private entrances. **Pros:** great food that's dietary-need friendly; helpful hosts live next door; breakfast and afternoon refreshments are included. **Cons:** half a mile from town; no room phones; ornate and frilly rooms are not for everyone. $ *Rooms from: $185* ⊠ *2284 Sunset Dr., Julian* ☎ *760/765–2179, 800/379–4262* ⊕ *www.butterfieldbandb. com* ⊸ *5 rooms* ⦿ *Free Breakfast.*

Julian Gold Rush Hotel

$ | **B&B/INN** | Built in 1897 by freed slave Albert Robinson and his wife, Margaret, this old hotel is Julian's only designated national landmark and the oldest operating hotel in Southern California. **Pros:** genuine historic hotel; convivial atmosphere; afternoon tea. **Cons:** small rooms; no TV or in-room phones; street parking only. $ *Rooms from: $160* ⊠ *2032 Main St., Julian* ☎ *760/765–0201, 800/734–5854*

⊕ *www.julianhotel.com* ⊸ *16 rooms* ⦿ *Free Breakfast.*

Julian Lodge

$ | **HOTEL** | Near shops, this small hotel is a replica of the late-19th-century Washington Hotel. **Pros:** in-town location; free parking; reasonable rates and online promotions. **Cons:** simple appointments; no breakfast; no view. $ *Rooms from: $180* ⊠ *2720 C St., Julian* ☎ *760/765–1420, 800/542–1420* ⊕ *www.julianlodge.com* ⊸ *23 rooms* ⦿ *No Meals.*

★ Orchard Hill Country Inn

$$ | **B&B/INN** | On a hill above town, this true country inn experience with a lodge and 12 Craftsman-style cottages offers luxurious accommodations decorated with antiques, original art, and handcrafted quilts, complemented by sweeping views of the countryside; some of the cottage suites have see-through fireplaces, whirlpool tubs, sitting areas, and private patios or balconies. **Pros:** most luxurious digs in Julian; quiet 5-acre property away from crowds; lovely views. **Cons:** limited amenities; not recommended for young children; whirlpool rooms don't have showers. $ *Rooms from: $325* ⊠ *2502 Washington St., Julian* ☎ *760/765–1700, 800/716–7242* ⊕ *www. orchardhill.com* ⊸ *22 rooms* ⦿ *Free Breakfast.*

Wikiup Hummingbird Hotel

$$ | **B&B/INN** | Best known for its herd of llamas and goats, this cedar-and-brick inn is decorated with romantic furnishings and offers theme guest rooms with fireplaces and outdoor hot tubs for stargazing. **Pros:** pleasant surroundings with private entrances; no resort fees or hidden charges; renovated rooms. **Cons:** limited facilities; no meals included; two-night minimum on weekends. $ *Rooms from: $210* ⊠ *1645 Whispering Pines Dr., Julian* ⊹ *1.4-miles outside of town* ☎ *800/694–5487* ⊕ *www.wikiupbnb.com* ⊸ *5 rooms* ⦿ *No Meals.*

Shopping

The Julian area has a number of unique shops that are open weekends, but midweek hours vary considerably. In autumn locally grown apples, pears, nuts, and cider are available in town and at a few roadside stands. The best apple variety produced here is a Jonagold, a hybrid of Jonathan and Golden Delicious.

CLOTHING
The Mountain Gypsy

JEWELRY & WATCHES | This shop is popular for its extensive collection of jewelry, apparel, and shoes for men and women. ⊠ *2007 Main St., Julian* ☎ *760/765–0643* ⊕ *www.themountaingypsy.com.*

GALLERIES
Santa Ysabel Art Gallery

ART GALLERIES | On display here are works of fine art, including paintings, stained glass, sculptures, and other creations by local artists, including James Hubbell and Joe Garcia. Many of the rotating works focus heavily on traditional and contemporary art. ⊠ *30352 Hwy. 78, Santa Ysabel* ☎ *760/765–1676* ⊕ *www. santaysabelartgallery.com* ⊗ *Closed Tues. and Wed.*

GIFTS AND HOME ACCESSORIES
The Barn Vintage Marketplace

ANTIQUES & COLLECTIBLES | Between Julian and Santa Ysabel, "The Barn" goes beyond standard antiques with one-of-a-kind vintage home decor, spanning industrial, primitive, rustic, and more. Be sure to greet the resident emus, Daisy and Duke. ⊠ *4559 Hwy. 78, Santa Ysabel* ☎ *760/310–8587* ⊕ *www.facebook.com/TheBarnVintageMarketplace* ⊗ *Closed Mon.–Thurs.*

California Wolf Center Nature Store

SOUVENIRS | In the heart of downtown Julian, education and shopping unite with wildlife-theme gifts and nature exhibits about conservation and history of the Mexican gray wolf. Proceeds help fund the California Wolf Center. ⊠ *2775 B St.,* *Julian* ☎ *760/765–0030* ⊕ *www.californiawolfcenter.org.*

The Cider Mill

OTHER SPECIALTY STORE | Family-owned and -operated for more than 45 years, this small cider-pressing factory sells honey, nuts, candy, apples, preserves, and, of course, fresh local cider. Don't ask how they make their pumpkin butter and homemade fudge—both are crafted from a secret recipe. ⊠ *2103 Main St., Julian* ☎ *760/765–1430* ⊕ *www.juliancidermill.com.*

Julian Mercantile

JEWELRY & WATCHES | With brands like Brighton jewelry, UNOde50, and Mud Pie, this gift shop is packed with crafts, carvings, soaps, jewelry, leather, and other imports from Bali, Mexico, Brazil, Spain, and Ecuador. ⊠ *2111A Main St., Julian* ☎ *760/765–0280* ⊕ *www.julianimports.net.*

★ The Warm Hearth

SOUVENIRS | With two levels in a historic feed barn from 1913, this is the store that keeps on giving. Step inside for all things Julian including honey, jams, clothing, books, jewelry, toys, and even thoughtful gift sets. ⊠ *2125 Main St., Julian* ☎ *760/765–1022* ⊕ *www.facebook.com/warmhearthjulian.*

Ramona

18½ miles east of Escondido via Route 78 E, 36 miles north of San Diego.

For many heading into the San Diego mountains or desert, Ramona is the last stop. It's where drivers fill up with gas (sometimes less expensive than in the city), pick up provisions at one of several supermarkets (there are none farther east), and have a bite to eat. Increasingly, visitors are spending time in Ramona for a couple of reasons: to play golf and to drop some cash at the Barona casino, located along a country road a few miles south of town. Ramona's history is intertwined with Julian's, the town 22 miles east, where a gold rush drew argonauts in the 1870s. Descendants of those settlers still run cattle on ranches extending from Ramona to Julian. Today Ramona is a growing unincorporated area of about 28,000 residents, most of whom have ranches. There's a budding wine-making industry with more than 30 wineries now open to the public on weekends. The main thoroughfare also houses the largest selection of antiques shops in the backcountry. With the exception of the Barona Resort, lodging and dining fall into the simple and comfortable category. Don't come here if you're looking for luxury.

◉ Sights

Milagro

WINERY | FAMILY | For quality wine and an enjoyable wine-tasting experience, Milagro leads the long list of wineries in Ramona. Overseeing production is Hugo D'Acosta, who trained in Bordeaux and is considered one of Mexico's preeminent winemakers. The classy tasting room is tucked inside a copse of ancient oak trees, surrounded by vineyards, fruit trees, and local animals. Their highly rated wines are Sauvignon Blanc, Barbera, and Sangiovese. ⊠ *18750 Littlepage La., Ramona* ☎ *760/787–0738* ⊕ *www.milagrowinery.com* 🍷 *Tastings $16* ⊗ *Closed weekdays.*

Restaurants

Barona Oaks Steakhouse

$$$ | STEAKHOUSE | The elegant, dinner-only restaurant at Barona Resort is one of the few fine-dining venues east of San Diego. It caters to high rollers whose culinary choice often involves steak, thus the menu here lists a large selection of USDA Prime, including dry-aged porterhouse and buffalo rib eye, but there are seafood options, too. **Known for:** dry-aged

steaks; seafood options; remarkable rack of lamb. ⑤ *Average main: $40* ⊠ *1932 Wildcat Canyon Rd., Ramona* ☎ *619/443–2300* ⊕ *www.barona.com* ⊗ *Closed Sun.–Wed. No lunch.*

D'Carlos

$ | AMERICAN | The parking lot in front of D'Carlos is always full, a sure sign that Ramonans like this casual family-style dinner house. The menu offers something for everyone: burgers, sandwiches, salads, steaks, barbecue, seafood, and pasta. **Known for:** daily drink specials; homemade meat loaf; good variety. ⑤ *Average main: $20* ⊠ *1347 Main St., Ramona* ☎ *760/789–4340* ⊕ *www. dcarlos.com.*

🛏 Hotels

San Vicente Golf Resort

$ | RESORT | Accommodations in this three-story resort popular with golfers are clean, pleasant, and have mountain or golf-course views from balconies or patios. **Pros:** scenic location; free parking; great-value golf packages. **Cons:** limited amenities (but there are great jogging and nature trails); casual service; breakfast not included. ⑤ *Rooms from: $150* ⊠ *24157 San Vicente Rd., Ramona* ☎ *760/789–3788, 800/776–1289* ⊕ *www. sanvicenteresort.com* 🛏 *28 rooms* ⊘| *No Meals* ⛳ *Green fee from $70.*

Activities

GOLF

Mount Woodson Golf Club

GOLF | This beautiful, heavily wooded club in a hilly area off Highway 67 is set amid a grove of ancient oak trees and granite boulder-strewn hillsides with spectacular views of the historic Woodson Castle, a private residence built in 1921 that is now one of San Diego's most popular wedding venues. The course features some challenging holes like the par 5 Windinface, a deep, three-tiered green, where accuracy is a must. The course also features wooden bridges and good views, particularly from Hole 17. There is a pro shop and a small café. This is a popular local tournament site. ✉ *16422 N. Woodson Dr., Ramona* ☎ *760/788–3555* ⊕ *www.mtwoodsongolfclub.com* ⌨ *From $80* ⌘ *18 holes, 6004 yards, par 70.*

HIKING

★ **Mount Woodson Trail** (*Potato Chip Rock*)

HIKING & WALKING | Due to San Diego's varied terrain, a range of hiking trails is accessible for any skill level. Aptly nicknamed the Potato Chip Rock hike, Mount Woodson is best known for a picturesque rock formation that juts out of the mountainside—providing a timely photo op for hikers. It's not uncommon for people to wait in line to climb up on the rock and have their photo taken, since the trail can get crowded on weekends. This steep hike located between Poway and Ramona isn't for the faint of heart, taking most people about three hours to complete the 8-mile loop. But if for no other reason, do it for the Insta-worthy photo. Be sure to take plenty of water and avoid hiking in the heat of the day. ✉ *Lake Poway Recreation Area, 14644 Lake Poway Rd., Poway, Ramona* ✛ *8 miles southwest of Ramona* ☎ *858/668–4772* ⊕ *poway.org/502/Trails-Hiking* ☞ *Parking $10.*

Anza-Borrego Desert State Park

88 miles from Downtown San Diego (park border due west of Borrego Springs).

GETTING HERE AND AROUND

You'll need a car to visit the Anza-Borrego Desert and Borrego Springs, which is totally surrounded by wilderness. The trip from San Diego is about 88 scenic miles, and it takes around two hours.

Once there be prepared to drive on dusty roads as there is no public transportation. The best route to Borrego Springs is via I–8 east out of San Diego; exit east on Highway 79 and take the scenic drive through the Cuyamaca Mountains to Julian, where Highway 79 intersects with Highway 78 going east. Follow Highway 78 into the desert to Yaqui Pass Road, turn left and follow the signs to Borrego Springs Christmas Circle. Take Borrego Palm Canyon west to reach the Anza-Borrego Desert State Park headquarters.

TOURS

California Overland Desert Excursions

ADVENTURE TOURS | For group or private adventures, California Overland Desert Excursions offers day tours and overnight excursions into hard-to-reach scenic desert destinations using climate-controlled and open-air, military-transport vehicles. Typical destinations include Font's Point, the Badlands, and Split Mountain. ✉ *1233 Palm Canyon Dr., Borrego Springs* ☎ *760/767–1232* ⊕ *www.californiaoverland.com.*

VISITOR INFORMATION

CONTACTS Anza-Borrego Desert State Park. ✉ *200 Palm Canyon Dr., Borrego Springs* ☎ *760/767–5311* ⊕ *www.parks.ca.gov.* **State Park Reservations.** ☎ *800/444–7275* ⊕ *www.reserveamerica.com.*

 Sights

Anza-Borrego Desert State Park

STATE/PROVINCIAL PARK | Today more than 1,000 square miles of desert and mountain country are included in the Anza-Borrego Desert State Park, one of the few parks in the country where you can follow a trail and pitch a tent wherever you like. There are 110 miles of hiking and riding trails that allow you to explore canyons, capture scenic vistas, tiptoe through fields of wildflowers in spring, and possibly see wildlife—the park is home to rare Peninsula bighorn sheep, mountain lions, coyotes, black-tailed jackrabbit, and roadrunners. Parts of state Highway 78, which runs east and west through the park, intersect with the Juan Bautista de Anza National Historic Trail, marking portions of the route of the Anza Colonizing Expedition of 1775–76 that went from northern Mexico to the San Francisco Bay area. In addition, 85,000 acres have been set aside in the eastern part of the desert near Ocotillo Wells for off-road enthusiasts. General George S. Patton conducted field training in the Anza-Borrego to prepare for the World War II invasion of North Africa.

Many of the park's sites can be seen from your vehicle, as 500 miles of paved and dirt roads traverse the park—note that you are required to stay on them so as not to disturb the park's ecological balance. On dirt roads it's easy to sink up to your wheel covers in dry sand, so rangers recommend using four-wheel-drive vehicles on the dirt roads. Also, carry the appropriate supplies: shovel and other tools, flares, blankets, and plenty of water. Canyons are susceptible to flash flooding; inquire about weather conditions before entering.

Wildflowers, which typically begin to bloom in late February and are at their peak in mid-March, attract thousands of visitors each spring. A variety of factors, including rainfall and winds, determine how extensive the bloom will be in a particular year. Following wet winters, spectacular displays often fill the dry washes in Coyote Canyon and along Henderson Canyon Road.

■ TIP→ The best light for photography is in the early morning or late afternoon.

Erosion Road is a self-guided, 18-mile auto tour along Route S22 on the way to the Salton Sea. The Southern Emigrant Trail follows the route of the Butterfield Stage Overland Mail, the route used by half of the argonauts heading for the gold fields in Northern California.

At Borrego Palm Canyon, a few minutes north of the visitor information center, is a 1½-mile trail that leads to a small oasis. Borrego Palm Canyon and Tamarisk Grove—12 miles southeast of Borrego Palm Canyon—are the only campgrounds with flush toilets and showers in the park. (Day use is $10 and camping is $35 in high season.)

Geology students from all over the world visit the Fish Creek area of Anza-Borrego to explore a famous canyon known as Split Mountain (⊠ *Split Mountain Rd. south from Rte. 78 at Ocotillo Wells*), a narrow gorge with 600-foot perpendicular walls that was formed by an ancestral stream. Fossils in this area indicate that a sea covered the desert floor at one time. Wind Caves Trail, a 2-mile nature trail west of Split Mountain, rewards hikers with a good view of shallow caves created by erosion. Dogs are not permitted on any of the hiking trails in the park. ⊠ *200 Palm Canyon Dr., Borrego Springs* ☎ *760/765–5311* ⊕ *www.parks.ca.gov.*

Anza-Borrego Desert State Park Visitor Center

VISITOR CENTER | Rangers and displays at this excellent visitor center can point you in the right direction. Most of the desert plants also can be seen in the demonstration desert garden here. A high-clearance vehicle is necessary. Bring plenty of water. ⊠ *200 Palm Canyon Dr., Borrego Springs* ☎ *760/767–4205* ⊕ *www.parks. ca.gov* ⊠ *$10 use fee.*

Borrego Springs

31 miles from Julian, east on Rte. 78 and Yaqui Pass Rd., and north on Rte. S3.

A quiet town with a handful of year-round residents, Borrego Springs is set in the heart of the Anza-Borrego Desert State Park and is emerging as a destination for desert lovers. It was named the first dark sky community in the world, meaning you can stargaze without any

Spring Wildflowers

Southern California's famous climate has blessed this corner of the continent with an ever-changing, year-round palette of natural color. It's hard to find a spot anywhere around the globe that produces as spectacular a scene as San Diego in spring—from native plant gardens found tucked away in mountain canyons and streambeds to carpets of wildflowers on the desert floor. You'll have to see it yourself to believe just how alive the deceptively barren desert really is.

When to Go

Spring debuts in **late February or early March**. Heavy winter rains always precede the best bloom seasons. And good blooms also bring even more beauty—a bounty of butterflies. A further boon: here in this generally temperate climate, the bloom season lasts nearly all year.

Some drought-tolerant plants rely on fire to germinate, and the years following wildfires generally produce a profusion of plant life not normally seen.

What to See

Look for rare western redbud trees erupting into a profusion of crimson flowers, sometimes starting as early as February. Native California lilacs (ceanothus) blanket the hillsides throughout the backcountry with fragrant blue-and-white blossoms starting in May and showing until August.

Native varieties of familiar names show up in the mountain canyons and streambeds. A beautiful white western azalea would be the star in anyone's garden. A pink California rose blooms along streambeds in spring and summer. Throughout the year three varieties of native dogwood show off white blooms and beautiful crimson fall foliage. The **Cuyamaca Mountains** usually put on a display of fall color as the native oaks turn gold and red. By winter the rare toyon, known as the California Christmas tree, lights up the roadside with its red berries.

Farther east in the **Anza-Borrego Desert State Park,** the spring wildflower display can be spectacular: carpets of pink sand verbena, yellow desert sunflowers, and white evening primrose as far as the eye can see. Rocky slopes yield clumps of beavertail cactus topped with pink blossoms, clumps of yellow brittlebush tucked among the rocks, and crimson-tipped ocotillos. For an introduction to desert vegetation, explore the visitor center demonstration garden, adjacent to the park's underground visitor center.

To see the blooms, take I–8 east to Route 79, go north to Julian, and then east on Route 78 into Anza-Borrego park.

light pollution. From September through June, temperatures hover in the 80s and 90s, and you can enjoy activities such as hiking, nature study, golf, tennis, horseback riding, and mountain-bike riding. Even during the busier winter season, Borrego Springs feels quiet in a town void of traffic signals. There are several golf resorts, B&B, and a community of winter residents, but the laid-back vibe prevails. If winter rains cooperate, Borrego Springs puts on the best wildflower displays in the low desert.

VISITOR INFORMATION
CONTACT Borrego Springs Chamber of Commerce. ✉ *786 Palm Canyon Dr., Borrego Springs* ☎ *760/767–5555, 800/559–5524* ⊕ *www.borregospringschamber.com.*

 Sights

★ Galleta Meadows
PUBLIC ART | FAMILY | At Galleta Meadows, camels, llamas, saber-toothed tigers, tortoises, and monumental gomphotherium (a sort of ancient elephant) appear to roam the Earth again. These life-size bronze figures are of prehistoric animals whose fossils can be found in the Borrego Badlands. The collection of more than 130 sculptures, created by Ricardo Breceda, was commissioned by the late Dennis Avery, who installed the works of art on property he owned for the entertainment of locals and visitors. Maps are available from Borrego Springs Chamber of Commerce. ✉ *Borrego Springs Rd., from Christmas Circle to Henderson Canyon, Borrego Springs* ☎ *760/767–5555* ✍ *Free.*

🍴 Restaurants

Carlee's Place
$$ | AMERICAN | This local watering hole seems to collect characters ranging from hippies to mountain men and is the place to go any night of the week. A large, dimly lighted room houses the bar and dining tables, and the menu lists pasta and pizza in addition to old-fashioned entrées such as liver and onions, ribs and steaks, and a mixed grill. **Known for:** classic entrées; long-standing roadhouse; extensive menu; good buffalo wings, burgers, and ribs. ⑤ *Average main: $21* ✉ *660 Palm Canyon Dr., Borrego Springs* ☎ *760/767–3262* ⊕ *www.carleesplace. com.*

Carmelita's Mexican Grill and Cantina
$ | MEXICAN | Before dawn, owner and chef Narciso Dorado preps all of

Unburied Treasure

The Anza-Borrego Desert is one of North America's most geologically active spots and a repository of paleontological treasure. Beneath the desert's surface are fossil-bearing sediments that provide clues to past geological activity, from climate change to tectonic activity and up-thrust. Reading the fossil record, scientists have learned that the badlands here were once a wonderland of green and home of saber-toothed tigers, flamingos, zebras, camels, and a flying bird with a 16-foot wingspan.

Carmelita's meat, sauces, and sides to create the generous portions served at this friendly family-run eatery tucked into a back corner of what is called "The Mall." Carmelita's draws locals and visitors all day whether it's for a hearty breakfast, a cooked-to-order enchilada or burrito, or a brew at the bar. If you're still hungry, they'll serve you plenty of chips and salsa. It's the best place to escape the heat with a margarita on the rocks. **Known for:** reasonably priced menu; large portions; festive cantina. ⑤ *Average main: $18* ✉ *575 Palm Canyon Dr., Borrego Springs* ☎ *760/767–5666* ⊕ *www. carmelitasborrego.com.*

Red Ocotillo
$ | AMERICAN | For inexpensive comfort food, this desert diner serves sandwiches, pasta, burgers, and chicken-fried steak with thick fries. This is the area's best breakfast joint, with menu highlights including cinnamon French toast and smoked salmon eggs Benedict. **Known for:** smoked salmon eggs Benedict; flavorful rosemary potatoes; hearty biscuits and gravy; pet-friendly patio. ⑤ *Average*

main: $15 ✉ *721 Ave. Sureste, off Christ-mas Circle, Borrego Springs* ☎ *760/767–7400* ⊕ *www.redocotillo.com.*

 Hotels

★ Borrego Valley Inn

$$ | B&B/INN | Those looking for desert landscapes and some stargazing—guests must be 21 or older—may enjoy the adobe Southwestern-style buildings here that house spacious rooms, which boasts plenty of natural light, original art, pine beds, and corner fireplaces. **Pros:** swim under the stars in the clothing-optional pool; exquisite desert gardens; simple knock-'n-drop breakfast at your door. **Cons:** no kids and no pets; rooms could use sprucing up; service inconsistent. ⑤ *Rooms from: $285* ✉ *405 Palm Canyon Dr., Borrego Springs* ☎ *760/767–0311, 800/333–5810* ⊕ *www.borregovalleyinn. com* ⌐ *15 rooms* ⓘ◯ *Free Breakfast.*

La Casa del Zorro

$$ | RESORT | FAMILY | Even though it has changed hands multiple times since it was first built in 1933, Casa del Zorro is still a secret desert hideaway for those looking for spacious and comfortable accommodations—many with private pools, surrounded by gorgeous desert mountains. **Pros:** colorful gardens; summer stargazing; amenities such as fitness center, spa, and pools. **Cons:** expensive restaurant; huge campus; spotty service. ⑤ *Rooms from: $229* ✉ *3845 Yaqui Pass Rd., Borrego Springs* ☎ *760/767–0100* ⊕ *www.lacasadelzorro.com* ⌐ *66 rooms* ⓘ◯ *Free Breakfast.*

The Palms at Indian Head

$$ | B&B/INN | Spectacular desert views can be had from this small, 1950s hotel that displays an authentic mid-century modern look, with Mondrian influences and original art by local artists. **Pros:** quiet, oasis-like atmosphere; mid-century design; great views. **Cons:** somewhat remote location; restaurant closed in summer; no room phones. ⑤ *Rooms from: $200* ✉ *2220 Hoberg Rd., Borrego Springs* ☎ *760/767–7788* ⊕ *www. thepalmsatindianhead.com* ⌐ *12 rooms* ⓘ◯ *No Meals* ⌐ *Families with children under 13 must book rooms 6 or 7.*

Index

278

Photo Credits

Front Cover: Prisma by Dukas Presseagentur GmbH/Alamy Stock Photo [Description: USA, United States, America, California, San Diego, City, La Jolla District, Seals Rock, coast, marina, seals, wildlife]. **Back cover, from left to right:** Sebastien Burel/Shutterstock. Viviane Teles. Dance Strokes/Shutterstock. **Spine**: Dance Strokes/Shutterstock. **Interior, from left to right:** McClean Photography/iStockphoto (1). Robert Matarazzo/iStockphoto (2-3). Jose Angel Astor Rocha/Shutterstock (5). **Chapter 1: Experience San Diego:** Dancestrokes/Shutterstock (6-7). Sierralara/Shutterstock (8-9). Adeliepenguin/Dreamstime (9). Melanie Stocker/Courtesy of Sandiego.org (9). Lisa Field/Courtesy of Sandiego.org (10). Visit California/Courtesy of Sandiego.org (10). Teri Virbickis/Shutterstock (10). Rob Atherton/Alamy (10). Sebastien Burel/Shutterstock (11). Brett Shoaf/Courtesy sandiego.org (11). Sandrafoyt/Dreamstime (11). San Diego Brewery Guide (11). Ilandavid/Dreamstime (12). Ganeshkumar Durai(Ganesh005)/ Dreamstime (12). Courtesy Sandiego.Org (12). Karen Grigoryan/ Shutterstock (13). Dancestrokes/Shutterstock (16). Joseph S Giacalone/Alamy (16). Sebastien Burel/Shutterstock (16). Julia Hiebaum/Alamy (17). Marcel Fuentes/Shutterstock (17). Striders/Courtesy Sandiego.Org (18). Africa Studio/Shutterstock (18). Lindsey Marie Photography (18). Anne Watson (19). Haley Hill Photography (19). Courtesy of Cutwater Spirits (20). Courtesy of Stone Brewing and Stone Brewing World Bistro & Gardens/Escondido (20). Todd Warshaw/Courtesy of Epping Brewing (20). Courtesy of You & Yours Distilling Co. (20). Courtesy of Karl Strauss (21). **Chapter 3: Downtown With the East Village, Embarcadero, The Gaslamp Quarter, Little Italy, and Barrio Logan:** F11photo/Shutterstock (55). Brett Shoaf/Artistic Visuals (73). Neilld/Dreamstime (76). **Chapter 4: Balboa Park, Bankers Hill, and San Diego Zoo:** Jon Bilous/Shutterstock (87). Appalachianviews/Dreamstime (99). Americanspirit/Dreamstime (101). Alisafarov/Shutterstock (101). Robert Holmes (102). Steve Snodgrass/Flickr (103). FPat/Flickr (104). FPat [CC BY 2.0]/Flickr (104). Edward Fielding/Shutterstock (104). Chris Gotz/ Shutterstock (104). Lequint/Dreamstime(104). Jose Angel Astor Rocha/Shutterstock (105). Sherry V Smith/Shutterstock (106). Exquisitexplorations/Dreamstime (106). NaturaLight / Alamy Stock Photo (107). Marin James/Shutterstock (107). Stefano Panzeri / Shutterstock (107). **Chapter 5: Old Town and Uptown:** Kongomonkey/Dreamstime (111). ZUMA Press Inc/Alamy Stock Photo (117). Brett Shoaf/Artistic Visuals (120). Kongomonkey/Dreamstime (126). **Chapter 6: Mission Bay and the Beaches**: Bonandbon/Shutterstock (137). Rinus Baak Photography 2014 (140). **Chapter 7: La Jolla With Clairemont, Kearny Mesa, and Miramar:** Brett Shoaf/Artistic Visuals (153). Alysta/Shutterstock (154). Lowe Llaguno/Shutterstock (155). San Diego CVB (155). Sebastien Burel/Shutterstock (156). Janet Fullwood/Sacramento Bee Staff Photo (157). Sebastien Burel/iStockphoto (157). Windo9888/Dreamstime (164-165). Brett Shoaf/Artistic Visuals (167). Sebastien Burel/Shutterstock (178). Kevin Baird/Flickr (181). **Chapter 8: Point Loma Peninsula With Harbor and Shelter Islands, Ocean Beach, and Liberty Station:** Sean Pavone/Shutterstock (185). San Diego CVB (186) .James Benet/ iStockphoto (187). Cass Greene/iStockphoto (187). Julius Fekete/Shutterstock (204). **Chapter 9: Coronado**: Gabriele Maltinti/Shutterstock (207). Bill Chizek/Shutterstock (210). HannaTor/Shutterstock (215). **Chapter 10: North County and Around:** Courtesy of Brett Shoaf, Artistic Visuals (221). James Kirkikis/Shutterstock (242). Aguina/Dreamstime (244). Msurdin/Dreamstime (260). Kitleong/Dreamstime (265). **About Our Writers:** All photos are courtesy of the writers except for the following: Kai Oliver-Kurtain, courtesy of 2015 Found Creative Studio.

*Every effort has been made to trace the copyright holders, and we apologize in advance for any accidental errors. We would be happy to apply the corrections in the following edition of this publication.

Notes

Fodor's SAN DIEGO

Publisher: Stephen Horowitz, *General Manager*

Editorial: Douglas Stallings, *Editorial Director;* Jill Fergus, Amanda Sadlowski, *Senior Editors;* Brian Eschrich, Alexis Kelly, *Editors;* Angelique Kennedy-Chavannes, *Assistant Editor;* Yoojin Shin, *Associate Editor*

Design: Tina Malaney, *Director of Design and Production;* Jessica Gonzalez, *Senior Designer;* Jaimee Shaye, *Graphic Design Associate*

Production: Jennifer DePrima, *Editorial Production Manager;* Elyse Rozelle, *Senior Production Editor;* Monica White, *Production Editor*

Maps: Rebecca Baer, *Senior Map Editor;* David Lindroth, Mark Stroud (Moon Street Cartography), *Cartographers*

Photography: Viviane Teles, *Senior Photo Editor;* Namrata Aggarwal, Neha Gupta, Payal Gupta, Ashok Kumar, *Photo Editors;* Jade Rodgers, *Photo Production Intern*

Business and Operations: Chuck Hoover, *Chief Marketing Officer;* Robert Ames, *Group General Manager*

Public Relations and Marketing: Joe Ewaskiw, *Senior Director of Communications and Public Relations*

Fodors.com: Jeremy Tarr, *Editorial Director;* Rachael Levitt, *Managing Editor*

Technology: Jon Atkinson, *Executive Director of Technology;* Rudresh Teotia, *Associate Director of Technology;* Alison Lieu, *Project Manager*

Writers: Claire Deeks van der Lee, Marlise Kast-Meyers, Kai Oliver-Kurtin, Jeff Terich

Editor: Alexis Kelly

Production Editor: Elyse Rozelle

34th Edition

ISBN 978-164097-636-8

ISSN 1053-5950

SPECIAL SALES
This book is available at special discounts for bulk purchases for sales promotions or premiums. For more information, e-mail SpecialMarkets@fodors.com.

PRINTED IN CANADA

10 9 8 7 6 5 4 3 2 1

About Our Writers

Veteran traveler **Claire Deeks van der Lee** feels lucky to call San Diego home. An East Coast transplant, she never takes the near-perfect weather for granted. Claire loves playing tourist in her own city, exploring San Diego's cultural attractions as well as its myriad neighborhoods. Claire has contributed to *Everywhere* magazine and several Fodor's guides. She updated the following chapters for this guide: Travel Smart; Balboa Park, Bankers Hill, and San Diego Zoo; and Mission Bay and the Beaches.

Journalist and author **Marlise Kast-Myers** has traveled to more than 80 countries and has lived in Switzerland, Dominican Republic, Spain, and Costa Rica. Before settling in Southern California, she completed a surfing and snowboarding expedition across the world. Following the release of her memoir, *Tabloid Prodigy,* Marlise co-authored over 45 Fodor's Travel Guides including books on Cancún, San Diego, Panama, Puerto Rico, Peru, Los Cabos, Corsica, Riviera Maya, Sardinia, Vietnam, California, and Costa Rica. She served as a photojournalist for *Surf Guide to Costa Rica* and authored *Day and Overnight Hikes on the Pacific Crest Trail.* Based in San Diego County, she writes travel features for the *San Diego Union-Tribune* and other publications. She currently lives at the historic Betty Crocker Estate where she and her husband, Benjamin, operate an antiques business, Brick n Barn. Her website is ⊕ *www.marlisekast. com.* She updated the La Jolla, Point Loma Peninsula, and North County and Around chapters.

Freelance journalist **Kai Oliver-Kurtin** specializes in travel, dining, and lifestyle topics. She contributes to various publications including *Marie Claire, HuffPost, Time Out,* and *San Diego Magazine.* Follow her on Twitter @kaiokay or Instagram @kaizie1. Kai contributed to the Experience chapter.

Jeff Terich is a freelance writer living in San Diego with his wife and two cats. His byline has appeared in *San Diego Magazine,* the *San Diego Union-Tribune, Spin, Bandcamp Daily, Stereogum,* ⊕ *StarTrek.com,* uDiscover Music, and ⊕ *Grammy.com.*You can follow his musical adventures on Twitter @1000TimesJeffs. Jeff updated the Downtown, Old Town and Uptown, and Coronado chapters.